Lay Presidency at the

Lay Presidency at the Eucharist?

An Anglican Approach

Nicholas H. Taylor

mowbray

Published by Mowbray
A Continuum imprint
The Tower Building, 11 York Road, London, SE1 7NX
80 Maiden Lane, Suite 704, New York, NY 10038

www.continuumbooks.com

British Library Cataloguing-in-Publication Data
A catalogue record for this book is available from the British Library.

ISBN: PB: 978-1-9062-8618-7

Typeset by Mark D. Chapman
Printed and bound in Great Britain by Ashford Colour Press Ltd., Gosport, Hants.

Contents

to Bishop Lawrence Zulu
with affection and esteem

Foreword by the Series Editor

Affirming Catholicism exists to promote education and informed theological discussion in the Anglican Communion. While it seeks to embrace the best of the catholic tradition it is not narrowly partisan and strives to encourage the kind of thinking that rises above the prejudices that so often characterize theological debate. Nicholas Taylor's impressive monograph, which is the first single-authored work in the Affirming Catholicism series, tackles the issue of lay presidency from a whole variety of perspectives. It offers an authoritative account of the subject in a masterful blend of biblical scholarship, church history, and contemporary theology. It will provide an invaluable resource for all those parts of the Anglican Communion who are contemplating the theological problems of lay presidency. In his pithy and trenchant style, Nicholas Taylor offers a robust critique of some advocates of lay presidency, while also sympathizing with others. He does not seek to promote a particular line, but raises significant questions about the nature of ministry and catholic order that need to be addressed before any decisions can be made. In his cautious conclusion, where he argues against lay presidency, he nevertheless sees it as a second-order issue. I hope that this book will provoke and stimulate thought and act as a reliable guide as the Anglican churches contemplate their mission and ministry in the twenty-first century.

Mark D. Chapman
Ripon College Cuddesdon
The Feast of the Transfiguration of Our Lord, 6 August 2008

Acknowledgements

This work has its seeds in my return to the United Kingdom in 2004, after nearly a decade serving as a priest and theological educator in different parts of Africa. The year spent at Ripon College Cuddesdon was an opportunity both to reacquaint myself with the nebulous workings of the Church of England, and to reflect on Anglican ministry as experienced in varied contexts. The peculiar genius of Anglicanism, and ways in which the ministry of Word, Sacrament, and pastoral oversight have mutated in different times and places and in different circumstances in Church and society, have been a particular preoccupation.

It is against this background, at a time when the Anglican Communion is experiencing apparently incomparable strain, both between and within its component provinces, that the subject of this study was chosen. This issue is less likely to excite the secular press than those of human sexuality and women priests and bishops, but it raises the same questions about how theology is done, and contentious and unprecedented questions addressed, in Anglicanism.

I would particularly like to thank the Rev. Dr Mark Chapman for his encouragement of this project through all stages, and invitation to include it in this series. The Rev. Dr Phillip Tovey, Canon Dr Robin Greenwood, and Canon Professor John Suggit have also read and commented on draft texts. Notwithstanding my appreciation for their insights and suggestions, I make the customary protestations about my own responsibility for what follows. I have been grateful also for correspondence with the Rev. Professor Bryan Spinks, Canon Dr Alan Hargrave, Bishop Steven Croft, Bishop Humphrey Southern, Bishop Stephen Pickard, the Rev. Dr Anni Pesonen, the Rev. Dr Peter Bolt, and Dr Philip Selden. Thanks are due also to staff of Ripon College Cuddesdon, the Bodleian and Theology Libraries in Oxford, the British Library, and St Deiniol's Library, Hawarden. Lastly, I would express my appreciation of the candidates for ministry of several denominations whom I have been privileged to teach, and from whom I have been privileged to learn, as well as the communities in which my priesthood has been exercised and challenged.

Nicholas Taylor

Abbreviations

1. Patristic Texts
Apostolic Fathers
1 Clem.	*1 Clement*
Did.	*Didache*

Shepherd of Hermas
Vis.	*Visiones*

Ignatius of Antioch
Eph.	*To the Ephesians*
Magn.	*To the Magnesians*
Smyrn.	*To the Smyrnaeans*
Phld.	*To the Philadelphians*
Rom.	*To the Romans*
Trall.	*To the Trallians*

2. Ante-Nicene Fathers
Clement of Alexandria
Quis div.	*Quis dives salvetur (Salvation of the Rich)*
Strom.	*Stromata (Miscellanies)*

Cyprian of Carthage
Laps.	*De lapsis (The Lapsed)*
Ep. 1	*Ad Donatum*
Ep. 4	*Ad Presbyteros*
Ep. 9	*Ad Clerum*
Ep. 10	*Ad Martyres*
Ep. 12	*Ad Clerum*
Ep. 22	*Ad Clerum Romae*
Ep. 24	*Ad Clerum*
Ep. 27	*Cyprianus Lapsis*
Ep. 33	*Ad Clerum et Plebem*
Ep. 34	*Ad Clerum et Plebem*
Ep. 35	*Ad Eosdem* [Clerum and Plebem].
Ep. 40	*Ad Plebem*
Ep. 55	*Ad Cornelium*

Ep. 61	*Ad Eucharatium*
Ep. 63	*Ad Caecilium*
Ep. 65	*Ad Rogatianum*
Ep. 66	*Ad Clerum et Plebem Furnis*
Ep. 67	*Ad Stephanum*
Ep. 68	*Ad Clerum et Plebem in Hispania*

Irenaeus of Lyon
Haer.	*Adversus Haereses (Against all Heresies)*

Justin Martyr
1 Apol	*1 Apologia (First Apology)*
Dial.	*Dialogus cum Tryphone Iudaeo (Dialogue with Trypho)*

Martyrdom of Polycarp
Mart Pol	*De Martyria Polycarpi (The Martyrdom of Polycarp)*

Origen
Cels.	*Contra Celsum (Against Celsus)*
Hom. Exod.	*Homiliae in Exodum (Homilies on Exodus)*
Hom. Lev.	*Homiliae in Leviticum (Homilies on Leviticus)*
Comm. Jo.	*Commentarii in evangelium Joannis (Commentary on John)*
Comm. Matt.	*Commentarium in evangelium Matthaei (Commentary on Matthew)*
Or.	*De Oratione (On prayer)*

Tertullian
An.	*De Anima (The Soul)*
Apol.	*Apologeticus (Apology)*
Bapt.	*De baptismo (Baptism)*
Cor.	*De corona militis (The Crown)*
Exh. cast.	*De exhortatione castitatis (Exhortation to Chastity)*
Fug.	*De fuga in persecutione (Flight in Persecution)*
Idol.	*De idololatria (Idolatry)*
Marc.	*Adversus Marcionem (Against Marcion)*
Mon.	*De monogamia (Monogamy)*
Praescr.	*De praescriptione haereticorum (Prescription against Heretics)*
Pud.	*De pudicitia (Modesty)*
Scorp.	*Scorpiace (Antidote for the Scorpion's Sting)*
Val.	*Adversus Valentinianos (Against the Valentinians)*
Virg.	*De virginibus velandis (The Veiling of Virgins)*

3. Apostolic Tradition and related texts

Const. ap.	*Constitutiones apostolicae (Apostolic Constitutions)*
Trad. ap.	*Traditio apostolica (The Apostolic Tradition)*
T Dom	*Testimentum domini*
Didasc	*Didascalia*
Can Hip	*Canones Hippolyti (Canons of Hippolytus)*

4. Nicene and Post-Nicene Fathers

Augustine

Enchir.	*Enchiridion de fide, spe, et caritate (Enchiridion on Faith, Hope, and Love)*
Pecc. merit.	*De peccatorum meritis et remissione (Guilt and Remission of Sins)*

Epiphanius

Pan	*Panarion (Adversus Haereses) (Refutation of all Heresies)*

Eusebius of Caesarea

Hist. eccl.	*Historia ecclesiastica (Ecclesiastical History)*

Jerome

Ep. 146	*Ad Evangelum*

5. Later texts:

Aquinas, *Summa*	Thomas Aquinas, *Summa Theologiae*
Calvin, *Inst.*	John Calvin, *Institutiones Religionis Christiani*
Cranmer, *Defence*	Thomas Cranmer, *A Defence of the True and Catholick Doctrine of the Sacrament*
Cranmer, *Quest and Ans.*	Thomas Cranmer, *Questions and Answers on the Sacraments and the Appointment and Power of Bishops and Priests*
Cranmer, *Sacr.*	Thomas Cranmer, *De Sacramentis*
Hooker, *Lawes*	Richard Hooker, *Of the Lawes of Ecclesiastical Polity*
Lombard, *Sent.*	Peter Lombard, *Sententiares*
Luther, *Inst Min.*	Martin Luther, *Institutiones Ministeriae*
Taylor, *Cler Dom.*	Jeremy Taylor, *Clerus Domini, or, A Discourse of the Divine Institution, Necessity, Sacredness, and Separation, of the Office Ministerial, together with the Nature and Manner of its Power and Operation*

6. Contemporary:

ACC	Anglican Consultative Council
ALW	*Archiv für Liturgiewissenschaft*
ARCIC	Anglican-Roman Catholic International Commission
ATR	*Anglican Theological Review*
BEM	*Baptism, Eucharist, and Ministry*
BMU	[Church of England] Board for Mission and Unity
FOCA	Fellowship of Continuing Anglicans
GAFCON	Global Anglican Futures Conference
HTR	*Harvard Theological Review*
JRS	*Journal of Roman Studies*
JTS	*Journal of Theological Studies*
Neot	*Neotestamentica*
PIO	Pontifical Oriental Institute
RB	*Revue Biblique*
ST	*Studia Theologica*
StL	*Studia Liturgica*
TDNT	*Theological Dictionary of the New Testament*
TEAC	Theological Education for the Anglican Communion
WCC	World Council of Churches

Introduction

For most Christians the celebration of the eucharist, holy communion, the Lord's Supper, or mass is central to their corporate spiritual and worshipping lives. This is most evident in Catholic and Orthodox traditions where the eucharist is celebrated at least on Sundays and major festivals, if not daily. In Anglicanism celebration of the eucharist on Sundays and major festivals, and also on Ash Wednesday, is prescribed by rubric in the Book of Common Prayer.[1] Daily celebrations are the custom in many cathedrals, religious communities, and parishes in the catholic tradition within Anglicanism. In many Protestant denominations there has been a significant increase in the frequency with which communion services are held. Even in communities where celebrations are infrequent, the rarity of the occasion can enhance its significance, both devotionally and socially. This is true both of Protestants for whom the ministry of the word has traditionally been the predominant and most regular aspect of corporate worship, and for Orthodox and Catholic communities, including many Anglicans, who do not benefit from the continuous presence and ministry of an ordained priest or presbyter.

The eucharist is a formal, structured, act of worship, following a particular rite or order, in Anglicanism that of the Book of Common Prayer or one of the modern liturgies authorized in the various Provinces of the worldwide Anglican Communion. However informally conducted, the essential shape and content are retained as the eucharist is an act of the universal Church, not that of any individual priest, or of any particular gathered community. Roles in the celebration are therefore assigned according to Church order. In most denominations only authorized persons, almost always ordained ministers of the word and sacraments, may preside or officiate at the eucharist. In Anglicanism, the Book of Common Prayer and the Articles of Religion, together with the canon law of the various Provinces of the Communion, prescribe that only a bishop or priest (presbyter) may preside, with the implication that the eucharist may not be celebrated unless such a person is present.

It is worth pausing to consider what we mean by the term "preside". It used to be conventional, particularly in more catholic circles, to refer to

---

1   Unless otherwise stipulated, reference to the Book of Common Prayer or the Ordinal designates those of 1662.

the officiating priest as the "celebrant" at the eucharist. This reflected notions of priesthood as being endowed with a particular power, almost supernatural or even magical, to perform rituals in which God's power (the Holy Spirit) is invoked over the bread and wine in order to transform them into the body and blood of Christ. Neither such notions of priesthood nor of transubstantiation have ever been official Anglican doctrine, at least since the Reformation, even though they have lingered in popular belief in some parts, and been adopted by some catholic Anglicans, both in England and in Provinces with a strongly Anglo-Catholic tradition. In contemporary thought, the eucharist is understood as an act, not of a single person, but of the gathered community, mystically joined with the universal Church, the Body of Christ which transcends space and time. The congregation as a whole is therefore the celebrant, and the priest who leads them in this, and recites words and performs actions on their behalf, is referred to as the president rather than the celebrant. This derives from the Greek term ὁ προεστώς, whose first recorded use in this connection is by the second-century Christian writer Justin Martyr.[2] The apostle Paul uses the same terminology of the leaders of the early Christian churches, though not explicitly of their role in the celebration of the eucharist.[3] The usage is clearly ancient, and was introduced to the liturgy of the Church of England with Series 3 in 1971. President is the generally preferred term for the officiant at the eucharist not only in the Anglican Communion but also in the Roman Catholic Church and ecumenically. This is reflected in the important World Council of Churches Report, *Baptism, Eucharist, and Ministry*, published in 1982.[4]

Recognition of the gathered community as the celebrant at the eucharist has generally not led to any change in the requirement that the president be an ordained, or in some denominations otherwise authorized, minister of the word and sacraments. The eucharistic prayer, consisting essentially of the institution narrative, recalling the words and deeds of Jesus at the Last Supper, including the injunction that his disciples "Do this in remembrance of me", and usually also the epiclesis or invocation of the Holy Spirit over the elements, is reserved for authorized ministers. Irrespective of whether the bread and wine are

---

2   *I Apol.* 67.1. Cf. C. O. Buchanan, 'Questions Liturgists Would Like to Ask Justin Martyr', in *Justin Martyr and His Worlds*, ed. S. Parvis and P. Foster (Minneapolis, MN: Fortress Press, 2007), pp. 153–4.

3   Rom. 12:8; 1 Thess. 5:12.

4   The Anglican Diocese of Sydney objects to this usage, which will therefore be avoided when their particular proposals are considered.

understood to undergo any change in their essential character, or to retain any sanctity beyond their immediate ritual use, the eucharistic prayer is a sacred and transformative act, reserved to those duly authorized so to function on behalf of the Church. Where the threefold orders of catholic ministry are retained, eucharistic presidency is reserved, with few exceptions, to bishops and presbyters or priests. In some denominations deacons and lay leaders are authorized to preside, usually only in specified circumstances when no presbyter or ordained minister is available, and often only in private ministry to the sick and housebound rather than in the public worship of the congregation.

In Anglicanism only a bishop or presbyter is authorized to preside at the eucharist, and such parts as the absolution, the greeting of peace, the eucharistic prayer, and the blessing, are reserved for ordained priests. The diocesan bishop is the normative president, and presbyters do not normally preside in the presence of the bishop. The medieval custom, which persisted in Anglicanism after the Reformation, whereby the bishop presided from his throne, while a simple priest acted as celebrant, is not in keeping with contemporary understandings of the episcopate or the presbyterate, or of the role of liturgical presidency, and accordingly is no longer considered appropriate.

The distinction between clergy and laity in the Church is ancient, even if its origins are disputed and the relationship between the ordained ministry and the laity has been variously understood throughout Christian history. The principle that functions of ministry were reserved to particular officers of the Church was clearly established at a very early date. By the end of the first century, the letter conventionally known as *1 Clement*, and attributed to the eponymous bishop of Rome, was modelling Christian ministry on the hierarchy established by Moses in ancient Israel, in which the priesthood of the temple in Jerusalem constituted a clearly defined caste. Only a few years later, Ignatius of Antioch was articulating, also in letters, an ecclesiastical hierarchy in which supreme authority was vested in the bishop. How the offices and ministries of bishops, presbyters, and deacons emerged from the apostolic Church is all but beyond historical reconstruction, though few would claim that the hierarchy of catholic ministries was directly established by the apostles, least of all in ways as depicted in the pseudepigraphical *Apostolic Constitutions*. What is clear is that the Church established at an early date a clear distinction between clergy and laity, defining their roles and status, and reserving the ministry of word and sacraments, and, in theory at least, administrative and pastoral oversight, to the clergy. Within the clergy there emerged the distinct

3

orders of bishop, priest or presbyter, and deacon, whose precise nature and functions mutated with time and changing circumstances. Lay people were from an early date forbidden to assume the functions of ministry, particularly in the celebration of the eucharist, but also in the administration of baptism.[5]

For over a millennium the Church order and discipline established in the first centuries went unchallenged, whatever doctrinal conflicts, disputes over authority, and other controversies may have beset the Church. During the medieval period, the question of lay people celebrating mass without a priest was raised, only to be dismissed, by the thirteenth-century French Dominican Guerric of St Quentin, as an exercise in scholastic casuistry.[6] The Reformation saw the fragmentation of Western European Christendom, but most Protestant denominations maintained a clear distinction between clergy and laity, with the former defined primarily as authorized ministers of the word rather than of the sacraments. Nevertheless, even where the doctrine of the priesthood of all Christians was espoused, administration of the sacraments continued to be reserved to ordained ministers. The Church of England, while adopting tenets of Protestant doctrine and discipline, retained Catholic orders of ministry, except during the brief interlude of the Commonwealth. Administration of holy communion has been reserved to bishops and priests by law in England since the Act of Uniformity of 1662. Until recently this has been the unchallenged tradition of Anglicanism. Neither the Book of Common Prayer, first published in 1549, with revised editions in 1552, 1559, 1604, 1627, and what has become the definitive edition of 1662, nor any other Anglican Prayer Book or authorized liturgy, has ever envisaged otherwise. This is true also of the Ordinal, conventionally bound with the Book of Common Prayer but technically distinct from it, and of the authorized ordination rites included in most modern Anglican Prayer Books.[7]

---

5   Administration of clinical baptism by lay people is a specific exception which will be considered below.

6   *Quaestio de Ordine*, cited A. McDevitt, 'The Episcopate as an Order and Sacrament on the Eve of the High Scholastic Period', *Franciscan Studies* 20 (1960): 142–44; cf. D. N. Power, *Ministers of Christ and His Church* (London: Geoffrey Chapman, 1969), p. 173.

7   For discussion of the development of the Book of Common Prayer see F. Procter and W. H. Frere, *A New History of the Book of Common Prayer* (London: Macmillan, 1951). For more recent developments see C. O. Buchanan (ed.), *Modern Anglican Liturgies* (London: Oxford University Press, 1968); *Further*

The established tradition has been challenged recently, both in Anglicanism and ecumenically, as a result of a variety of social and theological developments impinging on the life of the Church. Most crucial, perhaps, has been the increasing frequency of celebrations of the eucharist in Anglican parishes, and also in many Protestant congregations, over the past century. From the Reformation until the twentieth century, Matins would have been the principal Sunday morning service in nearly all Anglican churches, preceded or followed on occasion by a sparsely attended eucharist, often without a sermon. Except for some evangelical parishes, the eucharist has become the principal act of worship throughout the Church of England on most Sundays, at least when a priest is available. Even if this trend has diminished recently, on account of pressures to conduct worship conducive to young families and those who feel alienated by liturgical worship, frequent, and at least weekly, celebration of the eucharist has become normative Anglican practice. This development has coincided with a significant decline in the number of stipendiary clergy, and the consequent amalgamation of rural benefices in particular. Nowadays priests often serve several parishes, and can therefore not always be available to every congregation in their care, on all occasions on which a celebration of the eucharist would be desirable or considered appropriate.

The reduction in stipendiary clergy has occasioned an increasing role and prominence for lay ministries, throughout Western Christianity, and by no means only in the Anglican Communion. In the Church of England the order of Readers was established during the second half of the nineteenth century, in 1866 in the province of Canterbury, and in 1889 in the province of York. It was initially envisaged that Readers would assist with the ministry of the word, reading the lessons at Matins and Evensong, and conducting these services in the absence of the clergy. In recent decades Readers have been licensed to preach, the legality and desirability of which were still being debated during the early 1960s, and the order has been opened to women since the end of that decade. In 1970 the Convocations of Canterbury and York authorized the licensing of lay people, including Readers, to assist with the distribution at the eucharist. In addition to these roles, Readers are now permitted also to conduct baptisms and funerals. A detailed account of the origins of other forms of lay ministry in the Church of England and in other provinces of the Anglican Communion is not

---

Anglican Liturgies (Bramcote: Grove Books, 1975); *Latest Anglican Liturgies* (London: SPCK, 1985).

necessary in order to appreciate that acceptance has been a slow process which seems to have reached a critical point about 1970. During this period the charismatic movement was beginning not only to influence the worship and spirituality of many Anglican parishes but also to challenge latent assumptions that Christian ministry and the gifts of the Holy Spirit were restricted to the ordained clergy. As well as greater emphasis on worship, and in particular on the eucharist, the charismatic movement saw the establishment within Anglican parishes of lay-led prayer meetings and study groups, often known as house churches. While many of these groups eventually seceded from Anglicanism and became or joined Pentecostal denominations, their influence on Anglican ecclesiology, pneumatology, and lay identity has been considerable, and has persisted within both catholic and evangelical circles.

Until recently any question of lay presidency at the eucharist would have been inconceivable in the Church of England, except in theoretical discussion in evangelical circles. The extension of lay ministries, the influence of the charismatic movement, and the increasing dependence of the Church on the ministry, and other practical contributions, of lay people, has probably made the question inevitable. No contemporary treatment of lay ministry, or of priesthood, can ignore it. In 1983 an official discussion document *A Strategy for the Church's Ministry* emphasized that the principle needed to be addressed; the Church was not facing a temporary emergency during which bishops might authorize *ad hoc* arrangements, but a long-term shortage of (stipendiary) priests and so needed to made adequate and appropriate provision for the ministry of word and sacrament.[8] Over a decade later, in 1997, the House of Bishops published *Eucharistic Presidency*, a carefully balanced statement of the current position of the Church of England,[9] but is of necessity concise rather than comprehensive in its treatment, and has not ended debate on the issue, either in England or in the wider Anglican Communion.

The inability of Christian communities to celebrate the eucharist for lack of a priest was addressed as early as the late second-century by the Christian writer Tertullian.[10] In this sense it is nothing new, and it would

---

8   J. Tiller, *A Strategy for the Church's Ministry* (London: Church Information Office, 1983), commonly known as the Tiller Report.

9   *Eucharistic Presidency: A Theological Statement by the House of Bishops of the General Synod* (London: Church House Publishing, 1997), commonly known as the Ely Report – Bishop Stephen Sykes of Ely chaired the Theological Group in the House of Bishops which drafted the text.

10 *Exh. cast.* 7.3.

be little short of bucolic fantasy to suppose that every village in England was continuously served by a resident priest or priests from the seventh to the twentieth century. During the medieval period in Europe, the eucharistic spirituality of lay Christians focused on witnessing the celebration of the eucharist, and in particular the moment of consecration, often on a daily basis. Lay people rarely partook of the consecrated elements, with many communicating only at Easter. The absence of a priest would nonetheless have been a deprivation, ameliorated perhaps by alternative devotions in which the consecrated Host in the pyx or tabernacle would have been the focus. It was, as noted previously, only during the twentieth century that lay Anglicans became regular, even weekly, communicants, and Matins came in many places to be regarded as a less than satisfactory substitute for the eucharist when no priest was available. A shortage of clergy has been felt in the developing world for much longer than in Europe, with low population densities in rural areas, less developed transport infrastructures, and relative economic poverty in places where the Church has often expanded very rapidly. Particularly since the withdrawal of European missionaries, especially monastic orders which provided a relative concentration of priests in mission areas, solitary priests have been required to serve several congregations scattered over vast and often inaccessible geographical areas, some communities receiving priestly ministry as infrequently as once a year. Despite this, many Christian congregations have undoubtedly endured, and even grown, without the regular ministry of the sacraments, and perhaps with less than adequate ministry of the word and other Christian teaching, over extended periods. The deprivation needs nonetheless to be acknowledged.

It was precisely in a context of rapid church growth, with dioceses and missionary agencies unable to provide priests for young and scattered congregations, that the issue of authorizing lay people to preside at the eucharist was first raised in the Anglican Communion. As early as the beginning of the last century, Bishop Vedanayakam Samuel Azariah of Dornekal in India proposed that lay people be authorized to preside at the eucharist on occasion. At the 1963 Anglican Congress in Toronto, a similar proposal was made by Canon Frank Synge, Principal of Christchurch Theological College in New Zealand and formerly of St Paul's Theological College in Grahamstown, South Africa.[11] Alternative

---

11 F. C. Synge, 'The Challenge of the Frontiers', in *Anglican Congress 1963* (Toronto: Editorial Committee, 1963), pp. 155–64.

liturgies, including celebration of the eucharist without a priest, have almost certainly been performed in some evangelical and charismatic, and also feminist, Anglican communities, but these have served to make theological statements rather than pastoral provision for communities without priests.

The diocese of Sydney, Australia, began to consider lay administration of holy communion in 1970, and its Synod first endorsed the principle in 1985.[12] Opposition from other dioceses has meant that any measure to implement this would be unlikely to be approved at all necessary levels of ecclesiastical governance in the Anglican Church of Australia. Sydney has, moreover, traditionally occupied a distinctive and perhaps even liminal position on the evangelical fringe of Anglicanism, which has made its debates appear somewhat idiosyncratic and irrelevant to the wider Anglican Communion. With the ascendancy of a more radical and more militant form of evangelicalism in Sydney, and the increasingly prominent role of its archbishop in conservative movements in the Anglican Communion, developments in this Australian diocese have acquired greater significance for the wider Communion. Meanwhile, the issue of lay eucharistic presidency came to attention in the Anglican Communion when the Province of the Southern Cone of South America (Iglesia Anglicana del Cono Sur de America) raised the issue during the 1980s, and canvassed other provinces and the then nascent organs of the Communion, before debating the question in their provincial synod in 1986. Diaconal presidency was authorized in the Anglican province of Kenya in 1985, subject to special permission from the diocesan bishop; a development which did not receive much attention from the wider Anglican Communion.[13] The question has been taken more seriously since being pursued with renewed vigour in Sydney since the 1990s. Both in Sydney and in Latin America, appeal is made to the immediate missionary needs of the local church, with greater emphasis placed on a Reformed theological agenda in the case of Sydney. A similar missionary agenda has motivated many advocating lay presidency in the Church of England, particularly the church planting movement and the fresh expressions of church initiative which it has inspired.

---

12 Synodical and other documents from 1985 onwards, are available online at www.sydney.anglican.asn.au
13 This development is reported by C. O. Buchanan in *News of Liturgy* 126 (1985): 3, but appears otherwise to have passed unnoticed.

It needs to be emphasized that proposals to permit lay people to preside at the eucharist do not necessarily reflect any denigration of the rite. Even where there is an explicit subordination of the sacrament to proclamation of the word, the stated objective is to make the eucharist available to the people of God wherever and whenever appropriate, and not only on occasions when a priest is present. It should also be recognized that anarchy is not being proposed. On the contrary, it is almost always envisaged that lay people authorized to preside at the eucharist would be carefully selected, appropriately and adequately trained, and explicitly licensed by the bishop to function only in the absence of a priest, and for a limited period. Lay presidency is not always promoted apart from strict control over the interpretation of Scripture and ecclesiastical discipline, and does not necessarily entail surrender of clerical leadership and authority in the community. While licensing may acknowledge, co-opt, and perhaps hold accountable, those who already exercise leadership in communities without priests, it is nonetheless expected that bishops and priests, however remote, will retain their authority and oversight of those communities and their lay leadership.

A former Archbishop of Canterbury writes, with apparent lack of concern, that, while serving in the armed forces before his ordination, "we held services according to the Book of Common Prayer and I celebrated holy communion – quite illegally, of course".[14] Notwithstanding such retrospective prelatical nonchalance, the prolonged synodical debates over decades in the diocese of Sydney, and the deliberate consultation with other Anglican provinces by Iglesia Anglicana del Cono Sur de America, illustrate the profound issues of ecclesiology and sacramental theology involved. The nature of the Church, the eucharist, and the ministry, ordained and lay, are all at issue, and all require careful consideration, whether or not fundamental truths of the gospel are ultimately seen to be affected by the development which has been proposed in different parts of the Anglican Communion. These issues of ecclesiology and sacramental theology cannot be treated entirely in isolation, and are probably incapable of disentanglement. Furthermore, they will inevitably be perceived very differently from different theological perspectives. Discussion is complicated by continuing disputes over the ministry and ordination of women, and, at least at the levels of polemic and politicking if not of theological substance, human sexuality. Discussion of all these issues has become submerged in

---

14   G. L. Carey, *Know the Truth* (London: HarperCollins, 2004), p. 37.

prolegomena concerning authority in the Church, and specifically in the Anglican Communion. Some attention to Anglican theological method would therefore seem an essential, and neglected, prerequisite to addressing the question cogently.

This study will therefore begin with a discussion of Anglican theological method. This is an elusive and contentious concept, even among those who acknowledge that Anglicanism has any distinctive ethos, self-identity or theological approach. Anglicans who regard the Chicago–Lambeth Quadrilateral as somehow fundamental, and even those who define themselves more narrowly in terms of the Bible and the Book of Common Prayer, with which the Ordinal and the Articles of Religion are conventionally included, can differ quite significantly on issues of central importance to at least some of them. While the issues cannot be resolved within the parameters of this study, if at all, an approach will be defined in conformity with Scripture and continuity with tradition, which ought to be broadly acceptable across the Anglican spectrum.

In view of universal Anglican, and wider Christian, assent to the primacy of Scripture, the second chapter will investigate the biblical evidence. Beginning with the accounts of the Last Supper in the gospels and 1 Corinthians, the question to whom the dominical injunction to "Do this" was addressed will be considered. I shall discuss the issue of eucharistic presidency and the significance of rites akin to ordination for the exercise of ministry in the Church during the New Testament period. Chapter 3 will review the writings of a number of early Church Fathers on ministry and the eucharist, and then consider the emergence of ordination liturgies, before concluding with some discussion of the nature of priesthood in the early Church. This will be followed, in Chapter 4, by a study of the Anglican tradition on ministry and the eucharist from the Reformation onwards, with some consideration of the ecumenical context and patterns of collaboration in ministry of the word and sacraments.

Chapter 5 will discuss alternative provisions for worship in the absence of a priest to preside at the eucharist, in different parts of the Anglican Communion and in different traditions within Anglicanism. Chapter 6 will examine specific proposals for authorized lay eucharistic presidency in the Anglican Communion, and Chapter 7 will address theological issues relating to the question. The final chapter will identify and discuss outstanding issues, impacting directly or indirectly on the question of authorized lay presidency at the eucharist, before some concluding reflections are offered.

1

Authority and Theological Method in the Anglican Tradition

As with other controversies engulfing the Anglican Communion, so with the question of lay presidency at the eucharist, there is a quite profound issue of how theology is done. This concerns how truth is discerned and how decisions are made, and specifically how ecclesiological issues are explored and resolved, and at what level in the increasingly complex network of both legally constituted and informal structures which link dioceses and provinces in a single, nebulous but precarious, Communion. This is not simply an issue of canon law and process, of what can be decided by diocesan and provincial synods, or of what, in the case of the Church of England, would require parliamentary legislation. Rather, it is an issue of the theology which informs synodical debates and resolutions, and how the theological questions are approached, before Canons are formulated and adopted.

As is well known, Anglicanism is the product of the Reformation upon the long-established catholic Church in England, Wales, and Ireland.[1] While there are contemporary theologians, not only of evangelical persuasion, who regard Anglicanism as almost a Protestant *creatio ex nihilo*,[2] this was not the intention of the English reformers, political or ecclesiastical. As John Jewel, Bishop of Salisbury 1560–71, and one of the first major apologists of the Anglican settlement, expressed it: "We have planted no new religion but only have preserved the old that was undoubtedly founded and used by the Apostles of

---

1   A. G. Dickens, *The English Reformation* (London: Batsford, 1964); E. Duffy, *The Stripping of the Altars* (New Haven, CT: Yale University Press, 1992); C. A. Haigh, *English Reformations* (Oxford: Clarendon Press, 1993); W. P. Haugaard, *Elizabeth and the English Reformation* (Cambridge: Cambridge University Press, 1968); F. Higham, *Catholic and Reformed* (London: SPCK, 1962); S. C. Neill, *Anglicanism* (Harmondsworth: Penguin, 1965); J. J. Scarisbrick, *The Reformation and the English People* (Oxford: Oxford University Press, 1984).

2   Cf. P. D. L. Avis, *The Anglican Understanding of the Church* (London: SPCK, 2000); S. C. Neill, 'Britain, 1600–1780', in *The Layman in Christian History*, ed. S. C. Neill and H.-R. Weber (London: SCM, 1963), pp. 191–215.

11

Christ and other holy Fathers of the Primitive Church."[3] Whatever the
merits or otherwise of the theological and historical judgements which
informed the changes introduced during the sixteenth century, the
intention to recover the essence of ancient Christianity is clear. The
same principle inspired Richard Hooker (1554–1600), whose *Of the
Lawes of Ecclesiastical Polity*, published in five books between 1593 and
1597 (with three further volumes published some decades after his
death), has become a classic statement of Anglican ecclesiology, and to
which further reference will be made in this and subsequent chapters.[4]

It would be a fundamental misconception to regard the English
reformation as a single, consistent and coherent, process, guided by a
clear theological insight or agenda. Influences upon reform in England,
Wales, and Ireland, and also Scotland, were perhaps more varied than
was the case with the movements which gave rise to the Lutheran and
Reformed churches on the European continent; the Anglican Reformation was politically rather than theologically initiated, and continued to
be politically driven, but some important theological principles came to
be established through the process. Some of the issues will be considered
in further detail in Chapter 4. For the present, the point to recognize is
that some of the defining documents of Anglicanism, and the principles
which informed them, emerged in a climate of political and intellectual
volatility. The lack of consistent theological direction, and the shifting
and uncertain political context, could in part explain why authority has
become so crucial an issue in Anglican theology.[5]

Perhaps more than other reformed churches, Anglicanism recognized
the instability of the world in which it operated, and the inevitability and
necessity of change, and therefore of evolving tradition. The reform of
the Church was not perceived to be a single, final process which had
once and for all recovered and reconstituted the ancient Christian faith
and institutions. This is a legacy which has served the Church well, not
least in that it has enabled a national church to evolve, however
unconsciously, into a worldwide Communion, to accommodate and
even to embrace diversity, and to confront vigorously, and seek

3   *Apologia Ecclesiae Anglicanae; An Apologie or Aunswer in Defence of the Church of
    England*, 1562.
4   See esp. *Laws*, 3.1.10.
5   Cf. G. R. Evans, *Authority in the Church* (Norwich: Canterbury Press, 1990); R.
    A. K. Runcie, *Authority in Crisis?* (London: SCM Press, 1988); S. W. Sykes, *The
    Integrity of Anglicanism* (London: Mowbray, 1978); *Unashamed Anglicanism*
    (London: Darton, Longman and Todd, 1995); S. R. White, *Authority and
    Anglicanism* (London: SCM Press, 1996).

consensus on, divisive and contentious issues. This may seem to have failed in recent decades, as provinces of the Communion have experienced schism over the ordination of women, and the Communion as a whole faces further crisis over human sexuality. However, we cannot ignore the earlier schisms such as those which gave rise to Methodism and Congregationalism, or the more recent secession of untold numbers of Pentecostal groups and independent churches, particularly but by no means only in the developing world. The divisions of the present day, in which the very essence of Anglicanism is being fiercely contested, may reflect ways in which not only the pragmatism but, perhaps more importantly, the sense of evolving tradition which informed Anglican theology of the Reformation period, have been abandoned in some quarters. Conservative evangelicals have increasingly embraced a pan-Protestant biblicism, prone to bigotry and blind to the constricting influence of their own interpretive traditions, which are often in effect elevated above Scripture itself. Conservative Anglo-Catholics, on the other hand, have persisted in a romantic and reactionary, if selective, attachment to pre-Vatican II Roman Catholicism, with papal authority and fantasies about general councils of the Church deployed as a brake against the perceived threats of secular and liberal modernity. A return to the principles crystallized during the English Reformation, which enabled the Churches of England and Ireland to regain and retain stability, and to define their identity and theological method, may be timely.

It is often observed that the liturgy, and in particular the Book of Common Prayer, rather than any confessional declaration or systematic theological system, defines Anglican doctrine. There is certainly truth in this, not least in that the English Reformation was not dominated by a single figure whose writings have become definitive, as have the works of Luther, Calvin, and, later, Wesley, in the denominations to which their names have formally or informally been attached. Nor did the English Church publish or subscribe to a definitive confessional statement, other than the Creeds of the Universal Church. Where ecclesiology and ministry are concerned, the Book of Common Prayer cannot be read in isolation from the Ordinal, which is conventionally bound with it but is technically a distinct document.

Alongside successive editions of the Book of Common Prayer and the Ordinal, the Articles of Religion became a definitive expression of Anglican doctrine and discipline, but have never served as a confessional statement. These have a quite complex history from the promulgation of the Ten Articles in 1536, via the Forty-Two Articles of 1553, to the familiar Thirty-Nine Articles of Religion, promulgated in Latin in 1563 and, with some amendments, in English in 1571.[6] The Church of Ireland promulgated its own Articles in 1615, but subsequently adopted the Articles of the Church of England in 1635. Whereas until 1662 successive monarchs ordered and promulgated further revisions of the Book of Common Prayer and the Ordinal, the Articles have not been revised since 1571, and while attempts were made in some provinces during the last century no agreed definitive text was reached. On the other hand, the authority of the Articles has mutated and, in recent years, diminished considerably. The 1968 Lambeth Conference recommended that provinces review the status of the Articles, and that, should assent continue to be required, this be framed "in the context of a statement which gives the full range of our inheritance of faith and sets the Articles in their historical context".[7] Whereas in the Church of England those assuming ecclesiastical office were formerly obliged to "subscribe ... avoiding of all ambiguities ... willingly and *ex animo*" to the Articles as being "agreeable to the Word of God",[8] today all that is required is "assent",[9] informed by "sufficient knowledge"[10] of this and other "historic formularies".[11] In other Anglican provinces, where the Articles are retained at all, no more than similarly qualified acknowledgement is required.

Drafted by ecclesiastical authority and promulgated by the Crown, the Articles reflect particular theological and political concerns of the sixteenth century, and include assertions concerning royal authority, judicial process, and other matters which would be considered at best controversial today. Not all the Thirty-Nine Articles have therefore proved to be of equal or enduring value. Formularies which were subject to revision by lawful authority in their own day, can hardly be irrevocable and unalterable by lawful authority in another era. The Articles are therefore clearly subordinate in canonical authority to

---

6   For discussion of the development of the *Articles* see E. J. Bicknell, *A Theological Introduction to the Thirty-Nine Articles of the Church of England* (London: Longman, 1955); cf. O. M. T. O'Donovan, *On the Thirty Nine Articles* (Exeter: Paternoster Press, 1986).

7   Resolution 43. A complete archive of the resolutions of the Lambeth Conferences are available athttp://www.lambethconference.org/resolutions/index.cfm.

8   Canon XXXVI of 1603.

9   Canon A2, promulgated 1969.

10   Canon C7, amended 1972.

11   Canon C15, amended 1992; the Declaration of Assent.

synods charged with the governance of the Church today. Nevertheless, they are useful in illuminating how the Church of England sought to define its theological method and ecclesiological identity at the Reformation. Whatever reservations there may be about the Erastianism and the social values of the English ruling classes of the sixteenth century, the principles guiding the more theological and ecclesiological propositions remain valid, and many of the Articles express the Anglican spirit with enduring relevance, balance, and perspicacity.

Of most direct relevance to questions of authority and theological method are Articles VI and XX. These will be considered briefly.

All Anglicans would affirm, with Article VI, Of the Sufficiency of the Holy Scriptures for Salvation, that

> *Scriptura sacra continet omnia, quae ad salutem sunt necessaria, ita ut quicquid in ea nec legitur, neque inde probari potest, non sit a quoquam exigandum, ut tanquam Articulis fidei credatur, aut ad salutis necessitatem requiri putetur.*

> Holy Scripture containeth all things necessary to salvation: whatsoever is not read therein, nor may be proved thereby, is not to be required of any man, that it should be believed as an article of the Faith, or be thought requisite or necessary to salvation.

While this may at first sight seem entirely unequivocal, the Article is carefully nuanced, and what precisely it means in practice has been subject to dispute. The historical context is rejection by the Church of England of the decrees of the Council of Trent, which had attributed to ecclesiastical tradition an authority comparable with that of Scripture:

> ... *hanc veritatem et disciplinam contineri in libris scriptis et sine scripto traditionibus, quae ab ipsius Christi ore ab apostolis acceptae, au tab ipsis apostolis Spirito sancto dictante quasi per manus traditae ad nos usque pervenerunt,* ...

> ... this truth [the Gospel] and rule are contained in written books and in unwritten traditions which were received by the apostles from the mouth of Christ himself, or else have come down to us, handed on as it were from the apostles themselves at the inspiration of the Holy Spirit.[12]

It is in response to this attribution of equal authority to Scripture and tradition, with the papacy effectively deciding what was and was not

---

12   Sessio IV, Decr. 1, 1546.

authentic tradition, that Article VI asserts the sufficiency of Scripture in fundamentals of the Christian faith. The Article can be interpreted as endorsing the Protestant slogan of *sola Scriptura* only in a very qualified sense. The Bible is not equated with the Word of God, and all parts of it are not accorded equal inspiration and authority, as tended to be the case in the Reformed tradition.[13] Rather, the Bible *continet* (containeth) all authoritative teaching essential to human salvation.

Article VI has become a positive statement of Anglican conviction, and the principle is fundamental to addressing all issues of controversy in the Church. While the sufficiency of Scripture in matters pertaining to salvation is unequivocally declared, this does not mean that the Bible provides an easy or obvious solution to all issues with which Christians, or specifically Anglicans, are confronted. On the contrary, there are issues, of a secondary order rather than being "necessary to salvation", which cannot be resolved on the basis of explicit and unambiguous statements in the Bible. In such cases unwritten, and inherently unfalsifiable, tradition cannot bear the same apostolic authority as Scripture.[14] In matters of conviction, the liberty of the human conscience is to be respected, and a measure of freedom of belief unusual in sixteenth-century Europe is guarded. This clearly leaves room for differences of opinion within the Church, and proscribes coercion in matters not defined in Scripture. However, it does not mean that the Church is without the authority or the resources to address and to decide such matters, particularly where its life and worship are concerned.

This becomes clear when Article XX. *Of the Authority of the Church*, is considered:

> *Habet Ecclesia ritus sive caeremonias statuendi ius, et in fidei controversies auctoritatem; quamvis Ecclesiae non licet quicquam instituere, quod verbo Dei scripto adversetur, nec unum Scripturae locum sic exponere potest, ut alteri contradicat. Quare licet Ecclesia sit divinorum librorum testis et conservatrix, attamen ut adversus eos nihil decernere, ita praetor illos nihil credendum de necessitate salutis debet obtrudere.*

> The Church hath power to decree Rites or Ceremonies, and Authority in controversies of faith: And yet it is not lawful for the Church to ordain any thing that is contrary to God's Word written, neither may it so expound one place of Scripture that it be repugnant to another. Wherefore, although the Church be a witness and a keeper of Holy

---

13   Cf. N. L. Jones, *The English Reformation: Religion and Cultural Adaptation* (Oxford: Basil Blackwell, 2002), pp. 184–6.

14   Bicknell, *Articles*, pp. 125–7; O'Donovan, *Articles*, p. 52.

> Writ, yet, as it ought not to decree any thing against the same, so
> besides the same ought it not to enforce any thing to be believed for
> necessity of Salvation.

The application of this principle to the life and worship of the Church of
England is what promulgation of the Articles of Religion sought to
accomplish, in and for the period in which they were formulated. This
authority is clearly subordinated to that of Scripture, to which the
Church is *testis et conservatrix* (a witness and a keeper). The authority of
the Church is therefore to be exercised in continuity and conformity
with the Bible.[15] Nevertheless, the right (*ius*) of canonical ecclesiastical
authority to decide questions concerning worship, and to a lesser degree
(*auctoritas*) doctrine, where there is no explicit direction given in
Scripture, is unambiguously affirmed, and would undoubtedly apply to
the question of lay presidency at the eucharist. The principle is asserted
against sixteenth-century Puritan claims to the contrary, as well as
against Tridentine claims to a line of authoritative oral tradition
independent of Scripture. The Church can introduce changes to its
patterns of worship, provided only that these are consistent with
Scripture. Article XX implicitly rejects conservative and traditionalist
opposition to any and all change. Neither the catholic appeal to the
tradition of the Church, whether historically plausible or otherwise, nor
the evangelical insistence on particular received interpretations of
Scripture, as though these interpretations are not themselves tradition, is
compatible with Article XX. Where the Bible provides no clear
direction, it is the Church in the present, not the Church in the past,
which decides issues of controversy concerning its life and worship.
How Scripture is interpreted, and its authority applied within the
decision-making processes of the Church, is therefore crucial. This is an
issue to which we shall return.

That the Church can introduce changes into its life and worship is
clearly explicit in the Articles, but the question remains how these
changes are to be considered and implemented. The presupposition of
the Articles of Religion is the Royal Supremacy. Whatever authority
may have been vested in the Archbishops and Convocations of
Canterbury and York, and in bishops within their own dioceses, the
governance of the Church was exercised under the oversight of the
Sovereign. This is expounded in Article XXXVII, Of the Civil Magis-
trates:

---

15   Cf. Bicknell, *Articles*, pp. 313–35; O'Donovan, *Articles*, pp. 49,113–17.

Regia Majestas in hoc Angliae regno, ac caeteris ejus dominiis, ad quam omnium statuum hujus regni, sive illi ecclesiastici sint, sive civiles, ...

The Queen's Majesty hath the chief power in this Realm of England, and over her dominions, unto whom the chief government of all estates of this Realm, whether they be Ecclesiastical or Civil, ...

Cum Regiae Majestati summam gubernationem tribuimus, ... eam tantum praerogativam, quam in sacris Scripturis a Deo ipso, omnibus piis Principibus, videmus simper fuisse attributam: hoc est, ut omnes status atque ordines fidei suae a Deo commissos, sive illi ecclesiastici sint, sive civiles, in officio contineant et contumacies ac delinquents gladio civili coerceant.

Where we attribute to the Queen's Majesty the chief government, ... that only prerogative, which we see to have been given always to all godly princes in holy Scriptures by God himself; that is, that they should rule all estates and degrees committed to their charge by God, whether they be Ecclesiastical or Temporal, and restrain with the civil sword the stubborn and evildoers.

Quite apart from the question of how many godly princes are actually mentioned in Scripture, it is important to recognize that this Article antecedes any notion of a secular state. While some separation of powers between the Crown and its administrative and judicial agencies on the one hand, and the Church on the other, had been recognized during the medieval period, in practice the structures overlapped, ecclesiastical sinecures were used to finance what would today be called civil servants, and all authority was subject to that of the Sovereign. Such an understanding of state, Church, and society was common to Christendom until centuries after the Reformation, and is not distinctively English, or for that matter distinctively Christian. On the contrary, to many contemporary Christians this Article is morally and theologically repugnant, and has probably contributed a great deal to bringing the Articles as a whole into disrepute. It is, however, important to recognize that this Article does not introduce erastian notions into the governance of the Church of England. Its primary purpose is to repudiate any *externae jurisdictioni*, foreign jurisdiction, in the affairs of the Church of England. In particular, *Romanus pontifex nullam habet jurisdictionem in hoc regno Angliae* (The Bishop of Rome hath no jurisdiction in this realm of England).

Acknowledgement of the Sovereign as the supreme authority in the Church of England never implied that the monarch assumed the authority in doctrine and administration of the sacraments hitherto exercised, at least nominally, by the pope. The Article specifically guards against the ascription of sacerdotal functions and powers to the Sovereign: *non damus Regibus nostris, aut verbi Dei, aut Sacramentorum administrationem* (we give not to our princes the ministering either of God's Word, or of Sacraments). This point is important for understanding the distinction between ordination and nomination to ecclesiastical office, as will become clear in the discussion in succeeding chapters.

Anglican provinces outside England, including Wales since 1920 and Ireland since 1871, have formed polities independent of the state, and with supreme authority vested in their own synodical structures, subject only to their own fundamental declarations, which have generally included assent to Scripture as the final authority in all matters of doctrine, and to the Nicene and Apostles' creeds as the definitive statements of Christian doctrine. In many provinces the Book of Common Prayer, and in some the Thirty-Nine Articles of Religion, have also been cited as foundational documents. Most provinces give some form of expression to their spiritual and historical links with the Church of England and communion with the See of Canterbury, but, while some early appointments to overseas bishoprics were made by the Crown, this has in all cases been superseded by processes of canonical nomination or election according to local canon law. What has never been resolved is how these autonomous Anglican polities relate to each other, and the degree of independence and interdependence each should enjoy, not least in reaching decisions in matters of controversy. The Lambeth Conference, convened decennially since 1867, has never exercised any kind of governance in the Anglican Communion, and neither has the Anglican Consultative Council, established in 1970. Whatever the draft Anglican Covenant may achieve during the coming years, it will almost certainly precipitate, or perhaps aggravate, a discernible and pernicious shift from theology to law as the sphere in which decisions are reached in the Anglican Communion.

This illustrates a weakness, already noted, in Anglicanism. The possibly quite beneficial lack of a single and coherent governing theological agendum at the Reformation has meant that questions of authority have tended to predominate over issues of theological principle, particularly in addressing issues of contention. While the Royal Supremacy may effectively have resolved or pre-empted questions of authority for several centuries, this was at the cost of the freedom of the Church, as was illustrated by the débâcle over revision to the Book of Common Prayer during the 1920s. By this date not only had parliament functioning as a representative body of the laity of the

19

Church of England become an anachronism, but implicitly since the restoration of the monarchy in 1660 and by law since the Act of Supremacy of 1689, the legislature had progressively assumed the powers formerly exercised by the monarch, and ministers of the Crown accounted to parliament rather than to the Sovereign. The evolution of synodical structures in the Church of England during the twentieth century has been a response to the anomalous and aberrant situation which became evident in parliament's rejection of the revised Book of Common Prayer in 1928. The quasi-parliamentary procedures of General Synod have inevitably meant the predominance of legal and political considerations over theological, and this is a problem which those Anglican provinces which have operated synodically, and independently of the Crown and the Royal Supremacy, for centuries have also not been able to avoid. It is therefore vitally important that the legacy of the Royal Supremacy be recognized, and that synodical deliberations in modern Anglican polities be theologically informed.

After the Book of Common Prayer and the associated Ordinal and Articles, perhaps the greatest legacy of the English reformation is Richard Hooker's *Of the Laws of Ecclesiastical Polity*, already mentioned. Hooker's work has not acquired the quasi-canonical status Calvin's *Institutio Christianae Religionis* came to occupy within the Reformed tradition. Indeed, Hooker himself was critical of the way in which certain Reformed theologians regarded Calvin as "almost the very canon to judge both doctrine and discipline by", observing that this status was analogous to that accorded to Thomas Aquinas by the Church of Rome.[16] Hooker's articulation of the Anglican spirit during the Elizabethan stage of the English Reformation is nonetheless a defining statement of Anglican ecclesiology, even if his pre-eminence does not date from his own day but is the product of the ecclesiastical politics of the Caroline restoration.[17] Calvinists such as Perkins and Cartwright may have been more influential during their own day, at least in the universities,[18] but it is Hooker who has become paradigmatic for

---

16   *Laws*, Pref. 2.8.

17   P. D. L. Avis, *Anglicanism and the Christian Church* (London: T & T Clark, 2002), pp. 31–51; M. A. Brydon, *The Evolving Reputation of Richard Hooker* (Oxford: Oxford University Press, 2006); R. K. Faulkner, *Richard Hooker and the Politics of a Christian England* (Berkeley, CA: University of California Press, 1981); A. Pollard, *Richard Hooker* (London: Longman, 1966); P. B. Secor, *Richard Hooker* (Tunbridge Wells: Burns & Oates, 1999).

18   B. D. Spinks, *Two Faces of Elizabethan Anglican Theology* (Lanham, NY: Scarecrow, 1999), pp. 161–75.

Anglican theology. Notwithstanding his unpopularity with Calvinist Anglicans of his own day, Hooker's enduring value and influence have been such that contemporary Anglican evangelicals, as well as other streams of contemporary Anglican thought, all claim him for their own.[19]

It is accordingly not surprising that Hooker's approach to authority, and particularly the relationship between Scripture and other sources of authority, is disputed.[20] Hooker's presuppositions in reading the Bible are essentially pre-critical, as were those of his contemporaries, Catholic and Protestant alike.[21] His affirmation of the supremacy of Scripture[22] cannot be equated with the modern evangelical notion of *sola Scriptura*, especially not in its fundamentalist sense, as for Hooker reading the Bible in itself requires the use of reason.[23] While acknowledging the supremacy of "what Scripture doth plainly deliver", Hooker recognizes, as does Article VI, that such clear teaching is not always available. He accordingly acknowledges next "whatsoever any man can necessarily conclude by force of reason",[24] failing which "the voice of the Church succeedeth".[25] In this Hooker reflects the language and approach expressed in Article XX:

---

19 Cf. A. M. Allchin, *Participation in God* (London: Darton, Longman and Todd, 1988), p. 7; N. T. Atkinson, *Richard Hooker and the Authority of Scripture, Tradition and Reason* (Carlisle: Paternoster Press, 1997); J. E. Booty, 'Richard Hooker', in *The Spirit of Anglicanism*, ed. W. J. Wolf (Edinburgh: T. & T. Clark, 1979), pp. 1–45; 'The Judicious Mr Hooker and Authority in the Elizabethan Church', in *Authority in the Anglican Communion*, ed. S. W. Sykes (Toronto: Anglican Book Centre, 1987), pp. 94–115; Brydon, *Reputation*; J. S. Marshall, *Hooker and the Anglican Tradition* (London: A. and C. Black, 1963); P. Munz, *The Place of Hooker in the History of Thought* (London: Routledge and Kegan Paul, 1952); M. R. Percy, *Introducing Richard Hooker and the Laws of Ecclesiastical Polity* (London: Darton, Longman and Todd, 1999); Secor, *Hooker*.

20 Atkinson, *Hooker*; G. Hillerdal, *Reason and Revelation in Richard Hooker* (Lund: Gleerup, 1962); H. R. McAdoo, *The Spirit of Anglicanism* (London: Black, 1965), p. 6; Marshall, *Hooker*; W. D. Neelands, 'Hooker on Scripture, Reason, and "Tradition"', in *Richard Hooker and the Construction of Christian Community*, ed. A. S. McGrade (Tempe, AZ: Arizona State University, 1997), pp. 75-84; Secor, *Hooker*; N. Voak, *Richard Hooker and Reformed Theology* (Oxford: Oxford University Press, 2003); 'Richard Hooker and the Pirnciple of *Sola Scriptura*', *JTS* 59 (2008): 96–139.

21 Marshall, *Hooker*, pp. 45–55.

22 *Laws*, 1.8.4; 5.21.2–3.

23 *Laws*, 3.8.13; 9.1.

24 *Laws*, 5.6.2; 5.8.2.

25 *Laws*, 5.7; 8.2.

> The Church hath authority to establish that for an order at one time,
> which at another time it may abolish, and in both it may do well ...
> Laws touching matter of order are changeable, by the power of the
> Church; articles concerning doctrine not so.[26]

While doctrine is regarded as immutable, and fixed in Scripture, on matters on which there is no explicit direction in Scripture the Church is authorized to alter established traditions and to make innovations governing its life and discipline.[27] The same would of course have been substantially the position of Hooker's Calvinist opponents, whatever claims Puritans may have made to the contrary.[28] What is notable is that Hooker elevates reason above the tradition of the Church in the hierarchy of authority – but only where relevant teaching in Scripture is lacking or equivocal. Therefore, not only is tradition unequivocally subordinated to Scripture, in keeping with Article VI, but the responsibility of the Church to govern its life and regulate its worship in the present is not constrained by tradition or precedent, in keeping with Article XX.

During the Reformation period, in continuity with medieval scholasticism, the Bible was read and interpreted in an essentially pre-critical manner, as the book of the Church.[29] This is evident from the assumption of consistency and coherence between all parts of the Bible in Article XX, with which Luther would certainly have disagreed, and also from the assertion in Article VIII that the doctrines expounded in the Nicene, Apostles', and Athanasian Creeds *firmissimis Scripturarum testimonies probari possunt* (may be proved by most certain warrants of Holy Scripture). This approach to Scripture is reflected also in Hooker's *Lawes of Ecclesiastical Polity*, and across the full spectrum of Christian, and not only Anglican, writing of the period. Modern critical scholarship would demonstrate significant theological differences not only between the Bible and the creeds, but also within the Old and New Testament documents. But, in terms of the canons of interpretation prevalent at the time, the claim of Articles VIII and XX would have been uncontentious. Whatever advances had been made in knowledge of the Greek and Hebrew languages by the sixteenth century, these had not yet given rise to the critical scholarship, increasingly independent of

---

26 *Laws*, 5.8.2.
27 *Laws*, 5.8.1–2; 9.
28 Cf. Atkinson, *Hooker*, p. 71; Booty, 'Mr Hooker', p. 7.
29 For fuller discussion, see Jones, *Reformation*.

ecclesiastical authority, which developed from the eighteenth century. When contemporary Anglican scholars and theologians read the Bible in the light of critical scholarship, which no tradition of interpretation can ignore altogether in the present day, they are distinguishing Scripture from the interpretative tradition of the Church, and from the constraints of ecclesiastical authority, to a degree inconceivable at the time the classic Anglican formularies were devised.[30] The results of such research are of course very different, and, to use again the example of Article VIII, the relationship between the biblical writings and the creeds would be understood very differently. While critical exegesis may provide a means of challenging traditions of interpretation in the light of the text, and of historical reconstruction of its contexts, this does not mean that the Biblical text thereby becomes clear, unambiguous, and accessible to all readers. As well as differences of interpretation among scholars, irrespective of their religious beliefs and affiliations, there remains the tension between the historic, canonical, texts and the traditions of interpretation of those texts which have informed the theological tenets of the various Christian denominations.

Such differences among scholars, theologians, and ecclesiastical authorities may well concern what is and is not clearly stated in the Bible. Within the Anglican Communion, this has been quite apparent in the debates about the ordination of women, and is evident in the current controversies over human sexuality. How the Bible is interpreted in Anglican theology is perhaps in itself an issue which has received insufficient attention.[31] While evangelicals tend to join other Protestants in professing *sola Scriptura*, and Anglo-Catholics ascribe authority to the tradition of the Western Church, liberals tend either to exploit critical scholarship or to divorce Scripture from matters of Christian faith and practice, whichever is more expedient. None of these approaches is compatible with the letter or the spirit of Article XX, or consistent with the example of Hooker and other classical writers of the Anglican Reformation.

Few would claim that who may preside at the eucharist is an article of Faith as defined and governed by Article VI. There are, however, those who claim that Scripture is clear on this subject, albeit with a clarity that

---

30 Cf. O'Donovan, *Articles*, pp. 57–9.
31 Cf. Evans, *Authority*, pp. 6-16; R. H. Fuller, 'Scripture, Tradition and Priesthood', in *Scripture, Tradition and Reason*, ed. R. J. Bauckham and B. Drewery (Edinburgh: T & T Clark, 1988), pp. 101–14; Runcie, *Authority*, pp. 34–8; Sykes, *Unashamed Anglicanism*, pp. 109–12.

is paradoxically silent.[32] The evidence of Scripture regarding eucharistic presidency and the ordained ministry will be re-examined in the next chapter. In the meantime, we need to establish how Scripture functions in the Church, how its authoritative teaching is to be discerned, and how it is to be applied, in an age in which critical scholarship cannot be ignored. The insights and conclusions of scholarly exegesis are often disputed, not only by ignorant or fundamentalist Christians or by clergy with vested interests, but within the academic community itself, irrespective of confessional loyalties. In any event the results of critical exegesis, and even of scholarly consensus, cannot simply be equated with the teaching of Scripture. How biblical scholarship relates to ways in which Scripture has been received and interpreted in the life of the Church remains an issue. In acute awareness of this problem, the Archbishop of Canterbury has observed:

> Because some of our present difficulties are, at the very least, compounded by the collision of theologically inept or rootless accounts of Scripture, and it seems imperative to work at a genuine theology of the Bible as the sacred literature of the Church. Popular appeals to the obvious leave us battling in the dark; and the obvious, not surprisingly, looks radically different to different people.[33]

The questions are larger than can be resolved within the parameters of this study, but the issue with which we are concerned nonetheless needs to be explored in awareness of the wider exegetical and ecclesiological contexts. That there is no explicit directive in the Bible on the subject of eucharistic presidency could probably be agreed by nearly all parties,[34] even if the conclusions to be drawn from this are contested.[35] There are, however, outstanding questions as to what light critical scholarship can shed on this issue, and some attention will therefore be given to the origins of the eucharist and the emergence of the ordained ministry, and what may be extrapolated from the text of the New Testament, in the succeeding chapters.

---

32 Cf. Beckwith, *Elders*, pp. 70–72.
33 R. D. Williams, 'The Bible Today: Reading and Hearing', Larkin Stuart Lecture, Toronto, 2007.
34 Cf. P. F. Jensen, 'Lay Administration of Holy Communion', Address to the Clergy of the Diocese of Newcastle, 2004; J. Woodhouse, 'Lay Administration of the Lord's Supper', *St Mark's Review* 162 (1995): 15–16.
35 Cf. R. T. Beckwith, *Priesthood and Sacraments* (Abingdon: Marsham Manor, 1964), pp. 29–30; E. Schillebeeckx, *Ministry* (New York, NY: Crossroad, 1981), pp. 50–2.

A fundamental issue, for Anglicans as for all Christians, is how the tradition of the Church is transmitted, and how it can evolve, while remaining faithful to God as revealed in Scripture. As noted above, the inevitability and necessity of change was recognized at the Reformation, and most Anglican provinces have introduced significant liturgical change over the past decades. Many have begun to ordain women to the diaconate and priesthood, and some to the episcopate. There may be isolated congregations who genuinely believe that they still worship precisely as their forebears did when the Book of Common Prayer was first published. But for most change has been a constant, conscious or unconscious, contentious or uncontentious, aspect of the life of their church. The issue is whether specific changes being contemplated are desirable and, for some, whether they are lawful. The crucial question is who has the authority to initiate and authorize changes which seem, to at least to some Anglicans, a fundamental departure from the doctrine and discipline inherited from previous generations.

In recent decades the Anglican Communion, and several of its component provinces, have experienced very deep divisions, and on occasion schism, on issues not necessarily of doctrine but certainly of discipline. Such issues have included the remarriage of divorcees, polygynous marriages, the ordination of women to the priesthood and episcopate, and homosexual relationships, especially those involving clergy. When ways in which Scripture is understood and interpreted are themselves subject to change, and developments in exegesis cannot be controlled by ecclesiastical authority and are unlikely to lead to consensus on key issues, an indefinite period during which deeply held, but fundamentally opposed, convictions are held with equal sincerity is inevitable. The process of managing the tensions which arise, and maintaining dialogue between those who hold different views while all are committed to a continuing process of discernment, has come to be termed reception.[36] Even where innovations have already been introduced, and occasioned impaired communion between those who accept and those who reject such changes, the process of reception remains in principle open-ended, and the changes which have been

---

36 P. D. L. Avis, 'Reception: Towards an Anglican Understanding', in *Seeking the Truth of Change in the Church*, ed. P. D. L. Avis (London: T & T Clark, 2004), pp. 19–39; H. Chadwick, 'Reception', in *Christian Life and Witness*, ed. C. M. N. Sugden and V. Samuel (London: SPCK, 1997), pp. 200–13; G. R. Evans, *The Reception of the Faith* (London: SPCK, 1997); N. Sagovsky, *Ecumenism, Christian Origins and the Practice of Communion* (Cambridge: Cambridge University Press, 2000); Sykes, *Unashamed Anglicanism*.

introduced potentially reversible. An example of reception in practice has been the ordination of women to the priesthood in the Church of England. While the innovation has clearly been canonical, it has not been accepted by all parties, and during the period of reception provision is made for those who do not accept women priests to remain within the Church of England, in impaired communion with the majority who have welcomed, or at least accepted, the ordination of women to the priesthood.[37]

The example of the ordination of women as a test case for reception is worth considering, as a potential precedent for authorized lay presidency at the eucharist. In the unlikely event of consensus on women priests being attained in the Church of England, impaired communion would give way to the restoration of full communion. Provisions for the accommodation of those hitherto unable or unwilling to accept women priests would fall away, or, in theory at least, the ordination of women to the priesthood could be discontinued. In the meantime, at least some opponents of the ordination of women are campaigning to institutionalize permanently the pastoral arrangements introduced to accommodate them during the reception period, through the creation of a third province within the Church of England before women are consecrated to the episcopate. At the same time, there are those irrevocably committed to the ordination of women as deacons, priests, and bishops who find the anomaly of alternative episcopal oversight offensive, and are campaigning for the legislation enabling these provisions to be revoked. This suggests that neither party is committed to the spirit of reception. At the same time, reception has enabled significant numbers within the Church of England to engage in a discernment process, not least through experience of the ministry of women as deacons and priests.

Reception does not seem even to have been contemplated as an approach to the conflict within the Anglican Communion over human sexuality. There are Anglican clergy in many parts of the world openly or clandestinely living in same-sex partnerships, some legally recognized and registered by the civil authorities, with or without the official knowledge of the bishops of their dioceses. But positions seem too entrenched, particularly on the part of mainly evangelical forces implacably opposed to any deviation from what they regard as clear

---

37 P. D. L. Avis, 'The Episcopal Ministry Act of Synod 1993: A "Bearable Anomaly"?' in *Seeking the Truth of Change in the Church*, ed. P. D. L. Avis (London: T & T Clark, 2004), pp. 152–70.

biblical teaching, for this anomalous situation to be regarded as part of a process of reception. It has accordingly been presumed that consensus will never be achieved, and therefore that the options are compromise or schism. Resolution 1.10 of the Lambeth Conference of 1998 would seem to reflect the former option: paragraphs (c) and (f) speak of "listening" and "monitoring", as though there were commitment to an ongoing and open-ended learning process; on the other hand, paragraphs (b), (d), (e), and (g) pre-empt any such learning process. It is therefore hardly surprising that institutionalized schism, under the guise of an "Anglican Covenant", should be considered the only viable solution to the crisis in the Communion.

These observations would seem to suggest that reception may not be a viable avenue of discernment on the question of lay presidency at the eucharist. It would be possible hypothetically for canonical process to authorize, for a limited or indefinite period, the licensing by a diocesan bishop of certain lay people to preside at the eucharist in parishes or other pastoral charges which have agreed to participate in such a discernment process, with provision also for the pastoral and sacramental needs of those unable to participate in such celebrations of the eucharist. In a sense this is what was proposed in Iglesia Anglicana del Cono Sur de America, though sacramental provision for those unable to accept lay eucharistic presidency would not have been possible. By some accounts it is taking place, passively if not actively, in the diocese of Sydney, with a proverbial blind episcopal eye turned to lay administration of Holy Communion in some parishes. Whether this can meaningfully be described as a process of reception is doubtful, particularly in a diocese implacably opposed to any learning process on the ordination of women to the priesthood or on human sexuality. What is happening in Sydney is effectively change through the proverbial back door, in reaction to what is seen as intransigence on this issue on the part of the remainder of the Anglican Church of Australia. This does not mean that a bona fide process of Reception could not be initiated in some part of the Anglican Communion, with provisions similar to those described above. But alongside the experimental aspect there needs also to be a commitment to open-ended theological investigation and discernment.

In conclusion we may say that the English Reformation has bequeathed to the Anglican Communion its classic liturgies and some principles for addressing issues of contention in doctrine and discipline. This has resulted not in unanimity in theological method, but rather in a continuum along which different Anglican theologians have balanced the relative authority of Scripture, tradition, natural law, reason, and experience with differences in emphasis and choice of slogans, rather than in fundamental principle. Not all Anglicans have, during the succeeding centuries, kept within this broad framework, and there remain issues on which the parameters of tolerable diversity and dissent are fiercely contested. Rather than later fundamentalist notions of "scriptural omnicompetence",[38] Reformation Anglicanism embraced a variety of more subtle and sophisticated approaches to Scripture, employing the tradition of the Church and human reason in different ways to interpret the Bible and expound Christian doctrine in the cultural and intellectual milieu of early modern Europe. The example of Hooker is, once again, worth citing: Hooker affirmed unequivocally that God is revealed in ways other than through Scripture,[39] and that human reason derives from God and discerns what is good;[40] a process he associates with the guidance of the Holy Spirit.[41] While tradition, particularly that of the ancient Church and its most eminent and holy leaders, is to be esteemed, the allegiance he advocates is not supine, but critical, and open to discerning different truths from Scripture in the light of reason.[42]

In essential continuity with the Articles of Religion and the theological method articulated by Hooker is the notion of "dispersed authority" expounded at the 1948 Lambeth Conference:

> Authority, as inherited by the Anglican Communion from the undivided Church of the early centuries ... is single in that it is derived from a single divine source. ... It is distributed among Scripture, Tradition, Creeds, the Ministry of Word and Sacraments, the witness of saints, and the *consensus fidelium*, which is the continuing experience of the Holy Spirit through His [*sic*] faithful people in the Church.[43]

The bishops' statement reflects a clear concern for proverbial checks and balances, to avoid "the temptations to tyranny and the dangers of unchecked power". Positively, it also draws confidence from consensus and the "multiplicity of God's loving provision", assuming that

---

38 Atkinson, *Hooker*, p. 125; cf. Neelands, 'Hooker'; Voak, *Hooker*, p. 253.

39 *Laws*, 2.1.4.

40 *Laws*, 1.7.2–4.

41 *Laws*, 3.8.15,18.

42 *Laws*, 2.7.4.

43 Report IV, 'The Anglican Communion', *The Lambeth Conference 1948* (London: SPCK, 1948), pp. 84–5.

agreement between the various embodiments of authority, of which Scripture is listed first, will reflect the will of God. The emphasis also on the continuing process whereby God's revelation is to be discerned and interpreted by the Church of the present day, in critical but faithful continuity with the witness of the Church in previous generations, accords both with the openness of Reformation Anglicanism to learning and change, and with the modern notion of reception.

It is in keeping with the cardinal Anglican values of reverence for Scripture, and the responsibility of the Church in each age to discern God's will afresh, that this study will explore the question of authorized lay presidency at the eucharist.

2

Eucharist and Ministry in the
New Testament Church

Anglicanism recognizes that "Holy Scripture containeth all things necessary to salvation",[1] but also that there are matters on which the Bible provides no clear guidance, where the Church needs to govern its life in continuity with Scripture, but without being unduly circumscribed by tradition. That there is no passage in the Bible which states that "Only an episcopally ordained priest may preside at the Eucharist", or "Any baptised member of the church may preside at the Eucharist", or anything in between, ought readily to be acknowledged. This does not mean that Scripture is accordingly irrelevant to the ordering of public worship, and specifically the celebration of the eucharist. It remains important to learn what we can from the New Testament, and to be informed by the example of the Apostolic Church, so far as we are able to reconstruct it.

In this chapter we will consider such evidence as there is of the celebration of the eucharist in the New Testament, complementing allusions in the text with what we know from other sources of the social and cultural context in which the documents were written. We will consider also evidence for rites akin to ordination, and ways in which people were set apart for particular ministries. We need to begin, however, by considering the origins of the eucharist.

The institution of the eucharist

Christian tradition is all but unanimous in locating the origins of the eucharist in the "last supper" Jesus ate with his disciples shortly before his arrest and crucifixion.[2] The institution narrative is prominent in most eucharistic prayers, but precisely how the eucharist evolved from the rite instituted by Jesus is a matter of considerable scholarly controversy.[3] For

---

1   Article VI.

2   Mt. 26.20–35; Mk 14.17–31; Lk. 22.14–38; cf. John 13.2–17.26.

3   P. F. Bradshaw, *Eucharistic Origins* (London: SPCK, 2004), pp. 1-23; B. D. Chilton, *A Feast of Meanings* (Leiden: Brill, 1994); G. Dix, *The Shape of the Liturgy* (London: Dacre, 1945); K. A. A. L. Eichhorn, *The Lord's Supper in the New*

over a century a significant body of scholarship has believed that the accounts of the "last supper" reflect Christian reinterpretation of the meal in the light of Jesus' death and resurrection.[4] It is therefore all but impossible to be certain as to precisely what happened and what was said.

It is probable that the eucharist took a variety of forms in different places and different cultural contexts as Christianity spread during the early centuries. It is accordingly very difficult to identify any "original" form of the eucharist, from which all others somehow derived. The issues this raises can be discussed here only in so far as they are relevant to the question of eucharistic presidency in the church today. Several aspects of the "last supper" traditions in the gospels and 1 Corinthians have been discussed and disputed in the debates on presidency, and on what in the Church of England and some other Anglican provinces has become a related issue: extended communion.

It is often assumed that the "last supper" was a Passover meal, conducted according to established rites in Judaism of the day. These related assumptions are all problematic. Judaism of the first century was by no means monolithic, and there is no reason to suppose that the Passover liturgy was at all uniform. The Passover was a domestic rite, conducted in the home by the head of the family, even if the lamb was slaughtered by priests and Levites in the temple.[5] We therefore have singularly little information on how the meal was conducted, or would have been conducted, by Jesus and his disciples. We need to be aware, though, that all meals were ritual occasions, even if the Passover had a particular significance and its celebration involved distinctive foods and observances.

It is, furthermore, unclear that the "last supper" was always understood to have been a Passover meal by those who transmitted the tradition in its different versions. The Passover was an annual festival in the Jewish calendar, and all surviving evidence suggests that the eucharist was a more frequent event, integral to the corporate life of most if not all ancient churches. However, in the gospels of Matthew, Mark, and Luke it is clearly the understanding of the evangelists that the

---

Testament (Atlanta, GA: Scholars, 2007); J. Jeremias, *The Eucharistic Words of Jesus* (London: SCM Press, 1966); F. J. King, *More Than A Passover* (Frankfurt: Peter Lang, 2007); X. Léon-Dufour, *Sharing the Eucharistic Bread* (Mahwah, NJ: Paulist Press, 1982).

4   Eichhorn, *Lord's Supper*; X. Léon-Dufour, *Sharing the Eucharistic Bread* (Mahwah, NJ: Paulist Press, 1982); cf. Bradshaw, *Eucharistic Origins*.

5   E. P. Sanders, *Judaism* (London: SCM Press, 1992), pp. 132–8.

"last supper" was a Passover meal, and Christian tradition has tended to follow them. However, in John the meal takes place the day before Passover, and Jesus dies on the day of preparation as the lambs are being slaughtered in the temple (Jn 19.31). It is worth noting that this account does not include the institution of a new rite, and eucharistic overtones can be discerned elsewhere in the gospel, most particularly in the feeding miracle in Chapter 6. Irrespective of whose chronology is correct, it remains clear that, for all the evangelists, Jesus died at Passover time, and this would appear to be Paul's understanding also (1 Cor. 5.7).[6] It is unlikely that interpretation of this meal was ever divorced from paschal imagery.[7] It is, however, significant that it was not the lamb, a sacrificial animal, but bread and wine, which became the elements of the new ritual.[8]

The celebration of the eucharist is of course more ancient than the written accounts of the "last supper" in the gospels and 1 Corinthians. In other words, the traditions were put to writing at a time when liturgical traditions were already becoming well established in many churches. The transmission of the traditions behind the Gospel accounts of the "last supper" is complex, and has been influenced by the early Christian experience of the eucharist and of other ritual meals in ancient society.[9] Much of the detail has not been included in the written accounts, possibly because it was not deemed to be theologically relevant by the evangelists, but also because common assumptions about how meals were conducted would have made such information superfluous to the original readers, who in any event had probably heard very much more detailed oral accounts of the "last supper". Most scholars are agreed that while Matthew is essentially dependent on Mark, Luke draws from another tradition, known also to Paul.[10] More detailed historical

---

6   Jeremias, *Eucharistic Words*, pp. 36–41; C. F. D. Moule, *Worship in the New Testament* (London: Lutterworth Press, 1961), pp. 18–29.

7   1 Cor. 5.7; Heb. 11.28; cf. G. Feeley-Harnik, *The Lord's Table* (Philadelphia, PA: University of Pennsylvania Press, 1981), p. 116; Moule, *Worship*, pp. 21, 31–32.

8   Cf. Moule, *Worship*, pp. 11–12. This does not imply that these were invariably the elements of early Christian Eucharists, cf. Bradshaw, *Eucharistic Origins*, pp. 51–5; A. B. McGowan, *Ascetic Eucharists* (Oxford: Oxford University Press, 1999).

9   Cf. Bradshaw, *Eucharistic Origins*, pp. 1–23; Chilton, *Feast*; Feeley-Harnik, *Lord's Table*, pp. 113–16.

10   *Synopsis Quattuor Evangeliorum*, ed. K. Aland (Stuttgart: Württembergische Bibelanstalt Stuttgart, 1964), pp. 436–7; *Gospel Parallels*, ed. B. H. Throckmorton (Nashville, TN: Nelson, 1992), pp. 184-5; A. J. B. Higgins, *The Lord's Supper in*

reconstruction cannot be attempted within the parameters of this study, and the detailed arguments are not directly relevant to our immediate concerns.

In all traditions the "last supper" is clearly related as a ritual meal over which Jesus presided.[11] Jesus was not a priest of the hereditary caste which officiated in the temple. e functions as a lay member of Israel, the leader of the movement which had arisen out of his public ministry, and in some sense as a surrogate father to the disciples gathered for what was essentially a family festive meal. The questions pertinent to this study are, who was present at the "last supper"? and to whom was the dominical injunction τοῦτο ποιεῖτε εἰς τὴν ἐμὴν ἀνάμνησιν (Do this in remembrance of me),[12] addressed? While these words are found only in the Lukan and Pauline accounts, it is the act of remembrance which would have given significance and purpose to the rite: communal meals were commonplace and inherently ritual acts, and for the disciples to meet and eat together would in itself have required no dominical injunction.[13] Remembrance is implicit both in blessing the bread and wine and in the consumption thereof; it is not only the one who presides and blesses who fulfils the commandment of Jesus but all who eat and drink. The question is, who was to invoke the benediction over the bread and wine at future gatherings of the disciples, and, by extension, of the church?

It is generally assumed that there were thirteen men present at the "last supper", Jesus and the δώδεκα, "twelve" (Mk 14.17), the inner group of his disciples who came to be known as ἀπόστολοι, apostles, and are so identified in Lk. 22.14. The instruction to repeat the ritual Jesus was instituting would therefore have been addressed to the "twelve".[14] The continuation of the eucharist in the life of the Church would depend on the extension and transmission of the dominical injunction to the Church as a whole, and the question would be whether

---

the New Testament (London: SCM Press, 1952); Jeremias, *Eucharistic Words*; Léon-Dufour, *Sharing*.

11   Cf. P. F. Bradshaw, *The Search for the Origins of Christian Worship* (London: SPCK: 2002), p. 65; *Eucharistic Origins*, pp. 1–15; M. Barker, *The Great High Priest* (London: T & T Clark, 2003); Chilton, *Feast*; Dix, *Shape of the Liturgy*, pp. 48-78; Feeley-Harnik, *Lord's Supper*, pp. 113–16; Jeremias, *Eucharistic Words*, pp. 15–88; King, *Passover*.

12   Lk 22.19; 1 Cor. 11.24, 25.

13   Moule, *Worship*, p. 33; cf. W. R. Crockett, *Eucharist: Symbol of Transformation* (Collegeville, MN: Pueblo, 1989), pp. 21–8.

14   Cf. G. Wingren, *Gospel and Church* (Edinburgh: Oliver & Boyd, 1964), p. 127.

the act of blessing, as opposed to eating and drinking, should be restricted to an office or ministry derived from that of the apostles. The question may be more complicated, however.

As we have already noted, much of the detail, including precisely who was present, has not been transmitted in the written accounts of the "last supper". It is possible that a substantially larger group than thirteen men participated in this meal. Mark 14.17–18 could be understood to mean that Jesus and the "twelve" arrived at a venue where the wider circle of disciples had already gathered and awaited them.[15] Such a gathering would have included women disciples and the wives and children of male disciples.[16] In this case it would be a question not so much whether the injunction to celebrate the eucharist was directed only to the "twelve", or to everyone present, as of who could take the place of Jesus in initiating the rite and pronouncing the benediction. The canonical accounts would imply that everyone present was given the bread and wine over which Jesus had pronounced a distinctive blessing, and there is no explicit restriction as to who was permitted to articulate a blessing on future occasions. On this basis it might be possible to argue that any Christian may assume the role of presiding over the meal as Jesus had done at the "last supper".[17]

If only the "twelve" were present with Jesus, it would be possible to argue that the whole Church was enjoined to partake of the blessed bread and wine, but only some to break the bread and pronounce the blessing. Jesus clearly had other disciples who, if they were not included in the "last supper", could be construed not to have been authorized to preside over the ritual meals of the community at which particular benedictions were recited. If only the "twelve" were authorized so to act in the place of Jesus, then it could be argued that he instituted a new priesthood when he instituted a new cult, and that this was limited to the inner circle of his disciples, and by extension to their successors. The problem then would be to identify the successors of the "twelve", or to define the apostles and their heirs. But perhaps this is to misconstrue the issue.

The "last supper" was not an egalitarian or unstructured occasion. Jesus, as leader of the movement which was to become the Christian

---

15 Cf. P. M. Casey, *Aramaic Sources of Mark's Gospel* (Cambridge: Cambridge University Press, 1998), pp. 226–8.

16 Cf. also Q. Quesnell, 'The Women at Luke's Supper', in *Political Issues in Luke-Acts*, ed. R. J. Cassidy and P. J. Sharper (Maryknoll, NY: Orbis, 1983), pp. 59–79, on the Lukan account.

17 Cf. H. Küng, *The Church* (London: Burns & Oates, 1968), pp. 379–80.

Church, clearly presided over the gathering by virtue of that leadership. In other words, Jesus' presidency at the meal derives from the network of social relationships he had initiated by forming the group of his disciples. It is not incidental, but neither does it derive from the christological and soteriological significance which the "last supper", and Jesus' life, ministry, death, and resurrection subsequently acquired. The question therefore is, who was able to maintain and sustain that network of relationships, and to preside over the ritual and corporate life of the group in the anticipated absence of Jesus himself?

There clearly was already something of a hierarchy within the Jesus movement, and within the inner circle of Jesus' disciples known as the "twelve".[18] However disapproving Jesus may have been of rivalry within the "twelve",[19] the evidence that he chose this inner group himself is considerable.[20] In ancient communities patriarchy was taken for granted, and the cultural assumption would have been that one of the "twelve" would preside in Jesus' absence, presumably according to the precedence established within their company. Whatever may be made of the disputes about precedence within the "last supper" narrative, the question would have been crucial to the survival of the movement after the death of Jesus.[21] That Peter assumed the leadership in what became the earliest Christian community would seem entirely clear from the early chapters of Acts. This would have included ritual leadership, presiding over all corporate activities of the community, including gatherings for worship, and pronouncing the blessing over the food at the common meal.[22] "It would have been quite natural for Peter to take on the role of housefather by presiding over the bread-breaking celebration in the house with the upper room."[23] Whether the words of Jesus at the "last supper", or the cultural presuppositions which governed the ritual and communal life of the Early Church, imply that

18 Cf. O. Cullmann, *Peter* (London: SCM Press, 1953); S. V. Freyne, *The Twelve* (London: Sheed & Ward, 1968); H. Mosbech, 'Apostolos in the New Testament', *ST* 2 (1948): 166–200; W. Schmithals, *The Office of Apostle in the Early Church* (London: SPCK, 1971).

19 Cf. Mt. 18.1–4; 23.11; Mk 9.34; Lk. 9.46; 22.24–26.

20 Mt. 10.1–4; Mk 3.13–19; Lk. 6.13–16; Acts 1.15–26.

21 Cf. R. Stark, *The Rise of Christianity* (Princeton, NJ: Princeton University Press, 1996), p. 77.

22 Acts 1.15–26; 2.14–42; 5.3–10.29–32; etc.

23 R. W. Gehring, *House Church and Mission* (Peabody, MA: Hendrickson, 2004), p. 96.

an essentially patriarchal hierarchy should preside over the ritual and corporate life of the Church for all time, is another question.

Whatever disputes there may be in modern scholarship as to the historicity of the "last supper", it was well established in Christian tradition at a very early date. Paul, writing no more than a quarter of a century after the events, and reiterating what he had imparted during his mission to Corinth several years previously,[24] could state, quite uncontroversially, Ἐγὼ γὰρ παρέλαβον ἀπὸ τοῦ κυρίου, ὃ καὶ παρέδωκα ὑμῖν, ὅτι . ... ., "For I received from the Lord what I also passed on to you, that ... ."[25] It is clear that a Christian corporate ritual meal, in conscious recollection of Jesus' action at the "last supper" and in obedience to the dominical injunction, was observed by the middle of the first Christian century, in at least some parts of the Church.

Eucharistic presidency in the New Testament Church

A detailed discussion of the diversity of early Christian liturgical practice would not be possible within the parameters of this study.[26] Sources within and outside the New Testament are sparse and incomplete, and do not directly address the question with which we are concerned. It would also be beyond the scope of this study to engage in detailed discussion of early Christian theologies of the Church,[27] the eucharist,[28] or of ministry.[29] It is, however, important to recognize the intellectual

---

24 1 Cor. was written c. 54 CE, and Paul's mission to Corinth can be dated to 51 CE. Cf. N. H. Taylor, *Paul, Antioch and Jerusalem* (Sheffield: Sheffield Academic Press, 1992), pp. 46–7, 54–6.

25 1 Cor. 11.23. Cf. *1 Clem.* 40.1–3.

26 Cf. A. Bouley, *From Freedom to Formula* (Washington DC: Catholic University of America, 1981); Bradshaw, *Eucharistic Origins*; Chilton, *Feast*; Higgins, *Lord's Supper*; McGowan, *Eucharists*.

27 C. K. Barrett, *Church, Sacraments and Ministry in the New Testament* (Exeter: Paternoster Press, 1983); A. T. Hanson, *Church, Sacraments and Ministry* (London: Mowbrays, 1975); J. A. T. Robinson, *The Body* (London: SCM Press, 1952); R. Schnackenburg, *The Church in the New Testament* (New York, NY: Herder, 1965).

28 Bradshaw, *Eucharistic Origins*; Chilton, *Feast*; Jeremias, *Eucharistic Words*; E. La Verdiere, *The Eucharist in the New Testament and in the Early Church* (Collegeville, MN: Liturgical, 1996); McGowan, *Eucharists*; F. J. Moloney, *A Body Broken for a Broken People* (Peabody, MA: Hendrickson, 1997); E. Schweizer, *The Lord's Supper According to the New Testament* (Philadelphia, PA: Fortress Press, 1967); D. E. Smith, *From Symposium to Eucharist* (Minneapolis, MN: Fortress, 2003).

29 R. E. Brown, *Priest and Bishop* (London: Chapman, 1971); Hanson, *Church*; B. Holmberg, *Paul and Power* (Minneapolis, MN: Fortress Press, 1980); C. G. Kruse, *New Testament Models for Ministry* (Nashville, TN: Nelson, 1983); E.

milieu in which the academic study of early Christianity has evolved over the past century. Since the late nineteenth century scholarship has tended to view the development of the Church in terms of a decline from charismatic egalitarianism to an ecclesiastical order which came to be known pejoratively as "early catholicism".[30] That this process is discerned within the New Testament documents raises questions for the Church today; whereas Protestants have tended to deplore what they see as a corruption of, and decline from, apostolic Christianity, Catholics would argue that, even if there were development, this is reflected within the New Testament, and was therefore entirely valid and even essential. An analogy which may be worth noting is the ways in which the theological agenda has informed theories of the paganization of Christianity during the fourth century, following the conversion of Constantine.[31] The presumption that there was ever a pristine form of Christianity, with an idyllic corporate life and egalitarian approach to worship, tends to be presupposed, consciously or otherwise, in arguments for lay eucharistic presidency on the basis of New Testament and early Christian evidence.[32] If ancient Christianity was idyllic, free of scandal and of competition for power, then several of Paul's letters would never have been written. Before considering the implications of these observations for the question of eucharistic presidency, it would be useful to take note of some aspects of the religiosity of the ancient world.

Contemporary Judaism distinguished clearly between, on the one hand, cultic worship, in which sacrifices were offered in the temple in Jerusalem, at rites over which hereditary priests officiated, assisted by hereditary Levites, and, on the other, the less formal gatherings in local

---

Schillebeeckx, *The Church with a Human Face* (London: SCM Press, 1985); J. H. Schütz, *Paul and the Anatomy of Apostolic Authority* (Cambridge: Cambridge University Press, 1975); E. Schweizer, *Church Order in the New Testament* (London: SCM Press, 1975).

30   W. F. Bauer, *Orthodoxy and Heresy in Earliest Christianity* (Philadelphia, PA: Fortress Press, 1971); R. A. Campbell, *The Elders* (Edinburgh: T & T Clark, 1994); H. F. von Campenhausen, *Ecclesiastical Authority and Spiritual Power in the Church of the First Three Centuries* (London: Black, 1969); E. Käsemann, *Essays on New Testament Themes* (London: SCM Press, 1964); Schweizer, *Church Order*.

31   J. Z. Smith, *Drudgery Divine* (Cambridge: Cambridge University Press, 1990), pp. 21–46.

32   Beckwith, *Elders*; W. H. G. Thomas, *The Principles of Theology* (London: Vine, 1930), pp. 316-29; J. Pryor, 'Lay Presidency and the Ordained Ministry Today', *St Mark's Review* 138 (1989): 12–17; J. Woodhouse, 'Lay Administration of the Lord's Supper', *St Mark's Review* 162 (1995): 15–19.

communities in Palestine and the diaspora.[33] In these latter "synagogues" patterns of worship were not yet standardized, but sacrifices were not offered. Readings and exposition of Scripture, recitation of psalms and singing of hymns, and offering of prayers did not require the services of a priest. Other community activities could and did include corporate meals. Leadership was exercised by local elders, whose position may have been more formalized in the diaspora cities where relations with local rulers and Roman officials needed constantly to be negotiated.[34] While non-cultic, this leadership was patriarchal, and authority was demonstrated and entrenched through ritual. The same was true of patriarchal authority in the Jewish home, expressed in presiding over family meals and domestic rites.

While it is unlikely that the public cults performed in the pagan temples influenced early Christian ritual life, the impact of domestic cults and the ritual conventions governing meals and hospitality are more directly relevant to the celebration of the eucharist.[35] It is important to recognize just how omnipresent the symbols of paganism were in the home, as in public places, and accordingly just how constant a factor ritual observances were in daily life. While those who officiated in domestic cults were not priests, ritual function nonetheless corresponded with hierarchical and clearly defined patriarchal domestic relationships.

Modern Western Christians have come to regard ritual acts as symbolic, only indirectly corresponding to divine action. They would never attribute supernatural power, still less control over God's power or action, to the officiant. This is far from the religious consciousness of ancient people, and their cultic acts were intended to please, appease, and even manipulate, the deities to whom they offered prayers and sacrifices.[36] That this applies in part to the first Christians may seem

---

33   Cf. J. M. G. Barclay, *Jews in the Mediterranean Diaspora* (Edinburgh: T & T Clark, 1996); B. Olsson and M. Zetterholm (eds), *The Ancient Synagogue from its Origins until 200 C.E.* (Stockholm: Almqvist & Wiksell, 2003); Sanders, *Judaism*.

34   Cf. Barclay, *Jews*; Campbell, *Elders*, pp. 44–54; T. Rajak and D. Noy, '*Archisunagogoi*: Office, Title and Social Status in the Greco-Jewish Synagogue', *JRS* 83 (1993): 75–93.

35   Cf. P. Lampe, 'The Corinthian Dinner Party', *Affirmation* 4 (1991): 1–16; Smith, *Symposium*.

36   Cf. C. M. Bell, *Ritual Theory, Ritual Practice* (New York, NY: Oxford University Press, 1992); H.-J. Klauck, *Magic and Paganism in Early Christianity* (Minneapolis, MN: Fortress Press, 2003); G. van der Leeuw, *Religion in Essence and Manifestation* (London: Allen & Unwin, 1964); R. MacMullen, *Paganism in*

inconceivable, but it needs to be acknowledged if the ritual life of the Early Church is to be understood. Jews and Christians worshipped one God only, not a plethora of deities whose rivalries could be exploited, and power harnessed, by human worshippers for their own ends, good or evil. Nevertheless, the divine power invoked in prayer and ritual was perceived as real, and at least potentially dangerous. In the eucharist, blessing the bread and wine consists in a great deal more than simply thanking God for the gift thereof and what it represents; blessing invokes the power of God over the elements.[37] Irrespective of the nature of the transformation brought about through this benediction, the authority to invoke divine power on behalf of the community was socially significant. The notion that, as the χάρισμα, *charism*, of presiding at the eucharist is not mentioned in 1 Cor. 12, it was a matter of no consequence who conducted the liturgies of the Church,[38] is highly implausible. Whereas private devotions in the pagan temples could entail self-administered sacrifices, the eucharist was a corporate act of the church. To invoke the power of God over ritual food and drink on behalf of the gathered community was a socially significant act, and could be undertaken, with some trepidation, only by a person whose position in the community made such action appropriate, effective, and beneficial.

The presence of acknowledged leaders in the early Christian churches is entirely apparent from the New Testament, even if their precise roles are far from clear.[39] While the nature of the leadership, and the theological and sociological bases of the authority which substantiated it,[40] may not be clear, it is highly implausible that this leadership did not find expression in presiding over the rituals and liturgies of the communities.[41] On the contrary, if there were no office in the ancient

---

the Roman Empire (New Haven, CT: Yale University Press, 1981); J. Z. Smith, *To Take Place* (Chicago, IL: University of Chicago Press, 1987); V. W. Turner, *The Ritual Process* (New York, NY: de Gruyter, 1969).

37 Feeley-Harnik, *Lord's Supper*, p. 72.

38 Beckwith, *Elders*, pp. 70–72; Pryor, 'Lay Presidency'; Woodhouse, 'Lay Administration', p. 16.

39 Rom. 12.8; 1 Cor. 16.15–16; Phil. 1.1; 1 Thess. 5.12–13; cf. Heb. 13.7, 17, 24; 1 Pet. 5.1–4.

40 A. J. Blasi, *Making Charisma* (New York, NY: Peter Lang, 1991); A. D. Clarke, *Serve the Community of the Church* (Grand Rapids, MI: Eerdmans, 2000); Holmberg, *Paul*; R. H. Williams, *Stewards, Prophets, Keepers of the Word* (Peabody, MA: Hendrickson, 2006).

41 As argued by Beckwith, *Elders*, pp. 70–72; Pryor, 'Lay Presidency'; Woodhouse, 'Lay Administration', p. 16; pace, Campbell, *Elders*; Gehring, *House Church*; D.

Church defined by liturgical presidency,[42] this would indicate that the function of liturgical presidency could not be separated from other aspects of leadership and oversight in the community. The Roman empire was a highly stratified, ritualized, and patriarchal society,[43] in which status was expressed, entrenched, and enhanced through rituals, and in which honour depended on maintaining status and power.[44] In Graeco-Roman paganism, householders presided over domestic cults at which the ancestral spirits of their families were venerated. "The religious authority and the social position of the head of the household are ... good reason to assume that he or she participated in presiding over the Lord's Supper."[45] A Christian householder hosting a church would have deferred only to a more eminent figure such as an itinerant apostle or prophet in presidency at the eucharist.[46] Even this was to

---

N. Power, *Ministers of Christ and His Church* (London: Geoffrey Chapman, 1969), p. 173.

42   P. F. Bradshaw, *Liturgical Presidency in the Early Church* (Bramcote: Grove Books, 1983), pp. 8–9.

43   K. R. Bradley, *Slavery and Society at Rome* (Cambridge: Cambridge University Press, 1994); J. K.-M. Chow, *Patronage and Power* (Sheffield: Sheffield Academic Press, 1992); Clarke, *Serve the Community*, pp. 251–2; P. D. A. Garnsey, *Social Status and Legal Privilege in the Roman Empire* (Oxford: Clarendon Press, 1970); G. Herman, *Ritualised Friendship and the Greek City* (Cambridge: Cambridge University Press, 1987); R. MacMullen, *Roman Social Relations* (New Haven, CT: Yale University Press, 1974); G. E. M. de Sainte Croix, *The Class Struggle in the Ancient Greek World* (London: Duckworth, 1981); R. P. Saller, *Personal Patronage Under the Early Empire* (Cambridge: Cambridge University Press, 1982); A. Wallace-Hadrill (Ed.), *Patronage in Ancient Society* (London: Routledge, 1989).

44   B. J. Malina, *Christian Origins and Cultural Anthropology* (Atlanta, GA: John Knox, 1986); B. K. Malinowski, 'The Role of Magic and Religion', in *Reader in Comparative Religion*, eds W. A. Lessa and E. Z. Vogt (New York: Harper & Row, 1965), pp. 63–71; J. H. Neyrey (ed.), *The Social World of Luke-Acts* (Peabody, MA: Hendrickson, 1991); Smith, *To Take Place*; Turner, *Ritual Process*.

45   Gehring, *House Church*, pp. 194–5; cf. H.-J. Klauck, *Herrenmahl und Hellenistischer Kult* (Münster: Aschendorf, 1982), pp. 349–50; Williams, *Stewards*, pp. 21–54.

46   Cf. Bradshaw, *Liturgical Presidency*, p. 9; Campbell, *Elders*; Clarke, *Serve the Community*, pp. 251–2; H. C. B. Green, *Lay Presidency at the Eucharist?* (London: Darton, Longman and Todd, 1994), pp. 9–10; H.–M. Legrand, 'The Presidency of the Eucharist According to Ancient Tradition', *Worship* 53 (1979): 415; H. O. Maier, *The Social Setting of the Ministry* (Waterloo, Ontario: Wilfred Laurier University Press, 2002); M. Slee, *The Church of Antioch in the First Century CE* (Sheffield: Sheffield Academic Press, 2003), pp. 101-9. Cf. Jesus at Emmaus, Lk. 24.30.

become a matter of some delicacy at a very early date,[47] and could well have been a factor in the tensions between Paul and the Corinthian church. Paul is unequivocal in asserting his rights as an apostle, but careful to decline payment, which would have reduced him to the level of a client or retainer of a Christian householder.[48] As a client Paul could not have presumed to take precedence ahead of a Christian householder in presiding over the eucharist held in his home. Deference to an apostle or prophet, or other such figure, could well have been reluctant, as the visitor would have been perceived as posing an implied challenge to the honour and status of the householder, and therefore to his authority in the church. Such occasions would almost certainly have been managed, as were invitations from synagogue leaders to visiting personages, so as to contain any threat to established local leadership.[49] An apostle or other itinerant prophetic or church-founding authority figure, for example, would almost certainly have expected precedence to be ceded. However, we have noted that Paul's relationship with the church in Corinth suggests that the authority and status even of the founding apostle would not always be acknowledged.[50] Such tensions between local and itinerant leadership figures competing for supremacy may well have been more widespread than can be confirmed from the records. This is not to deny that active participation in worship by several if not all members of the church was encouraged, to the point that order was threatened, but the importance of maintaining order in the community is frequently emphasized, not least by Paul himself.[51] However, from the first, liturgical presidency would have been the ritual expression of leadership and authority in and over the Christian community.[52]

It is generally believed that the eucharist began as a community meal, or was at least celebrated in such a context. At some stage, though not necessarily as part of a uniform process, the eucharist came to be

47 Cf. *Did.* 10.7.

48 1 Cor. 9; 2 Cor. 11-12. Cf. Chow, *Patronage*.

49 Cf. Acts 13.15. For discussion Bradshaw, *Liturgical Presidency*; Clarke, *Serve the Community*, pp. 251–2; Legrand, 'Presidency', p. 415; Rajak and Noy, '*Archisunagogoi*'; Slee, *Church*, pp. 101–9; cf. A. Etzioni, *A Comparative Analysis of Complex Organizations* (New York, NY: Free Press, 1975).

50 Taylor, *Paul*, pp. 206–14.

51 1 Cor. 11; 14; cf. 1 Thess. 5.12-13.

52 Bradshaw, *Liturgical Presidency*; Gehring, *House Church*; Green, *Lay Presidency*, pp. 8–10; E. Schillebeeckx, *Ministry: Leadership in the Community of Jesus Christ* (New York, NY: Crossroad, 1981), pp. 50–52; Slee, *Church*, pp. 101–109; cf.

separated from the corporate meal or *agape*, with only token elements of food and drink retained for ritual consumption.[53] Reasons for this may have been quite varied, and practical rather than theological in motivation. Particularly during the periods of persecution during the first three centuries, Christian worship could not have taken place in public buildings, and the space available in private homes, even of the wealthy, would have been restricted. Serving a full meal to large numbers of people could have become inconvenient, particularly when prolonging the gathering would increase the risks of apprehension and its consequences. Reducing the celebration to a token meal would have been expeditious and expedient in the circumstances. There is no reason at all to suppose that a desire for more elaborate liturgies motivated this development, but neither should we suppose that a corporate meal would in any respect have been an informal event. It would have been contrary to the culture of ancient society for the eucharist in the context of a corporate meal to have been any less formal and ritualized than the rite apart from the meal.[54] Considerations of order and honour would have applied equally, whatever form the eucharist took.

We should note briefly at this stage that the distinction between eucharist and *agape* in the ritual life of the Early Church has recently been brought into question.[55] It has been suggested that the diversity of ancient Christian liturgies was such that no neat distinction between two categories of worship can be drawn. Without entering this debate, one observation regarding its implications for current issues is important. The recent revival of an *agape* as a Christian ritual meal which is not a eucharist, and does not depend on the presence or presidency of a priest,[56] may rest on a distinction which did not apply in the ancient Church. The pastoral issues will be considered in Chapter 5, but it is important to recognize that even if the distinction is valid, this would not have affected the issue of precedence and presidency in the corporate ritual life of the Early Church.

Holmberg, *Paul*; H. Küng, *Why Priests?* (London: Collins, 1971), p. 29; Legrand, 'Presidency', p. 415.

53 Cf. Bradshaw, *Eucharistic Origins*, p. 66.

54 Cf. Bradshaw, *Eucharistic Origins*; J. Inziku, *Overcoming Divisive Behaviour* (Frankfurt: Peter Lang, 2005); Lampe, 'Corinthian Party'.

55 Bradshaw, *Eucharistic Origins*, pp. 27–9.

56 Dix, *Shape of the Liturgy*; Higgins, *Lord's Supper*, pp. 56–63; cf. L. Boff, *Ecclesiogenesis* (Maryknoll, NY: Orbis, 1986), pp. 61–75; G. E. D. Pytches and B. Skinner, *New Wineskins* (Guildford: Eagle Press, 1991), p. 33.

Historical reconstruction of church life as reflected in the New Testament indicates that ritual and authority were inextricably related. Honour required that order be maintained through conformity to cultural expectations, particularly in the conduct of corporate rituals. This would have implied that the person of highest status, either the host or a visiting personage of greater eminence in the Church, would have presided over community rituals, including the celebration of the eucharist. If such protocols were not explicitly articulated in the New Testament documents, this was because the criteria of precedence in the household and in the Church were sufficiently well established for there to be no such need.

It is certainly true that there is no statement or instruction anywhere in the New Testament which stipulates, either for the exigencies of the immediate context or for the Church of all time, who may or may not preside at the eucharist.[57] Historical reconstruction such as we have undertaken has suggested that precedence was the criterion for presidency, but that precedence could be contested. It would be too simplistic to describe this as a struggle for supremacy between the social power of the householders and the spiritual authority of apostles, prophets, and other charismatic figures, but social position and ascribed spiritual qualities were clearly key factors in determining precedence during the earliest period of the Church.[58] We turn our attention to questions relating to ministry and evidence for ways in which people were set apart for particular functions in the local community or the wider Church, in particular through the imposition of hands.

Imposition of hands and ministry in the New Testament
The word "ordain" has come to acquire in modern English usage a technical meaning, and is used almost exclusively of the liturgy whereby ministers of religion are commissioned, in which imposition of hands by appropriate authorities on the head of the person being ordained is the defining ritual. It is important, particularly when using older translations of the Bible, to recognize that "ordain" has had a very much wider semantic range, with connotations of arranging, deciding, preparing, equipping, appointing, assigning, and directing. Usage to refer to the rite of commissioning Christian clergy is a technical and derivative application. Most other uses of the word have become archaic in

---

57 Cf. Küng, *Why Priests?*, p. 29; Moloney, *Body Broken*; Wingren, *Gospel*, p. 13.

58 Campbell, *Elders*; cf. J. T. Burtchaell, *From Synagogue to Church* (Cambridge: Cambridge University Press, 1992).

contemporary English, but were still current when older translations of the Bible and the Book of Common Prayer were produced, as well as concordances and other handbooks which have become standard but reflect English usage of earlier generations. We cannot therefore assume that every occurrence of "ordain" or "ordination" refers unambiguously to a distinctive Christian rite, still less a sacrament of conferring distinct and permanent orders. As we shall see, a diversity of vocabulary is used in the original Greek of the New Testament, which would militate against postulating either the emergence of distinct orders of ministry or a uniform rite of admission to such orders. Therefore, before considering accounts of and allusions to commissioning rituals in the New Testament, some consideration needs to be given to the patterns of ministry and leadership attested in the Apostolic Church.

We have noted in the previous section something of the significance of householders in the Early Church. During the period before local congregations were able to acquire or build premises of their own, they were dependent on hospitality and patronage for access to places where they could meet for worship and other corporate activities. Smaller churches could meet in tenements occupied by less prosperous households (cf. Acts 20.7-12), but as congregations grew, and particularly as converts were attracted from the more affluent and influential orders of Graeco-Roman society, it was these owners of larger houses, with sufficient space available for larger numbers of people to gather, who became the predominant patrons of the local churches. This is not to deny that public buildings and business premises could also have been used, but access to these venues would also have depended on patronage. Householders and other patrons who provided venues where the church could meet would also have been in a position to provide patronage in other ways to the community and its members, by virtue of their relative wealth and social connections. This could have included some measure of protection in an hostile environment. Patrons would therefore have been in a position of considerable influence in the life of the church, and scholars are increasingly convinced that this was a most significant factor in the emergence of the monarchical episcopate.[59] As we have noted, at meetings of the gathered church, whether a small

---

59 Campbell, *Elders*; Gehring, *House Church*, pp. 196–210, 257–81; Holmberg, *Paul*, pp. 99–121; H.-J. Klauck, *Hausgemeinde und Hauskirche Im Frühen Christentum* (Stuttgart: VKB, 1981); W. A. Meeks, *The First Urban Christians* (New Haven, CT: Yale University Press, 1983), pp. 134–6; Slee, *Church*, pp. 101–19; Williams, *Stewards*, pp. 21–54.

congregation meeting in a tenement or a larger one in a villa, it was the host who would normally preside over the celebration of the eucharist. When the householder was a woman (cf. Rom. 16.1), we should suppose that she presided.[60] Whether or not they received any kind of commissioning for their role in the life of the church, from the founding apostle or from the community, we have simply no information. However, in a highly ritualized society, some form of inauguration or commissioning may well very often have taken place.

The emergence of the householder as bishop of the local church saw the eclipse of itinerant authority figures whose stature extended more widely in the Church. While this process would appear to have culminated somewhat after the New Testament period, aspects of this development are apparent at an early date. Itinerant authority figures are most frequently described as ἀπόστολοι (apostles), and προφῆται (prophets), and would have included, but not been restricted to, the founders of the churches. Nor can those called apostles be restricted to the inner circle of Jesus' disciples, with a few exceptions such as Barnabas and Paul. While Luke tends to use the term more exclusively, the evidence from Paul's letters suggests a much wider group of people, including at least one woman (Rom. 16.15). Paul also implies that there were specific criteria of apostleship: having seen the resurrected Jesus, and being active in the proclamation of the gospel (1 Cor. 9.1; 15.7); possibly also being an ethnic Jew and having suffered in the cause of the gospel (cf. 2 Cor. 11.21-29). The account of the election of Matthias, in keeping with the lukan restriction of apostleship to the original circle of Jesus' disciples, suggests that all apostles should in principle have shared in Jesus' historical ministry, and have been baptized by John the Baptist or at least have associated with his movement before the commencement of Jesus' ministry (cf. Acts 1.21–22). Paul was to become an exception, and a controversial one, and he indicates not merely was his calling chronologically the last, but also in some respect anomalous (1 Cor 15.8), not only because he had persecuted Christians before his conversion, but because he had not been a disciple of Jesus during his earthly ministry. For our present purpose, the point of significance is that the apostles were not a self-regenerating group, and their role in the Church would therefore end within the first Christian generation.[61]

60 Gerhring, *House Church*, pp. 211–25; C. Osiek and M. Y. MacDonald, *A Woman's Place* (Minneapolis, MN: Fortress Press, 2006), pp. 144–63.

61 C. K. Barrett, 'Shaliah and Apostle', *Donum Gentilium*, eds E. Bammel *et al.* (Oxford: Clarendon Press, 1978), pp. 88–102; K. H. Rengstorf, ἀποστέλλω,

The role of many, and probably most, of those later known as apostles began in their discipleship of Jesus during his historical ministry. While there was evidently an inner core of Jesus' disciples, presumably twelve in number, they cannot simply be equated with the later apostles. Not only did Judas Iscariot never become an apostle, but the Gospel accounts contain several discrepancies as to who were members of this group (Mt. 10.2-4; Mk 3.16-19; Lk. 6.14-16). Barnabas and others never identified as members of the δώδεκα are later described as apostles (Acts 14.4, 14; Rom. 16.15; 1 Thess. 2.7). The same was probably true of many others disciples who, after their Easter experience, proclaimed the gospel but do not meet Luke's particular criteria of apostleship, and whose activities are not recorded.

It is instructive to consider briefly the gospel accounts of Jesus' selection of the "twelve". It is not possible within the parameters of this study to consider all the critical issues relating to these texts and their tradition history. The relevant passages will therefore simply be read as narrative accounts which however theologically significant to the evangelists, would have met the criteria of plausibility for those who first heard the stories told. Unlike the accounts of the calling of individual disciples (Mt. 4.18-22; 9.9-13; Mk 1.16-20; 2.13-17; Lk. 5.1-11, 27-32; Jn 1.35-51), these passages suggest a degree of formal designation, which would have been a ritual, status-altering process for the disciples concerned. The texts are worth considering briefly:

Mk 3.14:   καὶ ἐποίησεν ....δώδεκα᾿ οὓς καὶ ἀποστόλους ὠνόμασεν̂

And he appointed twelve [whom he also named apostles]

The verb ἐποίησεν literally means "made", and its usage in this context indicates a transition from one status to another. The phrase in parentheses is a variant reading, which may not be original to the text, but rather reflect later assimilation of the "twelve" to the apostles. The setting of this episode on a mountain in itself evokes the motif, common in the Old Testament, of encountering God in high places, most particularly at Sinai. This is not to suggest that the evangelist is consciously alluding to Moses' summoning Aaron and his sons before God and commissioning them as priests (Exod. 19.24; 28-29). The context of prayer in which the "twelve" are called is nonetheless clear. They are appointed or "made" from among the wider company of Jesus'

ἀπόστολος, *TDNT* 1: 319–412; W. Schmithals, *The Office of Apostle in the Early Church* (London: SPCK, 1971); Taylor, *Paul*, pp. 227–8.

disciples, both to accompany him more closely and to be sent on a preaching mission, during which they would also have power to exorcize. Separation from a larger group, prayer, commissioning, and empowerment are all present in this verse, which strongly suggests that a ritual act, performed by Jesus, accompanied this.[62]

Mt 10.1–2   καὶ προσκαλεσάμενος τοὺς δώδεκα μαθητὰς αὐτοῦ ἔδωκεν αὐτοῖς ε ἐξουσίαν ... τῶν δὲ ἀποστόλων τὰ ὀνόματά ἐστιν ταῦτα.

Summoning his twelve disciples, he gave them power . ... These are the names of the twelve apostles:

Here the twelve are portrayed as the full complement of Jesus' disciples, coterminous also with the apostles. They have power conferred on them for healing and exorcism. While the element of separation from a larger group is absent, commissioning is implicit and becomes explicit in the following verses, and power to overcome supernatural forces is conveyed. It is almost certain, therefore, that the evangelist envisages that a ritual process underlies the account.[63]

Lk. 6.13   προσεφώνησεν τοὺς μαθητὰς αὐτοῦ, καὶ ἐκλεξάμενος ἀπ' αὐτῶν δώδεκα, οὓς καὶ ἀποόστολους ὠνόμασεν.

He called his disciples, and chose from among them twelve, whom he also called apostles.

As in the case of Mark, the mountain setting and the explicit statement that Jesus had spent the night in prayer reinforce the significance of the occasion. Jesus chooses (cf. Acts 1.2) twelve of his disciples, and names them apostles. They are not sent out until 9.1, and it is at that point that they receive power for healing and exorcism while proclaiming the coming kingdom of God. In 10.1 seventy further disciples are sent out in pairs to prepare the ground for Jesus' mission to the towns and villages

---

62   J. R. Donahue and D. J. Harrington, *The Gospel of Mark* (Collegeville, MN: Liturgical, 2002), pp. 122–7; C. E. B. Cranfield, *Mark* (Cambridge: Cambridge University Press, 1963), pp. 126–32; M. D. Hooker, *The Gospel According to Mark* (London: Black, 1991), pp. 110–13; J. Marcus, *Mark 1–8* (New York, NY: Doubleday, 2000), pp. 262–9.

63   F. W. Beare, *Matthew* (Peabody, MA: Hendrickson, 1987), pp. 238–40; W. D. Davies and D. C. Allison, *Matthew I* (Edinburgh: T & T Clark, 1991), pp. 150–9; U. Luz, *Matthew 8–20* (Minneapolis, MN: Fortress Press, 2001), pp. 66–9; R. Schnackenburg, *Matthew* (Grand Rapids, MI: Eerdmans, 2002), pp. 94–7.

they would visit. They are instructed to proclaim the kingdom of God and to heal the sick, but while they are clearly commissioned they are not explicitly empowered. Nonetheless the commissioning is clearly a ritual act, even if Luke prefers to speak of election, and associates empowerment rather with a more specific task.[64]

This brief survey has shown that the evangelists portray Jesus' commissioning of the "twelve" in significantly different ways. The ritual event is most apparent in Mark, where separation from the larger body, appointment to a more distinct role, and empowerment for the task take place on a single occasion, after prayer. Manual acts and other ritual gestures are not mentioned, but contemporary culture would have expected such, and early readers of the texts would have assumed that Jesus laid hands on or breathed over the disciples, or similarly transmitted power to them, symbolically but effectively. The vocabulary used to describe the commissioning of the "twelve" varies, which would count against a uniform Christian ordination or commissioning rite being retrojected onto this event in Jesus' historical ministry.

The narrative in Acts includes several commissioning accounts, which can usefully be considered briefly in turn. As with the gospel accounts considered above, space does not permit a detailed discussion of the critical issues surrounding the historicity of Acts in general and the texts to be considered in particular. A significant body of scholarship believes that Luke retrojects ecclesiastical customs and institutions of his own day onto the Church of the apostolic period.[65] We have to be aware, therefore, that at least some episodes may reflect the practice of the Church, or some parts of the Church, during the last third of the first century, rather than recording actual historical events precisely as they took place. Furthermore, the speeches in Acts need to be recognized, in

---

64   C. F. Evans, *Luke* (London: SCM Press, 1990), pp. 317–22; J. A. Fitzmyer, *Luke* (New York: Doubleday, 1981), pp. 613–20; I. H. Marshall, *Luke* (Exeter: Paternoster Press, 1978), pp. 236–41; J. C. Nolland, *Luke* (Waco, TX: Word, 1989), pp. 264–72.

65   C. K. Barrett, *Acts* (Edinburgh: T & T Clark, 1994); H. G. Conzelmann, *Acts of the Apostles* (Philadelphia, PA: Fortress, 1987); J. A. Fitzmyer, *Acts* (New York, NY: Doubleday, 1998); E. Haenchen, *Acts* (Oxford: Basil Blackwell, 1971), pp. 98–110; cf. M. Hengel, *Acts and the History of Earliest Christianity* (London: SCM Press, 1979); L. T. Johnson, *Acts* (Collegeville, MN: Liturgical Press, 1992), pp. 3–9.

conformity with contemporary historiographical conventions, as the
literary creation of the author or of a source from which he drew.[66]

There has been a substantial amount of scholarship in recent years
which has considered the formation and leadership of the early Christian
communities against the background of analogous or comparable
voluntary associations, including Jewish synagogues, in the ancient
world, and in particular the eastern Mediterranean.[67] Much of this has
been informed by sociology as well as ancient history and archaeology.
It is not necessary to rehearse or debate the findings of this research to
recognize that it has transformed our understanding of early
Christianity, not least in the area of leadership. Recognition of the social
and relational aspect of "charisma", and of the social reality of
household structure and patronage, have rendered untenable the image
of unstructured and leaderless egalitarian charismatic communities. A
consequence is that many scholars are now less sceptical than they once
were of the emergence of ecclesiastical offices at an early date.

The first commissioning account is that of Matthias to replace Judas
Iscariot in the circle of the "twelve" (Acts 1.15-26). The process is
initiated by Peter, in a gathering of the ἀδελφοί, a group which includes
Jesus' mother and brothers as well as his disciples. Luke numbers these
as approximately 120, which is considerably less than the 500 who,
according to Paul, experienced the christophany of the risen Jesus (1
Cor. 15.6). There is nevertheless no reason to suppose that this was a
closed gathering of any authoritative body, to the exclusion of other
disciples of Jesus. Peter refers to τὸν κλῆρον τῆς διακονίας ταύτης,
"the share in the ministry [of Jesus]" in which Judas had participated (v.
17). κλῆρος here means "portion" or "lot", a share in a greater task
which has been assigned to a particular person; it would be
anachronistic to read into this text the usage of the term to denote the
clergy as distinct from the laity in the Church. διακονία refers to the
specific ministry or service of the "twelve", which, once Matthias has
been elected, is associated with ἀποστολή, the commission or

---

66 Conzelmann, *Acts*, pp. xliii–xlv; Fitzmyer, *Acts*, pp. 103–8; M. L. Soards, *The
    Speeches in Acts: Their Content, Context, and Concerns* (Louisville, KY:
    Westminster/John Knox, 1994).

67 Gehring, *House Church*; Holmberg, *Paul*; *Sociology and the New Testament*
    (Minneapolis, MN: Fortress Press, 1990); H. C. Kee, *Christian Origins in
    Sociological Perspective* (London: SCM Press, 1980); A. J. Malherbe, *Social Aspects
    of Early Christianity* (Philadelphia, PA: Fortress Press, 1983); Meeks, *First Urban
    Christians*; G. Theissen, *The Social Setting of Pauline Christianity* (Edinburgh: T &
    T Clark, 1982).

apostleship of proclaiming the gospel (v. 25), on which the "twelve" would begin on Pentecost, the next pericope in the Acts narrative. Peter proceeds to quote two passages from the Psalms, the second of which provides the rationale for the process: τὴν ἐπισκοπὴν αὐτοῦ λαβέτω ἕτερος, "let another take his office" (v. 20, citing Ps. 109.8). ἐπισκοπή is specifically the office of oversight, which came to be applied not only to the "twelve" but to local church leaders also, who were to acquire in due course the related word ἐπίσκοπος, overseer or bishop, as a title. This does not constitute an historical link between the "twelve" and the later monarchical episcopate, but it does demonstrate how concepts could become associated as the tradition and structures of the Church developed. What is important for the present purpose is the process that was followed: Peter called for nominations, and two names were proposed, presumably from the gathered assembly rather than the narrower circle of the surviving members of the "twelve". After prayer, the election was decided by casting lots. Irrespective of whether casting lots would be considered a commendable means of discerning the will of God today, and how it would compare with the machinations of contemporary electoral processes, Luke is clearly more concerned with the rationale attributed to Peter than with questions of procedure. The ending of the narrative is very brief, and, after Matthias has been elected, we are told simply that συγκατεψηφίσθη μετὰ τῶν ἕνδεκα ἀποστόλων, "he was numbered with the eleven apostles" (v. 26). Whereas lots rather than a democratic process were used to ascertain the will of God, once the choice was established, an act of the community to confirm this would seem to have followed. συγκατεψηφίσθη is suggestive of conducting a ballot, but is more likely here to denote a gesture to endorse the election of Matthias. Whether this consisted merely of verbal acclaim, or of a ritual act, is not stated, but the latter is more likely in the cultural context. At the very least, we should expect that the "twelve" would have made a gesture to signify to the gathering that Matthias had been admitted to their body, and complemented their number.[68]

The election of the "seven" is the first account of commissioning for office in the Early Church, in which the rite of imposition of hands is explicitly reported (Acts 6.1–6). We do not need to discuss either the traditional identification of Stephen and his companions as the first

---

68 Barrett, *Acts*, pp. 91–105; Conzelmann, *Acts*, pp. 10–12; Fitzmyer, *Acts*, pp. 217–28; Haenchen, *Acts*, pp. 157–65; Johnson, *Acts*, pp. 34–40.

deacons,[69] or whether in fact their role was the practical and administrative διακονία indicated. In the account of Stephen's death which follows this pericope (Acts 6.8–8.1), distribution of food to widows is certainly not among the accusations brought against him, but rather his activity in proclaiming the gospel[70] – precisely the activity for which his appointment was ostensibly intended to release the apostles. What is important for our purpose is that a need was identified, and the "twelve" responded by inviting nominations from the community of people whom "we" would appoint – καταστήσομεν – to address the problem, and stipulated the spiritual qualities required (v. 3). Whether "we" refers to the community as a whole or to the "twelve" is not clear. The seven selected by the community, by whatever process, are presented, either by the gathered assembly as a whole or by the designated representatives of the Hellenists to the apostles, οὓς ἔστησαν ἐνώπιον τῶν ἀποστόλων (v. 6). What follows is prayer and imposition of hands – προσευξάμενοι ἐπέθηκαν αὐτοῖς τὰς χεῖρας – whether by the entire assembly or by the apostles alone is disputed in scholarship.[71] Grammatically both readings are possible, even if the latter meaning could have been expressed unambiguously. On the other hand, the pericope as a whole suggests that the apostles were delegating to the "seven" a function that at least some in the community regarded as their responsibility. Moreover, scholars discern the influence on this passage of the accounts in the Pentateuch of the ordination of Aaron and his sons as priests of the tabernacle (Lev. 8.10), and of the appointment of Joshua to succeed Moses, to which imposition of his hands on Joshua, by Moses alone, was the defining ritual (Num. 27.15–23). While we cannot be certain, therefore, there are sound reasons for believing that the apostles alone laid their hands on the "seven" to signify blessing and conferral of authority for their new role.[72]

The church of Antioch-on-the-Orontes in Syria was one of the most significant during the early centuries of Christianity.[73] It was here that

---

69 First attested by Irenaeus, *Haer.* 3.12.10; 4.15.1. Cf. Rom. 16.1; 1 Cor. 3.5; 2 Cor. 3.6; 11.23; Col. 1.7; 1 Tim. 3.8–13.

70 N. H. Taylor, 'Stephen, the Temple, and Early Christian Eschatology', *RB* 110 (2003): 62–85.

71 Barrett, *Acts*, p. 315; cf. Fitzmyer, *Acts*, p. 351; Johnson, *Acts*, p. 107.

72 Barrett, *Acts*, pp. 302–17; Conzelmann, *Acts*, pp. 47–8; Fitzmyer, *Acts*, pp. 343–52; Haenchen, *Acts*, pp. 260–9; Johnson, *Acts*, pp. 105–13.

73 R. E. Brown and J. P. Meier, *Antioch and Rome* (London: Geoffrey Chapman, 1983); W. A. Meeks and R. L. Wilken, *Jews and Christians in Antioch* (Missoula,

the conversion of Gentiles is first recorded, and that the term Χριστιανοί, "Christians" was first applied to members of the Church (Acts 11.19-26). Furthermore, Antioch became a major centre for Christian mission, in which Barnabas and Paul were to play a major role. The key text is Acts 13.1-3. This begins by identifying a number of προφῆται, prophets, and διδάσκαλοι, teachers in the community, of whom Barnabas is listed first and Paul (here still identified by the Semitic version of his name, Saul) last. Attempts to identify some of the five names as those of prophets and others as teachers are inevitably speculative, and the terms may not be mutually exclusive. Irrespective of the functions Barnabas and Paul had hitherto played in the church, what is important is the significant change in their role and status which takes place in this pericope. The setting is a gathering of the church for worship, as indicated by λειτουργούντων with its connotations of public service, and not a prayer meeting of the leadership. This gathering had presumably been preceded by fasting, as a regular discipline rather than an extraordinary observance, unless there was a prior intention to seek divine revelation on a matter of concern. The revelation as recorded is simultaneously clear and unspecific:

Ἀφορίσατε δή μοι τὸν Βαρναβᾶν καὶ Σαῦλον εἰς τὸ ἔργον ὃ προσκέκλημαι αὐτούς.

Set apart for me Barnabas and Saul for the work to which I have called them (v. 2).

The verb for separate or set apart, ἀφορίζω, is also used by Paul to describe his calling to be an apostle (Rom. 1.1; Gal. 1.15). The precise nature of their new task is apparently not specified in the revelation, but becomes clear as the narrative unfolds. Presumably at a subsequent gathering for worship, after further fasting, Barnabas and Paul are formally set apart and commissioned for their new work. This is ritually signified by the imposition of hands, τὰς χεῖρας αὐτοῖς ἀπέλυσαν (v. 3). It is not stated who carried out this rite, the remaining prophets and teachers or the church as a whole. Either way, this signifies the assent of the church to the new commission Barnabas and Paul have received, and invokes God's blessing on their work. The nature of this work becomes apparent only in the subsequent narrative, when Barnabas and Paul, significantly described as having been ἐκπεμφθέντες ὑπὸ τοῦ

MO: Scholars, 1978); Slee, *Church*; Taylor, *Paul*; M. Zetterholm, *The Formation of Christianity in Antioch* (London: Routledge, 2003).

ἁγίου πνεύματος, sent out by the Holy Spirit (v. 4), embark on what is commonly but incorrectly known as Paul's first missionary journey. Presumably the church of Antioch was well aware that Barnabas and Paul were setting out to proclaim the gospel and establish churches in other centres, even if they could not foresee where they would meet with a favourable reception. This episode marks, in the Acts narrative, the beginning of Paul's work as an apostle, and it is only in the account of this mission that Barnabas and Paul are described as apostles (14.4, 14).[74]

At the conclusion of the account of Barnabas and Paul's mission, it is reported that they χειροτονήσαντες δὲ αὐτοῖς κατ' ἐκκλησίαν πρεσβυτέρους, "appointed elders [presbyters] in each of the churches they had founded" (Acts 14.23). The narrative would seem to suggest that this took place not when Barnabas and Paul left the city after founding the church but on their return journey. This would imply that the young churches were left to manage themselves without designated leadership, which could suggest that the appointment by the founding apostles would have confirmed the leadership which had become established in the interim, in all likelihood that of the householders who hosted the churches. Alternatively, this summary passage could indicate a general practice of installing local leadership in churches founded by missionaries from Antioch.[75] The verb used is χειροτονέω, literally meaning to stretch out the hand, which could denote casting a vote rather than of imposing hands on the person elected, but probably implies the latter ritual.[76] However, the language is that of formal appointment, and of transmission of authority and commission. We should expect that these appointments were formalized ritually in a gathering of the church, and confirmed or assented to by the community in some formal way.[77]

The other reference to appointed local church leadership in Acts occurs in the account of Paul's address to τοὺς πρεσβυτέρους, the presbyters of the church of Ephesus, whom he summoned to meet him in Miletus (20.18–38) when passing on his final journey to Jerusalem. The church in Ephesus had been founded rather later than those to

---

74 Barrett, *Acts*, pp. 598–611; Conzelmann, *Acts*, pp. 98–9; Fitzmyer, *Acts*, pp. 494–500; Haenchen, *Acts*, pp. 394–6; Johnson, *Acts*, pp. 220–7; Taylor, *Paul*, pp. 88–95.

75 Campbell, *Elders*, p. 166.

76 Campbell, *Elders*, p.167; Johnson, *Acts*, p. 254.

77 Barrett, *Acts*, pp. 687–8; Conzelmann, *Acts*, pp. 112; Fitzmyer, *Acts*, pp. 534–5; Haenchen, *Acts*, p. 436; Johnson, *Acts*, pp. 254–5.

which reference is made in Acts 14.23, during Paul's period of missionary activity in Greece and Asia Minor. It therefore represents a very different stage in Paul's career as a Christian apostle to his period working from Antioch.[78] In the Acts narrative Paul's speech to the Ephesian presbyters functions as a farewell discourse, and is set shortly before his arrest in Jerusalem and the end of his recorded career as a Christian missionary. In a sense, therefore, the Ephesian presbyters represent the leadership of all the churches Paul had established as a Christian apostle. For our present purpose, one particular sentence of this speech is of crucial importance:

Προσέχετε ἑαυτοῖς καὶ παντὶ τῷ ποιμνίῳ, ἐν ᾧ ὑμᾶς τὸ πνεῦμα τὸ ἅγιον ἔθετο ἐπισκόπους ποιμαίνειν τὴν ἐκκλησίαν τοῦ θεοῦ ...

Keep watch over yourselves and the whole flock, of which the Holy Spirit has appointed you overseers [bishops], to shepherd the church of God ... (Acts 20.28).

Several aspects of this are of interest. Those who are identified as πρεσβύτεροι in the narrative are here described as ἐπίσκοποι, overseers or bishops. That the two terms are applied to the same people, individually or collectively, does not imply that they are identical in meaning, any more than προφῆται and διδάσκαλοι have the same meaning in Acts 13.1. Their appointment is attributed to the Holy Spirit, which does not mean that Paul and the local church had no part in this process. Rather, the guidance of the Holy Spirit was invoked over the process of discernment whereby these particular leaders emerged. How this guidance was discerned is not explained, nor is the process whereby the community acknowledged the appointment attributed to the Holy Spirit. We should expect, however, that some formal ritual process would have given expression to this. There is no further information as to who these presbyters and bishops were, except that we may deduce that persons able to make the journey from Ephesus to Miletus at Paul's bidding would have enjoyed some control over their daily lives. This in itself would point to the householders who hosted meetings of the church, perhaps in several different congregations, and possibly others of equal or comparable standing in society. The application of pastoral imagery to the leadership of Christian communities is deeply rooted in the Old Testament,[79] and its application here to church leaders requires

78 Taylor, *Paul*, pp. 146–52.
79 Cf. Ps. 74.1-2; Jer 23.1-4; Ezek. 34.1-6; Zech. 11.4-17.

no detailed consideration other than to observe that it does not imply that the presbyters are of a different species to other members of their congregation.[80]

In summary, the accounts of commissioning and references to church leadership in Acts tend to confirm what one would expect to find: that the selection of leaders was attributed to the direction of the Holy Spirit, invoked through prayer and on at least some occasions by fasting. This does not exclude a guiding role, at least, for such authority figures as the founding apostles of the communities. Nor does it exclude the social power of patrons whose influence in the community and the wider society was co-opted or acknowledged. In at least some cases, and probably all, the appointment of leaders or acquiescence in the leadership already being exercised, was given ritual expression. Imposition of hands to invoke God's blessing on the leaders, and to symbolize assent by the community to their appointment, was at least one such rite. There is some fluidity in the terminology used to describe the leaders, and no indication at all that different titles reflected significantly different roles in the community.

The prevailing view in scholarship is that Acts reflects some degree of anachronism in ascribing structures and offices known in the church of Luke's day to earlier periods and perhaps also to different parts of the church where the same traditions did not develop in the same way or at the same time. However, we have also noted that Luke does not impose a bland uniformity on all Christian communities to which he alludes. The emergence of local leadership is not merely inherently plausible, but would have been essential to the survival of those communities from the initial impetus and fervour which accompanied their foundation, and certainly by the time founding missionaries departed. That these leaders should have been ritually acknowledged, and the power of the Holy Spirit invoked upon them for their work, is also inherently plausible. None of the accounts makes explicit reference to presiding at the eucharist, or indeed to any other specific ministry, with the exception of the "seven" in Acts 6. The only account of an actual celebration of the eucharist in Acts, as opposed to frequent passing allusions, is set in Troas (Acts 20.7–12).[81] In this episode, it is clear that Paul is presiding,

---

80   Barrett, *Acts*, pp. 974–7; Conzelmann, *Acts*, pp. 174–5; Fitzmyer, *Acts*, pp. 678–80; Haenchen, *Acts*, pp. 592–3; Johnson, *Acts*, pp. 362–3.

81   That this was a celebration of the Eucharist is disputed (Barrett, *Acts*, pp. 950–1). This argument rests on a doubtful distinction between eucharist and *agape*, and attaches insufficient weight to the explicit dating ἐν δὲ τῇ μιᾷ τῶν σαββάτων,

and that, as well as preaching all night (vv. 7,11), he κλάσας τὸν ἄρτον, "broke the bread" (v. 11). As founding apostle, Paul takes precedence over local leadership in this celebration. As this gathering seems to have taken place in a tenement rather than a villa, the householder who would normally have presided would have been of lesser status in society than the more powerful patrons whose predominance gave rise to the monarchical episcopate. His deference to Paul on this occasion may therefore also have been less reluctant than on some occasions in other cities.

Much of the material in Acts which we have reviewed concerns the work of Paul and the churches he founded. Particularly given that Luke wrote at a later period, it is important to compare the evidence we have gathered in Acts with references to local church leadership in Paul's letters.

In what most scholars believe is the earliest of Paul's letters, 1 Thessalonians, we find an explicit affirmation of the leadership that is being exercised in the local church. The context would appear to be that the authority of the leaders is not being acknowledged by all members of the church, and their efforts on behalf of the community not appreciated. These leaders are described at some length:

> . . . τοὺς κοπιῶντας ἐν ὑμῖν καὶ προϊσταμένους ὑμῶν ἐν κυρίῳ καὶ νουθετοῦντας ὑμᾶς . . .
>
> ... those who labour among you and watch over you in the Lord and who admonish you (1 Thess. 5.12).

The descriptive nature of Paul's reference in itself suggests that these are not titled officers, but nonetheless those whom he acknowledges as the legitimate leaders of the community, whose identity would have been perfectly clear to the recipients, whom he expects also to acknowledge them. Working hard in or on behalf of the community does not in itself imply leadership, but mentioning this aspect of their role first subtly reminds the Thessalonian Christians of their reciprocal obligation to these leaders. The connotations of watching over or presiding are very similar to those associated with bishops: oversight and leadership in the community. That Paul qualifies this, rather than the other activities of the leaders, as being ἐν κυρίῳ (in the Lord), counts against interpreting προϊσταμένους to mean "showing concern for" as favoured by previous

---

the first day of the week, in commemoration of the resurrection of Christ (v. 7). Cf. Fitzmyer, *Acts*, p. 669; Haenchen, *Acts*, pp. 584–6; Johnson, *Acts*, p. 356.

generations of predominantly Protestant scholarship, and continues to be defended by some evangelicals.[82] The same term clearly designates authority figures in Rom. 12.8; 16.2. At a later date προϊσταμένος is used specifically of the leader who presides over the celebration of the eucharist. While it would be anachronistic to read that meaning into Paul's usage here, the role of leadership and oversight in the community would have included presiding over its ritual life, including the celebration of the eucharist. If these figures are also the patrons who host meetings of the church in their homes, they would certainly have expected to preside over those gatherings, in the absence of Paul and the co-founders of the Thessalonian church, Silvanus and Timothy.[83] Whether their leadership was conferred ritually is not specified, but there would appear from the text to be no doubt as to who these people were, even if their authority is not acknowledged appropriately by all members of the community.

It is in the Corinthian correspondence that we have the most substantial body of extant literature concerning a single church of the first century. Recent scholarship has emphasized the role of patronage in the Corinthian church, and also ways in which powerful patrons were able to undermine the authority Paul exercised over the community he had founded, and to enlist the support of unidentified but evidently prestigious apostolic figures in doing so. Internal rivalries, reflecting competition among patrons for status and power in the church and in the wider society, are also apparent.[84] Paul was confronted at various times both with the social power of the patrons and with the charismatic authority ascribed to other prominent Christians, some of whom also styled themselves apostles. His comments on leadership and ministry need to be understood in this light, bearing in mind that the leaders of the church seem to have been a significant part of the problem.[85] The text most frequently cited is of course 1 Cor. 12, and in particular the catalogue of gifts of the Holy Spirit, or rather of those manifesting such gifts, in v. 28. The list is presumably not intended to be comprehensive, and the examples cited are probably directly relevant to the particular

---

82 R. Banks, *Paul's Idea of Community* (Exeter: Paternoster, 1980), p. 141.

83 E. Best, *A Commentary on the First and Second Epistles to the Thessalonians* (London: A. & C. Black, 1972), pp. 224–7; Holmberg, *Paul*, pp. 99–118; C. A. Wanamaker, *The Epistles to the Thessalonians* (Grand Rapids, MI: Eerdmans, 1990), pp. 191–4.

84 Chow, *Patronage*; D. G. Horrell, *The Social Ethos of the Corinthian Correspondence* (Edinburgh: T & T Clark, 1996); Theissen, *Social Setting*.

85 Campbell, *Elders*, p. 105; cf. Chow, *Patronage*.

situation prevailing in the church in Corinth at the time of writing. It is noteworthy that, after itemizing apostles, prophets, and teachers, Paul refers not to titles or offices but to people who perform certain functions and manifest certain gifts. As well as manifestations of supernatural power, Paul lists more mundane services to the church, including κυβερνήσεις, administration. There is no explanation as to how these gifts were recognized, or whether they were ritually invoked or conferred, even if there are indications that some gifts were more actively sought than others (vv. 29-31). Nor is there any clear indication as to how the diverse gifts relate to each other in the life of the church, other than the principle of an organic and interdependent relationship within a single body (vv. 7-26). Paul's concern for order in the community, and particularly in its gatherings for worship, is especially apparent in 1 Cor. 11 and 14. In 1 Cor. 16.15-18 Paul affirms the authority of Stephanas, his first convert, ἀπαρχή, in Corinth, and evidently a householder of some substance. While not the only patron providing hospitality to Christian gatherings in Corinth, and probably not the most wealthy or powerful, he is the only one mentioned in connection with the service, διακονία, of the church.[86] This could indicate that Paul is less willing to endorse the leadership of patrons in Corinth than elsewhere, on account of the conflicts among them.[87]

It is only in Phil. 1.1 that titled officers are mentioned in an undisputed letter of Paul's. For this reason there has been considerable scholarly discussion of this brief reference. As the ἐπίσκοποι and διάκονοι, bishops and deacons, are addressed only in the epistolary prescript, and are not mentioned again in the letter, there is no explanation of their roles and functions. The connotations of ἐπισκοπή suggest leadership and oversight in the community, and, as we have noted previously, quite probably patronage.[88] The connotations of διακονία are more ambiguous, suggesting service or servanthood, but capable of disguising power as service, and in particular as service which incurs the reciprocal obligation of compliance. Paul uses διακονία

---

86 Crispus and Gaius (1 Cor. 1.14) are almost certainly also patrons. Gaius in Rom. 16.23 is probably the same as the latter, while the former was previously ἀρχισυνάγωγος, leader of the synagogue in Corinth (Acts 18.8). Chloe (1 Cor. 1.12) may also be a patron in Corinth, but her whereabouts are uncertain.

87 Campbell, *Elders*; R. F. Collins, *1 Corinthians* (Collegeville, MN: Liturgical Press, 1999); D. L. Bartlett, *Ministry in the New Testament* (Minneapolis, MN: Fortress Press, 1993), pp. 46–50; Chow, *Patronage*; Horrell, *Social Ethos*; B. W. Winter, *After Paul Left Corinth* (Grand Rapids, MI: Eerdmans, 2001).

88 Campbell, *Elders*, pp. 123–4.

elsewhere of the service rendered by leaders in the community, not least himself (Rom. 16.1; 1 Cor. 16.15; cf. 1 Thess. 5.12). It is also noteworthy that Paul and Timothy describe themselves as δοῦλοι, slaves, of Christ (Phil. 1.1; cf. 2.7), by no means intending thereby to renounce their authority in relation to the Philippian Christians. There is no indication as to how those called bishops and deacons emerged to leadership, other than what can be surmised from our knowledge of patronage and household structures in Graeco-Roman antiquity. Nor is there any indication as to whether or how Paul or the community publicly acknowledged their leadership and authority. Nevertheless, that they are addressed in itself implies that they played a role of some significance in the Philippian church at an early date. While these officers cannot be equated with the bishops and deacons of succeeding generations, neither can their existence in Philippi during the middle years of the first century be regarded as an isolated or insignificant phenomenon.[89]

In the opinion of most, but not all, critical scholars, the letters addressed to Timothy and Titus, collectively known as the Pastoral letters, were not written by Paul himself, but were ascribed to him by another writer some years after his death.[90] The prominence of ecclesiastical office bearers in 1 Tim. and Tit. is attributed to changing conditions in the Church of the apostolic period. Several points are worth noting. In 1 Tim. 4.14 Timothy is reminded of the χαρίσματος ὃ ἐδόθη σοι διὰ προφητείας μετὰ ἐπιθέσεως τῶν χειρῶν τοῦ πρεσβυτερίου, "the gift [of the Holy Spirit] which you were given through prophecy with the imposition of the hands of the college of presbyters". The gift in question is presumably that of teaching and preaching mentioned in the preceding verse. Prophecy and bestowal of

---

89 F. W. Beare, *Philippians* (London: Black, 1988), pp. 49–50; M. N. A. Bockmuehl, *Philippians* (London: Black, 1997), pp. 53–5; J. B. Lightfoot, *Saint Paul's Epistle to the Philippians* (London: Macmillan, 1896), pp. 82, 95–9; P. Oakes, *Philippians* (Cambridge: Cambirdge University Press, 2001).

90 Pauline authorship is defended by G. D. Fee, *1 & 2 Timothy, Titus* (Peabody, MA: Hendrickson, 1995); L. T. Johnson, *Letters to Paul's Delegates* (Valley Forge, PA: Trinity Press International, 1996); J. N. D. Kelly, *The Pastoral Epistles* (London: Black, 1963); pseudepigraphy argued by M. F. Dibelius and H. G. Conzelmann, *The Pastoral Letters* (Philadelphia, PA: Fortress Press, 1972); H. Koester, *History and Literature of Early Christianity. II* (Philadelphia, PA: Fortress Press, 1982), pp. 297–305; cf. Campbell, *Elders*, pp. 176–9; D. G. Meade, *Pseudonymity and Canon* (Grand Rapids, MI: Eerdmans, 1987), pp. 130–9; S. G. Wilson, *Luke and the Pastoral Epistles* (London: SPCK, 1979).

charismatic gifts accompany the rite of imposition of hands, the corporate act of a body of elders or presbyters. Who constituted this body is not specified, but it is implied that they acted collegially. This is not necessarily a separate occasion to that referred to in 2 Tim. 1.6, where Paul emphasizes τῆς ἐπιθέσεως τῶν χειρῶν μου, "the imposition of my [Paul's] hands". The difference may be one of emphasis, with drawing attention on one occasion to his own role, and on the other to the collegial nature of ordination. The other alternative is that Timothy was understood to have received the imposition of hands in commissioning for Christian ministry on more than one occasion, initially by a college of presbyters in a rite of commissioning for Christian mission, perhaps at a point in the Acts narrative near 16.2-3; and subsequently by Paul alone for his work as Paul's delegate in oversight of certain churches. The letter presupposes that Timothy is exercising some kind of oversight of a number of churches, and teaching and preaching form a part of this ministry, but by no means all of it. Timothy himself is χεῖρας ... ἐπιτίθει, to "lay hands" on others (1 Tim. 5.22), but to exercise caution in doing so. This can justifiably, and without anachronism, be called ordination. Titus is also instructed to καταστήσῃς κατὰ πόλιν πρεσβυτέρους, "appoint presbyters in every city" (Tit. 1.5). The verb καθίστημι has connotations of formally admitting to office, as well as of election to such a position. The qualities required of office-bearers are spelled out in some detail, including those of bishops (1 Tim. 3.2-7; Tit. 1.7-8); presbyters (1 Tim. 5.17; Tit. 1.6),[91] and deacons (1 Tim. 3.8-12). A question of some consequence not only for understanding the emergence of ecclesiastical structures, but of enduring ecclesiological concern, is whether ἐπίσκοπος and πρεσβύτεροι apply to the same officers, or whether they can be distinguished, and on what basis. That the former term occurs always in the singular and the latter in the plural is suggestive of some distinction. More significant, perhaps, is that the bishop alone is required to be hospitable (1 Tim. 3.2; Tit. 1.8). This would seem to imply that a bishop should be a householder able to host meetings of the church. The requirement that he be also of good repute in the wider society (1 Tim. 3.7) indicates that a bishop should be able to wield influence on behalf of the church and its members. The prohibition on appointing recent converts (1 Tim. 3.6) suggests that potentially useful patrons might

---

91   Campbell's argument in *Elders*, that πρεσβύτερος is a generic term of persons of eminence is more than plausible, even it became the title of a distinct office. The implications of this insight will be discussed below.

otherwise be elevated prematurely to leadership. It is a requirement that bishops be able to teach (1 Tim. 3.2), and presbyters able to do so are regarded as somewhat superior to their less endowed colleagues (1 Tim. 5.17). It is notable also that the same verb, προΐστημι, is used of bishops and presbyters in these letters (1 Tim. 3.4, 5, 12; 5.17; Tit 3.8,14) as of the leaders of the Thessalonian church (1 Thess. 5.12) at an early date. Whatever uncertainties may remain about the ecclesiastical structures reflected in the Pastoral letters, the existence of the offices is presupposed, but not theologically, still less polemically, articulated.[92]

To summarize the evidence gathered from the Pauline corpus, there is no substance at all to the egalitarian charismatic anarchy idealized by some scholars. Paul viewed some charismatic manifestations, and claims to authority asserted on the basis thereof, as disruptive of the life of the community, and as not authentically reflecting the presence and activity of the Holy Spirit. The differentiation of functions, inspired by different gifts of the same Spirit, in itself implies that individuals were not free to assume whatever roles they chose in the corporate life of the community.[93] The patronage networks and structures of ancient society impacted on church organization and leadership from an early date. While there is no explicit reference to ordination before the Pastoral letters, it is apparent that office-bearers of various kinds were active in the churches from an early date. It would have been consistent with the culture of the day for them to have been formally and ritually commissioned for their roles in the community, and the blessing and guidance of the Holy Spirit invoked over them.

The emergence of church leaders known as πρεσβύτεροι, elders or presbyters, is attested more widely in what are generally regarded as later writings of the New Testament. James addresses a number of issues to entire communities, including matters pertaining to order in worship (2.1-4), and the conduct of those who teach (3.1-2). The only role of the πρεσβυτέρους τῆς ἐκκλησίας, the presbyters of the church, that is discussed in the letter, is an intercessory one: to anoint and pray for the sick, effecting healing and forgiveness (5.14-16). It is of course highly unlikely that their role was limited to this; rather, the writer is encouraging Christians to make use of the services of the presbyters in this way.[94] The

---

92   Cf. Brown, *Priest*; Campbell, *Elders*, pp. 176–204; Johnson, *Letters*, pp. 14–15; *1 & 2 Timothy* (New York: Doubleday, 2002), pp. 212–25.

93   1 Cor. 12.1–31. Cf. Collins, *1 Corinthians*, pp. 441–71; Green, *Lay Presidency?*, p. 9.

94   Cf. S. Laws, *The Epistle of James* (London: Black, 1980), pp. 225–32.

author of 1 Peter identifies himself as a συμπρεσβύτερος, a fellow-presbyter addressing other presbyters (5.1). They are directed to ποιμάνατε, shepherd the flock of God, ἐπισκοποῦντες, overseeing or watching over those in their care; Christ himself being the chief shepherd (5.2-4), described elsewhere in the letter as τὸν ποιμένα καὶ ἐπίσκοπον τῶν ψυχῶν ὑμῶν, the shepherd and guardian [=bishop] of your souls.[95] In 2 John 1 and 3 John 1 the author identifies himself as ὁ πρεσβύτερος, the presbyter, and asserts a jurisdiction over a number of churches, perhaps not dissimilar to that which Paul had exercised. In 3 John this oversight is being resisted by the local leadership.[96] In Revelation, 24 πρεσβύτεροι, elders, appear in a heavenly scene (4–7; 11.16; 14.3; 19.4), twelve of whom are identified with the apostles, and there is no direct link with any presbyters who may have been exercising oversight of the seven churches or any other terrestrial community. In none of these passages is there any defence of the office of presbyter, or any detailed description of the role, or of how certain people assumed this position in their communities. Nor is there any reason to suppose that the leadership, or even the credentials of leadership, were at all uniform, though local patronage would have been increasingly prominent as founding apostles and prophets receded from the ecclesiastical scene.[97] Nevertheless, the cumulative evidence confirms that some form of presbyteral leadership was widely established in the Church in the first century.

None of the texts discussed makes any explicit reference to the celebration of the eucharist, still less stipulates who should preside at such gatherings. The conclusion we are led to is not that it was a matter of indifference as to who presided over the gatherings of the churches of the first generation, but rather that this was an issue settled in terms of established cultural conventions, and in particular notions of order and precedence. The structure of the household, and the social power of the patron hosting the church, would have been sufficient to ensure that the householder providing hospitality to the community also presided over its gatherings. It would have been only persons of greater and wider

---

95   P. J. Achtemeier, *1 Peter* (Minneapolis, MN: Fortress Press, 1996), pp. 320–34; J. H. Elliott, *1 Peter* (New York, NY: Doubleday, 2000), pp. 809–44; J. N. D. Kelly, *A Commentary on the Epistles of Peter and Jude* (London: Black, 1969), pp. 196–204.

96   R. E. Brown, *The Letters of John* (New York, NY: Doubleday, 1979), pp. 93–144; G. Strecker, *The Johannine Letters* (Minneapolis, MN: Fortress, 1996), pp. 218–22, 255–65.

97   Cf. Campbell, *Elders*, pp. 206–9.

eminence in the Church, such as apostles and prophets, who would have been accorded precedence ahead of established local church leadership in the form of patrons and householders.

The evidence of the Pauline letters is essentially corroborated by Acts. The earliest Christian churches were not unstructured egalitarian communities, but formal bodies inextricably interwoven with the fabric of ancient society and in particular the household. Ritual and order defined the community, shaping both its internal structure and its portrayal of itself to the surrounding society. There is some evidence of formal commissioning rites, including imposition of hands as a sign of conferral of authority, assent to appointment, or invocation of the Holy Spirit for blessing and guidance. Where such rites were not administered, the consent of the community, willing or otherwise, to the exercise of ministry and authority is "tantamount to ordination".[98] There is also evidence that titled offices emerged at an earlier date than has often been maintained. This does not imply that structures or rituals were uniform in all parts of the Church at any date, early or later. While later church orders cannot be traced back to the New Testament, the essential structures and roles, at least some of the nomenclature and their theological premises, are apparent from an early date.

Conclusions

Historical critical reconstruction of the life of the Church during the New Testament period, such as we have cursorily undertaken in this chapter, cannot simply be equated with Scripture, but it can illuminate it. The dominical injunction to celebrate the eucharist is well attested in Scripture. How the eucharist was celebrated in the Apostolic Church, and how the orders of ministry of Word and Sacraments emerged, can only be partially reconstructed on the basis of the New Testament evidence. Our study has been supported by the fruit of scholarship investigating the culture of ancient society, and patterns of association for worship and other purposes. Even here the answers are provisional, and the question of authorized lay presidency at the eucharist cannot be resolved without recourse to secondary authorities. Our investigation therefore turns in the next chapter to the ancient Church Fathers, and the light they shed on the emerging customs of the ancient Church, as well as their pronouncements concerning the eucharist, and church order.

---

98   Brown, *Priest*, pp. 41–2.

3

Eucharist, Ministry and the Early Church Fathers

The writings of the early Fathers do not enjoy the same prestige or authority in any part of the Church as does canonical Scripture. Nevertheless, both catholic and reformed traditions recognize that the witness of the Early Church, through the writings of the Fathers, provides a useful and authoritative foundation for Christian doctrine and practice. While tensions and significant differences within the patristic corpus have long been recognized, it has traditionally been maintained that these writings reflect the united witness of early Christianity, at least through the seven universally acknowledged ecumenical councils, culminating in Chalcedon in CE 451. This ignores the Jewish Christian churches, which remained significant, at least in Syria and to the east, until the Muslim conquests. It also ignores those churches which did not subscribe to the orthodoxy propounded by the Councils, and those of the Oriental Orthodox tradition, such as the Armenians, which were outside the Roman empire, and therefore not part of the conciliar processes.

Nevertheless, the most ancient patristic writings are of the greatest significance for our understanding of the development of Christianity. Indeed, some of these may be more ancient than some of the later New Testament documents, in which case they shed invaluable light on the earliest phases of Christianity, often addressing questions with which the canonical writings seem less concerned. These include issues of order and ministry, and we will begin by examining a number of texts which shed light on the celebration of the eucharist and the emergence and crystallization of ordered ministry. Thereafter we will consider briefly the development of ordination rites and, finally, notions of priesthood in the Early Church.

The Early Fathers

The writings of the Church Fathers do not form part of the New Testament. The earliest of these, however, may be at least as ancient as some of the canonical documents, and can therefore usefully complement the historical information which can be gleaned from the New

Testament. These writings can also illustrate ways in which the Church evolved during the late first and early second centuries. As a source of historical information they are therefore invaluable, irrespective of whether they form part of an authoritative tradition which can inform and interpret Christian doctrine and regulate the life of the Church.

The Didache

A document of considerable significance in discerning the development of early Christian liturgies and ministries is the *Didache*.[1] Scholars tend to the view that this work was composed in western Syria, and that it reflects issues and circumstances in the life of the church in Antioch.[2] Widely regarded as contemporaneous with much of the New Testament material, and possibly even as a source of the gospel of Matthew,[3] the *Didache* can be used to trace developments and illuminate issues of contention in at least a small part of the Early Church. However, as the *Didache* is clearly a composite document, incorporating different strands of tradition from different periods, with scholars deeply divided on much of the detail, the material needs to be used with some circumspection. Nevertheless, given the importance of the church of Antioch in the expansion of early Christianity,[4] and its subsequent prestige and influence in the wider Church, how issues were perceived and resolved there would have been, at least potentially, of wider significance. The traditions found in the *Didache* are clearly not the only ones representative of Christianity in western Syria at that period, but at least

1   P. F. Bradshaw, *Eucharistic Origins* (London: SPCK, 2004), pp. 24–42; R. E. Brown and J. P. Meier, *Antioch and Rome* (London: Geoffrey Chapman, 1983); A. J. P. Garrow, *The Gospel of Matthew's Dependence on the Didache* (London: T & T Clark, 2004); C. N. Jefford, *The Apostolic Fathers and the New Testament* (Peabody, MA: Hendrickson, 2006); R. R. Noll, *Christian Ministerial Priesthood* (San Francisco, CA: Catholic Scholars Press, 1993), pp. 257–326.

2   Brown and Meier, *Antioch*; Garrow, *Gospel*; M. Slee, *The Church of Antioch in the First Century CE* (Sheffield: Sheffield Academic Press, 2003); M. Zetterholm, *The Formation of Christianity in Antioch* (London: Routledge, 2003); cf. K. Niederwimmer, *The Didache* (Minneapolis, MN: Fortress Press, 1998), pp. 42–54.

3   Questions relating to the tradition history behind the *Didache* cannot be addressed here, but material can be dated to c. 50–100 CE; cf. Bradshaw, *Eucharistic Origins*, pp. 24–42; Brown and Meier, *Antioch*, pp. 81–4; Garrow, *Gospel*; Niederwimmer, *Didache*, pp. 42–52.

4   Cf. Brown and Meier, *Antioch*; N. H. Taylor, *Paul, Antioch and Jerusalem* (Sheffield: Sheffield Academic Press, 1992).

they do represent one or perhaps more perspectives in what was a contested tradition.

Conduct of the eucharist (9–10; 14) and the related issues of authority and ministry (11; 13; 15) feature prominently in the text. *Did.* 14 directs that the eucharist be celebrated κατὰ κυριακὴν δὲ κυρίου, "on the Lord's day of the Lord", i.e. Sunday. Significantly, the rite is described as θυσία, offering or sacrifice (14.2), introducing explicit cultic language to the rite. While the text clearly presupposes that authority is exercised in the gathered community, it does not stipulate by whom. *Did.* 9–10, possibly not originally of the same tradition as *Did.* 14, stipulates in greater detail how the eucharist is to be celebrated. This consists very largely of a form of the Eucharistic Prayer, possibly separate prayers for the common meal (*Did.* 9) and the eucharist (*Did.* 10). No instruction is given, however, as to who should recite the words, but prophets, προφῆται, are to be exempt from these prescriptions, and allowed to conduct the eucharist as they see fit (10.7). This is significant, given that the reception of itinerant authority figures, designated ἀπόστολοι, προφῆται, and διδάσκαλοι, apostles, prophets, and teachers, is clearly a sensitive issue (11; 13). *Did.* 15 instructs: χειροτονήσατε οὖν ἑαυτοῖς ἐπισκόπους καὶ διακόνους, "appoint for yourselves bishops and deacons". Their ministry, λειτουργία, is identified as the same as that of the prophets and teachers, and they themselves as worthy of equal honour in the community. The instruction to appoint bishops and deacons is presumably addressed to the local church, and χειροτονέω suggests that an election be conducted by a show of hands, or confirmed by imposition of hands, which would constitute ritual induction to office. While it is clearly envisaged that bishops and deacons should become the effective leaders of the local church, it is nonetheless recognized that prophets should be granted some guarded measure of precedence, including, evidently, the right to preside at the eucharist with freedom from local custom (10.7). The eucharist is nevertheless an ordered rite, with prescribed forms, and the implication is presumably that a bishop would normally preside over the gathering of the church for worship.

1 Clement

Another first-century document which sheds some light on the issues with which this study is concerned is *1 Clement*. This letter is traditionally attributed to the third successor of the apostle Peter as bishop of

Rome,[5] but it is doubtful whether Clement, or for that matter Peter, ever occupied a position of unrivalled supremacy in the Christian community or communities of Rome. It is more likely that Clement was one of a number of presiding presbyters or bishops who led Christian congregations in Rome during the second half of the first century; a pattern of leadership still reflected in Rome during the first half of the second century if not later.[6] *1 Clem.* has conventionally been dated to the closing years of the first century CE, during the reign of Domitian. More recently, a date during the 60s or 70s of the first century has been proposed.[7] If this were correct, the letter would be later than Paul's undisputed letters, but possibly earlier than Acts and any deuteropauline writings. *1 Clem.* was sent from the church in Rome to that in Corinth in response to the removal from office in the latter church of those regarded as its legitimate leaders (44), referred to as ἐπίσκοποι and διάκονοι, bishops and deacons (42.4), and at least the former also as πρεσβύτεροι, presbyters (44.5). This has usually been understood to mean that long-established leaders had been ousted from office by probably younger rivals, but could also reflect the increasing dominance of a single bishop, and the consequent demotion of presbyter-bishops who had hitherto exercised autonomy in the oversight of the several churches which met in their houses.[8]

Clement is concerned with order in the προσφορὰς καὶ λειτουργίας, "offerings and (public) services", insisting that they be conducted according to the commandments of Christ (40.1–2). This includes that the worship be conducted by those whom Christ has chosen (40.3–4). A typological relationship is suggested between Christian ministry and the priesthood of the Old Testament cult (40.5; 41; 43), with its hierarchy of high priest, ἀρχιερεύς, priests, ἱερεῖς, levites, λευῖται and, for the first time in extant Christian literature, the baptized members of the church described as laity, λαϊκοὶ (40.5), a term which can refer to "the people" as a whole, but which can have the pejorative connotations of ordinary

---

5   Cf. Irenaeus, *Haer.* 3.3.3.

6   Hermas, *Vis.* 2.4.3. Cf. A. Brent, *Hippolytus and the Roman Church in the Third Century* (Leiden: Brill, 1995).

7   T. J. Herron, 'The More Probable Date of the First Epistle of Clement to the Corinthians', *Studia Patristica* 21 (1989): 106–21; Jefford, *Apostolic Fathers*, pp. 18–19, 163; J. A. T. Robinson, *Redating the New Testament* (London: SCM Press, 1976), pp. 327–5; cf. B. E. Bowe, *A Church in Crisis* (Minneapolis, MN: Fortress Press, 1988), pp. 2–3.

8   Cf. R. A. Campbell, *The Elders* (Edinburgh: T & T Clark, 1994), pp. 213–16; R. M. Grant, *The Apostolic Fathers* (New York, NY: Nelson, 1964), p. 164.

and profane.[9] Clement expounds a notion of apostolic succession, whereby Christ sent the apostles to proclaim the gospel, and in each place where they established a church καθίστανον τὰς ἀπαρχας αὐτῶν . . . εἰς ἐπισκόπους καὶ διακόνους, "to appoint their firstfruits ... as bishops and deacons" (42.4), with provision for these to be succeeded by others when they died (44.1–2).

It would seem that *1 Clement* represents a significant development from the ecclesiology reflected in the New Testament, and in particular the undisputed letters of Paul. Paul's sacrificial interpretation of Christ's death (Rom. 3.24-26; 8.3; 1 Cor. 5.7; etc.) would invite analogies with the temple cult, and his account of the institution of the eucharist is at the least suggestive of immolation (1 Cor. 11.23-26). Paul emphasizes order in worship, and affirms the local leadership, not least the first-fruits (1 Cor. 16.15), but nowhere identifies a distinct cadre whose prerogative was not merely to preside over the worship of the community, but to present the eucharistic elements as though offering a sacrifice. As well as distinguishing clergy from laity, it has justifiably been argued that *1 Clement* contains the earliest extant prohibition of laity from presiding at the eucharist.[10]

Ignatius of Antioch
The letters of Ignatius of Antioch reflect a preoccupation with church order, centred on monarchical episcopacy, at the beginning of the second century.[11] Whether his own rule over the church of Antioch had been so absolute, or the church there so united, as Ignatius suggests, is open to serious doubt.[12] But Ignatius is nonetheless forthright in his claims on behalf of all bishops, of whom there should be only one in any city. He is correspondingly hostile to itinerant authority figures, quite

---

9   Cf. Bowe, *Church*; H. O. Maier, *The Social Setting of the Ministry* (Waterloo, Ontario: Wilfred Laurier University Press, 2002), pp. 87–135; Noll, *Priesthood*, pp. 70–81.

10   P. F. Bradshaw, *Liturgical Presidency in the Early Church* (Bramcote: Grove Books, 1983), p. 11.

11   Bradshaw, *Eucharistic Origins*, pp. 27–9; Brown and Meier, *Antioch*; Maier, *Social Setting*, pp. 149–87; Noll, *Priesthood*, pp. 87–124; W. R. Schoedel, *Ignatius of Antioch* (Philadelphia, PA: Fortress Press, 1985); Slee, *Church*.

12   W. F. Bauer, *Orthodoxy and Heresy in Earliest Christianity* (Philadelphia, PA: Fortress Press, 1971); Brown and Meier, *Antioch*; W. A. Meeks and R. L. Wilken, *Jews and Christians in Antioch in the First Four Centuries of the Common Era* (Missoula, MO: Scholars, 1978); Slee, *Church*; Zetterholm, *Formation of Christianity*.

possibly the prophets and teachers viewed with some suspicion in the *Didache (Eph.* 9; 16). The bishop is not merely the undisputed leader of the local church, but a representative also of the universal Church (*Smyrn.* 8.2).[13] The bishop relates to Christ as Christ to God the Father, and therefore merits unquestioning obedience (*Eph.* 3.2; 6.1; *Magn.* 3–5; 13.2). Presbyters and deacons are also accorded representative roles in relation to God, Christ, and the apostles. Ignatius does not stipulate how bishops, presbyters, and deacons are to be appointed, or by whom, or how the office is to be conferred, other than that they are ἀποδεδειγμένοις ἐν γνώμῃ Ἰησοῦ Χριστοῦ, "set in place by the decision of Jesus Christ" (*Phld.* inc). While the bishop is portrayed as acting together with the πρεσβύτηριον or College of Presbyters (*Eph.* 2.2; 4.1; *Magn.* 7; 13.1; *Smyrn.* 8.1; 12.2; *Phld.* 4; 7.1; *Trall.* 2.2; 7.2) and the deacons (*Magn.* 2; *Phld.* 4), it is upon the bishop's person and doctrinal and disciplinary authority that the life of the church depends (*Magn.* 7; *Trall.* 2–3; 7.1). Worship is valid only if offered in union with the bishop (*Eph.* 5–6.1; *Phld.* 4). A particularly important passage is *Smyrn.* 8.1-2:

Ἐκείνη βεβαία εὐχαριστία ἡγείσθω ἡ ὑπο τὸν ἐπίσκοπον οὖσα ἤ ᾧ ἂν αὐτὸς ἐπιτρέψῃ. . . . οὐκ ἐξόν ἐστιν χωρὶς τοῦ ἐπισκόπου οὔτε βαπτίζειν οὔτε ἀγάπην ποιεῖν.

Let that Eucharist be considered valid which is [celebrated] under the bishop, or one whom he has authorised ... It is not lawful apart from the bishop either to baptize or to hold a love feast [*lit.* to make love].

There are a number of critical issues in this text. It is unclear whether the ἀγάπη or love-feast is to be identified with the εὐχαριστία, eucharist, or is a communal meal, distinct from the context in which the eucharist is celebrated. In either case, the presidency of the bishop or his authorized representative is essential, for baptism as well as for the eucharist. Whether the person acting on behalf of the bishop need be a presbyter is a crucial point. Most scholars assume that a presbyter is implied,[14] but Ignatius does not actually say so.[15] However autocratic Ignatius' depiction of the bishop, he is consistently portrayed as acting together with the presbyters and deacons. It is therefore most likely that delegated authority to officiate in the absence of the bishop would be

13 Cf. *Mart. Pol.* 41.
14 R. E. Brown, *Priest and Bishop* (London: Geoffrey Chapman, 1971), p. 42; cf. Schoedel, *Ignatius*, pp. 238–44.
15 Cf. F. C. Synge, 'The Challenge of the Frontiers', in *Anglican Congress 1963: Report of Proceedings* (Toronto: Editorial Committee, 1963), pp. 155–64.

conferred on a presbyter, or possibly a deacon. Ignatius models himself on Paul, both as a writer of letters to churches (*Trall.* inc) and as one who sought martyrdom, and particularly in Rome (*Rom.* 1; 7). His ecclesiology, however, is significantly removed from that of Paul. Ecclesiastical authority is empowered by the Holy Spirit (*Phld.* inc.; 7.1-2), but representation of God in the church is the primary basis and rationale for episcopal authority. How ministerial office is conferred on presbyters and deacons is not indicated, but it would be consistent with Ignatius's notions of episcopal authority for the bishop to have presided over an inaugural ritual. The patriarchy of the household has been superseded by an ecclesiastical patriarchy whose theological rationale Ignatius presupposes and sometimes reflects in his letters, rather than articulating it consistently or comprehensively.

Justin Martyr

The apologist Justin Martyr provides some insight into the way the eucharist was celebrated and understood, at least within his circle in Rome about the middle of the second century. In continuity with Clement, he uses sacrificial imagery of the eucharist in his polemical writing against Judaism, the *Dialogus cum Tryphone Iudaeo* (41; 117). Justin's first *Apologia* is addressed to the emperor Antoninus Pius, and does not presuppose intimate knowledge of the Christian faith and tradition, and seems to avoid using obscure terminology when describing Christian worship. In his account of baptism Justin refers to ἄγοντος, "the one who leads" the convert into the baptismal waters (*1 Apol.* 61). The baptised is subsequently brought into the gathering of the church by those who have carried out the baptism (*1 Apol.* 65). There is no indication as to who conducts the baptism, and no mention of church leaders until the celebration of the eucharist which follows. The elements are received by τῷ προεστῶτι τῶν ἀδελφῶν, "the president of the brothers", who recites the eucharistic prayer. Thereafter the elements are distributed by διάκονοι, deacons. The origins and significance of the εὐχαριστία are explained (*1 Apol.* 66), before an account of the weekly gathering of the church for worship (*1 Apol.* 67). ὁ προεστώς, the president, διὰ λόγου τὴν νουθεσίαν καὶ πρόκλησιν τῆς τῶν καλῶν τούτων μιμήσεως ποιεῖται, "instructs by word and urges the imitation of these good things" read from Scripture. After this sermon and prayers, ὁ προεστώς receives the elements and, evidently extempore, ὅση δύναμις αὐτῷ, "according to his ability", εὐχὰς ὁμοίως καὶ εὐχαριστίας, "offers prayers and thanksgivings".

Further aspects of Justin's account of Sunday worship will be considered in a subsequent chapter, as they concern distribution of consecrated elements to absent members of the church. For the present we need to consider what precisely Justin means by ὁ προεστώς. As we have noted, Justin seems to avoid distinctive Christian terminology. As well as serving his apologetic purpose, this could also reflect a wish to avoid causing bishops or other Christian leaders to be singled out for persecution.[16] Justin does make explicit reference to deacons (*1 Apol.* 65; 67), and it is clear from οἱ καλούμενοι παρ' ἡμῖν διάκονοι, "those whom we call deacons" (*1 Apol.* 65), that διάκονος is the title of office-bearers in the church. Deacons are clearly subordinate to ὁ προεστώς, the president. Furthermore, the expression τῷ προεστῶτι τῶν ἀδελφῶν (*1 Apol.* 65) suggests an enduring relationship with the church, rather than an individual who happens to be officiating on a particular occasion. This is confirmed by the responsibility of this personage for the subsequent distribution of alms. Justin's near contemporary Hermas makes reference to τῶν πρεσβυτέρων τῶν προϊσταμένων τῆς ἐκκλησίας, "the presbyters presiding over the church", naming Clement and one Grapte.[17] While there may be no reason to suppose that Justin belonged to the same Christian group in Rome as Hermas or Clement, the cumulative evidence suggests that ὁ προεστώς is a deliberately vague designation of the bishop or presbyter who leads the life and worship of the particular Roman church of which Justin was a member.[18] In another passage Hermas refers to οἱ ἀπόστολοι καὶ ἐπίσκοποι καὶ διδάσκαλοι καὶ διάκονοι οἱ . . . ἐπισκοπήσαντες καὶ διδάξαντες καὶ διακονήσαντες, "the apostles and bishops and teachers and deacons who ... oversaw and taught and served" (*Vis.* 3.5.1). This suggests either that presbyters were associated particularly with teaching, or that presbyters and bishops were essentially the same, and a distinct order of teachers was recognized in the Roman church. There is

---

16 Cf. C. O. Buchanan, 'Questions Liturgists Would Like to Ask Justin Martyr', in *Justin Martyr and his Worlds*, eds S. Parvis and P. Foster (Minneapolis, MN: Fortress Press, 2007), p. 158.

17 *Vis.* 2.4.3. Most scholars would identify this Clement with that of 1 Clement, as does tradition.

18 Cf. Bradshaw, *Eucharistic Origins*, pp. 85–6; E. F. Osborn, *Justin Martyr* (Tübingen: J. C. B. Mohr, 1973), pp. 181–3; K. W. Stevenson, *Do This* (Norwich: Canterbury Press, 2002), p. 85; G. H. Williams, 'The Ancient Church, AD 30–313', in *The Layman in Christian History*, eds S. C. Neill and H.-R. Weber (London: SCM Press, 1963), p. 33.

no evidence that Justin was a presbyter, but it may nonetheless be anachronistic to describe him as a "lay" theologian.

Irenaeus of Lyon

For writers of the late second century, ecclesiastical offices, and in particular the episcopate in succession from the apostles, serve as a guarantee of doctrinal orthodoxy during a period when christological issues in particular were the subject of bitter disputes, and Gnostic groups competed for the allegiance of members of "orthodox" Christian communities. Irenaeus of Lyon describes the gospel, as interpreted by those he considers orthodox, as *traditionem quae est ab apostolis quae per successiones presbyterorum in ecclesiis custoditur*, "tradition which is from the apostles, which is maintained by the succession of presbyters in the churches".[19] He refers also to those *qui ab apostolis institui sunt episcopi*, "who were instituted as bishops by the apostles",[20] and to τῶν ἐν ταῖς ἐκκλησίαις προεστώτων, "those who preside over all the churches", who proclaim the same gospel irrespective of their geographical location and cultural origins.[21]

It would seem clear that Irenaeus recognizes little if any distinction between the offices of bishop and presbyter; both stand in the apostolic succession. While he refers to clergy as belonging to a *presbyterii ordine*, a distinct cadre in the Church,[22] apostolic succession consists at least as much in the transmission of orthodox doctrine as in the inheritance of ecclesiastical office, and there is no suggestion that the mechanical transfer of orders is at all relevant. Irenaeus does make reference to bishops of a previous generation having been *ab apostolis institui*, the semantic range of the verb including to appoint, train, or set in order, as well as to ordain. But he provides no information as to how presbyters and bishops were appointed or admitted to office in his own day. In both the Greek and the Latin transmissions of Irenaeus' work, the terms for bishop and presbyter are used interchangeably,[23] except that the former term is preferred in succession lists.[24]

Irenaeus' treatment of the eucharist emphasizes the incarnation against Gnostic dualism, and correspondingly the sanctification of

---

19   *Haer.* 3.2.2.
20   *Haer.* 3.3.1.
21   *Haer.* 1.10.2.
22   *Haer.* 4.26.4.
23   Cf. *Haer.* 4.26.2,5 (citing Isa. 60.17).
24   *Haer.* 3.3.3-4.

matter. While such expressions as γίνεται εὐχαριστία καὶ σῶμα Χριστοῦ, "the eucharist[ic elements] become the Body of Christ",[25] may be compatible with later doctrines of transubstantiation, no mention is made at all of bishops or presbyters in this connection. Irenaeus also, in contrasting the eucharist to the sacrificial cult of Judaism, uses sacrificial language of the Christian rite, but makes no mention of any officiating caste in either cult.[26] All this means is that the liturgical role of bishops and presbyters was not at issue in the controversies with which Irenaeus was engaged, and his emphasis on the role of presbyters and bishops in the Church is strongly indicative of their presidency over the worship and corporate lives of the Christian communities.

Tertullian

A more complex and enigmatic figure, but of immense importance for the present study, is Tertullian, a lay theologian from Carthage. His influence on Western theology has been immense, notwithstanding the ambiguities surrounding his relationship with the Church.[27] It was long believed that Tertullian left the Catholic Church and became a Montanist, and possibly subsequently left the latter also to found his own sect.[28] More recent scholarship would suggest, rather, that Tertullian joined a rigorist, Montanist-inspired, "New Prophecy" movement within the fractious African church.[29] While a shift in his theological perspective and interests can still be discerned, Tertullian's later writings should be understood as emanating not from schism, but from a renewal movement, loyal to and firmly within the Catholic Church, despite tensions and frustrations.

While committed to the enduring presence of prophecy in the Church,[30] Tertullian was equally insistent upon order, and on the highest standards of conduct on the part of those who held office, particularly during times of persecution. He ridicules bishops who assume titles

---

25   *Haer.* 5.2.2-3; cf. 4.18.5.

26   *Haer.* 4.18.

27   Cf. C. B. Daly, *Tertullian the Puritan and his Influence* (Dublin: Four Courts, 1993); E. F. Osborn, *Tertullian* (Cambridge: Cambridge University Press, 1997); D. I. Rankin, *Tertullian and the Church* (Cambridge: Cambridge University Press, 1995); D. E. Wilhite, *Tertullian the African* (Berlin: de Gruyter, 2007).

28   H. F. von Campenhausen, *Ecclesiastical Authority and Spiritual Power in the Church of the First Three Centuries* (London: Black, 1969), p. 227; E. Evans, *Tertullian's Homily on Baptism* (London: SPCK, 1964), pp. x–xi.

29   Rankin, *Tertullian*, pp. 27–51.

30   *An.* 3; cf. *Pud.* 21.

derived from the imperial cult, such as *pontifex*,[31] reserving such for Christ.[32] He is critical also of (unidentified) heretical groups for their lack of stable and ordered leadership, and lack of principle in *ordinationes*, the conferral of office.[33] Clergy are described as *maiores*, a term with connotations of social hierarchy, in relation to *laici*, the laity.[34] Apostolic succession in ecclesiastical office functions primarily as a guarantee of right doctrine; appointment and ordination by the apostles substantiates the transmission of sound doctrine in churches of apostolic foundation.[35] There is no suggestion that sacramental power is transferred thereby. Tertullian in his later writing distinguished between *doctrinam apostolorum et potestatem*, the doctrine handed down by the apostles and their authority to forgive sins, insisting that the power of the keys can rightly be exercised only in the Spirit.[36] The administration of church discipline during a period of sporadic and at times intense persecution was of crucial importance. By *Praesident probati quique seniores*, "elders of proven character preside over us", he refers probably to presbyters: *seniores* being equivalent to *presbyteres*, or possibly to a panel of eminent laity.[37] While acknowledging that prophets acting in the Spirit have authority to forgive sins, Tertullian repudiates pronouncement of absolution by confessors outside the disciplinary processes of the church.[38] His condemnation of the practice in itself suggests that it was widely believed that martyrs and confessors, by virtue of their sufferings, acquired such authority. While those who endure persecution thereby attain a higher status in the church, they do not thereby attain authority or office.[39] The administration of baptism is the prerogative of

> *summus sacerdos, si qui est episcopus; dehinc presbyteri et diaconi, non tamen sine episcope auctoritate, propter ecclesiae honorem quo salvo salva pax est; alioquin etiam laicis ius est …baptismus …b omnibus exerceri potest.*
>
> the high priest, who is the bishop; next the presbyters and deacons, but not without authorization from the bishop, for the honour of the

---

31 *Pud.* 1.6; *Val.* 37.1.
32 *Marc.* 4.9.9; 13.4; 5.35.7.
33 *Praescr.* 41.2–8.
34 *Bapt.* 17.
35 *Praescr.* 25–26; 32; cf. *Fug.* 13.3.
36 *Pud.* 21.1.
37 Rankin, *Tertullian*, pp. 139–40.
38 *Pud.* 22.
39 *Fug.* 11.1.

Church, for when that is secure there is peace. Otherwise the laity
certainly have the right. ... Baptism can be administered by all.[40]

Tertullian's concern is for unity and order in the community, and the
way in which it reflects on the public image of the Church. Lay people
may exercise their right to baptize only *in necessitatibus*, by implication
only when the person concerned would otherwise die unbaptized; they
are not to arrogate to themselves *episcopi officium* at will. Tertullian's
concern is not sacramental validity, even if his observation about the
apostles not having been ordained bishop, presbyter, or deacon,
indicates that he was arguing against a nascent sacerdotalism. Elsewhere
he describes baptism as being administered *sub antistitis manu*, "under the
hand of the priest".[41] *Antistes* designates specifically a cultic functionary,
and presumably refers to the bishop, or to a presbyter acting on his
behalf. The eucharist, by divine institution taken in the context of an
ordinary meal, is celebrated *nec de aliorum manu quam praesidentium
sumimus*, "under the hand of none but the presidents".[42] The *praesidentes*
are presumably bishops and presbyters, who appear in the plural in the
same paragraph as the single *antistes* who administers baptism.

As with baptism, so with the eucharist Tertullian is both rigid in
reserving presidency to designated officers and flexible in recognizing at
least a potential need for the sacraments to be administered in the
absence of clergy: the only explicit provision comparable to lay
presidency at the eucharist in extant patristic writings. He seems to
envisage two possible situations: an individual who finds himself in a
place where *ecclesiastici ordines*, the clerical orders, have not been
constituted, exercising an incipient priesthood, *ius sacerdotis*, "the right of
a priest", functions as *sacerdos tibi solus*, "a priest to yourself alone".[43] As
Tertullian mentions baptism as well as the eucharist in this connection,
it is difficult to conceive of a real or hypothetical situation to which he
may be referring.[44] Even if a solitary eucharist may be conceivable, one
who baptizes is not functioning as a priest for himself alone, but for at
least one other person.

Tertullian also envisages the possibility of a group of laity constituting
a church without clergy: *ubi tres, ecclesia est, licet laici*, "where three are, it

---

40   *Bapt.* 17.
41   *Cor.* 3.
42   *Cor.* 3.
43   *Exh. cast.* 7.4.
44   Bradshaw, *Search for the Origins of Christian Worship*, p. 101.

is a church, although they be laity".[45] By implication, where the Church is, there the eucharist is celebrated, although Tertullian does not develop this point, but returns to the issue of individual faith. His agenda in this passage is to persuade lay people to adopt the standard of moral probity prescribed for bishops in 1 Tim. 3, in particular not to marry a second time. The rhetorical question, *Nonne et laici sacerdotes sumus?*, (Are not we laity also priests?), implies that laity, as members of the order from which clergy were drawn, ought to conduct themselves as potential priests.[46] While conceding that male lay Christians could conceivably on occasion be justified in assuming the functions of bishops and presbyters in administering baptism and the eucharist, and emphasizing that the Church is not constituted by the clerical order alone,[47] Tertullian maintains a rigid distinction between the *ordo sacerdotalis* [48] or *ordo ecclesiasticus*[49] and the laity:

> *Differentiam inter ordinem et plebem constituit ecclesiae auctoritas et honor per ordinis consessum sanctificatus.*

> It is the authority of the Church, and the honour sanctified through the assembly of the Order, which has established the difference between the Order and the laity.[50]

Within the clerical caste Tertullian distinguishes the *ecclesiastici ordines* of bishops, presbyters, and deacons.[51] He uses the verb *ordinare* of admission to the clerical order,[52] and *adlegere* and the related noun *adlectio* to designate admission to the three clerical orders and that of widows, but not for those of virgin, *lector* (reader), *doctor* (teacher), and prophet.[53] While he provides no description of the ritual or process of admission, it is clear that a distinctive form of admission is used for clergy, which, with the exception of widows, is not used of those in what came to be known as minor orders. In Tertullian, therefore, while we

---

45 *Exh. cast.* 7.3; cf. P. van Benenden, 'Haben Laien die Eucharistie ohne Ordinierte Gefeiert? Zu Tertullians ,De Exhortatione Castitatis' 7.3', *ALW* 29 (1987): 31–46.

46 *Exh. cast.* 7.6; *Mon.* 11–12.

47 *Pud.* 21.17.

48 *Exh. cast.* 7.2.

49 *Idol.* 7.

50 *Exh. cast.* 7.3. Cf. Cyprian, *Ep.* 67, *Ad Stephanum.*

51 *Mon.* 12.2; *Exh. cast.* 13.4.

52 *Praescr.* 32.3; 41.6; cf. *Apol.* 21.23; *Scorp.* 12.1.

53 *Mon.* 12.1; *Idol.* 7.3; *Exh. cast.* 7.2.

find a clear distinction between clergy and laity, a deep concern for order in the Church, and the language of priesthood, there is also a recognition that the Church must continue to exist, and its sacraments be celebrated, even where there are no bishops or presbyters. However, it is important also to note that, despite the evident tensions with prevailing ecclesiastical authorities, where Tertullian proposes that lay people could assume the functions of clergy, it is not to subvert established authority but to constitute a church where none would otherwise exist.

Clement of Alexandria

By the third century church order had stabilized, with a clear distinction between clergy and laity, at least in the minds of the authors of such writings of the period which have survived. The bishop had emerged to predominance in the presbyterate, assisted undoubtedly by the notion of apostolic succession, and the increasing confidence that episcopal office originated in ordination by the apostles. Clement of Alexandria depicts John the apostle ἐπισκόπους καταστήσων, "appointing bishops", one of whom is also called a πρεσβύτηρ, and κλῆρον . . . κληρώσων τῶν ὑπὸ τοῦ πνεύματος σημαινομένων, "ordaining as clergy those indicated by the Spirit".[54] Clement also suggests that those Christians who conduct themselves in a manner worthy of presbyters, even if οὐχ ὑπ' ἀνθρώπων χειροτονούμενος ... ἐν πρεσβυτερίῳ καταλεγόμενος, "though not ordained by men ... are enrolled in the presbyterate" on account of their righteousness, and would enjoy that status in heaven.[55] This suggests not only that Clement believed some were excluded from office for no good reason, possibly including himself, but also that some who had been ordained conducted themselves unworthily.

Origen

Clement's student Origen is another early critic of ecclesiastical office-bearers, reflecting the same tension between lay intellectuals and the increasingly autocratic clerical hierarchy in Alexandria.[56] While clearly distinguishing the role of the laity from that of the bishop and presbyterate at the eucharist,[57] Origen rejects both the identification of apostolic succession with any ecclesiastical office, and the typological

---

54 *Quis div.* 42.
55 *Strom.* 6.13.
56 Cf. J. W. Trigg, *Origen* (London: SCM Press, 1983).
57 *Hom. Lev.* 3.

interpretation of the Levitical priesthood of the Old Testament in terms of Christian ministry. All Christians anointed with chrism at baptism are priests,[58] but the highest qualities are nonetheless expected in clergy, and in bishops in particular.[59] He condemns those who seek ecclesiastical office for unworthy motives, and abuse their positions.[60]

Like Tertullian, Origen believed that absolution could be given only in the Spirit, and not by virtue of any office in the Church, including that of bishop.[61] Developing the Platonist notion of Clement, Origen asserts that truly spiritual Christians, by which he means the most competent expositors of Scripture, are the genuine bishops and presbyters of the Church.[62] As with the other great lay theologians of his period, Tertullian and Clement of Alexandria, Origen[63] reflects tensions with the ecclesiastical hierarchy. Like Clement he asserts a spiritual office, unrecognized in the present world, which stands in closer succession to the apostles than do bishops and presbyters. But neither proposes that these spiritual elites should assume the functions of the clergy or otherwise subvert order in the Christian community.

Cyprian of Carthage

Cyprian of Carthage represents a consolidation in theology, if not in practice, of the trends in ecclesiastical structure and eucharistic theology which have been observed over the two centuries under review.[64] Authority in the church is concentrated in the office of the bishop, with Jesus' commission to Peter (Mt. 16.18–19) interpreted accordingly:

> *inde per temprum et successionum vices episcoporum ordinatio et ecclesiae ratio decurrit ut ecclesia super episcopos constituatur et omnis actus ecclesiae per eosdem praepositos gubernetur.*

> thereafter, through the vicissitudes of time and successions, the ordering of bishops and the doctrine of the Church continue, so that the Church is founded upon bishops and every act of the Church is governed by these overseers.[65]

---

58   *Hom. Lev.* 6.5; 9.9.
59   *Cels.* 3.48, citing Tit. 1.9-11.
60   *Comm. Matt.* 15.
61   *Or.* 28.8–10; *Comm. Matt.* 12.14.
62   *Comm. Matt.* 10; *Comm. Jo.* 32.12. Cf. J. J. Alviar, *Klesis* (Dublin: Four Courts Press, 1993), pp. 187–91.
63   Origen was ordained to the presbyterate in Caesarea Maritima c. CE 230, but was a layman throughout his association with the church of Alexandria.
64   J. D. Laurance, *'Priest' as Type of Christ* (New York, NY: Peter Lang, 1984).
65   *Ep.* 27, *Cyprianus lapsis* 1.

This is probably the strongest surviving statement on behalf of episcopal authority since Ignatius of Antioch, and, as with most of Cyprian's correspondence, was written during a period when he had withdrawn from Carthage during a time of persecution, leaving the church there in the care of the remaining presbyters and deacons. Cyprian takes exception to having received letters written in the name of the church, on the grounds that *ecclesia in episcopo et clero et in omnibus stantibus sit constituta*, "the church is formed of the bishop and clergy, and all who have stood firm". In other words, the church of Carthage cannot act without him, and certainly not address him as the bishop without whom they are not constituted a church. The episcopate is of dominical institution: *apostolos, id est episcopos et praepositos, Dominus elegit*, "the Lord chose apostles, that is bishops and overseers"; the diaconate, on the other hand, was instituted by the apostles, and is therefore inferior to the episcopate: *Deum . . . episcopos facit*, "God . . . made bishops", and bishops make deacons.[66] Even if *praepositos* includes presbyters, the plenary authority of the bishop is nonetheless clear. In keeping with this principle, bishops are to be ordained by the bishops of neighbouring sees, who similarly stand in succession to the apostles.[67] While the authority of the bishop is still linked to that of the college of presbyters, he alone is described as *sacerdos*, a priest.[68] The celebration of the eucharist belongs to the *officio sacerdotii nostri*, "the office of our priesthood".[69] Sacrificial language is used of the eucharist, and priesthood has acquired cultic overtones:

> *Si Iesus Christus Dominus et Deus noster ipse est summus sacerdotus Dei Patris, et sacrificium Patri se ipsum primus obtulit, et hoc fieri in sui commemorationem praecipit, utique ille sacerdos vice Christi veri fungitur qui id quod Christus fecit immitatur, et sacrificium verum et plenum tunc offert in ecclesia Deo Patri, si sic incipiat offere secundum quod ipsum Christum videat obtulisse.*

> If Jesus Christ, our Lord and God, is himself the chief priest of God the Father, and has first offered himself in sacrifice to the Father, and has instructed that this be done in commemoration of himself, certainly that priest truly functions in place of Christ who imitates what Christ did, and offers a full and true sacrifice in the church to God the Father,

---

66   *Ep.* 65, *Ad Rogatianum* 3.
67   *Ep.* 68, *Ad clerum et plebem in Hispania* 5.
68   *Ep.* 55, *Ad Cornelium* 5.
69   *Ep.* 63, *Ad Caecilium* 19.

when he begins to offer according to what he sees that Christ himself offered.[70]

While this is clearly pre-eminently an episcopal function, it is also clear that presbyters do on occasion preside at the eucharist,[71] and thereby share in the priesthood of the bishop:

> *singuli divino sacerdotio honorati et in clerico ministerio constituti non nisi altari et sacrificiis deservire et precibus atque orationibus vacare debeant.*
>
> everyone honoured with the divine priesthood and ordained into clerical service should serve only the altar and sacrifices, and have leisure for prayers and supplications.[72]

While in the absence of the bishop the church is in the care of the presbyters assisted by the deacons, Cyprian imposes clear limits on their authority to function in his absence. In particular, he condemns presbyters who reconcile to the church members who had lapsed during the persecution:

> *Quod enim non periculum metuere debemus de offensa Domini quando aliqui de presbyteris, nec Evangelii nec loci sui memores, sed neque futurum Domini iudicium nunc neque sibi praepositum episcopum cogitantes, quod numquam omnino sub anticessoribus factum est, cum contumelia et contemptu praepositi totum sibi vindicent?*
>
> What danger should we not fear from the Lord's displeasure, when certain of the presbyters, remembering neither the Gospel nor their own place, and, furthermore, mindful neither of the Lord's future judgment nor of the bishop set over them, outrageously and contemptuously arrogate to themselves plenary authority, something which never happened under our predecessors?[73]

Elsewhere, Cyprian does enjoin a more lenient regime in reconciling those who had lapsed, or at least those in danger of death.[74] But the role of presbyters, and of confessors, is clearly subordinate to that of the bishop in administering ecclesiastical discipline.[75] Presbyters and

---

70   *Ep.* 63.14.

71   *Ep.* 4, *Ad presbyteros* 2; with confessors in prison: *apud confessores offerunt*, cf. *Ep.* 9; *Ad clerum* 3.

72   *Ep.* 66, *Ad clerum et plebem furnis*, 1.

73   *Ep.* 9, *Ad clerum* 1.

74   *Ep.* 12, *Ad clerum* 1, where a more lenient regime is enjoined.

75   *Ep.* 10, *Ad martyres* 1; cf. *Ep.* 22, *Ad clerum Romae.*

deacons are to be ordained in the presence of the gathered church.[76] Confessors attain no ecclesiastical office apart from appointment and ordination by the bishop.[77]

The Apostolic Tradition

The *Apostolic Tradition* was for a long time associated with Hippolytus,[78] identified as a bishop of Rome early in the third century. More recently the precise identity of Hippolytus, and his relationship with the Christian communities of Rome, have been shown to be a great deal less certain.[79] The *Apostolic Tradition* has been shown to be composite document, with a complex tradition history and a varied manuscript tradition, from which such later works as the *Apostolic Constitutions*, the *Canons of Hippolytus*, and the *Testimonium Domini* have also drawn material.[80] The Greek text survives only in fragments, and the extant manuscript in Latin represents a different recension to the family of manuscripts preserved in Sahidic (southern Coptic), Arabic, Ethiopic, and Bohairic (northern Coptic). Even if an original text could be reconstructed, this would no longer be considered reliable testimony to church order in Rome or anywhere else before the fourth century. Rather, the *Apostolic Tradition* preserves customs, rules, and rites from different periods, adapted differently in the churches in which they were used.

The provision for the ordination of a bishop by neighbouring bishops (*Trad.* a*p.* 2.2-5; cf. *Const. ap.* 3.2.20; 8.2.4-5; *T. Dom.* 1.21) reflects muta-tion from the earlier practice of ordination by the College of Presbyters to the custom first attested in the middle years of the third century,[81] and prescribed by canon at the Council of Nicaea (325 CE).[82] Similarly, the

---

76 *Ep.* 68.4, *Ad clerum et plebem in Hispania.*

77 *Ep.* 22, *Ad clerum Romae; Ep.* 24, *Ad clerum; Ep.* 33, *Ad clerum et plebem; Ep.* 34, *Ad Clerum et Plebem;* it is noteworthy that *ordinatio* is used of a *lector* (reader); *Ep.* 35, *Ad Eosdem* [Clerum and Plebem].

78 Cf. G. Dix, *The Shape of the Liturgy* (London: Dacre, 1945); cf. H. Chadwick, 'Preface to the Second Edition', G. Dix, *The Treatise on the Apostolic Tradition of St Hippolytus of Rome* (London: Alban Books, 1992), pp. d–I; A. Stewart–Sykes, *Hippolytus, on the Apostolic Tradition* (New York: St Vladimir's Seminary, 2001), pp. 22–32.

79 Brent, *Hippolytus.*

80 Bradshaw, *Search for the Origins of Christian Worship*, pp. 206–10; P. F. Bradshaw et al., *The Apostolic Tradition* (Minneapolis, MN: Fortress Press, 2002).

81 Cyprian, *Ep.* 55, *Ad Cornelium*, 8; *Ep.* 67, *Ad Stephanum*, 5.

82 Bradshaw *et al., Apostolic Tradition*, p. 27; E. C. Ratcliff, 'Apostolic Tradition', *SP* 8 (1966): 266–70.

participation of the college of presbyters in the ordination of a presbyter (*Trad. ap.* 7; cf. *Const. ap.* 8.3.16; *T. Dom.* 1.30), reflects early usage before the monarchical bishop had fully emerged to supremacy in the local church.[83] The bishop alone ordains deacons, in a passage clearly intended to emphasise the subordination of deacons and to exclude them from the *clerus*, clergy, and, more particularly, the *sacerdotium*, priesthood – a term not used in the rites for the ordination of bishops and presbyters (*Trad. ap.* 8; cf. *Const. ap.* 8.3.17-18,19 [deaconesses]; *T. Dom.* 1.38). Confessors who have been imprisoned are to assume the office of presbyter by virtue thereof, without receiving episcopal ordination (*Trad. ap.* 9; *Can. Hip.* 6; *T. Dom.* 1.39); a tradition not attested elsewhere which must antedate the Edict of Milan (312 CE), and which is contradicted in the later variant tradition preserved in *Const. ap.* 8.3.23. While it is only in *Trad. ap.* 9, and there only by implication, that confessors acquire the authority to preside at the eucharist, it is nonetheless clear that they constituted an alternative, quasi-charismatic, alternative source of authority to bishops and presbyters in at least some churches, well into the third century, and possibly until the end of the persecutions under Constantine.

The *Apostolic Tradition* makes a clear distinction between ordination to the episcopate, presbyterate, and diaconate, and appointment to the range of offices later commonly known as minor orders; imposition of the bishop's hands being forbidden in the case of the latter (*Ap. trad.* 10–14; cf. *Const. ap.* 8.2.4–3.22). *Trad. ap.* 22, extant only in Ethiopic, is concerned with order in the distribution of the elements rather than with the celebration of the eucharist itself (cf. *Can. Hip.* 30-31; *T. Dom.* 2). It is presupposed that the bishop is the president at the eucharist, at least on Sundays, and it is deemed desirable that he should distribute the bread to the entire congregation; presbyters may assist with the distribution if necessary, and they and the deacons are to assist with the fraction.[84] Later developments in the tradition tend to emphasise the distinction in roles between the ranks of clergy in baptism and at the eucharist, and in pronouncing blessings and absolutions (*Trad. ap.* 21; *Const. ap.* 2.7.57; 3.1.10–11; 8.2.12; 3.28), and to condemn the assumption by lay people of clerical functions (*Const. ap.* 2.6.26).

The *Apostolic Tradition*, therefore, would seem to reflect the emergence of the monarchical episcopate, with increasingly concentrated powers, particularly in the area of ordination. It suggests also a relegation of the

---

83   Bradshaw et al., *Apostolic Tradition*, p. 58.
84   Cf. Bradshaw et al., *Apostolic Tradition*, pp. 136–7.

diaconate to a subordinate office, stripped of independent liturgical functions, particularly in the administration of the sacraments. Mutation in the liturgies of the Church to reflect these developments is also apparent. But there is no evidence that the right to preside at the eucharist was an issue of contention at any stage in the development of the tradition.

Conclusion

It is widely argued, and generally accepted, that ecclesiastical structures acquired an increasingly formal, rigid, and hierarchical character in the context of the doctrinal disputes of the early centuries. Abstract theological arguments cannot be separated from the social, cultural, and political forces which defined the shape of the Church, and its boundaries, but the point remains that episcopal monarchy gained supremacy and control over liturgical and teaching offices in and through these struggles.[85] As has been clear from the preceding study of biblical and patristic texts, this process represents some degree of mutation and rationalization in the structures of the Church, but not the introduction of patriarchal structures and authority that were absent at its inception. The crystallization of the clerical orders, with increasing concentration of power in the episcopate, is the most conspicuous development. The formalization and standardization of liturgies is less well attested in surviving documents, but certainly accompanied this process. The culmination in these developments can perhaps best be represented by Canon 14 of the second Council of Nicaea:[86]

ὅτι τάξις ἐμπολιεύεται ἐν ἱερωσυνῃ καὶ πᾶσιν ἀρίδηλον καὶ ὅτι τὸ ἐν ἀκριθείᾳ διατηρεῖν τὰς ἱερωσύνης ἐγχειρήσεις θεῷ ἐστιν εὐάρεστον.

It is manifest to all the world that in the priesthood there is order and distinction; and to observe the ordinations and elections of the priesthood with strictness and severity is work pleasing to God.

---

85 Bradshaw, *Liturgical Presidency*, pp. 15–17; cf. Bauer, *Orthodoxy*; Brown and Meier, *Antioch*; W. H. C. Frend, *The Rise of Christianity* (London: Darton, Longman and Todd, 1984); J. N. D. Kelly, *Early Christian Creeds* (Harlow: Longman, 1980).

86 Second Council of Nicaea, 787 CE.

Objections to "hierarchical legalism" in the Church as contrary to the nature of the Lord's Supper[87] may be effective polemic against contemporary authoritarianism and the disempowering of the laity in many communities, but are essentially anachronistic. Ecclesiastical hierarchies preceded by several centuries the sacerdotal developments in eucharistic theology and the priesthood characteristic of the mediaeval period. The doctrine of transubstantiation, sacrificial interpretations of the eucharist, and the consequent accrual of magical connotations to the priesthood, are all developments subsequent to the establishment of catholic orders of ministry, and liturgical order.[88] The Anglican repudiation of medieval doctrines at the Reformation[89] therefore cannot provide a sufficient basis for renouncing the ancient practice of episcopal and presbyteral presidency at the eucharist.[90] Before turning our attention to Anglicanism, however, it would be helpful to draw together our observations concerning the development of ordination rites and of the priestly connotations ascribed to Christian ministry, and to the presbyterate in particular.

Early ordination rites

The earliest extant ordination rites are those preserved in the *Apostolic Tradition*, discussed briefly above.[91] While this document was for some time confidently dated to the late second or early third century, assumed to describe the liturgy of the church of Rome, and therefore to be representative of early Christian practice, these assumptions are now all questioned if not altogether repudiated. The document, as it stands, dates from the fourth century, and corresponding traditions preserved in the *Apostolic Constitutions* date from much the same period. The other extant ordinal from the fourth century is that in the *Sacramentary* of

87 J. Moltmann, *The Church in the Power of the Spirit* (London: SCM Press, 1977), pp. 245–6; cf. A. Bieler and L. Schottroff, *The Eucharist* (Minneapolis, MN: Fortress Press, 2007).

88 P. McPartlan, *Sacrament of Salvation* (Edinburgh: T & T Clark, 1995), pp. 1–44; D. N. Power, *Ministers of Christ and His Church* (London, Geoffrey Chapman, 1969), pp. 163–7.

89 R. T. Beckwith, *Priesthood and Sacraments* (Abingdon: Marcham Manor, 1964), p. 28; W. H. Griffith Thomas, *The Principles of Theology* (London: Vine, 1930), pp. 318–19.

90 G. R. Evans, *Authority in the Church* (Norwich: Canterbury Press, 1990), p. 37; H. C. B. Green, *Lay Presidency at the Eucharist?* (London: Darton, Longman and Todd, 1994), pp. 4–5; pace, Griffith Thomas, *Principles*, pp. 318–19.

91 P. F. Bradshaw, *Ordination Rites of the Ancient Churches of East and West* (New York, NY: Pueblo, 1990).

Serapion, bishop of Thmuis in Egypt.[92] However uncertain the provenance of some of the traditions, and however complex the relationships between them, the evidence is nonetheless clear that, by the fourth century at the very latest, episcopal ordination of bishops, presbyters, and deacons had become normative if not universal Christian practice.[93] Imposition of episcopal hands with invocation of the Holy Spirit is the central and defining act in the ordination rites. The only power mentioned in the *Apostolic Tradition* is that conferred on the bishop to forgive sins (3.5), and by extension to exercise his rule over the community appropriately. There is no suggestion, in the ordination of either bishops or presbyters, that baptism and offering the gifts at the eucharist require any particular empowerment by the Holy Spirit.

As has been shown, the rite of ordination to Christian ministry is much more ancient than the fourth century, but detail is sparse and uniformity of custom cannot be assumed. Most, if not all, early Christian customs and liturgies would have been administered *extempore*, and transmitted orally, possibly for several generations, before being committed to writing. While the *Didache* and, much later, the *Apostolic Tradition*, may reflect attempts to establish some measure of uniformity in doctrine and practice, there is little if any evidence of this during the early centuries. There is substantial evidence that the offices of bishop, presbyter, and deacon emerged at an early date, but also that they varied and mutated considerably before the pattern of monarchical episcopacy, a collegial but increasingly dispersed presbyterate and attendant deacons became established.

We have noted that in the ancient world ritual induction to office was normal practice. This included initiations into the plethora of pagan cults and their priesthoods, and, by the second century at least, the ordination of rabbis in Judaism.[94] Transfer of symbols of office, either from superior to inferior or, less frequently, from predecessor to successor, was a common form of ritual induction. There is no evidence of any such custom in Judaism. While in the Pentateuch an elaborate liturgy is recounted in which Moses inaugurated Aaron and his sons to be the first priests of the new cult (Lev. 8), the priesthood was

---

92   F. E. Brightman, 'The Sacramentary of Serapion of Thmuis', *JTS* 1 (1899): 247–77; M. E. Johnson, *The Prayers of Serapion of Thmuis* (Rome: PIO, 1995).

93   Bradshaw, *Search*, p. 210.

94   E. Ferguson, 'Jewish and Christian Ordination', *HTR* 56 (1963): 13–19; L. A. Hoffman, 'Jewish Ordination on the Eve of Christianity', *StL* 13 (1979): 11–41; E. Lohse, *Die Ordination im Spätjudentum und im Neuen Testament* (Berlin: Evangelische Verlag, 1951).

hereditary, and any purificatory or other ritual which preceded a priest's first assumption of duty in the temple would not have been an ordination, but rather a confirmation of his identity as a priest, his physical fitness to officiate in the temple, and his ritual purity.

There is no evidence of the use of symbols of office in the Early Church, in ordination or other commissioning rites or in any other context. The offices of bishop, presbyter, and deacon seem to have been defined primarily in terms of relationships within the community, and of representing God within such relationships, and not in terms of particular functions. Proclamation of the gospel, exposition of the Word, and administration of the sacraments clearly became the functions pre-eminently of the episcopate, and secondarily of the presbyterate, assisted by deacons and a wide range of ministers in what came to be known as minor orders. But the offices of bishop, presbyter, and deacon were not defined by any role for which any of the later symbols of office issued at ordinations would have been appropriate.

The evidence of the New Testament, considered above, indicates that manual gestures were from the first the predominant mode of ritual induction into Christian ministry. Two particular forms seem to be indicated: extension of one or both hands in the direction of the person set apart for ministry, an act in which the community as a whole could possibly have participated, and ritual imposition of hands on the person concerned, which is likely to have been restricted to such authority figures as apostles and prophets, endowed with charismatic authority and accordingly considered able to invoke the Holy Spirit to empower the person commissioned for ministry. While these commissioning rites are attested from the earliest days of the Church, it is impossible to ascertain at what stage such ordinations came to be linked to particular titled offices. Imposition of hands became the normative ritual for the ordination of bishops, presbyters, and deacons,[95] while manual gestures not involving direct contact may have influenced rites of admission to such offices as sub-deacon and *lector*. In both cases, ordination or commissioning became increasingly the prerogative of the bishop, even if the very assertion of this prerogative[96] indicates that this concentration of power in episcopal hands did not go unchallenged. Presbyteral ordination, of bishops as well as of presbyters and deacons, was normative in many places into the fourth century, and it is at least

---

95   E. Ferguson, 'Laying on of Hands', *JTS* 26 (1975): 1–12.
96   *Const. ap.* 3.1.11; 8.3.28; Cyprian, *Ep.* 65, *Ad Rogatianum* 3; *Ep.* 68, *Ad clerum et plebem in Hispania* 4–5.

arguable that the *Apostolic Tradition* and *Apostolic Constitutions* represent attempts to suppress the more ancient practice in favour of episcopal ordination.[97]

While bishops such as Ignatius and Cyprian made explicit claims to plenary authority on behalf of the episcopate, and are to some extent supported by lay theologians such as Tertullian, the emergence of monarchical bishops to pre-eminence in their churches, and the corresponding demotion of presbyters in function and status, would seem to have been a prolonged and far from uniform process.[98] As well as teaching authority, the right to ordain presbyters and deacons, and fellow bishops, became a crucial aspect of episcopal power. In the eastern regions of the Church the structure of monarchical bishop, college of presbyters, and attending deacons seems to have been settled fairly early, irrespective of whether Ignatius' claims reflected the reality of ecclesiastical polity in Antioch of his period. In Western regions, and not least in Rome, the distinction between presbyter and bishop seems to have taken rather longer to crystallize. In subsequent Western theology, when authority to preside at the celebration of the eucharist had come to be regarded as the defining quality of priesthood, bishop and presbyter were considered no more than different ranks within a single order of priesthood.[99] Bishops had come to be distinguished more by their temporal power than their spiritual qualities and pastoral office, and dioceses functioned primarily as revenue-generating units to subsidize the lifestyle, patronage, and political intrigues of aristocratic prelates. If the plenitude of Christian priesthood was vested in the presbyterate, it followed that priests had the power not only to preside at the eucharist but also to confer Orders. The ambiguous status of the episcopate is reflected in both Catholic and Protestant ecclesiologies during the Reformation period, as will become clear in the following chapter. For the present, it is important to recognize that writers such as Ignatius and Cyprian, and those who transmitted the *Apostolic Tradition* and related liturgical and other texts, did not settle the question of episcopacy for all time, at least where the Western Church was concerned.

Furthermore, apostolic succession was originally conceived not in terms of mechanical transmission of sacramental power, but of custodianship of orthodox doctrine. It is therefore an error of Anglo-

---

97 Cf. Bradshaw et al., *Apostolic Tradition*, pp. 28–9, 58.

98 Cf. Campbell, *Elders*.

99 Peter Lombard, *Sententiares* 4.24; Thomas Aquinas, *Summa Theologiae* 3. Sup. 35.2; 37.1–3.

Catholic theology in particular to assert that episcopacy in the apostolic succession, and episcopal ordination of bishops, priests, and deacons, define legitimate Christian ministry, even though this is assumed in such documents as the Chicago–Lambeth Quadrilateral, and reflected also in the Canon Law of many Anglican provinces. The presidency of a priest, ordained by a bishop consecrated in the apostolic succession, can therefore not be regarded as an absolute prerequisite to valid celebration of the eucharist. Collegial presbyteral governance, from which monarchical bishops subsequently emerged, is attested at an early date, and almost certainly functioned *de facto*, in the form of patrons hosting gatherings of the local church, before titles, liturgical office, and theological rationale were attached to the role. The evidence we have reviewed, in both the New Testament and the early Fathers, suggests that ordination, or at the very least rites akin to ordination, were administered in the Church from its earliest period. While such rites may have been normative from the first, we cannot claim that this was universal or uniform practice during the apostolic age, or a prerequisite to the exercise of authority and liturgical presidency in the Church. The earliest extant evidence of ordination being regarded as an episcopal prerogative is not until the early fifth century.[100] We cannot be certain that everyone who presided over the life and worship of the ancient churches had received any form of ritual recognition and inauguration to office before first presiding at the eucharist, still less ordination in the form which has been normative since at least the third century.

Priesthood in the Early Church

In the world of early Christianity, priesthood was associated with the cults of the multitudinous pagan temples scattered throughout the Graeco-Roman world,[101] with the exception of those parts of Palestine under Jewish and Samaritan rule. For Jews and the first Christians, the pre-eminent temple was that in Jerusalem.[102] This was served by an hereditary priesthood, traditionally drawn from the tribe of Levi in ancient Israel, and specifically descendants of Aaron in the male line. John the Baptist was born into this priesthood (Lk. 1.5-25,57-66), and, according to Acts 6.7, the church in Jerusalem made converts from

---

100 Jerome, *Ep.* 146, *Ad evangelum*, 1.
101 H.–J. Klauck, *Magic and Paganism in Early Christianity* (Minneapolis, MN: Fortress Press, 2003); R. MacMullen, *Paganism in the Roman Empire* (New Haven, CT: Yale University Press, 1981).
102 E. P. Sanders, *Judaism* (London: SCM Press, 1992), pp. 45–146.

among the temple priesthood. There is no evidence that such priests played any distinctive role in the Early Church, in Jerusalem or elsewhere.

In ancient Israel, priesthood served essentially three functions, summarised in Moses' blessing on the tribe of Levi in Deut. 33.8-10:[103] discerning the will of God, traditionally accomplished by casting lots – the Urim and Thummim (cf. Josh. 18-19; 1 Sam. 10.17-24); teaching and interpreting the Law (cf. Lev. 13–14; Num. 5; Neh. 8); officiating in the cult, initially in the tabernacle in the wilderness, subsequently at Shiloh and ultimately in the temple in Jerusalem (Lev. 9; 14–16; Josh. 18.1; 1 Sam. 1–3; 1 Kings 8; cf. Lk. 1). A development which may seem all to familiar to Christian clergy today is that, by the close of the Old Testament period it was only the cultic duties that remained an exclusive priestly function. For centuries prophets had been acknowledged by many as those who spoke in God's name. Some, such as Jeremiah (Jer. 1.1), Ezekiel (Ezek. 1.3), and John the Baptist (Lk. 1.5), and possibly Isaiah (Isa. 6.1–8), had been priests, but the majority were lay Israelites like Amos (Amos 7.14). Similarly, during the post-exilic period scholarship and the interpretation of the Law of Moses had ceased to be a priestly prerogative, and lay scribes and expositors of the Law competed with priests and with each other to influence the lives and devotions of the people. While Ezra is identified as a priest (Ezra 7.1–6), such eminent rabbis as Hillel and Shammai, and also Gamaliel (Acts 5.34), were all, so far as surviving records indicate, lay Jews, as was the future Christian apostle Paul (Phil. 3.5).

Christianity emerged in an environment in which the temple in Jerusalem was the dominant cultic institution, until its destruction by the Romans in 70 CE. It may be that the continued functioning of the temple, and the participation of Christians in Jerusalem in its worship, militated against the formation of a Christian priesthood during the apostolic period.[104] Other factors, however, do need to be considered. Jesus had proclaimed the destruction of the temple (Mk 13.1-4 and par; Jn 2.19), and this was a major factor, if not the actual catalyst, in the process that led to his crucifixion.[105] Opposition to the temple system

---

103 Cf. Brown, *Priest*, pp. 8–10.

104 Brown, *Priest*, pp. 16–17.

105 E. P. Sanders, *Jesus and Judaism* (London: SCM Press, 1985); *The Historical Figure of Jesus* (London: Penguin, 1994); N. H. Taylor, 'Prolegomena to Reconstructing the Eschatological Teaching of Jesus', *Neot* 33 (1999): 145–60; 'Jerusalem and the Temple in Early Christian Life and Teaching', *Neot* 33

similarly contributed to the death of Stephen (Acts 6.8–8.1),[106] and there is very little evidence to suggest that Stephen's views were significantly different to those of other Christians in Jerusalem.[107] Rejection of the temple, or at the very least its supersession by the death of Jesus – sacrificially interpreted – is overt in such New Testament writings as the letter to the Hebrews and the book of Revelation.

Protestant scholarship in particular has argued that such interpretations of the death of Jesus postdated the destruction of the temple, and reflect Christian attempts to present the death of Jesus as having ended the role of animal sacrifices in the worship of God and in human redemption. It is doubtful whether this process began as late as the last quarter of the first century, however, as sacrificial allusions and overt sacrificial language are widely used of the death of Jesus in the New Testament. The interpretation of such passages from Scripture as Isaiah 53, and the martyr theology it had inspired in Judaism since at least the Maccabaean period, are also important.[108] In Mk 10.45 (Mt. 20.28) Jesus alludes to his death as λύτρος ἀντὶ πολλῶν, "a ransom for many". In modern parlance this may be the language of hijacking and kidnapping, but it derives from the cult, and in particular the offering of sacrifices for redemption. A martyrological interpretation could be suggested as an alternative to a cultic one,[109] but it is doubtful whether the two notions can be entirely separated: whatever distinctions may be drawn between the formality of liturgical sacrifices and the brutality of persecution, the latter is given meaning by the former. Also in Mark, in the "last supper" narrative,[110] Jesus describes the wine: τοῦτο ἐστιν τὸ

(1999): 445–61; contra, J. Klawans, *Purity, Sacrifice, and the Temple* (Oxford: Oxford University Press, 2006), pp. 222–41.

106 N. H. Taylor, 'Stephen, the Temple, and Early Christian Eschatology', *RB* 110 (2003): 62–85.

107 Cf. M. Simon, *St. Stephen and the Hellenists in the Primitive Church* (London: Longman, 1958); *pace*, M. H. Scharlemann, *Stephen* (Rome: PBI, 1968).

108 D. Boyarin, *Dying for God* (Stanford, CA: Stanford University Press, 1999); P. Middleton, *Radical Martyrdom and Cosmic Conflict in Early Christianity* (London: T & T Clark, 2006).

109 M. D. Hooker, *The Gospel According to Mark* (London: Black, 1991), pp. 250–1; R. T. France, *The Gospel of Mark* (Grand Rapids, MI: Eerdmans, 2002), pp. 419–21.

110 There are several variant readings of the synoptic accounts of the Last Supper, and in particular of the words of institution. These do not substantially affect the issues under discussion here, and can be attributed largely to the oral transmission of the tradition, both in recounting the Gospel and in the

αἷμα μου τῆς διαθήκης τὸ ἐκχυννόμενον ὑπὲρ πολλῶν, "this is my blood of the covenant, poured out for many" (14.24). Irrespective of how the wine relates to the blood of Jesus, that it represents blood not coursing through the veins but shed into a vessel, is in itself indicative of death, and ritualized death in particular. Together with the vicarious nature of the death, these words are at the very least suggestive of a sacrificial victim.[111] Matthew emphasizes this further, and specifies that the sacrifice represented by the cup of wine is offered εἰς ἄφεσιν ἁμαρτιῶν, "for the forgiveness of sins" (26.28).[112] Luke, representing a tradition independent of that preserved in Mark and Matthew, refers both to a new covenant, and to Jesus' blood being ritually shed for the disciples: τοῦτο τὸ ποτήριον ἡ καινὴ διαθήκη ἐν τῷ αἵματί μου τὸ ὑπὲρ ὑμῶν ἐκχυννόμενον, "this cup is the new covenant in my blood, poured out for you" (22.20).[113] In John, Jesus is described as ὁ ἀμνος τοῦ θεοῦ ὁ αἴρων τὴν ἁμαρτίαν τοῦ κόσμου, "the lamb of God who takes away the sin of the world" (1.29), reflecting both the interpretation of Isaiah 53 in terms of Jesus, and also the attribution of atoning qualities to Jesus as the Passover lamb.[114] The cultic language is less overt in Jn 3.16, which alludes to the incarnation as well as the passion, but the sacrificial connotations of the verse are nonetheless clear.[115] It is not necessary to equate any of these allusions with any specific sacrifice prescribed in the Torah, and routinely offered in the temple in Jerusalem. All four canonical gospels presuppose that Jesus' death was interpreted as self-immolation in the cause of human salvation. The undoubted relevance of the Jewish martyr tradition does not alter this.[116]

While the gospels may be relegated to dates relatively late in the first century, and Matthew and Luke postdate the fall of Jerusalem, Paul's undisputed letters date from no later than the middle years of the first

celebration of the Eucharist in the early Christian communities. For references see discussion above.

111 Cf. Exod. 24.8. Hooker, *Mark*, p. 340; France, *Mark*, pp. 569–72.

112 Cf. W. D. Davies and D. C. Allison, *Matthew. III* (Edinburgh: T & T Clark, 1997), pp. 472–4; U. Luz, *Das Evangelium nach Matthäus* (Berlin: Benziger, 2002), pp. 373–85.

113 J. A. Fitzmyer, *The Gospel according to Luke, X–XXIV* (New York, NY: Doubleday, 1985), pp. 1385–1403; I. H. Marshall, *The Gospel of Luke* (Grand Rapids, MI: Eerdmans, 1978), pp. 801–7.

114 R. E. Brown, *The Gospel according to John (i–xii)* (New York, NY: Doubleday, 1966), pp. 55–63; B. F. C. Lindars, *The Gospel of John* (London: Marshall, Morgan and Scott, 1972), pp. 108–10.

115 Brown, *John*, pp. 133–49; Lindars, *John*, p. 359.

116 Cf. Boyarin, *Dying for God*; Middleton, *Martyrdom*.

century. Paul was undoubtedly a creative and innovative interpreter of the gospel, and may well not be representative of his generation of Christian theologians, but he is nonetheless of seminal importance for Christian doctrine. The sacrificial interpretations of Jesus' death found in his letters therefore cannot be disregarded. In Rom. 3.24-25 Paul refers to Jesus as follows: ὅν προέθετο ὁ θεὸς ἱλαστήριον διὰ πίστεως ἐν τῷ αὐτοῦ αἵματι (Jesus Christ, whom God offered as an atoning sacrifice, through faith in his blood).[117] In 1 Cor. 5.7 Paul identifies Jesus with the Passover lamb which has been sacrificed for the Church, τὸ πάσχα ἡμῶν ἐτύθη Χριστός. The context provides abundant references to the symptoms and manifestations of sin, even if ἁμαρτία is not used.[118] In the same letter Paul includes his account of the institution of the eucharist (11.24-25), which he associates explicitly with the death of Jesus (11.26). In 2 Cor. 5.19 Paul writes: θεὸς ἦν ἐν Χριστῷ κόσμον καταλάσσων ἑαυτῷ (God was in Christ reconciling the world to himself). By ἐν Χριστῷ Paul means in the death of Christ, accomplishing that which the sacrificial cult was established to bring about, through sin offerings for individuals and the atonement sacrifice for all Israel.[119] In Eph. 2.14-16 Paul or a deuteropauline author writes of Christ ἐν ἑνὶ σώματι . . . διὰ τοῦ σταυροῦ (in his one body by the cross), effecting reconciliation not only between particular people and God, but between people also.[120] However shocking the reference to the cross as cultic apparatus may have been to the recipients of the letter, this implication would have been quite apparent to recipients of previous letters who would have been well aware of just how Jesus died. Titus 2.14 also alludes to Jesus' death in sacrificial terms. While Paul and the Pauline tradition use sacrificial imagery of the death of Jesus, the

---

117 The relationship between clauses in a very long Greek sentence is debated in scholarship, with considerable diversity of interpretation. The use of sacrificial language in this passage is nonetheless unambiguous. Cf. J. D. G. Dunn, *Romans* (Waco, TX: Word, 1988), pp. 163–70; J. A. Fitzmyer, *Romans* (New York, NY: Doubleday, 1993), pp. 348–50; R. Jewett, *Romans* (Minneapolis, MN: Fortress Press, 2007), pp. 268–83.

118 R. F. Collins, *First Corinthians* (Collegeville, MN: Liturgical, 1999), pp. 205–15; G. D. Fee, *The First Epistle to the Corinthians* (Grand Rapids, MI: Eerdmans, 1987), pp. 214–20.

119 C. K. Barrett, *A Commentary on the Second Epistle to the Corinthians* (London: Black, 1973), pp. 176–8; V. P. Furnish, *II Corinthians* (New York, NY: Doubleday, 1984), pp. 301–5; M. E. Thrall, *II Corinthians* (Edinburgh: T & T Clark, 1994), pp. 392–400.

120 E. Best, *Ephesians* (Edinburgh: T & T Clark, 1998), pp. 247–66; J. Muddiman, *The Epistle to the Ephesians* (London: Continuum, 2001), pp. 123–36.

metaphor does not correlate with any single or specific rite of the temple in Jerusalem. The specific reference to Passover in 1 Corinthians may well have derived from earlier tradition. That the Passover lamb was not a sin offering, still less the sacrificial lamb of the Day of Atonement, does not in any way negate Paul's overt interpretation of Jesus' death as a sacrificial self-immolation which effected redemption.

Sacrificial imagery is also found in other traditions within the New Testament. This is most conspicuous in the Letter to the Hebrews, in which Jesus is described as ἀρχιερεὺς κατὰ τὴν τάξιν Μελχισέδεκ, (a high priest according to the order of Melchizedek) (5.10; similarly 6.20; cf. 7.15-19). The high priesthood of Jesus is eternal (7.20-25), his sanctuary is celestial (8.1–2), and he is κρείττονός ἐστιν διαθήκης μεσίτης (the mediator of a greater covenant) (8.6) which has rendered the first covenant obsolete (8.13). Jesus replaces the cycles of the sacrificial cult, and in particular the rites of the Day of Atonement, τοῦ ἰδίου αἵματος, with his own blood (9.12),[121] offered once and for all (9.25-28; 10.10,12). Whether Hebrews was written before or after the destruction of Jerusalem and abolition of the temple cult, it interprets the death of Jesus as a single, eternal, sacrifice, compared with which that of the temple is inadequate and irrelevant.[122]

In 1 Pet. 1.18-19 the addressees are described as having been ἐλυτρώθητε, ransomed or delivered, τιμίῳ αἵματι ὡς ἀμνοῦ ἀμώμου καὶ ἀσπίλου Χριστοῦ, "with the precious blood of Christ, like that of a blameless and unblemished lamb". The metaphor of Christ as a sacrificial victim, whose death is effective for human redemption, is unambiguous.[123] In 1 Jn 1.7 the blood of Jesus καθαρίζει ἡμᾶς ἀπὸ πάσης ἁμαρτίας, "cleanses us from all sins". In the same letter Jesus is twice described as ἱλασμός, a propitiation or atoning sacrifice (2.2; 4.10). Finally, in Rev. 5.6-10 Jesus is symbolised as ἀρνίον ἑστηκὸς ὡς ἐσφαγμένον, a "lamb standing as though it had been slaughtered", and acclaimed as having ἠγόρασας τῷ θεῷ ἐν τῷ αἵματι σου, "ransomed for God by your blood" those described as τῷ θεῷ ἡμῶν βασιλείαν καὶ

121 H. W. Montefiore, *The Epistle to the Hebrews* (London: Black, 1064), pp. 153–4.

122 See also H. W. Atteridge, *The Epistle to the Hebrews* (Philadelphia, MN: Fortress Press, 1989); P. Ellingworth, *The Epistle to the Hebrews* (Grand Rapids, MI: Eerdmans, 1993).

123 P. J. Achtemeier, *1 Peter* (Minneapolis, MN: Fortress Press, 1996), pp. 123–30; J. N. D. Kelly, *A Commentary on the Epistles of Peter and Jude* (London: Black, 1969), pp. 74–5.

ἱερεῖς, "a kingdom of priests to our God"; an idea reflected also in Rev. 1.6 and 20.6.

It is immediately apparent that despite the abundance of sacrificial imagery employed to interpret the death of Jesus as a salvific event, it is only in the passages relating the "last supper" that a direct if mystical link is posited between the crucifixion of Jesus, sacrificially interpreted, and the eucharist. Furthermore, there is no reference in any of the texts cited to a priesthood which officiated at the cultic commemoration of Jesus' sacrificial death. In the Letter to the Hebrews it is Jesus himself who is both priest and sacrificial victim, and the eucharist is nowhere mentioned. The kingdom of priests depicted in Rev. 1.6 and 5.10 (cf. 20.6) is a corporate entity, modelled on Israel at Sinai (Exod. 19.6), the eschatological community of those redeemed through Jesus' death, and no liturgical role is attributed to them. The Sinai traditions, moreover, in their canonical form at least, maintain a clear distinction between the Levitical priesthood, originating with Aaron and inherited by his male descendents, and the other tribes of Israel, and include accounts of the divine wrath visited on those who presume to usurp the liturgical office of Aaron and his sons (Num. 16–17). The corporate priesthood in Revelation does not immolate the sacrifice, which is Jesus, the lion of Judah, depicted as a slaughtered lamb.[124] Similarly, ἱεράτευμα is used in 1 Pet. 2:5, 9 to denote the corporate identity and status of the elect people of God. Even though they are depicted as offering πνευματικὰς θυσίας, spiritual sacrifices, this does not designate any cultic role, and is, if anything, equated with the proclamation of the gospel.[125] This is not to suggest that the priestly aspect of Christian identity in these passages is at all unimportant, merely that the priesthood reflected does not consist in cultic office.

The only occurrences in the New Testament of priestly and sacrificial language used of Christian ministry are self-designations by Paul. In Rom. 15.15–16 Paul describes his apostleship as λειτουργὸν Χριστοῦ Ἰησοῦ, the public service of Jesus Christ, and ἱερουργοῦντα, priestly service. This consists not only in the proclamation of the gospel, but also in facilitating ἡ προσφορὰ τῶν ἐθνῶν, the offering of the Gentiles, not

---

124 D. E. Aune, *Revelation 1–5* (Waco, TX: Word, 1997), p. 362; S. S. Smalley, *The Revelation to John* (London: SPCK, 2005), pp. 137–38.
125 Achtemeier, *1 Peter*, pp. 149–68; Kelly, *Peter*, pp. 91–98; H.–M. Legrand, 'The Presidency of the Eucharist According to Ancient Tradition', *Worship* 53 (1979): 414; E. G. Selwyn, *The First Epistle of St. Peter* (London: Macmillan, 1961), pp. 160–68.

necessarily to be understood in a cultic sense but at least suggestive thereof.[126] In Phil. 2.17 Paul suggests that he might be σπένδομαι ἐπὶ τῇ θυσίᾳ καὶ λειτουργίᾳ, "poured out as a libation over the sacrifice and [public] service" of the faith of the Philippians. He does not attribute any priestly role to himself, but rather depicts himself as a secondary and complementary offering to the sacrifice presented by the Philippian Christians.[127] In neither passage is the sacrificial language to be understood literally, even if Paul is conscious of the possibility of martyrdom ahead of him. Neither can the sacerdotal language in Rom. 15.16 be understood as an assertion of Christian priesthood, cultic or otherwise.

There is no Christian priesthood, in the sense of a cadre of cultic functionaries, attested in the New Testament. This does not mean there was no hierarchy in the Church, but leadership and precedence in the Christian communities, and with them liturgical function, were not defined in terms of cultic office. Where a Christian priesthood is mentioned, this is a corporate entity, embracing the entire Church, and not an office within it.

Corporate notions of the Church as a Christian priesthood persist into the second century, not least in the writings of Justin and Irenaeus.[128] The same Fathers also developed the idea of Christ as priest.[129] The conjunction of these images demonstrates that the images were not understood as mutually exclusive. This presupposes not so much a mystical identification of Christ with the Church as a distinction between the sacrificial self-offering of Christ and the lives and witness of Christian believers.

In *Did.* 13.3 prophets are described as ἀρχιερεῖς, high priests. It will be recalled that the *Didache* reflects some tension between prophets and the increasingly powerful local leadership in the churches, so such a designation might appear anomalous. However, what is being referred to is the privilege of receiving the firstfruits of the harvest, which is restricted to prophets who have decided to settle in a particular community, and therefore to have accepted its discipline and acknowledged its leadership. The analogy between the right to material support of the Christian prophet and the high priest of the Old

---

126 C. E. B. Cranfield, *Romans* (Edinburgh: T & T Clark, 1979), p. 755; Dunn, *Romans*, pp. 858–61; Fitzmyer, *Romans*, pp. 711–12; Jewett, *Roman*, pp. 905–8.
127 G. F. Hawthorne, *Philippians* (Waco, TX: Word, 1983), pp. 104–7.
128 Justin, *Dial.* 116.3; Irenaeus, *Haer.* 4.8.3; 5.34.3.
129 Justin, *Dial.* 116.1; Irenaeus, *Haer.* 4.8.2.

Testament is at issue. This text does not imply that the prophet is otherwise regarded as a priest, and it is stipulated that the same benefits should be given to the poor if there is no prophet to receive them.

The tradition of modelling Christian worship, and in particular the eucharist, on the cult of the Jerusalem temple as described in the Old Testament, is exemplified by *1 Clement*, as we have noted above. The analogy between the hierarchy of the temple and that of the Church, and the divine institution of both, require that order be maintained in the Church. While *1 Clem.* 40-44 may stop short of explicitly attributing sacerdotal qualities to Christian ministry,[130] it certainly represents a stage towards such interpretations.

When the language of priesthood was first explicitly used of Christian ministry, the imagery and nomenclature is attributed specifically to the bishop, and to presbyters by derivation if at all.[131] This development presupposes the establishment of a monarchical episcopate, to which the college of presbyters is clearly subordinate. It also reflects a stage in the evolution of church structures in which presbyters rarely functioned independently of the bishop. In other words, the bishop is assumed to exercise pastoral and liturgical oversight of a single local community, and not a cluster of distinct groups in which a presbyter exercised these functions.

Tertullian describes the bishop as *summus sacerdos*, high priest.[132] This does not imply that this was a formal title of the bishop, and we have noted above that Tertullian was wary of ways in which bishops were beginning to acquire the trappings and nomenclature of office hitherto associated with the pagan cults. The priestly qualities attributed to the episcopate do not in any way diminish the priesthood in which all members of the Church share through baptism.[133] Tertullian cites Rev. 1.6 to reinforce his point that lay Christians are also *sacerdotes*.[134] Tertullian's concern for Christian moral living, and his regarding lay people as potential bishops and presbyters, led him to demand the same standards of conduct of lay people as were required of clergy.[135] He also allowed that there were circumstances in which lay people could assume the functions of priesthood.[136] Tertullian would appear to use the term

---

130 Bradshaw, *Search for the Origins of Christian Worship*, p. 202.
131 Brown, *Priest*, p. 47; cf. Bradshaw, *Search*, p. 203.
132 *Bapt.* 17.1.
133 *Bapt.* 7.
134 *Exh. cast.* 7.3.
135 *Exh. cast.* 7.4.
136 *Exh. cast.* 7.3.

sacerdos, where not applied to all baptized Christians, primarily of bishops, but possibly also of presbyters.[137]

Cyprian of Carthage is another North African early Church Father who uses *sacerdos* of bishops.[138] Presbyters are associated with the priesthood of the bishop, and exercise it in his absence, but are not in themselves invested with sacerdotal status.[139] Cyprian, as we have noted, represents with Ignatius of Antioch the most vigorous assertion of monarchical episcopacy attested in the Early Church. He was also constrained to be absent from his church for extended periods when it was under persecution, and therefore to leave his community dependent on the ministry of presbyters and deacons.

Origen similarly designates the bishop as *sacerdos*, but attributes a lesser priesthood to presbyters.[140] If Eusebius' account of Origen's self-castration is historical, and was deemed an impediment to ordination to the presbyterate,[141] this could be further circumstantial evidence that by the third century Christian ministry was acquiring attributes associated with the priesthood of the temple in the Old Testament.

In the *Apostolic Tradition*, the language and symbolism of priesthood are employed in the ordination prayer for a bishop,[142] but not of a presbyter.[143] In the prayer for the bishop the Old Testament allusions are to Abraham and a succession of priests who served from that time onwards, perhaps an oblique reference to Melchizedek, and the bishop is consecrated to a high priesthood, and the Holy Spirit is invoked to empower him for his ministry. The presbyter, on the other hand, is modelled on the elders who were appointed to assist Moses in his oversight of Israel in the desert, and governance and counsel are the roles envisaged in the exercise of presbyteral ministry.

Catholic tradition has come subsequently to associate priesthood essentially with the presbyterate, and often to deem the episcopate a rank or office within this priesthood rather than a distinct order of ministry. This ambivalence in the relationship between presbyter and bishop is one to which we will have occasion to return. For the present, we need to note that the appropriation of sacerdotal nomenclature by

137 Cf. Bradshaw, *Search*, p. 203.
138 *Ep.* 1, *Ad Donatum*, 1.1; 61, *Ad Eucharatium*, 3.1; 63, *Ad Caecilium*, 14.
139 *Ep.* 1, *Ad Donatum*, 1.1; 40, *Ad plebem*, 1.2; 61, *Ad Eucharatium*, 3.1; 67, *Ad Stephanum*, 4.3.
140 *Hom. Ex.* 11.6; *Hom. Lev.* 6.6.
141 *Hist. eccl.* 6.8.1-2,5.
142 3.2-5; cf. *Didasc.* 2.26.4; *Const. ap.* 2.6.34; *Can. Hip.* 3; *T. Dom.* 1.
143 *Trad. ap.* 7; cf. *Can. Hip.* 4.

and on behalf of the clergy developed after the monarchical episcopate had emerged from the presbyterate, and applied specifically to bishops, and at most secondarily and derivatively to presbyters. Sacrificial interpretations of the death of Jesus, with which the eucharist was closely associated, evolved much earlier, and quite apart from questions of church order and ministry.

Conclusions

This chapter has covered, somewhat cursorily, a substantial body of material, much of which is little known outside specialist academic circles. The early Church Fathers reflect continuity with the New Testament, in that developments in theology, ministry, and church order already attested in the Apostolic Church continued through the early centuries. The eucharist was central to the spiritual life of the Christian communities throughout this period, and at no time was its conduct a matter of indifference. On the contrary, order in the liturgy reflected order in the community, and presbyters and bishops presided over the worship and communal life of their churches.

The establishment of church order was accompanied by the development of rituals of admission to office, the antecedents of which were as ancient as the Church itself, even if ordination rites evolved more gradually, and may not have acquired a common form or have become universal custom until a later date.

The appropriation of priestly connotations to the ministry of bishops, and subsequently of presbyters, took place independently of eucharistic theology and the development of church order. The restriction of the right to preside at the eucharist to bishops and presbyters preceded, and was in no sense dependent upon, either sacerdotal notions of ministry or sacrificial interpretations of the eucharist.

4

Sacramental Ministry in the Anglican Tradition

Notwithstanding assumptions or assertions which may be made to the contrary,[1] Anglicanism does not begin with the Reformation.[2] It is a misconception that the English church of the preceding millennium and more was part of a monolithic foreign entity, rather than a distinctive and indigenized branch of the Western catholic Church, which had developed its own traditions, many of which mutated quite radically but continued to be valued and meaningful in the reformed Church of England. Local custom had been and continued to be suppressed in Wales and Ireland, in the cause of English rather than Roman domination, and indeed in England itself in the cause of Anglo-Norman hegemony. The English reformers were very conscious of their continuity with the ancient Church, catholic as well as English. This is not to say that their judgements as to what was ancient and universal, and what was not, were always sound. Nor does it mean that Anglicans today would retain or abolish the same aspects of the medieval heritage as did some of the reformers. But the principle reflected in the Book of Common Prayer and expounded in the Ordinal and the Articles of Religion is nonetheless clear, of a tradition that was being purified, not abandoned.

The Reformation was a period of considerable instability in the English church and society, and indeed in the state, to the point that it can be doubted whether this was a single process: "the various (and varied) Reformations in sixteenth-century England were haphazard and had only limited success, at least by comparison with Protestant aims".[3] This is not the occasion to debate the merits or otherwise of the various phases of reform in the Church of England, or of the financial and dynastic motives of Henry VIII in instigating a process of ecclesiastical reform, several aspects of which he rescinded during his final years. We do need to be aware, however, that the English medieval church was not

---

1   P. D. L. Avis, *Anglicanism and the Christian Church* (London: T & T Clark, 2002); S. C. Neill, *Anglicanism* (Harmondsworth: Penguin, 1965).

2   Hooker, *Of the Lawes of Ecclesiastical Polity* 3.1.10; cf. A. M. Ramsey, *The Anglican Spirit* (London: SPCK, 1991).

3   C. A. Haigh, *English Reformations* (Oxford: Clarendon Press, 1993), p. 12.

inevitably collapsing or disintegrating under the weight of its own corruption (many aspects of which the Reformation did nothing to abolish). Reform was not eagerly anticipated, but was in places quite vigorously resisted, while in others acquiescence was grudging and iconoclasm avoided as far as possible.[4] The more radical reforms of the reign of Edward VI were driven largely by lay aristocracy whose wealth and power had been substantially increased and entrenched through the dissolution of the monasteries and redistribution of confiscated church property. The reign of Mary saw a reversion to the ecclesiastical status quo of the last year of Henry VIII – and not to an unreformed medieval Catholicism which the Queen and her Archbishop of Canterbury, Cardinal Reginald Pole, were ardently committed to reforming. The settlement which evolved gradually under Elizabeth I was neither inevitable nor uncontested, even if it did realize some stability in Church and nation. This was modified by James I and Charles I, and temporarily overthrown by the Commonwealth, until finally entrenched under Charles II with what became the definitive edition of the Book of Common Prayer in 1662, and accompanying legislation. Whatever the intentions of James II, his overthrow by William III entrenched Protestantism, and brought further repression in Scotland and Ireland, but attempts at further reform of the Church of England were thwarted.

Whatever the merits or otherwise of customs and doctrines which were retained or abolished during different phases of the English Reformation, a number of observations relevant to this study must be made. The first is that the catholic orders of ministry, i.e. bishops, priests (presbyters), and deacons, were retained, and administration of the sacraments was reserved to bishops and priests. The predominantly lay preaching orders were suppressed, and preaching was with few exceptions restricted to ordained and specifically licensed clergy. At the same time, while public worship was to be conducted in the vernacular, provision was initially made only for English; the Book of Common Prayer was published in French in 1549, 1552, and 1662, but in Welsh not until 1567, and in (Irish) Gaelic for the first time in 1608. As well as English being less familiar than Latin in significant parts of the two kingdoms, many liturgical and extra-liturgical observances, as well as visual artworks, which had been fundamental to the spirituality of the laity for centuries, were abolished. Notwithstanding increasing literacy during the late medieval and Renaissance periods, reading remained the

---

4   Cf. E. Duffy, *The Stripping of the Altars* (New Haven, CT: Yale University Press, 1992); Haigh, *Reformations*.

preserve of a minority, and access to literature was limited, notwith-standing the provision of a Bible in every parish church. In significant ways, therefore, the laity of the Church of England were spiritually disempowered by the Reformation. This was exacerbated by the suppression of the monasteries and preaching orders, and the opportunities these provided for women as well as for men.[5]

While the Reformation heritage of the Church of England has been contested during the subsequent centuries,[6] it is incontrovertibly the case that many of what have become the defining documents of Anglicanism originated during this period, and many of the principles governing Anglican theology and worship were formulated. The question whether lay people should be authorized to preside at the eucharist in Anglican churches therefore cannot be adequately considered without attention to the Reformation process and settlement.

The Reformation Settlement in England

Some observations have already been made about the English Reformation, and ways in which an Anglican theological method was developed. The diverse nature of the Church of England is such, however, that not all Anglicans assent to the relationship between Scripture, tradition, and reason defined at the Reformation, articulated in Article VI and expounded by Hooker. This study, however, will seek to apply this method, in which Scripture was acknowledged as the supreme authority in all matters relating to faith, but it was also acknowledged that there are issues of concern in the life of the Church on which Scripture gives no explicit direction, and which may therefore give rise to legitimate differences of opinion within the Church. The question of lay presidency at the eucharist is one such issue.

There was at times some flexibility in admitting to office in the Church of England ministers of continental European Protestant churches who had been presbyterally, but not episcopally, ordained. In the medieval Church, the priesthood had been widely regarded as a single order of ministry; bishops enjoyed an elevated religious and secular rank and status, and exercised administrative functions and powers within their jurisdiction, but were nonetheless priests of the same

---

5   For discussion see Duffy, *Stripping of the Altars*; Haigh, *Reformations*; D. N. J. MacCulloch, *Thomas Cranmer* (New Haven, CT: Yale University Press, 1996); F. Procter and W. H. Frere, *A New History of the Book of Common Prayer* (London: Macmillan, 1951).

6   Cf. Avis, *Anglicanism*.

order as were presbyters.[7] This position is articulated by Peter Lombard[8] and Thomas Aquinas,[9] and continued to be maintained during the Reformation period and subsequently among Roman Catholics as well as Protestants, not least by Henry VIII and Thomas Cranmer, his loyal if not supine Archbishop of Canterbury.[10] If presbyters were endowed with the plenitude of apostolic ministry, it followed that they could confer Orders, and this right was exercised during the medieval period by abbots in particular. It was only in 1563 that the Council of Trent reserved the *potestas* of conferring Orders to bishops, removing it from abbots and any other dignitaries who had hitherto administered ordination, but were not bishops.[11] This was after the Church of England had repudiated papal authority, and after the subsequently contested consecration of Matthew Parker as Archbishop of Canterbury,[12] but before the final excommunication of the Church of England by the Pope in 1570.

Notwithstanding the above observations, the principle of an episcopally ordained ministry was never conceded in the Church of England, except during the Commonwealth. The question "Whether the wordes of institucion of the supper of the Lorde spoken to the apostles are to be understonde at spoken to laye persons as to preistes or preistes only"[13] is raised in an anonymous manuscript, but led to no change in the discipline of the English Church. Bishops alone were authorized to ordain, and any lingering ambiguity on the requirement of "Episcopal Consecration or Ordination" was finally resolved in the Preface to the Ordinal of 1661. Preaching was restricted to bishops and specifically licensed presbyters and deacons.[14] Administering the sacraments was the prerogative of priests, and the role of lay people in sacramental ministry was, if anything, reduced through restrictions on clinical baptism, which

---

7   A. McDevitt, 'The Episcopate as an Order and Sacrament on the Eve of the High Scholastic Period', *Franciscan Studies* 20 (1960): 96–148.

8   *Sententiares*, 4.24.

9   *Summa Theologiae* 3 Sup 35.2; 37.1–3.

10   MacCulloch, *Cranmer*, p. 277.

11   Session xxiii, Canon *De Sacramento Ordinis* 7. This, and the preceding Canon 5, repudiate the claims of the magisterial reformers that ordination is unnecessary or that appointment by secular rulers sufficed.

12   E. J. Bicknell, *A Theological Introduction to the Thirty-Nine Articles of the Church of England* (London: Longman, Green & Co., 1955), pp. 337–8.

13   *Questiones de missa cum responcionibus eisdem*, cited G. P. Jeanes, *Signs of God's Promise* (London: T & T Clark, 2008), p. 108.

14   An exception was Cranmer's licensing as Preachers two lay members of the universities in 1535, MacCulloch, *Cranmer*, p. 138.

had hitherto frequently been administered by midwives, who of course were not merely lay people but women.[15] Any notion that the Reformation in England increased the participation of lay people in the life of the Church is therefore highly questionable.

Cranmer

The English Reformation was not the programme of a single theological campaigner, which is not to suggest that that in any other European country this was so. But developments in England perhaps vacillated rather more than in Germany or Switzerland, largely on account of the role and agenda of the Crown in directing reform. The dominant figures during the initial period were clearly Henry VIII, for a time his vicegerent Thomas Cromwell, and Cranmer. Cranmer's significance has been perceived to have been such that most parties in subsequent Anglicanism have wished to claim him for their own. His role in the composition of successive liturgical texts is a legacy which has continued to be widely appreciated.[16] But Cranmer's "theological views shifted so subtly and secretly that analysis of [it] is a historical industry in itself".[17] Through the theological vacillations reflected incompletely in his writings, and his role in the fluctuating political and ecclesiastical developments of his day, consistency can be discerned only in his allegiance to the Crown, and particularly to the Royal Supremacy in the Church of England. This dogma, defined by Henry VIII to fill the canonical void created by his repudiation of papal jurisdiction in his realms, was endorsed by Convocation in 1530 and by parliament in 1534, and later enshrined in Article XXXVII. Cranmer's entire archiepiscopate was therefore exercised on the premise that the king was "the only supreme head on earth of the Church of England". Despite or because of his subservience to royal authority, Cranmer was at times, if not always, able to influence the course of reform over a period of two decades, until the first of two future queens whom he had declared a bastard, ascended the throne.

A distinction needs to be recognized between Cranmer's theological opinions and the liturgical and other official documents of the Church of England in whose composition and promulgation he had played a

---

15 Private baptism by a lay person in an emergency was authorized by rubric in the Prayer Book of 1549, but restricted to "lawful ministers" from 1604. For discussion, Proctor & Frere, *Book of Common Prayer*, pp.585–8; cf. R. Hooker, *Laws*, 5.60–62; J. Taylor, *Clerus Domini*, 4.2,14.

16 An exception being G. Dix, *The Shape of the Liturgy* (London: Dacre, 1945).

significant, if not a formative, role. The Ordinals published in 1550 and 1552, corresponding with the two Prayer Books of Edward VI, emphasize the role of the priest in representing the congregation at the celebration of the eucharist, and the mediatorial nature of priesthood in the "ministry of salvation", embracing word, sacrament, and discipline.[18] However unambiguous this may be, as expressing the legal and theological position of the Church of England, Cranmer's expressed theological opinions also merit close scrutiny.

Under Lutheran influence, Cranmer did not regard ordination as a sacrament, on the grounds that it was not *instituta ad significandam remissionem peccatorum*, "instituted to signify the remission of sins".[19] This does not mean that he regarded the rite as unimportant or unnecessary, at least during the early years of his archiepiscopate, during the ascendancy of Cromwell, but before the influence of Zwingli, Bucer, and Calvin overshadowed that of Luther: *ministros ecclesiae ordinandos esse per impositionem manuum sacerdotis*, "the Church's ministers are to be ordained by the laying on of the priest's hands".[20] It is notable that Cranmer uses *sacerdos* to designate the officiating minister of ordination, rather than *episcopus*, bishop. In continuity with medieval scholasticism, as noted above, he maintained that priests and bishops constituted a single order of ministry, and both were empowered to confer orders through the imposition of hands.[21] The validity ascribed to presbyteral ordination was not a Protestant novelty, and does not represent any repudiation of the catholic heritage of the Church of England.

It has been claimed that Cranmer made allowance for "lay ordination" and thereby, by implication at least, for lay presidency at the

---

17 Haigh, *Reformations*, p. 14.

18 C. O. Buchanan, 'Some Anglican Historical Perspectives', in *Lay Presidency at the Eucharist?* ed. B. T. Lloyd (Bramcote: Grove Books, 1977), pp. 11–12; H.–J. Feulner, *Das "Anglikanische Ordinale": Eine Liturgiegeschichtliche und Liturgietheologische Studie* (Neuried: Ars Una, 1997); E. G. Rupp, 'The Age of the Reformation, 1500–1648', in *The Layman in Christian History*, eds S. C. Neill and H.–R. Weber (London: SCM Press, 1963), pp. 135–50; S. W. Sykes, *Unashamed Anglicanism* (London: Darton, Longman and Todd, 1995), pp. 42–3.

19 *De Sacramentis*, G. P. Jeanes, 'A Reformation Treatise on the Sacraments', *JTS* 46 (1995): 178–9. While this document is anonymous, the case for Cranmer's authorship in c. 1537/8 has been cogently argued by Jeanes, pp. 149–60.

20 *De Sacramentis*, Jeanes, 'Reformation Treatise', p. 169.

21 *Questiones and Answers* 10; *De Sacramentis*, Jeanes, 'Reformation Treatise', p. 178. Cranmer anteceded Canon VII of the Council of Trent, which restricted authority to confer Orders to bishops.

eucharist.[22] This misrepresents Cranmer's position, largely because it overlooks his Erastianism. In *Questions and Answers on the Sacraments and the Appointment and Power of Bishops and Priests*, written in 1540, Cranmer notes that the apostles did not have the benefit of "Christian princes, by whose authority ministers of God's word might be appointed", and were therefore reliant on their own judgement in establishing ministries to continue their work.[23] Presumably, if Paul had succeeded in converting Agrippa II,[24] he would thereby have placed not only himself but all Christian missionaries and churches under the jurisdiction of the vassal of infamous emperor Nero. At his trial several years later, the by then deposed Archbishop was forced to concede that, in terms of the logic of his theology of royal supremacy, Nero had in fact been head of the Church.[25] This in itself might be cause for hesitation in subscribing uncritically to Cranmer's theology, but his formative influence on Anglican worship requires that we clarify his position.

Cranmer's provisions applied specifically to the powers of anointed and crowned Christian monarchs, in whom a quasi-sacerdotal quality and peculiar rights of ecclesiastical governance, evidently the *ius ordinis* as well as the *ius iurisdictionis* which had been claimed by Henry VIII, were deemed to be vested.[26] Maintaining that civil and ecclesiastical functionaries alike hold office under the Christian king, and denying that Scripture requires the consecration of bishops and priests, Cranmer concludes that lawful, i.e. royal, appointment to office is sufficient without ordination.[27] When a king appoints a bishop or priest, the rite of ordination is "comely" and "seemly", but superfluous.[28] In effect, the act of the monarch in making the appointment is the functional equivalent of ordination, and the person so appointed thereby becomes a bishop or priest. As Cranmer does not count ordination a sacrament, this does not imply the ascription to the monarch of sacramental powers, a notion such as Article XXXVII was later to exclude. Cranmer suggests further that were a "prince christian-learned to conquer certain dominions of infidels" or an ecclesiastical hierarchy in his realm to have been

---

22   B. T. Lloyd, *Lay Presidency at the Eucharist?* (Nottingham: Grove Books, 1977), p. 5.

23   *Quest. and Ans.* 9.

24   Acts 26.28-29.

25   MacCulloch, *Cranmer*, p. 577. cf. Jeanes, *Signs of God's Promise*, p. 9.

26   Haigh, *Reformations*, p. 14; MacCulloch, *Cranmer*, p. 278; cf. Avis, *Anglicanism*, p. 5.

27   *Quest. and Ans.* 11–12.

28   *Quest. and Ans.* 9.

obliterated, the said "prince christian-learned" might institute new hierarchies without those appointed to clerical office receiving ordination.[29]

The *Questions and Answers* are an exercise in casuistry, and reflect Cranmer's private views, and not the official position of the Church of England as expounded in the Ordinal. Nevertheless, it is important to be clear as to what his argument was. Cranmer does not propose that lay persons could or should preside at the eucharist. Rather, he argues that a person lawfully appointed by a Christian monarch to an ecclesiastical office thereby becomes a bishop or a priest, irrespective of whether or not he has received the "comely" and "seemly" rite of ordination.

In *A Defence of the True and Catholick Doctrine of the Sacrament*, written in 1550, Cranmer wrote that "Christ made no such difference between the priest and the layman, that the priest should make oblation and sacrifice of Christ for the layman".[30] This document, from the reign of Edward VI, arguably represents Cranmer at his least inhibited by royal constraints, and increasingly under the influence of the Swiss reformers, in particular Bucer. Despite his apparent denial of any distinction between priest and laity, Cranmer does not proceed to suggest that lay people should preside or "minister" at the eucharist.[31] Rather, his emphasis is on the role of the priest as an act of service, and on the active participation of the laity in the eucharist. It is medieval patterns of priesthood, private masses, with lay people reverencing rather than partaking of the consecrated elements, which are his concerns in this text. While Cranmer emphasizes the active if silent role of the laity in the eucharistic prayer, and their equal standing with priests before God, it is the role of the priest alone "to initiate the action of celebrating the Lord's Supper".[32]

Cranmer's recorded theological opinions, no more than his liturgical compositions which substantially became the two editions of the Book of Common Prayer and the Ordinal of the reign of Edward VI, provide any precedent for lay presidency at the eucharist. If Cranmer's views on the ministry and ordination are fully reflected in the texts just considered, and have any enduring significance, it is surely to challenge the distinction drawn in many of the debates we will be considering in

---

29 *Quest. and Ans.* 13–14.

30 *Defence*, 5.11.

31 Cf. J. Woodhouse, 'Lay Administration of the Lord's Supper', *St Mark's Review* 162 (1995): 18.

32 Sykes, *Unashamed Anglicanism*, pp. 42–3.

subsequent chapters, between authorization (licensing) and ordination.[33]
In terms of Cranmer's theology, a lay person lawfully authorized to
exercise the functions and office of a priest, such as preaching or
administering the sacraments, thereby becomes a priest, even if not
episcopally ordained. The crucial question would be how this principle
should be applied in the absence of anointed and crowned supreme head
or governor of the (established) Church, as is the case throughout the
Anglican Communion, with the exception of the Church of England.
Furthermore, while complicit in the scheme to place Lady Jane Grey on
the throne in 1553, Cranmer does not seem to have considered how this
principle would apply if the reigning monarch were female, which might
pose further problems for proponents of lay presidency committed to the
principle of male headship in the Church.

The Articles of Religion
The Articles of Religion reached their definitive form as part of the
Elizabethan settlement of the Church of England, and were for centuries
a definitive statement of doctrine and discipline to which clergy were
required to declare their unqualified allegiance. Their provisions for the
exercise of ministry are therefore of crucial importance to understanding
the position of the Church of England, in the absence of any subsequent
legislation which might revise the principles expressed in the Articles.

Article XXIII: *Of Ministering in the Congregation*, stipulates that ministry
may be exercised only by those *legitime vocatus et missus*, "lawfully called,
and sent". There is no explicit reference to ordination, or identification
of bishops, priests, and deacons as the ministers of the Church. It has
accordingly been claimed that this Article makes provision for, or at
least leaves open the possibility of, lay presidency at the eucharist.[34]
This, as will become clear, depends on reading Article XXIII in isolation
not only from the other Articles, but also from the Book of Common
Prayer and the Ordinal. Furthermore, any ambiguity in Article XXIII
reflects the longstanding and continuing disputes about the sacramental
character of episcopacy, in distinction from the priesthood of the
presbyterate, noted above. Ordination as the prerequisite to exercising

---

33 Cf. A. T. Hanson, *Church, Sacraments and Ministry* (London: Mowbrays, 1975),
    pp. 105–6.
34 W. H. Griffith Thomas, *The Principles of Theology* (London: Vine, 1930), pp.
    313–38; cf. R. T. Beckwith, *Priesthood and Sacraments* (Abingdon: Marsham
    Manor, 1964), pp. 42–6.

the ministry of word and sacraments is not at issue.[35] As with Cranmer's personal opinions, this Article could conceivably imply that royal appointment was sufficient empowerment without ordination, if read in isolation from the Book of Common Prayer, the Ordinal, and Article XXXVI: *Of Consecration of Bishops and Ministers*.

Article XXXVI stipulates the ministry of consecrated bishops and ordained priests and deacons, and defends the validity of Anglican ordination rites, in particular those of the reign of Edward VI whose wording and "intention" were subsequently to prove contentious. The Article refers to *consecratione Archiepiscoporum, et Episcoporum*, "Consecration of Archbishops and Bishops", and to *ordinatione Presbyterorum et Diaconorum*, "ordering of Priests and Deacons". It should be noted that neither this Article nor the Ordinal envisages that a bishop translated to an archbishopric would undergo a further consecration. Rather, it reflects a context in which it was not at all unusual for priests who were not yet bishops, such as Parker, to be appointed to the archiepiscopal sees, and therefore to be consecrated to an archbishopric rather than to a diocesan (or suffragan) see. While ambiguity about the episcopate as a distinct order of ministry may possibly be discerned, this Article was formulated in 1563, the same year as the Council of Trent resolved this issue in Roman Catholic doctrine and discipline, and reserved ordination to bishops.[36]

Lawful practice in the Church of England since the Reformation has consistently been that ordination be administered by bishops on the authority of the Crown, before ecclesiastical offices and functions are assumed.[37] Article XXIII was revised and clarified from *Nemo in Ecclesia ministret nisi vocatus*, "Nobody may minister in the Congregation unless called", when the Article was promulgated in 1563, to the more specific and unambiguous definitive version of 1571:

> *Non licet cuiquam sumere sibi munus publice praedicandi, aut administrandi Sacramenta in Ecclesia, nisi prius fuerit ad haec obeunda legitime vocatus et missus.*
>
> It is not lawful for any man to take upon him the office of publick preaching, or ministering the Sacraments in the Congregation, before he be lawfully called, and sent to execute the same.

---

35   O. M. T. O'Donovan, *On the Thirty Nine Articles* (Exeter: Paternoster Press, 1986), p. 119.

36   Bicknell, *Thirty Nine Articles*, pp. 321–2.

37   Cf. P. F. Bradshaw, *The Anglican Ordinal* (London: SPCK, 1971); Bicknell, *Thirty Nine Articles*, p. 323.

The emphasis on legal process in the calling of clergy is not at all unusual in the Reformed tradition, and the use of "Congregation" to render *Ecclesia* does not imply any kind of parochial calling or presentation by patrons independent of the Crown; rather the "Congregation" is the setting in which clergy fulfil and exercise their ministries. It is worth noting that Article XIX. *Of the Church* renders *Ecclesia* with "Church", and uses the term both of the universal and the local body.

Anglicanism since the Reformation has been theologically and in other respects somewhat fractious, even if some vague consensus around allegiance to the principles expounded in the Book of Common Prayer, Ordinal, and Articles of Religion can be discerned.[38] The proverbial fault lines have shifted somewhat as the issues confronting the Church have changed, and using such expressions as "high" and "low" to trace continuity between competing tendencies during different periods is potentially misleading. For instance, John Wesley would have been considered "high", but would also be classified as "evangelical", a label that would more commonly be associated with "low". The intellectual and spiritual forces were rather more complex than such characterizations would suggest. It would therefore be virtually impossible to select a representative sample of Anglican theological thinking during the centuries following the Reformation, particularly on an issue which was never discussed as a practical proposition, but at most obliquely in theoretical and abstract terms. Therefore, in surveying briefly some contributions to the development of Anglican theology on the eucharist and ministry, the texts considered will be those which have proved of enduring value, rather than any which might be deemed more representative of their day.

Richard Hooker

Richard Hooker may not be representative of academic theology in the Church of England of his day, but he has nonetheless acquired a pre-eminence which requires that any survey of Anglican theology from the Reformation onwards begin with him. Hooker's *Of the Lawes of Ecclesiastical Polity* is unequivocal in regarding the "ministry of things divine" as not to be undertaken without "lawful authority": "Ministerial power is a mark of separation, because it severeth them that have it from other men, and maketh them a special *order* consecrated unto the service

---

38 Cf. Avis, *Anglicanism*.

of the Most High in things wherewith others may not meddle."[39] While subordinating the ministry of the Church to the royal supremacy, Hooker also emphasizes its subjection to God, and proceeds to divide the Church into two entities, the "order" of clergy and the laity, described as ἰδιώτας (i.e. private individual, common or lay person – in sense of having no specialized knowledge) citing 1 Cor. 14.16, 24. Modern Christians might recoil from the use of ἰδιώτας, with or without the connotations of the English word "idiot", but Hooker's clear distinction in both character and function between clergy and laity can nonetheless not be ignored. Referring specifically to the apostolic Church, Hooker proceeds to divide the clergy into the two orders of presbyters and deacons, debating somewhat equivocally whether "priest" or "presbyter" is the more appropriate designation of the latter.[40] He refers also to bishops as a distinct "order" who replaced the apostles, and signals an intent to discuss episcopacy in Book VII.[41] In this latter volume, drafted but not published at the time of his death, Hooker asserts that "A thousand five hundred years and upward the Church of Christ hath now continued under the sacred regiment of bishops."[42] While defending the antiquity and normativity of episcopal church governance and ordination, Hooker desists from regarding these as essential:

> The whole Church visible being the original subject of all power, it hath not ordinarily allowed any other than bishops alone to ordain: howbeit, as the ordinary course is ordinarily in all things to be observed, so it may be in some cases not unnecessary that we decline from the ordinary ways.[43]

The principle that the Church as a whole, and not the individual bishop or any other functionary, has received from God the authority to ordain, informs Hooker's repudiation of mechanical conceptions of apostolic succession as essential to the validity of Christian ministry. What is indispensable is authorization by lawful authority, normatively conferred through episcopal ordination, but in exceptional circumstances conferred through ordination by other agents.

---

39 *Laws*, 5.77.1-2.
40 *Laws*, 5.78.2-3.
41 *Laws*, 5.78.9.
42 *Laws*, 7.1.4.
43 *Laws*, 7.14.11.

In defending the ordination to the diaconate and presbyterate of persons who had not been appointed to benefices or curacies, Hooker asserts that "Presbyters and Deacons are not by ordination consecrated unto places but unto functions."[44] This would imply that the functions which clergy, and in particular priests, are authorized to perform at their ordinations are of the essence of their ministry, and cannot be undertaken without the empowerment of the Holy Spirit for "those actions that appertain to our place and calling".[45] This principle is integral to his theology, and fundamental to his ecclesiology, and cannot be disregarded by those who claim his legacy for their own. Clergy are the "means of making the gifts of the Incarnation available to the Church, and, through the Church, to the world".[46] It is reasonable to suppose that, were Hooker aware of any arguments for lay eucharistic presidency, he would have addressed these explicitly in Book V, or at least have indicated his intention to do so in a subsequent Book. But there is no indication of this at all, and Hooker is unequivocal in distinguishing clergy from laity in status as well as function. He defends baptism by lay people, including women, in specific circumstances "by occasion of urgent necessity" where no cleric is available to officiate, citing ancient precedent and the absence of any explicit prohibition in Scripture.[47] On the other hand, Hooker makes no similar provision regarding the eucharist, maintaining a high theology of the ordained ministry which he regards as of apostolic institution in both office and function, albeit not dependent upon mechanical notions of apostolic succession.[48]

The historical and exegetical basis of Hooker's position may not be tenable in the light of modern critical biblical and patristic scholarship, and his pre-eminence owes more to Anglican consensus than to official endorsement or promulgation of his works. Nevertheless, while his positions on the issues of his day cannot prescribe solutions to the questions with which subsequent generations of Anglicans are

---

44   *Laws*, 5.80.6.

45   *Laws*, 5.77.8.

46   J. S. Marshall, *Hooker and the Anglican Tradition* (London: A & C Black, 1963), pp. 146–7; cf. C. W. Dugmore, *Eucharistic Doctrine in England from Hooker to Waterland* (London: SPCK, 1942); *The Mass and the English Reformers* (London: Macmillan, 1958); B. D. Spinks, *Two Faces of Elizabethan Anglican Theology* (Lanham, NY: Scarecrow, 1999).

47   *Laws*, 5.61-62.

48   *Laws*, 5.76-77.

confronted, he nonetheless provides a model for principled and rigorous exploration of matters of contention in the Church.

William Laud

Whereas Hooker may have been somewhat controversial in his own day, William Laud, Archbishop of Canterbury under Charles I, was positively divisive, not only in England but, perhaps more catastrophically, in promoting the king's ecclesiastical policy in Scotland. In theology, he was rather more moderate, and unequivocally committed to reform, however much he regretted the fragmentation of Christendom this had caused. It is in dialogue with Roman Catholicism that Laud, claiming agreement with the "dissenting churches", discusses the eucharist, relating this directly to questions of ministry. Laud distinguishes three "sacrifices" in the eucharist:

> One by the priest only; that is the commemorative sacrifice of Christ's death, represented in bread broken and wine poured out. Another by the priest and people jointly; and that is, the sacrifice of praise and thanksgiving for all the benefits and graces we receive by the precious death of Christ. The third, by every particular man for himself only; and that is, the sacrifice of every man's body and soul, to serve Him in both all the rest of his life, for this blessing thus bestowed on him.[49]

The clear distinction in roles between priest and congregation, within a common act of worship, would clearly preclude any discussion of lay presidency. Whether Protestant theologians, Lutheran or Calvinist, let alone Anabaptist, would have acquiesced in Laud's use of "sacrifice" and "priest" may be debatable. But denial of a distinctive priesthood of the clergy, and rejection of sacrificial language of the eucharist, did not realize any diminution in the distinction between ministers and laity in the reformed Church of England.

Jeremy Taylor

A theologian of more enduring significance, as well as a notable spiritual writer, was Jeremy Taylor, who became Bishop of Down and Connor, and subsequently also of Dromore, in the Church of Ireland at the Restoration of Charles II. His writings span the period from Charles I to his own episcopate, but perhaps the most significant of his works for our purpose was written during the early years of the Commonwealth, at a

---

49   *A Relation of the Conference between William Laud late Lord Archbishop of Canterbury and Mr. Fisher the Jesuit*, pp. 358–9.

time when the restoration of the monarchy, the episcopate, and public worship according to the Book of Common Prayer was neither inevitable nor foreseeable.

Clerus Domini, or, A Discourse of the Divine Institution, Necessity, Sacredness, and Separation, of the Office Ministerial, together with the Nature and Manner of its Power and Operation, represents an ecclesiology, as its title suggests, preoccupied with questions of order. Taylor regards the orders of ministry as being of divine institution, a continuation of that exercised by the apostles.[50] The Petrine privileges of "binding and loosing" and the "power of the keys" are accordingly vested in the priesthood.[51] Preaching the gospel,[52] and the administration of the sacraments of baptism[53] and the eucharist,[54] are accordingly functions reserved to bishops and priests. Consecration of the eucharistic elements is effected by the Holy Spirit "not by the force of syllables . . . [but] by the prayer of the church, presented by the priests".[55] Ordination takes place by imposition of human hands, but the grace is God-given, and "All power of ordination descends from God".[56] Taylor emphasizes that the power invoked in the sacraments is mystical rather than magic, *facultas* and not *vis* "to intervene between God and the people".[57] Lay people cannot therefore validly or effectively perform priestly functions.

Taylor is concerned to regulate what in contemporary terms would be considered charismatic manifestations, "given extra-regularly", apart from ecclesiastical office: gifts of the Holy Spirit were conferred on lay men and women as well as on the apostles in the New Testament, but did not constitute a basis for public ministry.[58] He is reluctant to see lay people administer baptism, as "the ordinary minister of baptism is a person consecrated", and the sacrament "most notoriously and signally"

---

50 *Cler. Dom.* 1.8; 2.2–3; 6.7.

51 *Cler. Dom.* 2.4–5; 4.3–12.

52 *Cler. Dom.* 3.2–15.

53 *Cler. Dom.* 4.3–12. Cf. B. D. Spinks, 'Two Seventeenth Century Examples of *Lex Credendi, Lex Orandi*: The Baptismal and Eucharistic Theologies of Jeremy Taylor and Richard Baxter', *StL* 21 (1991): 167–72.

54 *Cler. Dom.* 5. Cf. H. R. McAdoo, *The Eucharistic Theology of Jeremy Taylor Today* (Norwich: Canterbury Press, 1988); Spinks, 'Seventeenth Century Examples', pp. 179–84.

55 *Cler. Dom.* 7.10.

56 *Cler. Dom.* 6.7; 7.2,15.

57 Authority or capacity rather than force, *Cler. Dom.* 7.3.

58 *Cler. Dom.* 3.4–6.

involves the power of the keys, which has been conferred on the apostolic ministry.[59]

Regarding the eucharist, Taylor argues that the dominical injunction, *Hoc facite*, "Do this", was addressed to the "apostles in the capacity of ministers: not as receivers, but as consecrators and givers",[60] and cites patristic sources in support for his assertion that only a priest may officiate at the altar. While acknowledging the royal priesthood of the Church, Taylor denies that individual lay people are accordingly priests.[61] The apostles received "power of consecration of the eucharist, at the institution of it", before, and quite apart from, the conferral of the Holy Spirit on the whole Church at Pentecost.[62] It would therefore be sacrilegious for a lay person to execute a priestly function:[63] "[I]t is most consonant to the analogy of the mystery, that this commemorative sacrifice be presented by persons as separate and distinct in their ministry, as the sacrifice itself is from, and above, the other parts of our religion."[64]

While continuity with Hooker can readily be discerned, Taylor represents perhaps the most forthright distinction and separation between clergy, and particularly priests, on the one hand, and Christian laity on the other, between the Reformation and the Anglo-Catholic revival. Particularly in distinguishing between the gift of the Holy Spirit to the Church at Pentecost and the empowerment of the apostolic ministry by Christ, Taylor separates the ordained ministry from, as well as within, the life of the Church as a whole. The celebration of the eucharist belongs to the latter category, and is accordingly a function of the ordained priesthood. Taylor cannot be regarded necessarily as representative of the Church of England, or of Ireland, of his period.[65] But neither is there any evidence that contrary opinions on eucharistic presidency were espoused, either within the established church or in dissenting circles, during this period.

59　*Cler. Dom.* 4.2,13–14.

60　*Cler. Dom.* 5.4.

61　*Cler. Dom.* 5.9.

62　*Cler. Dom.* 8.1.

63　*Cler. Dom.* 8.18.

64　*Cler. Dom.* 5.5.

65　Cf. Avis, *Anglicanism*, pp. 111–17; McAdoo, *Eucharistic Theology*; Spinks, 'Seventeenth Century Examples'.

John Cosin

Taylor's contemporary, John Cosin, who became Bishop of Durham at the Restoration, is remembered as a liturgist and a catholic voice in the Caroline church. Nevertheless, he was extremely reluctant to declare invalid the ministry and sacraments of the French Reformed church, in whose fellowship he had lived in exile:

> Though we may safely say, and maintain it, that their ministers are not so duly and rightly ordained, as they should be, by those prelates and bishops of the church, who since the Apostles' time have only had the ordinary power and authority to make and constitute a priest, yet that by reason of this defect there is a total nullity in their ordination, or that they be therefore no priests or ministers of the church. ... I would loath to affirm and determine against them.[66]

This, however cautious and qualified, acknowledgement of the ecclesial character and integrity of Protestant denominations which had not retained episcopacy is significant in that it demonstrates that validity of ordination is not defined absolutely on the basis of the operation of bishops in the apostolic succession. A distinctive ministry is acknowledged, set apart from the laity, and charged with the ministry of word, sacrament, and pastoral oversight.

Restoration: The Book of Common Prayer

The Restoration of the monarchy in 1660 saw also the restoration and entrenchment of episcopacy in England and Ireland. Episcopacy was restored also in Scotland, until William III established Presbyterianism there in 1689, and the body which evolved into the Scottish Episcopal Church was not merely disestablished but subjected to at times repressive measures for over a century. Restoration of Anglican church order was accompanied by publication of rites for public worship in the forms which were to become definitive not only for the Church of England, but, symbolically at least, for worldwide Anglicanism.

The *Book of Common Prayer* of 1662 reflects some revision of Cranmer's earlier liturgical compositions, negotiated at the Savoy Conference between the bishops and a Presbyterian delegation. The rubrics to the order for Holy Communion are explicit in directing that "the Priest" say the Lord's Prayer, read the Decalogue, say the Collect for the Sovereign, read the Epistle and Gospel, read the Offertory sentence(s) and prepare

---

66   Letter to Mr Cordel, P. E. More and F. L. Cross, *Anglicanism* (London: SPCK, 1935), pp. 398–402.

the elements, say the Prayer of the Church Militant, read the Exhortation, call the congregation to Confession, pronounce the Absolution (deferred to the bishop when present), read the Comfortable Words, recite the *Sursam Corda* and the Preface, lead the Prayer of Humble Access, recite the Prayer of Consecration while performing the prescribed manual acts, lead the congregation in the Lord's Prayer, and pronounce the Blessing (deferred to the bishop when present). The officiant is referred to as "the Minister" in the rubric governing the distribution, to distinguish him from other clergy present, but it is nonetheless entirely clear that the minister of the eucharist is a priest. To avoid interpretations of the eucharist as repeating the sacrifice of Christ, the altar is consistently referred to as "the Table" or "the Lord's Table", and "there, by his one oblation of Himself, once offered" in the Prayer of Consecration gives this point verbal expression. The restriction of presidency to priests is therefore not a matter of sacerdotalism or residual medieval eucharistic theology, but one of Church order. Any ambiguity about the episcopate as a distinct order of ministry has given way to an unequivocal commitment to the threefold orders of ministry, and the Preface to the Ordinal declares:

> It is evident unto all men diligently reading holy Scripture and ancient Authors, that from the Apostles' time there have been these Orders of Ministers in Christ's Church: Bishops, Priests, and Deacons.

Modern Biblical and patristic scholarship, as reviewed in the previous chapters, would suggest that this confidence is somewhat misplaced, but it is nonetheless the premise upon which Anglican Church order is founded:

> Which Offices were evermore had in such reverend estimation, that no man might presume to execute any of them, except he were first called, tried, examined ... And also by publick Prayer, with Imposition of Hands, were approved and admitted thereunto by lawful authority.[67]

The *Ordinal* intends to continue the orders of ministry believed to be firmly rooted in the apostolic Church, and the rites of episcopal ordination contained therein are a prerequisite to exercising any of the functions of the three orders of ministry. Priests are identified as ministers of the Word and sacraments, and an authority is conferred on them which they have not hitherto possessed as lay people:

---

67   Preface to the Ordinal.

[at the imposition of hands] ... be thou a faithful dispenser of the Word of God, and of his holy Sacraments.
[at the delivery of the Bible] Take thou authority to preach the Word of God, and to minister the holy Sacraments in the Congregation ...

Whatever ambiguities there may be in the words "consecrate" and "administer",[68] that the authority to carry out these acts is conferred on priests alone is entirely clear. These provisions of the Ordinal are enforced by the Act of Uniformity of 1662,[69] which explicitly restricts consecration of the eucharistic elements to episcopally ordained priests and bishops.

The promulgation of the Book of Common Prayer in 1662 can be regarded as the culmination of the Reformation in England, by default if not intention. It has become the standard by which Anglican doctrine, order, and discipline are measured, any departure from which has required carefully considered synodical measures in the various provinces of the Communion. The historical and theological premises upon which the Book of Common Prayer, Ordinal, and accompanying legislation are founded may be debatable. But for Anglicans for whom the Book of Common Prayer is, alongside but theoretically subordinate to the Bible, the definitive and unalterable statement of doctrine and Church order, the unambiguous restriction of eucharistic presidency to priests – in the sense of episcopally ordained presbyters – would surely pre-empt discussion, let alone implementation, of lay presidency.

The Anglican tradition, from the beginnings of the English Reformation to the Restoration of the monarchy, embraces considerable theological diversity, greater than could be considered here. The only explicit discussion of eucharistic presidency clearly excludes lay people from this role, while others exclude lay presidency at least by implication. The paucity of debate on this issue suggests that the Church of England was united in insisting that ministries be authorized, and that authority was conferred through ordination. While the tradition considered thus far is unanimous, this is not to deny that tradition is inherently dynamic, and therefore subject to change.[70] We turn now to consider Anglicanism during the modern period.

---

68 *Eucharistic Presidency: A Theological Statement by the House of Bishops of the General Synod* (London: Church House Publishing, 1997), p. 62 n. 8.

69 *Act for the Uniformity of Publick Prayers, and Administration of the Sacraments...*, XIV Carol II.

70 Beckwith, *Priesthood*, pp. 29–30.

The Anglican Communion in the nineteenth and twentieth centuries
While the eighteenth century was not necessarily in all ways as arid a
period in the Church of England and the Church of Ireland as is
sometimes portrayed, it saw no significant developments in the theology
of the eucharist or of ministry pertaining to this study. The decision of
John Wesley, towards the end of his life, to ordain elders for what was
to become the Methodist Church, significantly altered the religious
landscape not only of England and Wales, but of many other parts of the
world, and has major continuing ecumenical implications which will be
considered further below. However, it was after the evangelical revival,
in the aftermath of the Oxford Movement and with the emergence of
critical biblical and patristic scholarship, that theological contributions
of lasting significance were written, particularly on Christian ministry,
and especially the priesthood and episcopate.

F. D. Maurice
Frederick Denison Maurice was an enigmatic and controversial
theologian, who belonged to no party, and was rejected by most in his
own day, but has subsequently been claimed by virtually all. He was
ejected from his chair at King's College, London, and, after pioneering
adult and women's education for the "working classes", ended his days
as Professor of Moral Philosophy at Cambridge. Maurice had been
reared in East Anglian Unitarianism, with its tradition of independent
intellectual rigour, and when he was received into the Church of
England he brought this with him, as well as a commitment to the
Reformation heritage and the breadth of Anglican tradition.

Maurice sought in the Articles of Religion a definitive Anglican
theological method, which he applied in his own writings. The most
important of these is *The Kingdom of Christ*, which is structured largely as
a dialogue with other Christian denominations. Maurice defends
Anglican ecclesiology, as he understands it, on both historical and
theological grounds. He attaches great importance to baptism and the
eucharist as being formative of the Church, and affirms the ordained
ministry as being not merely of ancient provenance, but as deriving from
Christ: "If the Incarnation mean anything, if the Church be not a dream,
all offices exercised by her on behalf of humanity must be offices first
exercised by Christ."[71] Conferral of the Holy Spirit by Christ on the
apostles is the foundation of Christian ministry. Priesthood and
episcopacy in the apostolic succession are "one of the appointed and

---

71   F. D. Maurice, *The Kingdom of Christ* (London: Rivington, 1842), vol. 2, p. 184.

indispensable signs of a spiritual and universal society".[72] Continuity between the cultic institutions of the Old Testament and the institutions and ministry of the Church is also emphasized, and, significantly, rooted in the eucharist:

> It has been believed, as a necessary consequence of the importance attached to the Eucharist, that an order of men must exist in the Christian Church corresponding to the priests of the old dispensation, with the difference that the sacrifice in the one case was anticipatory, in the other commemorative.[73]

Maurice identifies the authority to administer absolution as a defining characteristic of priesthood, and regards this as integrally linked with the celebration of the eucharist:

> the same person to whom the function of absolving is committed has also the function of administering the Eucharist. These two duties never have been separated, and it is most needful that they should be contemplated in their relation to each other ... [the priest's] whole object is to present Christ to men and men to Christ really and practically.[74]

Maurice is sensitive to the integrity and sincerity with which positions different to his own are held, especially in denominations with different ecclesiologies, including not only Presbyterians but also the Society of Friends. But, as an Anglican theologian whose convictions have been confirmed through critical investigation, he is unambiguous in affirming the catholic foundations of Anglicanism. His affirmation of apostolic succession in the ordained ministry, its typological antecedents in the Old Testament, and its representative function may not be at all original or distinctive, except perhaps in the critical rigour with which they are investigated. The inextricability of the authority to confer absolution and that to preside at the eucharist may be less familiar to Anglicans conscious of their Protestant heritage, but shows clear continuity with catholic conceptions of priesthood. Therefore, while Maurice would have been considered a radical by many, and while he did not identify with what he saw as the reactionary character of the Oxford Movement, still less the neo-Gothic romanticism which followed, his position on the

---

72 *Kingdom*, vol. 2, pp. 147–8.
73 *Kingdom*, vol. 2, p. 139.
74 *Kingdom*, vol. 2, p. 193.

Church and ministry is nonetheless unambiguously Catholic.[75] Presidency at the eucharist is a function of ordained priests.

J. B. Lightfoot

One of the most important historical and theological treatments of ministry to emanate from the Church of England during the late nineteenth century is by Joseph Barber Lightfoot, the Cambridge professor and noted scholar of ancient Christianity who became Bishop of Durham. "On the Christian Ministry" was published as an excursus to his commentary on Philippians. It will be recalled that of Paul's undisputed letters, Philippians alone addresses titled officers of the local church. Lightfoot's treatment of ἐπίσκοπος, particularly in relation to πρεσβύτερος, represents the culmination of nineteenth-century historical critical research and the consensus which prevailed for most of the twentieth. For the present purpose, however, Lightfoot's historical reconstructions are less important than the corollaries he posits for contemporary Christian ministry. He rejects notions of ministry as vicarious, in the sense of clergy being endowed with spiritual qualities and enjoying an access to God not possessed by the laity they represent. He suggests also that, while ordained ministries have become normative, circumstances could arise where normal legal provisions should be dispensed with:

> It may be a general rule, it may be under ordinary circumstances a practically universal law, that the highest acts of congregational worship shall be performed through the principal officers of the congregation. But an emergency may arise when "the spirit" and not the letter must decide ... the higher ordinance of the universal priesthood will overrule all special limitations. The layman will assume functions which are otherwise restricted to the ordained minister.[76]

It is immediately noticeable that the confidence with which prevailing Anglican structures had been retrojected into the New Testament Church by previous generations of scholarship, as is reflected in the Book of Common Prayer and the Ordinal, and less stridently as recently as Maurice, is no longer tenable. While Lightfoot is more concerned

---

75 Cf. Avis, *Anglicanism*, pp. 289–300; Ramsey, *Anglican Spirit*, pp. 69–77; W. J. Wolf, 'Frederick Denison Maurice', in *The Spirit of Anglicanism*, ed. W. J. Wolf (Edinburgh: T. & T. Clark, 1979), pp. 49–99.

76 J. B. Lightfoot, *Saint Paul's Epistle to the Philippians* (London: Macmillan, 1896), p. 266.

with the historical attestation of ecclesiastical structures than with the theology of ministry, his deductions for contemporary church discipline on the basis of his findings are nonetheless significant. The suggestion that, in the absence of ordained clergy, lay people might assume their role in public worship, is a departure from the more rigid discipline which the Church of England had hitherto maintained, and the flexibility and pragmatism would seem to be unprecedented in catholic tradition since Tertullian.

Charles Gore

The most important rejoinder to Lightfoot came from Charles Gore, later to become bishop, successively, of Worcester, Birmingham, and Oxford, as well as the founder of the Community of the Resurrection. Gore exercises considerably greater critical rigour than had the earlier Anglo-Catholics criticized by Maurice. Nevertheless, in *The Church and the Ministry*, first published in 1882, Gore tends to defend traditional catholic interpretations of the New Testament and patristic evidence, which Lightfoot had argued to be untenable or at best uncertain. He defends the episcopate as a distinct order of ministry, and the apostolic succession therein,[77] as well as the sacramentality of episcopal ordination as conferring distinctive powers on priests and bishops.[78] He is nonetheless unequivocal in asserting the priesthood of the Church as a whole, from which that of the ordained clergy derives, and repudiating notions of priesthood as a separated and privileged caste:

> It is an abuse of the sacerdotal conception, if it is supposed that the priesthood exists to celebrate sacrifices or acts of worship in the place of the body of the people or as their substitute ... The ministry is no more one of vicarious action than it is one of exclusive knowledge or exclusive spiritual relation to God. ... [T]he Church is one body. ... and this body has different organs through which the functions of its life find expression, as it was differentiated by the act and appointment of Him who created it.[79]

Gore proceeds to describe the role of the priest in the eucharist, which is fundamentally an act of the body, as that of "the necessary organ" of the body. The ministry is, furthermore, "the instrument as well as the

---

77   C. Gore, *The Church and the Ministry* (London: Longman, 1919), pp. 53–165.

78   *Church and the Ministry*, pp. 166–94.

79   *Church and the Ministry*, pp. 85–6.

symbol of the Church's unity".[80] In a later work, *The Body of Christ*, Gore argues that "the ministerial priest is but the divinely appointed and empowered organ of the whole priestly body", and points to the abolition of private or secret prayers by the priest during the eucharist, and the proscription of silent recitation of the *Anaphora* so as to diminish or obstruct the full participation of the congregation.[81] Nevertheless, only an episcopally ordained priest can effectively preside at the eucharist, as the representative and instrument of the Church, the Body of Christ. Gore's interpretations of the ancient documents have proved less sustainable than those of Lightfoot, but recent scholarship would recognize that he is more sensitive to the corporate nature of the Church, and to the inevitability of authority structures in any human community. This of course does not in itself imply that Gore, and the Catholic tradition he represents, are correct in attributing divine institution to the structures and offices which emerged.

R. C. Moberly

A theological exposition of Christian ministry, deeply indebted to Gore, which has proved to be of lasting significance, is *Ministerial Priesthood* by Robert Campbell Moberly, Regius Professor of Pastoral Theology in Oxford University. This book, first published in 1897, was envisaged as a preliminary study to a treatment of the Ordinal, a project which Moberly was unable to bring to completion. Moberly interacts critically with Lightfoot, and draws on Gore in his defence of traditional interpretations of New Testament and patristic passages which Lightfoot had shown to be uncertain. Moberly defines ministry as "the instrument which represents the whole Spirit-endowed Body of the Church; and yet withal is itself so Spirit-endowed as to have the right and the power to represent instrumentally".[82] He does not suggest that clergy function on behalf of those who have not been empowered with the Holy Spirit, but rather that by divine commission and the particular empowerment received through ordination, ministers are enabled to function representatively for the Church.

While accepting that the forms of ministry evolved gradually, and that it is impossible rigidly to distinguish ἐπίσκοπος from πρεσβύτερος in New Testament usage, Moberly nonetheless maintains the notion of apostolic succession in ministry. His understanding of priesthood derives

---

80   *Church and the Ministry*, p. 86.
81   C. Gore, *The Body of Christ* (London: John Murray, 1901), p. 271.
82   R. C. Moberly, *Ministerial Priesthood* (London: SPCK, 1969), p. 99.

from the priesthood of Christ and the doctrine of the Church as the Body of Christ: "what Christ is, the Church, which is Christ's mystical body, must also be".[83] The Church is identified with the priestly sacrifice of Christ, and therefore corporately endowed with priesthood. The priesthood of the ordained ministry derives from this:

> If the priesthood of the Church consists *ceremonially* in her capacity of self-identification, through Eucharistic worship, with the eternal presentation of Christ's atoning sacrifice, and *spiritually* in her identification of inner life with the spirit of sacrifice which is the spirit of love uttering itself in devoted ministry to others, so it is by necessary consequence with the priesthood of the ministry.[84]

Moberly argues further that ordained priests

> are, by ordination, specialized and empowered to exercise ministerially and organically the prerogatives which are the prerogatives of the body as a whole. They have no greater right in the Sacraments than the laity: only they, and not the laity, have been authorized to stand before the congregation, and to represent the congregation in the ministerial enactment of the Sacraments.

He places considerable emphasis on authorization, not so much as a legal category as of consecration, commissioning, and spiritual empowerment:

> Those who stand before the congregation, either as its representatives to Godward, or as the accredited ministers of God to it, must be authorized and empowered so to do. ... They are Priests because they are personally consecrated to be the representatives and active organs of the priesthood of the Church.[85]

Moberly goes on to argue that it is inherent in the apostolic office, and in the ministry of bishops and priests which derives from it, that those who exercise pastoral oversight in Christian communities should also preside at the celebration of the eucharist. The silence of the New Testament on this subject serves to confirm that there was no alternative, and by implication spiritually more exalted, office of liturgical oversight.[86]

---

83 *Ministerial Priesthood*, p. 251.
84 *Ministerial Priesthood*, pp. 257–8.
85 *Ministerial Priesthood*, pp. 258–9.
86 *Ministerial Priesthood*, pp. 266–72.

Unlike Lightfoot, Moberly finds implicit in the New Testament the teaching on ministry and the eucharist which becomes explicit in the Apostolic Fathers. There can be little question that Moberly is less rigorously critical than Lightfoot in the examination of historic texts. His distinction between clergy and laity is somewhat laboured, and his defence of the liturgical prerogatives of the priesthood tortuous. But it has nonetheless to be recognized that he addresses a crucial problem in relating the priesthood of the Church to that of the ordained ministry, and that he seeks to do so in continuity both with Scripture and ancient tradition and with the Book of Common Prayer and the Ordinal. His methodology is therefore thoroughly Anglican, even if his conclusions require some revision in the light of more rigorous critical scholarship.

Ecumenism and Anglican consciousness

A significant shift in theological emphasis during the twentieth century was occasioned by the emergence of the ecumenical movement. The most urgent questions concerning ministry dealt neither with the essential character of priesthood nor with the role of lay people in the life and worship of the Church. Rather, at least so far as Anglicans, and particularly Anglo-Catholics, were concerned, the crucial issue was the validity of the ordained ministries of the various Protestant denominations which had not retained episcopacy in the apostolic succession. For many, this has remained the case, to the extent that its novelty may not be readily appreciated. As will be recalled, it was not until the Council of Trent that episcopal ordination became a defining criterion of valid ministry in the Roman Catholic Church. The Church of England since the Reformation had wavered between ambivalence and pragmatism in receiving ministers ordained into Protestant denominations. German and Danish Lutheran ministers served in Anglican missions in India, without receiving episcopal ordination, and also in the Anglo-Prussian Jerusalem Bishopric, arguably the original Local Ecumenical Project. It was partly in response to this initiative that the Tractarian movement became preoccupied with the question of validity of Orders, as well as a wider sense of alienation from the established constitutional order in England.[87]

During the same period, the historic episcopate came to be enshrined as all but an article of faith, or at least a fundamental principle, in the United States. Anglican identity was being redefined, and structures

---

87 Cf. M. D. Chapman, *Bishops, Saints and Politics* (London: T & T Clark, 2007), pp. 10–23.

evolved, in congregations politically severed from the British Crown, and therefore from the constitutional basis of the established Church in England. When the constitution of the Protestant Episcopal Church of the United States of America was adopted in 1789, the Articles of Religion would clearly have been an inappropriate doctrinal foundation for Anglicanism in the novel setting of a secular republic, to whose citizens the monarch of Great Britain was an, at least potentially hostile, foreign ruler. Despite the relatively late introduction of bishops and diocesan structures to unite and oversee the scattered Anglican congregations in the United States, "the historic episcopate" came to be identified as an essential mark of the Catholic Church. It should be noted that this took place in a context of early ecumenism, with an explicit commitment to "heal the wounds of the Body of Christ", and to seek "the restoration of the organic unity of the Church". The House of Bishops in 1886 identified "as essential to the restoration of unity among the divided branches of Christendom", the following:

The Holy Scriptures of the Old and New Testaments as the revealed Word of God.
The Nicene Creed as the sufficient statement of the Christian Faith.
The two Sacraments, – Baptism and the Supper of the Lord, – ministered with unfailing use of Christ's words of institution and of the elements ordained by Him.
The Historic Episcopate, locally adapted in the methods of its administration to the varying needs of the nations and peoples called of God into the Unity of His Church.

This formulary was brought to the Lambeth Conference of 1888, and discussed also in the context of ecumenical engagement and seeking the reunification of the Church. What has come to be known as the Lambeth or Chicago–Lambeth Quadrilateral was adopted as "a basis on which approach may be by God's blessing made towards Home Reunion":

The Holy Scriptures of the Old and New Testaments, as "containing all things necessary to salvation", and as being the rule and ultimate standard of faith.
The Apostles' Creed, as the baptismal Symbol; and the Nicene Creed, as the sufficient statement of the Christian faith.
The two Sacraments ordained by Christ Himself – Baptism and the Supper of the Lord – ministered with unfailing use of Christ's words of institution, and of the elements ordained by Him.

The Historic Episcopate, locally adapted in the methods of its administration to the varying needs of the nations and peoples called of God into the Unity of His Church.[88]

It is immediately apparent that substantial amendments were made to the first two items, and a minor but significant amendment to the third. Crude reference to Scripture as "the revealed Word of God" is replaced with a statement inspired by Article VI and more in keeping with the Anglican theological tradition. The subtle distinction between the gospel sacraments of baptism and the eucharist and those of confirmation, reconciliation, unction, matrimony, and orders, similarly reflects closer continuity with received tradition, as well as sensitivity to the growth of the catholic movement in many Anglican provinces. This raises questions as to why the fourth item was adopted without amendment, when a more nuanced reference to ordered ministry, with or without explicit reference to bishops, priests, and deacons, would have been a more accurate depiction of Anglican ministry, in closer keeping with Anglican tradition, and easier to defend on the evidence of Christian antiquity. Irrespective of whether the professed cause of Christian unity has been well served by the Chicago–Lambeth Quadrilateral, we should note that its third item, concerning the sacraments, makes reference to "words of institution" and "elements" ordained by Christ, but does not stipulate by whom these sacraments should be administered.

Anglican consciousness was deeply affected by the papal encyclical *Apostolicae Curae* of 1896, in which Leo XIII declared *Ordinationes ritu anglicano actas, irritas prorsus fuisse et esse omninoque nullas*, "Ordinations according to the Anglican rite have been, and are, absolutely null and utterly void".[89] In a sense this merely confirmed what had been the prevailing opinion in the Roman Communion for centuries, but its definitive pronouncement contributed to a defensiveness among Anglicans which impacted negatively on ecumenical relations during the twentieth century. We do not need to discuss the circumstances leading to the promulgation of *Apostolicae Curae*, or the supposed *formae defectu*, defect in the ritual form in the Ordinals of Edward VI, or even the *defectus intentionis*, defect in the intention of the Ordinal, cited in evidence by the Pope. What is important to recognize is that validity of ministry, defined by episcopal ordination in the apostolic succession,

---

88 Resolution 11. The archive of resolutions of the Lambeth Conferences is available at http://www.lambethconference.org/resolutions/index.cfm

89 *Apostolicae Curae* 36, *AAS* 30 (1895), pp. 193–203; T. A. Lacey, *A Roman Diary* (London: Longman, 1910).

became a dominant issue, and often an insurmountable obstacle, to the growth of closer relations between Anglicans and Protestant denominations. This applied particularly to questions of authority in the administration of the sacraments.

Some Anglo-Catholics have continued to maintain, as historical fact as well as ecclesiological principle, notions of apostolic succession in the historical episcopate. This position was discredited by Lightfoot, before the promulgation of *Apostolicae Curae*, and was not adequately defended on historical grounds by Gore, Moberly, and their successors, and persists today in uninformed polemic rather than in literate theological discourse. Furthermore, the historical basis of apostolic succession is no longer defended by critical Roman Catholic scholars,[90] whatever enduring value may be attached to the ecclesiological principles represented. The basis for ascribing legitimacy or validity to the administration of the sacraments, or any other aspect of Christian ministry, in terms of apostolic succession is therefore very weak.

More liberal-minded Anglican theologians have understood authority bestowed by the Church to act on behalf of the Church as the defining criterion for administering the sacraments, and not any real or contrived ministerial pedigree. During the twentieth century this position was strongly supported by Archbishop William Temple.[91] Perhaps even more significantly for catholic-minded Anglicans, "authorization by the whole Church" was regarded as the defining criterion of ministry by Archbishop Michael Ramsey.[92] As well as being theologically more congenial to modern critical minds, and less susceptible to falsification, this position is closer to that represented by Cranmer and the historic Anglican tradition. The emphasis on lawful authority in the exercise of ministry, rather than the transmission of a distinctive power through ordination, has not been confined to the more Protestant tendencies in the Church of England.

The current position in the canon law of the Church of England is unequivocal: "No person shall consecrate and administer the holy sacrament of the Lord's Supper unless he shall have been ordained priest by Episcopal ordination in accordance with the provisions of Canon C 1."[93] Whatever ambiguity there may be in this canon[94] concerns abstruse

---

90   Cf. Brown, *Priest*, pp. 47–86.
91   Cf. W. Temple, *Thoughts on Some Problems of the Day* (London: Macmillan, 1931), pp. 110–11.
92   A. M. Ramsey, *The Gospel and the Catholic Church* (London: Longman, 1936), p. 219.
93   Canon B12.1, as amended 1994.

points of metaphysical speculation on the meaning and consequences of the word "consecrate", allowing some diversity of eucharistic theology within the Church of England. There can be no doubt that "administer" in this particular context means to officiate or preside at the eucharist, as Canon B12.3 uses "distribute" of the subsidiary function of serving the elements to the communicants. The current canonical position in the Church of England is therefore entirely clear, and revision or rescinding of Canon B12.1 by General Synod, subject to parliamentary ratification and royal assent, would be necessary to change this. The procedure required by canon law in other Anglican provinces would of course be different, but it is nonetheless the case that such an innovation would represent a quite fundamental change in the way ministry is exercised and the sacraments administered, as to require complex synodical processes to be completed.

This is not to suggest that the question of lay eucharistic presidency has not been raised, and perhaps with increased urgency, in recent decades. In the context of ecumenical relations in Britain, the issue was recognized as a "grave problem" during the discussions of the Anglican–Methodist Unity Commission in Britain during the 1960s.[95] At the Anglican Congress held in Toronto in 1963, the authorization of lay presidency to enable communities without the regular ministry of a priest to celebrate the eucharist was proposed by Canon Frank Synge, at the time principal of Christchurch Theological College in New Zealand.[96] This was not implemented in practice in any Province of the Anglican Communion, but the issue was acknowledged at the 1968 Lambeth Conference, in the context of an affirmation that "All Christians share in the priesthood of their Lord". The distinctive ministry of the ordained priest as an agent of Christ, the Church, and the bishop was also affirmed, as was the distinctive character and ministry of the bishop.[97] The divisive potential of any proposal to authorize lay presidency at the eucharist was noted in the report *The Theology of Ordination*, submitted by the Faith and Order Advisory Group of the Board of Mission and Unity to the General Synod of the Church of

94 *Eucharistic Presidency*, p. 62, n. 8.
95 *Conversations between the Church of England and the Methodist Church* (London: Church Information Office and Epworth Press, 1963), sect. 3 (6); *Anglican–Methodist Unity: Report of the Anglican–Methodist Unity Commission* (London: SPCK and Epworth Press, 1968), p. 181.
96 F. C. Synge, 'The Challenge of the Frontiers', in *Anglican Congress 1963* (Toronto: Editorial Committee, 1963), pp. 155–64. See discussion below.
97 *Renewal of the Church in Ministry* (London: SPCK, 1968), p. 100.

England in 1975. The universality of the ordained priesthood was emphasized, as being reflected in the act of presiding at the eucharist.[98] In 1978 a section at the Lambeth Conference convened to consider the question suggested that there "may be circumstances" in which lay eucharistic presidency should be considered, should there be no other way for the bishop to discharge his responsibility for provision of sacramental ministry to congregations in his care.[99]

During the 1970s, the ordination of women emerged as perhaps the dominant and most divisive issue of Anglican ministry, within the Church of England and other provinces of the Communion, as well as between provinces. The Anglican Consultative Council was formed in response to a resolution of the 1968 Lambeth Conference, and became perhaps the most significant forum in which the structure and character of the modern Anglican Communion were negotiated. It would be a gross distortion to suggest that the proverbial fault-lines emerged in response to a single issue, and to ignore the post-colonial reconfiguration of international relations in all areas of life, of which the Anglican Communion was a distinctive but not necessarily untypical example.

Nor should the constantly shifting character of the fault-lines in the Communion, as successive contentious issues were perceived and experienced differently in different Anglican provinces, be overlooked. Nevertheless, with the emergence of the question of ordaining women to the priesthood there emerged also a tendency to polarization on issues which transcended the older tensions of ritual and liturgy, and a tendency also for a single issue to dominate all aspects of church life. This was particularly evident when the expansion and growth of lay ministry became inextricably bound to the issue of the ordination of women. This is not to suggest that this was detrimental to the development of lay ministry in practice, but it did impact negatively on theological reflection on the role of the laity in the Church. The extension of lay ministry into areas of church life which had hitherto been the preserve of the clergy was frequently promoted by opponents of the ordination of women, precisely on the grounds that ordaining women was not necessary to their fulfilling their role in ministry. The promotion of lay ministry, particularly among women, accordingly served as a diversion from the debate about the ordination of women. The progressive and unreflective transfer to lay people of priestly and

---

98 (London: Church Information Office, 1975), p. 55.

99 *The Report of the Lambeth Conference 1978* (London: Church Information Office, 1978), p. 83.

diaconal roles, particularly but not exclusively in worship, has contributed significantly to the situation where "the practical distinction between minister and layman is the ability to say one prayer at the communion service".[100] Ironically, perhaps, it was in some feminist groups during the struggle for the ordination of women that (unauthorized) eucharistic rites came to be celebrated without a priest.[101]

New Patterns of Ministry

During the period in which the ordination of women emerged as a contentious but pressing issue in the Church of England and other parts of the Anglican Communion, the Church was in several provinces also experiencing a conspicuous decline in clergy numbers. The preceding decades had also seen the emergence of the parish eucharist as the principal act of worship in an increasing number of Anglican congregations, and accordingly raised new questions about the provision of ministry in congregations not benefiting from the regular presence of a priest. A range of alternative patterns of ministry began to be considered in response to these developments. These consisted essentially of increasing the scope of lay ministry and ordaining clergy whose vocations would entail neither full-time service nor the formation process which had come since the late nineteenth century to be regarded as standard. Within the diversity of options considered, one question to emerge was whether it would be permissible or appropriate to license lay people to preside at the celebration of the eucharist, and in what specific circumstances.

In the Church of England, this issue was acknowledged in the 1983 report of Canon John Tiller, the Chief Secretary of the Advisory Council for the Church's Ministry. In *A Strategy for the Church's Ministry*, Tiller analyses the state of ministry in the Church of England, and explores options for meeting its projected needs over the ensuing decades. Authorized lay eucharistic presidency is one possible strategy for provision of ministry of word and sacrament, but it is suggested that this would be a theologically inadequate approach, in that the distinction between authorization and ordination would then require further clarification, and in that the representative role of the priesthood, and of presidency in the eucharist, would be better served by ordaining a "local

---

100 Buchanan, 'Anglican Historical Perspectives', p. 14.

101 T. Pitt, *At the Head of the Table, or Under the Carpet?* (York: Dean and Chapter of York, 1994), p. 1.

priesthood".[102] The subsequent report of the Board of Mission and Unity, *The Priesthood of the Ordained Ministry*, submitted to General Synod in 1986, makes no reference to the issue of lay eucharistic presidency, but does emphasize eucharistic presidency as central to the distinctiveness of the ordained ministry.[103]

Pressure for change in the discipline of the Church of England has come principally from within the evangelical tradition, motivated at least as much by a desire for more frequent celebration of the eucharist as by any theological agendum. The relative infrequency of celebrations of the eucharist in many evangelical parishes meant that the issue of lay presidency did not become prominent until the eucharist itself became a more prominent and regular feature of evangelical Anglican worship.

> Despite commitment to the priesthood of all believers, Evangelical tradition has remained, for reasons which were as much sociological and practical as theological, quite satisfied with the restriction of a eucharistic ministry to those ordained as priests. However, as the sociological and practical ground shifted, the theological issues began to be discussed.[104]

The 1977 Grove booklet *Lay Presidency at the Eucharist?*, in which some diversity of evangelical theologians argue for and against the proposition,[105] reflects a debate that was not new at the time, and which remained unresolved for decades thereafter. The issue had for several years been on the agenda of the notably conservative evangelical diocese of Sydney in Australia. The principle of a "controlled form of lay presidency" was supported by majorities at the 1983 and 1987 Evangelical Conferences in Britain.[106] During the same period, the overwhelmingly evangelical province of Kenya authorized diaconal presidency at the eucharist in 1985, and the predominantly evangelical Iglesia Anglicana del Cono Sur de America considered and narrowly rejected the authorization of lay eucharistic presidency at its 1986

---

102 J. Tiller, *A Strategy for the Church's Ministry* (London: Church Information Office, 1983), pp. 120–21.

103 (London: Board for Mission and Unity, 1986), para. 133, 143.

104 C. J. Cocksworth, *Evangelical Eucharistic Thought in the Church of England* (Cambridge: Cambridge University Press, 1993), p. 168.

105 Lloyd, *Lay Presidency?*

106 Cocksworth, *Eucharistic Thought*, p. 169.

Synod, having previously canvassed opinions across the Anglican Communion.[107]

The South American proposal was formulated in response to particular missiological and pastoral issues, which will be considered further below. The Anglican Consultative Council, at its sessions in 1984[108] and 1987,[109] favoured provision for the regular celebration of the eucharist through the ordination to the priesthood of suitable local people, even though these might not meet the normal educational criteria of ordination. This approach was favoured also by the Lambeth Conference of 1988, which had "note[d] the received tradition that the president at the eucharist should be a bishop or presbyter", and suggested that "ordination of local persons" and "the 'extending' of communion through space and time" would be the more acceptable approaches to the shortage of clergy and difficulties many experienced in travelling to remoter congregations in some parts of the world.[110] These pronouncements, and the near unanimity with which they were formulated, ended neither discussion of the issue nor pressure to authorize some form of lay eucharistic presidency in different parts of the Anglican Communion, including the Church of England. The matter was considered, perhaps from a slightly different perspective, by the International Anglican Liturgical Consultation, held in Dublin in 1995. The liturgiologists opposed both the introduction of lay presidency at the eucharist and "extended communion" as measures to remedy the shortage of ordained priests in many parts of the Communion. Rather, in continuity with the Lambeth Conference and the Anglican Consultative Council, they advocated the ordination of local church leaders to the presbyterate in order to meet the need of communities to celebrate the eucharist.[111]

It was not until *Eucharistic Presidency*, commonly known as the Ely Report, was published by the House of Bishops in 1997 that the question was systematically addressed by an official organ of the Church of

---

107 A. L. Hargrave, *But Who Will Preside?* (Nottingham: Grove Books, 1990).

108 *Bonds of Affection* (London: Anglican Consultative Council, 1984), p. 65.

109 *Many Gifts, One Spirit* (London: Anglican Consultative Council), p. 57.

110 Resolution MM 205, *The Truth Shall Make You Free* (London: Church House Publishing, 1988).

111 *Renewing the Anglican Eucharist: Findings of the Fifth International Anglican Liturgical Consultation, Dublin, Eire, 1995*, ed. D. R. Holeton (Cambridge: Grove Books, 1996), p. 11; *Anglican Orders and Ordination: Essays and Reports from the Interim Conference at Jarvenpää, Finland, of the International Anglican Liturgical Consultation, 4–9 August 1997*, ed. D. R. Holeton (Cambridge: Grove Books, 1997).

England. The issue of lay eucharistic presidency was raised in General Synod in 1994, coincidentally the year in which women were first ordained to the priesthood in the Church of England. The context was the debate about authorizing extended communion, another approach to enabling congregations without a priest to partake of the sacrament. Synod acknowledged that authorized lay presidency at the eucharist would be "incompatible with the Anglican tradition", but noted also a need for clarification of the roles of clergy and laity in the eucharist, and requested that the House of Bishops provide this. In *Eucharistic Presidency*, the bishops briefly reviewed the relevant biblical and patristic texts, and considered the various theological arguments for authorizing lay eucharistic presidency. Their interpretation of the evidence of the early Church is essentially consistent with that which has been presented in greater detail in this study: the apparent silence of the New Testament suggests that eucharistic presidency was linked to leadership in the community.[112] The priesthood of all baptized Christians is corporate, and does not involve liturgical office or leadership on behalf of the whole Church.[113] The bishops accordingly affirmed the traditional Anglican position, that presidency at the eucharist is the function of bishops and presbyters who represent the whole Church in and to the gathered community over whose celebration they preside.[114] Rather than introducing lay eucharistic presidency, the bishops recommended the extension of ordained local ministries, evidently in preference also to extended communion. Furthermore, they recommended that lay people exercising in their communities the pastoral oversight that is proper to the priesthood should be ordained to the presbyterate.[115]

The conclusions of the Ely Report would seem to represent something of an Anglican consensus, from which a variety of primarily evangelical parties dissent. Whatever expectations there may have been that *Eucharistic Presidency* would end the discussion, in the Church of England if not throughout the Anglican Communion, the case for lay presidency has continued to be argued, both among evangelicals who pledge unequivocal loyalty to the Anglican heritage and among those who regard their Anglicanism as at best incidental. The theological question needs to be whether a departure from the long-established custom and discipline, not merely of the Anglican Communion but of

---

112 *Eucharistic Presidency*, p. 53.
113 *Eucharistic Presidency*, p. 53.
114 *Eucharistic Presidency*, p. 54.
115 *Eucharistic Presidency*, p. 61.

the universal Church, well rooted in Scripture and tradition, can be justified in changed circumstances, while maintaining allegiance to Scripture and continuity within the Anglican tradition.[116] The consistency in the biblical, patristic, and Anglican traditions might seem to place the burden of proof, in the light of the gospel, on those who would implement change. But it should also be recalled that ancient tradition, as represented by the admittedly enigmatic and controversial figure of Tertullian, could envisage circumstances in which the assumption of priestly functions by lay people could be justified. Anglican tradition has not been monolithic, and many of the premises upon which Anglican and Roman Catholic opposition to lay eucharistic presidency is founded have been shown to be tenuous. The biblical evidence, which would ideally settle the matter for all Christians, is inconclusive and subject to a wide range of interpretations.

In order to move the debate forward, it is necessary to consider the current situation of the Anglican Communion, the requirement of its communities to celebrate the eucharist and its members to participate therein, and the variety of approaches available to addressing these needs. Before pursuing this, however, we need to take into account the traditions and disciplines of the major ecumenical partners with which the Church of England and other provinces of the Anglican Communion are engaging and collaborating in different parts of the world.

Ecumenical Implications
In the Church of England ecumenical acts of worship, in terms of the Church of England (Ecumenical Relations) Measure 1988, are governed by Canon B43.[117] This makes provision, subject to stipulated procedures for obtaining consent from canonical authorities, for clergy and lay ministers of other denominations to participate in public worship in Church of England parishes. They are authorized to preach[118] and to assist in the administration of baptism[119] and the eucharist,[120] if authorized to exercise these functions in their own denominations.

---

116 Cf. Beckwith, *Priesthood*, pp. 29–30; P. F. Jensen, 'Lay Administration of Holy Communion', Address to the Clergy of the Diocese of Newcastle (2004); J. Pryor, 'Lay Presidency and the Ordained Ministry Today', *St Mark's Review* 138 (1989): 17.
117 Promulgated 1989.
118 Canon B43 1. (1) (c).
119 Canon B43 1. (1) (e).
120 Canon B43 1. (1) (f).

Corresponding provisions govern the acceptance by a bishop,[121] or by a priest or deacon,[122] of an invitation to perform these roles in the public worship of another denomination. Any invitation to preside at the eucharist in such circumstances requires the approval of the bishop or, in the case of a bishop, the archbishop, who would need to be "satisfied that there are special circumstances which justify acceptance of the invitation and ... the rite and the elements to be used are not contrary to ... the doctrine of the Church of England".[123]

Clergy of other denominations are authorized to preside at the eucharist in the Church of England only in canonically constituted Local Ecumenical Partnerships, governed by Canon B44.[124] The bishop may authorize clergy of the Church of England to use the rite of any participating denomination,[125] and "ministers" of participating denominations to preside at the eucharist in an Anglican place of worship within the partnership.[126] Such celebrations, however, are not deemed to be "a celebration of the Holy Communion according to the use of the Church of England".[127] Reservation of any elements consecrated at such a eucharist is prohibited, save when it is to be distributed the same day to a person who has expressly requested it.[128] It is stipulated that "minister" in this canon refers to a "person ordained to the ministry of word and sacraments".[129] Lay ministers, such as Methodist Local Preachers, who may be authorized to administer the sacraments in their own denomination, may therefore not preside at the eucharist in an Anglican church which is part of a Local Ecumenical Partnership.

In Roman Catholicism, and in the various Old Catholic churches, as also in the various Eastern and Oriental Orthodox churches, administration of the sacraments is of the essence of priesthood, and lay presidency at the eucharist would be unconscionable, at least at the level of official teaching.[130] This has been fully recognized in their dealings with the Anglican Communion, most particularly in the series of

---

121 Canon B43 2.
122 Canon B43 3.
123 Canon B43 4.
124 Promulgated 1989; amended 1994.
125 Canon B44 4. (1) (d).
126 Canon B44 4. (1) (f).
127 Canon B44 4. (3) (b).
128 Canon B44 4 (3) (c).
129 Canon B44 9.
130 Vatican 2, *Lumen Gentium* 28; *Presbyteres Ordinationes* 2; 6; 12.

discussions and quite substantial agreements which have been reached by the Anglican–Roman Catholic International Commission over the last four decades: ordained ministry is "not an extension of the common Christian priesthood but belongs to another realm of the gifts of the Spirit".[131] Whatever outstanding issues may remain concerning the nature of the eucharist and of Christian ministry, not least the validity of Anglican Orders, that presiding at the eucharist is the function of the bishop and presbyterate has been mutually understood throughout the proceedings. Where there has been dissent among Roman Catholic theologians, this has concerned the ontological nature of priesthood as the basis for restricting presidency which has been questioned, and the criteria for ordination, not the principle of priestly eucharistic presidency itself.[132] On both counts, it could be argued that such theologians stand in closer proximity to a traditional Anglican understanding of priesthood than they do to the official teaching of their own denomination, and that they are proposing new patterns of priestly ministry in many ways similar to recent initiatives in the Anglican Communion. We should also note in passing that among some Roman Catholic liberation theologians and other radical thinkers in the developing world it has been proposed that in Latin American base communities and in other marginalized or deprived groups, where a priest is not available to preside at a celebration, a eucharist-like fellowship meal should be held, as a less-than-adequate substitute for the eucharist.[133] Such a practice would not reflect the official teaching of the Roman Catholic Church, but it has been influential in some Anglican circles, and will accordingly be considered further below.

As we have noted, the ministry of lay people in the Church was not an issue at the Reformation, and, if anything, the abolition of popular cults and ritual observances rendered lay people more rather than less dependent on the clergy for their spiritual sustenance. In the Protestant denominations which emerged during the sixteenth and subsequent

---

131 *Ministry and Ordination: A Statement on the Doctrine of the Ministry Agreed by the Anglican–Roman Catholic International Commission* (London: SPCK, 1973), p. 13. Cf. J. W. Charley (ed.), *Agreement on the Doctrine of the Ministry* (Nottingham: Grove Books, 1973).

132 E. Schillebeeckx, *Ministry* (New York, NY: Crossroad, 1981), pp. 72–3,138–9; cf. H. Küng, *Why Priests?* (London: Collins, 1971).

133 L. Boff, *Ecclesiogenesis* (Maryknoll, NY: Orbis, 1986), pp. 61–75; cf. T. Balasuriya, *The Eucharist and Human Liberation* (London: SCM Press, 1979), in which the matter is not raised. Cf. also V. J. Donovan, *Christianity Rediscovered* (London: SCM Press, 1982), pp. 122–8, 149–59.

centuries, changes in patterns of ministry were effectively to "substitute a clericalism of the pulpit for the medieval clericalism of the altar".[134] This does not mean that new patterns of lay ministry did not emerge in time, which relate directly to evolving ecumenical relations today, and these need to be considered briefly.

Lutheran Churches

In recent decades, there have been significant developments in relations between Anglican provinces and churches in the Lutheran tradition in Europe and North America. The Meissen Agreement of 1988 between the Church of England and the Evangelische Kirche in Deutschland effected a measure of mutual recognition as authentic churches, but did not realize full intercommunion or full recognition of ministries. The Porvoo Agreement of 1993, on the other hand, effected full mutual recognition between the four Anglican bodies in Britain and Ireland and the churches of Norway, Sweden, Finland, Iceland, Estonia, and Lithuania, with the churches of Denmark and Latvia as observers. Within the Porvoo Communion there is full intercommunion with provision for interchange of ministries. The *Common Statement* reflects greater concern with the nature of episcopacy and, secondarily, the revival of the diaconate, than it does with questions to do with priesthood and the eucharist.[135]

The Lutheran tradition on ministry and the sacraments is nonetheless of immense significance for Anglicans. Earlier Anglican–Lutheran dialogue in Europe has presupposed that ministry of Word and sacrament are administered by ordained clergy,[136] which reflects perhaps a commitment to realizing a common discipline rather than shared theological reflection on the subject. Luther had argued, strongly if somewhat polemically, that all aspects of priesthood were entrusted to the entire people of God, even if they could lawfully be exercised only with the consent of the congregation.[137]

In the Lutheran tradition, the ministry of the ordained clergy is understood as deriving from the priesthood of all Christians, rather than

---

134 H. C. B. Green, *Lay Presidency at the Eucharist?* (London: Darton, Longman and Todd, 1994), p. 5.

135 *Together in Mission and Ministry: The Porvoo Common Statement with Essays on Church and Ministry in Northern Europe* (London: Church House Publishing, 1993).

136 *Anglican–Lutheran Dialogue: The Report of the European Commission* (London: SPCK, 1982), p. 47.

137 *De Ministeria; Institutiones Ministeriae* 3.

as being essentially different, and the question of lay eucharistic presidency tends to be viewed in these terms. In some Lutheran churches lay people can be commissioned to preach and conduct the eucharist in the absence of an ordained minister. Even where not officially authorized, it is not unknown for deacons and lay pastoral workers to conduct private celebrations of the eucharist in hospital wards and homes, even if not in gatherings of the congregation. This may reflect continuation of an older practice, to make pastoral provision for those unable to attend public worship to receive the sacrament, in churches in which the reservation and distribution of consecrated eucharistic elements is not permitted. In the Evangelical Lutheran Church of America, on the other hand, diaconal ministers routinely distribute consecrated elements to congregations on Sundays, where an ordained minister is not available.

While Lutheran theology may be more uniform than Anglican, discipline regarding ministry and the sacraments varies among the various national churches in Europe and Lutheran churches in other parts of the world. It has nevertheless been possible for Anglicans to reach a common mind and reciprocity of ministries to a greater extent than has generally been possible with other denominations from whom Anglicans have been separated for centuries.

Methodism

It is with the Methodist Church, particularly in Britain, that closer ecumenical ties have been both more urgently sought and more painfully frustrated, largely on matters to do with ministry and the sacraments. There is some ambiguity in the Methodist tradition concerning the administration of Communion by local preachers, and the circumstances in which this can be authorized.[138] This issue overshadowed the Anglican–Methodist dialogues of the 1960s, and contributed to the failure of the Church of England to accept the unity proposals. It was recognized in the report of the Commission that lay presidency at the eucharist, as practised by the Methodists, posed a "grave problem for the Church of England".[139] One might wonder whether the issue would have been perceived in quite the same way had the Commission been

---

138 Buchanan, 'Anglican Historical Perspectives', pp. 13, 16; D. J. Davies, 'Some Historical and Theological Arguments Against', in *Lay Presidency at the Eucharist?* ed. B. T. Lloyd (Bramcote: Grove Books, 1977), p. 21.

139 *Conversations*, sect. 3 (6).

reporting a decade or two later, after the Church of England had embraced the principle of non-stipendiary ordained ministry.

Another factor in Anglican intransigence on this point was a premature euphoria among Anglicans about the Second Vatican Council and conciliatory gestures received from the Roman Catholic Church. The unity proposals of 1963 envisaged that existing provisions for lay presidency in Methodist congregations would continue for a defined period in cases of pastoral need, where approved by all levels of ecclesiastical authority; nevertheless, bishops and presbyters were acknowledged as the normative, and should become the only, eucharistic presidents.[140]

This was the practice which had been adopted, in effect if not in intention, in the Church of South India,[141] the first and most successful, as well as the most significant, church unity scheme of the twentieth century, in which both Anglicans and Methodists participated fully. It is reasonable to suppose, therefore, that such an arrangement could have worked in Britain, whether or not all parties in both churches found it theologically acceptable as a compromise, or the outcome as compatible with their theology of ministry. Had ordination of local preachers to a non-stipendiary diaconate and presbyterate been an option during the 1960s, the issue would have been experienced quite differently, and the two churches might have been able to devise a common pattern of ministry theologically compatible with their traditions and able to harness and utilize to the full the gifts of those offering ministry in both Anglican and Methodist congregations. The issue of lay eucharistic presidency was raised in writings responding to the 1963 proposals,[142] and also in those reflecting on the final collapse of the unification process in 1968.[143]

The current position in the Methodist Church in Britain is that local preachers may be authorized, for a limited period, to preside at the eucharist in the absence of an ordained minister "where Eucharistic deprivation would otherwise exist". Despite the wider range of ministries now offered in the Church of England, the question remained unresolved in the *Anglican–Methodist Covenant* of 2001, which suggests

---

140 *Anglican–Methodist Unity*, pp. 179–82.

141 L. Newbigin, 'Lay Presidency at the Eucharist', *Theology* 99 (1996): 366.

142 Beckwith, *Priesthood*.

143 C. O. Buchanan, *et al.*, *Growing into Union* (London: SPCK, 1970).

that it requires further scrutiny within both denominations as well as jointly.[144]

Reformed Churches

In the Reformed tradition, authority to preach is generally the basis for that to administer the sacraments.[145] Notwithstanding the primacy accorded to the ministry of the Word, Calvin regarded eucharistic presidency as integrally related to pastoral oversight of the community.[146] "[T]he minister should repeat the words of institution of the Supper."[147] The "minister" is the pastor appointed and ordained to the ministry of Word and sacraments.[148] This remains the discipline of most denominations in the Reformed tradition, including those with which Anglicans have been engaged in ecumenical dialogue. The issue is clearly not eucharistic theology or sacramental power, but primarily one of teaching authority and order.[149] The nature of the ordained ministry, and particularly of episcopacy, remain issues of contention between Anglican provinces and their Presbyterian, Congregational, and other neighbours in the Reformed tradition, but there is perhaps a great deal more in common between Reformed patterns of ministry and those of the ancient Church than is widely appreciated in Anglicanism.

It should be noted briefly that Anglican engagement with the ecclesiology and sacramental theology of the Baptist and Pentecostal traditions, as with the independent and indigenous Christian traditions which have emerged in Africa, Latin America, and Asia, is hitherto significantly less developed than with the Roman Catholic, Eastern Orthodox, Lutheran, and Methodist traditions in particular. There has been some ecumenical engagement with various Baptist and Pentecostal churches, but as yet there have been no schemes for unity which would make the ecclesiological issues and sacramental discipline of the various denominations a pressing issue or potential cause for breakdown in developing relations.

---

144 *An Anglican–Methodist Covenant: Commont Statement of the Formal Conversations between the Methodist Church of Great Britain and the Church of England* (London: Methodist Publishing House/Church House Publishing, 2004).

145 Cf. P. D. L. Avis, *A Ministry Shaped by Mission* (London: T & T Clark, 2005), pp. 72–6; Cocksworth, *Eucharistic Thought*, pp. 223–4; L. Newbigin, *The Good Shepherd* (London: Mowbrays, 1977), p. 30.

146 *Institutio Christianae Religionis*, 4.3.16.

147 *Inst. Rel. Chr.* 4.17.43.

148 *Inst. Rel. Chr.* 4.3.7–8, 16.

149 Cf. D. W. Hegg, *Appointed to Preach* (Fearn: Christian Focus, 1999).

Baptism, Eucharist and Ministry

It would not be possible to treat comprehensively the position of all Christian denominations on questions of ministry and the sacraments, or even more narrowly on presidency at the eucharist. The comprehensive survey of the World Council of Churches, *Baptism, Eucharist and Ministry (BEM)*, published in 1982, together with the several volumes of responses published during the following decade, illustrates the significance which Christians of all persuasions have attached to these issues.

BEM notes that in most denominations the presidency of Christ at the eucharist "is signified by an ordained minister".[150] The point is not developed, nor is an ecumenical rationale for this expounded, as was observed in the digest of the six volumes of responses to *BEM* by both member and observer churches of the World Council of Churches.[151] This suggests a lack of ecumenical consensus on the reasons for reserving eucharistic presidency to the ordained ministry, if not on the principle itself. The dispensations from what is evidently considered normative, noted above, further suggest a lack of clarity and consistency on the issue, even among those Protestant denominations which Anglicans have traditionally found most congenial, and with which the Church of England and other Anglican provinces have enjoyed close ecumenical relations, and have made significant moves towards unity. However, there is also evidence that the Methodist and Lutheran churches may be moving away from authorized lay eucharistic presidency in favour of alternative provision for participation in the eucharist in the absence of an ordained minister.

Before discussing the proposals to authorize lay eucharistic presidency in the Anglican Communion, consideration will be given to alternative approaches to the problem posed by the desire for more frequent celebration of the eucharist than the priesthood, as traditionally conceived, can service. Some of these provisions have been adopted in other denominations, but the primary focus will be on Anglican worship.

---

150 Eucharist III.29.

151 *Baptism, Eucharist and Ministry 1982–1990* (Geneva: WCC, 1990), pp. 70–1.

5

Worship, Ministry, and Eucharistic Deprivation: Alternative Approaches

As has been noted, proposals for authorized lay presidency at the eucharist arose initially in contexts where a shortage of priests meant that congregations could not benefit from celebration of the sacrament as frequently as was felt appropriate. The increasing centrality of the eucharist to Anglican worship, and that of many Protestant denominations, during the twentieth century was accompanied by a decline in the number of ordained clergy in many parts of the world. There was a considerable expansion in the scope of lay ministries, and in the quality of training available to support it, in many parts of the Anglican Communion during the same period. It was in this context that lay presidency at the eucharist was initially proposed. This was not the only suggested approach to the spiritual and pastoral needs which had arisen, and the alternatives also need to be considered. This is not to deny that in some circles the issue of lay eucharistic presidency has become a theological and ecclesio-political agenda in its own right. Nevertheless, it is primarily with the pastoral considerations that we are concerned at present.

Few would deny that regular, and more frequent, celebrations of the eucharist have become normative in Anglicanism, representing a quite fundamental shift in the pattern of Sunday worship within the space of considerably less than a century. In addition to the principal act of worship on a Sunday, there has been demand for celebrations on weekdays, not only in the consecrated places of worship in which congregations have been accustomed to gather, but also in less formal, often quasi-private, domestic settings in which smaller, often self-selected, groups have gathered for prayer, Bible study, and fellowship. Whether the desire for eucharistic worship in such private contexts, rather than in the regular public worship of the gathered congregation, is entirely wholesome is a matter which itself requires further reflection.[1]

---

1 *The Theology of Ordination: A Report by the Faith and Order Advisory Group* (London: Church Information Office, 1975), pp. 58–9; cf. B. T. Lloyd (ed.), *Lay Presidency at the Eucharist?* (Nottingham: Grove Books, 1977), pp. 7–8.

On the other hand, the pastoral and spiritual need of worshipping communities to celebrate the eucharist regularly would be universally acknowledged. In situations where such a community is without the ministry of a priest, several approaches to meeting the spiritual need, or compensating for the lack of such provision, have been proposed. These will be considered briefly in turn.

Ministry of the Word apart from the Eucharist
The International Anglican Liturgical Consultation in 1995 recommended that, where a congregation is without the regular presence and ministry of a priest, the local lay leaders who exercise pastoral care in the community ought to be ordained to the diaconate and presbyterate, so as to be able to provide a sacramental ministry to those over whom they already exercise pastoral care and oversight. They recommended further that, until these leaders had completed their training and been ordained, a service of the word without the sacrament should be the normal principal act of worship in such congregations.[2]

The question of ordaining local church leaders will be considered in the following section; for the present we are concerned with whether ministry of the word can substitute for that of the sacrament. We need to recognize also that, far from being a temporary or transitional arrangement, a service of the word, whether Morning or Evening Prayer or less formal substitute, has long been the normal act of worship on Sundays for many Anglican congregations. In remote rural communities in the developing world, a priest may be able to celebrate the eucharist with the congregations in his care only once a month or once a quarter. The regular provision of pastoral care and liturgical ministry has fallen to catechists, many of whom have served with considerable distinction and unwavering faithfulness, but very few have been ordained. The reasons for this may in many cases have more to do with alien and not necessarily relevant notions of formal education, as well as social class and kinship connections or lack thereof. This raises questions as to the appropriate criteria for ordination, an issue which requires serious consideration in its own right. In the meantime, the use of services of the word as a substitute for the eucharist needs to be considered bearing in mind communities for whom the remoteness of priestly ministry and infrequency of sacramental worship has been normative for decades.

---

2   *Renewing the Anglican Eucharist*, ed. D. R. Holeton (Cambridge: Grove Books, 1996), p. 12.

Ministry of the word is an essential component of Anglican worship, and one perhaps neglected in many places on account of declining Sunday evening services and more frequent celebrations of the eucharist on Sunday mornings. That its importance should be affirmed, for all Anglican worshipping communities, ought therefore not to be in the least contentious. Whether word and sacrament can ever adequately compensate for lack of the other is another issue entirely, when both would normally be considered essential and integral to Christian life and worship. It is with the practical aspects of this proposal, that the ministry of the word be offered where that of the sacrament is not available, that we are presently concerned.

Ministry of the word requires, as well as readings from Scripture in the context of worship, sound and competent preaching "by public ministers apt and authorized thereunto".[3] Lack of a priest can therefore present precisely the same problem for ministry of the word as for that of the sacrament, unless authorized lay preachers are available where priests are not. Where such preachers are exercising an effective ministry of the word, the question of their ordination arises, an issue which will be considered further below. Where there is no lay or ordained person competent to expound the Scriptures in worship, then the ministry of the word is not being adequately provided, and this needs to be recognized just as much as lack of provision for celebration of the eucharist. The extempore or inadequately prepared, and often highly subjective and emotional, reflections and orations of people neither trained to preach nor educated in the exposition of Scripture and the doctrine and discipline of the Church, may reflect deep piety and faithfulness. But the potential of teaching of this quality to build up the community as the Body of Christ, and to respond adequately and appropriately to the challenges of Christian life and witness in a rapidly changing world, is very limited. During the medieval period, when few priests were licensed to preach, published homilies were read. It would not be inconceivable for homilies based on contemporary lectionaries to be produced, but proclamation of the word dependent on such a source would inevitably be divorced from the pastoral context of the community offering worship and receiving the ministry of the word. This can never be entirely satisfactory. Provision for adequate ministry of the word apart from the sacrament may therefore prove practically as problematic as providing appropriately for the celebration of the

---

3   R. Hooker, *Lawes of Ecclesiastical Polity*, 5.22.7; cf. A. B. Bartlett, *A Passionate Balance* (London: Darton, Longman and Todd, 2007), pp. 102-11.

eucharist in particular communities, as well as failing to ensure that there is regular and adequate ministry of both word and sacrament in every Christian worshipping community.

In places where lay people have been trained and licensed to preach, such as Readers in the Church of England and some other provinces of the Communion, a ministry of the word can be continued apart from the sacrament. Whether such Readers and other lay ministers ought to be ordained, and become ministers of the sacraments as well as of the word, is a question which obviously arises where celebrations of the eucharist are needed but cannot take place. In principle, if not in practice, Readers exercise a delegated teaching authority under the oversight of a priest who retains pastoral responsibility for the community.[4] Many Readers do in practice exercise pastoral oversight, especially in multi-parish benefices where the incumbent and any other clergy are not immediately accessible. It would therefore be an oversimplification and a generalization to argue that Readers do not exercise pastoral leadership, and accordingly should not become ministers of the sacraments.[5] The introduction of non-stipendiary ordained ministries, and increasing acceptance of the ordination of women and divorcees, in the Church of England and many other provinces of the Anglican Communion, mean that ordination is now an option available to the Church and to many competent and dedicated lay ministers, to whom this would not have been an option at the commencement of their ministries. The question may therefore be whether the order of Readers has now served its purpose, and rather than being perpetuated, should be superseded by ordination to the diaconate, and in at least a significant proportion of cases, to the presbyterate, of those who have hitherto served the Church as Readers or in comparable lay ministries.

The Church has an ancient and distinguished tradition of lay people such as Justin, Tertullian, Clement, and Origen exercising an effective teaching ministry in their congregations and more widely, and contributing significantly to the development of Christian doctrine. Whether this teaching ministry included liturgical preaching, however, is another matter entirely, and in the case of the Alexandrians Clement

---

4   *Eucharistic Presidency: A Theological Statement by the House of Bishops of the General Synod* (London: Church House Publishing, 1997), p. 56; cf. R. Brown, *Being a Deacon Today* (Norwich: Canterbury Press, 2005).

5   S. K. Pickard and L. Johnston, 'Lay Presidency at Holy Communion: An Anglican Dilemma', *St Mark's Review* 161 (1995): 14.

and Origen the evidence is to the contrary.[6] Academic theologians in the contemporary world are increasingly often lay men and women, many of whom exercise a teaching ministry within the Church as well as in the university. In this they exercise a degree of independence of ecclesiastical authority, both in that academic knowledge is developed in a context not governed by the Church, and in that lay people are not subject to their bishops and the doctrinal statements of the Church to the same degree as are clergy. The processes of academic theology, in which participation is not contingent upon any confessional commitment, are therefore in significant respects to be distinguished from the teaching of the Church. The ministry of the word is an aspect of the teaching of the Church, delivered in a context of worship and under ecclesiastical authority. Whatever their academic qualifications and homiletical training, which may indeed equip lay people for the task of preaching,[7] intellectual ability and rhetorical skill do not constitute or guarantee commitment to Christian doctrine and church discipline. It is the bishop's licence to preach, issued on the basis of assurance of the soundness of life and doctrine, as well as the competence, of the person concerned, that constitutes this authority to preach on behalf of the Church in a particular place. The questions remain whether this authority would more appropriately be conferred through ordination, an issue to which we will return in the following discussion. More challengingly, perhaps, the conferral of bishop's licences as authorization to preach raises the question whether corresponding authority might similarly be issued to administer the sacraments.[8] This is an issue to which serious attention will be required in subsequent chapters.

Delegated ministry of the word, apart from the sacraments, is at best a partial solution to the problem of what has been termed eucharistic deprivation. Its provision requires that an authorized, preferably trained, lay minister or deacon be available in a place where a priest is not available. It requires, in other words, a category of ministry bearing considerable responsibility in preaching and other forms of teaching, as

---

6   J. J. Alviar, *Klesis* (Dublin: Four Courts Press, 1993); J. W. Trigg, *Origen* (London: SCM Press, 1983).

7   Pickard and Johnson, 'Lay Presidency', p. 14.

8   Cf. *Eucharistic Presidency*, p. 56; D. J. Davies, 'Some Historical and Theological Arguments Against', in *Lay Presidency at the Eucharist?* ed. B. T. Lloyd (Bramcote: Grove Books, 1977), pp. 23–5; P. F. Jensen, 'Lay Administration of Holy Communion', Address to the Clergy of the Diocese of Newcastle, 2004, pp. 8–10; Pickard and Johnston, 'Lay Presidency'.

well often as pastoral care, without the commensurate authority. In particular, the person exercising pastoral care and oversight, and delivering the ministry of the word, would be unable to preside at the eucharist in that community. This disjunction between pastoral leadership and teaching on the one hand, and liturgical presidency on the other, is deeply questionable.[9] The Church has not been well served by such arrangements, and the theology of priesthood which informs such provisions requires rigorous critical scrutiny.

That the provision, however adequate in itself, of ministry of the word apart from the sacrament, is a far from satisfactory substitute for the ordination and deployment of priests who can function effectively as ministers of the word and sacraments and exercise effective pastoral oversight in their communities, has been widely recognized.[10] Other approaches to the spiritual and pastoral needs generated by the shortage of priests in many parts of the Anglican Communion therefore need to be considered.

Ordination of Community Leaders

As has been noted above, the solution which has enjoyed the widest support, within the Anglican Communion and ecumenically, to the sense of deprivation experienced in communities not served by a resident stipendiary priest, and therefore unable to celebrate the eucharist regularly, is the ordination of the lay leaders who exercise pastoral leadership in those congregations.[11] It is generally accepted that

---

9   Davies, 'Historical and Theological Arguments', p. 25; K. W. Stevenson, *Do This: The Shape, Style and Meaning of the Eucharist* (Norwich: Canterbury Press, 2002), p. 6.

10   *Ministry and Ordination: A Statement on the Doctrine of the Ministry Agreed by the Anglican–Roman Catholic International Commission* (London: Church Information Office, 1973), p. 11. Cf. Calvin, *Institutiones Religionis Charistiani*, 4.3.6; Hooker, *Laws* 5.21.4; R. W. Hovda, *Strong, Loving, and Wise: Presiding in Liturgy* (Collegeville, IN: Liturgical, 1976), pp. 7–8. Brown continues to defend Readers as representing a ministry of the word, apart from sacramental (and pastoral) ministry, fundamentally different to the ministry of deacons; see *Being a Deacon*, pp. 45–84; cf. P. D. L. Avis, *A Ministry Shaped by Mission* (London: T & T Clark, 2005).

11   Holeton (ed.), *Renewing the Anglican Eucharist*, p. 11; *Bonds of Affection* (London: Anglican Consultative Council, 1984), p. 65; *Many Gifts, One Spirit* (London: Anglican Consultative Council, 1987), p. 57; *Eucharistic Presidency*, pp. 55, 61; cf. R. Allen, *Missionary Methods* (London: World Dominion, 1960), pp. 105–7; H. C. B. Green, *Lay Presidency at the Eucharist?* (London: Darton, Longman and Todd, 1994), pp. 16–17; R. P. Greenwood, *Transforming Priesthood* (London:

such priests would receive some form of training, but not necessarily the same formation as undergone by candidates for the stipendiary ministry, and that they might not be required to meet the same criteria of selection for training. It is also accepted that they could not as easily be redeployed to other pastoral charges, but it is nonetheless emphasized that, once ordained to the priesthood, they become members of the diocesan college of presbyters.

An early proponent of the ordination of community leaders to the priesthood, even in recently established congregations consisting entirely of recent converts, was Roland Allen. In a book pointedly entitled *Missionary Methods: St Paul's or Ours?*,[12] Allen reflected on his experiences as a missionary in China, and perhaps also on his less happy experience in ministry in the Church of England as well as field research in India, Canada, and Kenya. He offered a trenchant critique of prevailing approaches to inculturation and indigenization in European, and particularly Anglican, missions in other parts of the world. He challenged the imposition of missionary leadership, and their alien culture and customs in worship, in new churches, and argued that concerns about education in (Western and Anglican interpretations and expressions of) Christian doctrine were fundamentally misplaced. Allen's reconstruction of Paul's missionary methods may not be entirely accurate, not least in that he overlooks the rootedness in Judaism of early Christianity. According to the Acts of the Apostles, Paul initiated his missions through contact with the local Jewish community, and preaching in the synagogues when invited to do so. His initial converts were therefore either Jews or godfearers, Gentiles who worshipped in the synagogue and conformed in some respects to Jewish beliefs and way of life.[13] The householders among these who exercised leadership in

---

SPCK, 1994), pp. 155–79; H. Küng, *Why Priests?* (London: Collins, 1971), pp. 60–64; H.–M. Legrand, 'The Presidency of the Eucharist According to Ancient Tradition', *Worship* 53 (1979): 437; T. Pitt, *At the Head of the Table, or Under the Carpet?* (York: Dean and Chapter of York, 1994), pp. 16–21; E. Schillebeeckx, *Ministry: Leadership in the Community of Jesus Christ* (New York, NY: Crossroad, 1981), p. 72; M. Thurian, *Priesthood and Ministry* (London: Mowbrays, 1983), p. 125.

12   *Missionary Methods: St Paul's or Ours?* (London, World Dominion, 1912); see also R. Allen, *The Case for Voluntary Clergy* (London: Eyre and Spottiswoode, 1930).

13   S. J. D. Cohen, 'Crossing the Boundary and Becoming a Jew', *HTR* 82 (1989): 13–33; N. H. Taylor, 'The Social Nature of Conversion in the Early Christian World', in *Modelling Early Christianity*, ed. P. F. Esler (London: Routledge, 1995), pp. 128–36. Cf. L. Hartman, *'Into the Name of the Lord Jesus': Baptism in the Early Church* (Edinburgh: T & T Clark, 1997), esp. p. 78.

the churches Paul founded were accordingly at the very least familiar with the fundamental tenets of Judaism, and therefore with the essentials on which Christianity was founded. The reinterpretation of Jewish beliefs in the light of Christ would not have represented as radical a change in convictions and way of life as would have been required of converts to the Christian gospel in other contexts. Nevertheless, Allen's critique of nineteenth- and early twentieth-century missionary methods has more recently come to be seen as prophetic, and the challenge of contextualizing the gospel and Christian ministry remains.

The ordination of community leaders is founded on the presupposition that each Christian congregation is not merely entitled to receive the ministry of both word and sacraments regularly, but that the gifts to exercise such ministry have been given to the Church, and are to be discerned within each congregation. As the Archbishop of Canterbury has expressed it:

> [W]hen the sensitive issue of lay people presiding at Holy Communion comes up for discussion, perhaps the question to be asked is not about the 'validity' in the abstract of such a practice, but about whether it is really true that God has left this or that community without the particular grace represented by the presbyter's ministry of presiding, of drawing together the prayers of the people into the single prayer of Jesus Christ. If God has given such grace, then the natural expression of it is in the public affirmation of this by the wider Church – in ordaining someone to take this responsibility.[14]

Few would advocate ordaining "sacramental priests" who perform rituals but exercise no ministry in the community outside the public liturgy.[15] Even where it is recognized that priests who have obligations to employers or have otherwise to earn their livelihood will not be able to commit their time fully to the ministry of the Church, it is nonetheless expected that their commitment will consist of rather more than presiding over public worship, and include some form of pastoral engagement with the community. There have, however, been advocates, however reluctant, of ordaining to the priesthood lay leaders who otherwise manifest the requisite qualities and commitment, but who are

---

14 R. D. Williams, 'Theological Resources for Re-Examining Church', in *The Future of the Parish System*, ed. S. J. L. Croft (London: Church House Publishing, 2006), p. 56.

15 W. S. Adams, 'The Eucharistic Assembly – Who Presides?' *ATR* 64 (1982): 315.

unable to preach.[16] Such clergy might be very effective in pastoral care, and competent and sensitive in presiding over the worship of the communities they serve, but they would not be ministers of the word in any meaningful sense. This would clearly not be entirely satisfactory, and it is hardly surprising that reservations have been expressed about such a course of action. In reality, however, prospective priests who are entirely unable to preach would be an extreme situation, particularly if some form of training and formation is provided before ordination. There is a considerable difference between expecting competent and relevant, but uncomplicated, proclamation of the word during public worship on a regular basis, and the capacity to articulate in a wider arena theologically informed responses to the major issues of the day, and to relate these both to the life of the Church and to the wider society. The latter would not normally be the vocation of priests ordained to exercise a pastoral and liturgical ministry in their local communities. At the same time, ordination, if not preceded by training which equips those chosen to be ministers of the word as well as the sacraments could perpetuate the perception that quasi-magical power to celebrate the eucharist is the defining quality in a priest.[17]

Self-supporting ordained ministry is complementary to, and not identical with, stipendiary priesthood.[18] It must nonetheless be recognized as integral to the same priesthood. Every person ordained as a deacon or presbyter by an Anglican bishop thereby becomes a deacon or presbyter of the universal Church. While clergy normatively exercise their ministry in the place and office to which they are licensed by their bishop, their ministry is nonetheless collegial and belongs primarily to the diocese in which they serve, but in principle to the Church catholic. The notion of an ordained ministry valid only within a specific pastoral charge or geographical remit, as Ordained Local Ministry in the Church of England is commonly understood to be, is contrary to the theology of ordination which Anglicans share not only with the Roman Catholic Church but with the Eastern and Oriental Orthodox Churches.[19]

---

16 Hooker, *Laws*, 5.81; Green, *Lay Presidency?*, pp. 15–16; H. Küng, *The Church* (London: Burns and Oates, 1968), p. 379.

17 J. Dallen, *The Dilemma of Priestless Sundays* (Chicago, IL: Liturgy Training Publications, 1994), p. 117; cf. A. E. Harvey, *Priest or President?* (London: SPCK, 1975), p. 29.

18 Cf. D. R. Etchells, *Set My People Free* (London: Collins Fount, 1995), pp. 146–7.

19 Lloyd, *Lay Presidency*, p. 10; Pitt, *At the Head*, pp. 6–7. Cf. the emphasis on the catholicity of the ministry in *Baptism, Eucharist, and Ministry* (Geneva: WCC, 1982), Eucharist III.29.

"Presbyters and Deacons are not by ordination consecrated unto places but unto functions."[20] The vocation, even if rooted in a particular congregation, is of the universal Church, and is in principle transferable to service in another community, potentially under the jurisdiction of another bishop. Furthermore, it needs to be understood that, in Anglican ecclesiology, the local community from which people are called to ministry, and into which they are ordained, is the diocese, not the parish.[21] Ministry is inherently collegial, and it is through the collegiality of the presbyterate with the bishop in the diocese, and through the collegiality of the episcopate in the province and throughout the Communion, that the universal Church is represented in the life and worship of local communities, and definitively so in the celebration of the eucharist.[22]

If locally ordained priests are identified fully with the diocesan college of presbyters, then many of the specific problems anticipated or actually experienced with ordained local ministries might be resolved, or even pre-empted.[23] Arguments that ordained local ministers are potentially divisive, lacking in professionalism and not responsive to change,[24] would seem indiscriminate at best. Stipendiary clergy are not necessarily any different when it comes to sowing dissension in communities, or conducting themselves in a manner which falls short of the standard the Church and society expect of the clergy, even where there are codes of conduct comparable to those which govern the work of other professionals. It is, furthermore, difficult to conceive how these problems could be avoided by licensing as lay eucharistic presidents the same men and women who might otherwise be ordained to a non-stipendiary priesthood. Sweeping, and often speculative, generalizations and *ad hominem* arguments alike are a particularly weak basis for preferring authorized lay eucharistic presidency to ordained local ministry.

Reservations about ordaining local leaders to the priesthood seem to be founded on essentially two categories of concerns, both of which may

---

20   Hooker, *Laws*, 5.80.6.

21   Hooker, *Laws*, 5.80.13; G. R. Evans, *Authority in the Church* (Norwich: Canterbury Press, 1990), p. 31. See above discussion of Article XXIII.

22   C. J. Cocksworth and R. Brown, *Being a Priest Today* (Norwich: Canterbury Press, 2002), pp. 74–80; D. W. Hardy, *Finding the Church* (London: SCM Press, 2001), p. 93; R. Moloney, *The Eucharist* (London: Geoffrey Chapman, 1995), p. 204.

23   Cf. *Eucharistic Presidency*, p. 54.

24   J. Tiller, *A Strategy for the Church's Ministry* (London: Church Information Office, 1983), p. 121.

be anecdotal rather than substantial. The first is what can crudely be described as the professional competence of those ordained, whether they are intellectually and spiritually equipped to preach the gospel and teach the Christian faith and morals in conformity with the doctrine and discipline of the Church. The second is whether they are able to exercise pastoral care and oversight, and manage relationships within the community, appropriately. It needs to be recognized that, on both grounds, competence is inherently contextual, and universal standards may be not merely irrelevant and inappropriate but actually harmful to the work of the gospel. The implicit ideal of the Anglican priest, as the younger son of a landed English family, educated at a public school and at Oxford or Cambridge, and formed for ministry in the pseudo-monastic environs of a residential theological college, segregated at all stages from the religious and secular lives of the general population, is at best anachronistic, anglocentric, and elitist. It is also worth observing that the ascendancy of the residential theological colleges was, to say the least, not accompanied or followed by spectacular growth in the Church of England. This in itself ought to suggest that alternative patterns of ministry and of ministerial formation ought to be favourably considered.

The capacity to exercise the ministry to which prospective clergy are to be ordained does of course need to be ascertained, as objectively as is possible. It is also important that this ministry be acknowledged in the communities to be served, and that it is seen to be supported by the bishop and the wider Church without having been imposed by outside authority. Those to be ordained need to identify fully with the wider Church they are to represent in their ministry, and they are to submit to canonical authority, and not be unduly influenced or compromised by local interests and pressures. These concerns relate essentially to the pre-existing relationships of lay leaders in and with the community they are to serve as priests, and whether these would impinge inappropriately on the exercise of priestly ministry, or could undermine accountability and canonical authority. It is of course also the case that at times stipendiary clergy can form inappropriate relationships or be influenced unduly by local interests, which are just as compromising to the exercise of their ministry. The difficulties in redeploying self-supporting clergy, if pastoral relations in the local community and the pastoral needs of the wider Church should require this, may often be considerably greater, and this needs also to be taken fully into account. Ordination in itself, however, does not create these real or potential problems, though it may on occasion make them more difficult to resolve. The same issues can confront lay ministry, and would be considerably exacerbated, were such lay ministries to be enhanced through acquiring public ritual functions such as presiding at the eucharist.

The objections and reservations which have been raised to the ordination of local church leaders to the diaconate and priesthood, after due training and with appropriate pastoral support and oversight, are less than persuasive. The same difficulties can be experienced in the ministry both of lay ministers and of stipendiary clergy. Authorized lay eucharistic presidency would therefore not avoid the problems which may arise, and as an alternative provision for sacramental ministry in congregations without a resident priest, lay presidency would in itself be no more satisfactory. The merits of lay presidency are yet to be considered in this study, but the benefits to the Church of the priestly ministry of those who exercise pastoral care and ministry of the word have been considerable, and have appropriately been enhanced by the ordination of these ministers and the extension of their role to the administration of the sacraments.

Visiting Priests

Recourse to a visiting priest not charged with the cure of souls in the particular community has of course long been the common practice in the temporary situation when the incumbency of a parish or other pastoral charge is vacant, or in the absence of the parish priest or chaplain on holiday or on other duties. Such visiting clergy have generally served as ministers of the word as well as of the sacrament, even if Readers and other lay ministers have assumed full responsibility for Morning and Evening Prayer, and for those occasional offices which do not require the ministry of a priest.

In the Church of England and other Anglican provinces where several years elapsed between the ordination of the first women to the diaconate and synodical legislation removing the bar to their ordination to the priesthood, there were parishes served, as *de facto* if not *de iure* incumbent, by women in deacon's orders, often of proven competence and with considerable pastoral experience. On occasion these deacons may even have been inducted as incumbent of the parish, thereby sharing with the bishop the cure of souls in those communities. Except of course where the incumbent in deacon's orders had a staff or ministry team including a stipendiary or non-stipendiary curate in priest's orders, such parishes would have depended for the celebration of the eucharist on visiting priests with little if any pastoral involvement in the community.

Such arrangements, whether temporary or permanent, separate presidency at the eucharist from pastoral oversight of the congregation.[25] In a sense this would be the ritual counterpart of devolving what is regarded as an essentially priestly function, that of pastoral oversight in the community, to a deacon or lay person, or of allowing such oversight to lapse altogether. During a vacancy the cure of souls reverts to the bishop, on whose behalf the visiting priest proclaims the word and presides at the eucharist on an interim basis. This does not substantially alter the absence of priestly pastoral oversight in the congregation, except in the little more than symbolic sense in which it is exercised by the bishop. In the situation in which pastoral oversight is to all practical purposes being exercised by a deacon or lay person, there is the very real danger that priesthood, experienced in the presidency of a visiting ritual functionary at the eucharist, could acquire quasi-magical connotations, which would be quite contrary to the nature of Christian priesthood as inherited from the primitive Church and continued in Anglicanism.

While recognizing the pastoral and theological issues in dependency upon priests from outside the local congregation, it would nevertheless be inappropriate to describe the use of visiting clergy as "sacramentally incomplete".[26] The definitive local community is the diocese, not the particular parish or congregation. Visiting priests represent the bishop and the college of presbyters of which they are a part and to which the priest serving the particular congregation would ordinarily belong. A visiting priest would also represent the universal Church, on the same basis as a resident priest, but would represent that aspect of priesthood very much more powerfully.[27] Such representative presence, if articulated appropriately both in the liturgy and informally, can be of positive pastoral benefit. This would be true particularly in geographically isolated congregations, giving ritual expression to the integral place of such communities in the diocese and the universal Church, an aspect of their Christian identity which might not otherwise be experienced or appreciated.

Whatever its pastoral usefulness, particularly on an interim basis, dependence of a Christian community on the ministry of a visiting priest for the celebration of the eucharist, or for the ministry of the word, is no long-term alternative to the regular eucharistic ministry of a priest with

---

25 A. Hargrave, *But Who Will Preside?* (Nottingham: Grove Books, 1990), p. 7.
26 L. Boff, *Ecclesiogenesis* (Maryknoll, MD: Orbis, 1986), pp. 72–3.
27 *Eucharistic Presidency*, p. 56.

whom the congregation has a continuing pastoral relationship.[28] Against authorized lay presidency, the ministry of a visiting priest would have the advantage during a vacancy of symbolizing and expressing the place of the community in the wider Church. Whether lay presidency would be more satisfactory than the ministry of a visiting priest in some circumstances remains to be considered. Authorized lay presidency, however, would not in itself address the questions and concerns which have been raised in the preceding discussion, regarding adequate and appropriate provision for the ministry of the word in communities temporarily or indefinitely without the ministry of a priest.

Extended Communion
By extended communion is meant, in Anglican, Roman Catholic, and some Lutheran churches, the distribution in public worship, in practice by deacons or lay ministers, of eucharistic elements which have been consecrated previously at a celebration of the eucharist, and reserved for administration to worshippers on another occasion. The Methodist rite of the same name is not intended for public worship, but provides for "elements previously set apart at a service of *Holy Communion*" to be distributed to the sick and housebound.[29] The provision for distribution from the reserved sacrament to the sick and housebound is covered by separate legislation in the Church of England, and is not directly at issue, except in so far as the principle of consecration for later use, on which both rites are founded, remains controversial in some circles, particularly though not exclusively among evangelicals.[30]

Extended communion was authorized, in its present form, in the Church of England in 2001.[31] The provision has been authorized for rather longer in the Roman Catholic Church; the current rite and accompanying rubrics having been promulgated by the Holy See in

---

28 Cf. Hovda, *Strong, Loving, and Wise*, pp. 7–8.
29 *The Methodist Worship Book*, p. 229.
30 Cf. C. J. Cocksworth, *Evangelical Eucharistic Thought in the Church of England* (Cambridge: Cambridge University Press, 1993), pp. 130–31; also, from a Lutheran perspective, R. F. Ziegler, 'Should Lutherans Reserve the Consecrated Elements for the Communion of the Sick'? *Concordia Theological Quarterly* 67 (2003): 113–47.
31 *Public Worship with Communion by Extension*. This superseded previous diocesan schemes and authorized and unauthorized *ad hoc* arrangements in use during the preceding decades.

1988.[32] The practice is also authorized in some Lutheran churches, but by no means all.[33] In the case of the Roman Catholic Church, the current provision is the culmination in a series of global and regional innovations since the Second Vatican Council, largely in response to an increasing shortage of priests, particularly in parts of the developed world hitherto accustomed to having a priest for every congregation.[34] These rites are innovative in authorizing deacons and lay people, including women, to preside over public worship at which the reserved sacrament is distributed to the communicant worshippers. In distinction from the private, and in some circles still controversial, communication of the reserved sacrament to the sick, the liturgies at issue here have been defined as "the distribution of previously consecrated elements to a congregation by a layperson (or a deacon) at a public service in the absence of a priest".[35] However, this distinction is not always sustainable, particularly in contexts such as nursing homes, where common rooms are in some respects public space, but in other respects private.[36] The distinction between public worship and pastoral ministry to individuals is nonetheless relevant.

Reservation of the eucharistic elements is at least as ancient as the second century CE. Justin Martyr records a custom whereby, at the conclusion of the eucharist, the deacons

τοῦ εὐχαριστηθέντος ἄρτου καὶ οἴνου καὶ ὕδατος ... τοῖς οὐ παροῦσιν ἀποφέρουσι

give to each of those present to partake of the bread and wine mixed with water ... and to those who are absent they carry away a portion.[37]

The reasons for absence of those to whom reserved elements are taken by deacons are not explained, but the implication would seem to be that this is involuntary, due perhaps to sickness, the constraints of servitude,

32 P. N. Tovey, 'The Theory and Practice of Extended Communion, with Particular Reference to Parishes Within the Anglican Diocese of Oxford' (Ph.D. thesis, Oxford Brookes University, 2006), p. 1; forthcoming as *The Theory and Practice of Extended Communion* (Aldershot: Ashgate, 2009).
33 Cf. Ziegler, 'Should Lutherans Reserve?'
34 Tovey, 'Extended Communion', pp. 50–78.
35 Tovey, 'Extended Communion', p. 2.
36 Cf. Tovey, 'Extended Communion', p. 6.
37 *1 Apologia* 65.

or imprisonment.[38] Justin is not explicit on the point, but the suggestion would seem to be that the distribution to absentees follows immediately upon the conclusion of the eucharist, and does not involve storage of the elements for any length of time.

It has been argued that Cyprian of Carthage, a century after Justin, alludes to a custom whereby reserved elements were taken from the celebration of the eucharist for private consumption during the week; those who partake when not in a fit state on account of their participation in idolatrous cults thereby incurring retribution.[39] However, it would seem more likely that Cyprian is referring to "lapsed" Christians who had succumbed to pressure during persecution, and offered sacrifices to the pagan imperial gods, partaking of the eucharist in public worship before undergoing penitential discipline and being reconciled to the church. This would seem to be indicated by *ad sanctum Domini ... accedunt*, with the singular of the adjective denoting a singular object: "they approach the holy [place] of the Lord". This is suggestive of, if not a sanctuary or consecrated church building, then the place where the local Christian community gathers, and where it celebrates the eucharist. The consecrated eucharistic elements would more probably have been alluded to in the plural, *ad Sancta Domini*, "holy things", denoting both the Body and the Blood of Christ. Furthermore, Cyprian's criticism is primarily of the church which restores lapsed Christians, i.e. apostates, to fellowship without appropriate penitential discipline, which he regards as both pastorally necessary and essential to the spiritual wellbeing of those being reconciled to the Church.

It is only the *Apostolic Tradition*, the date and provenance of whose component traditions is very much more difficult to ascertain, which attests the practice of worshippers taking home with them elements from the eucharist, to be consumed privately during the week.[40] The instructions for the care of the reserved elements, and prevention of their consumption by animals, non-Christians or demonic spirits, suggests that the elements have been handed over from the care of the church to its various members, and are being stored and consumed without direct supervision by ecclesiastical authority. Self-administration of the

---

38 Cf. N. Mitchell, *Cult and Controversy* (New York, NY: Pueblo, 1982), pp. 10–11; P. N. Tovey, *Communion Outside the Eucharist* (Nottingham: Grove Books, 1993), p. 6.

39 *De Lapsis* 15–16. Cf. Mitchell, *Cult*, pp. 11–12; Tovey, *Communion*, p. 17.

40 *Trad. ap.* 37–8. Cf. P. F. Bradshaw *et al.*, *The Apostolic Tradition* (Minneapolis, MN: Fortress, 2002), pp. 182–5; Mitchell, *Cult*, pp. 11–12; Tovey, 'Communion', p. 17.

eucharistic elements as a private devotion in the home, whatever its value may have been in the spiritual lives of members of the Christian communities reflected in this tradition, cannot be equated with extended communion, which is an act of public worship. A less well attested portion of the *Apostolic Tradition* may, however, reflect a custom more akin to extended communion. The various recensions of the *Apostolic Tradition* differ, and it is not entirely clear precisely what rite these texts and the *Canons of Hippolytus* are seeking to regulate. *Can. Hip.* 35 would seem to suggest that a deacon presides at the eucharist in the absence of a bishop or presbyter, but this may refer to a non-eucharistic fellowship meal at which a diaconal president recites prayers over the food in place of a bishop or presbyter;[41] should there be no clergy at all present, a lay president would distribute the food silently, without any benediction. *Trad. ap.* 28 is even less clear, except in that it is the procedure to be followed in the absence of the bishop which is at issue. Reference is made in the Egyptian family of texts (Sahidic, Arabic, Ethiopic) to ΕΥΛΟΓΙΑ, literally a blessing, being received at the hand of a presbyter or deacon, when the bishop is not present. ΕΥΛΟΓΙΑ has been understood to denote eucharistic bread which has previously been consecrated by the bishop, so that it could be distributed to the gathered church by a presbyter or deacon in his absence.[42] The action of the presbyter and deacon are described in precisely the same terms, the apparent implication being that, if the deacon is not described as presiding at a celebration of the eucharist, then neither is the presbyter. While the ordination prayer for presbyters in *Trad. ap.* 7 makes no reference to administration of the sacraments, any rule prohibiting presbyters from presiding at the eucharist in the absence of the bishop is otherwise unattested. Any reading of this tradition must therefore remain uncertain.

Reservation of elements from the eucharist for subsequent reception is attested from the second century, but only for distribution to those members of the church who are unable to attend that celebration of the eucharist. The custom attested in the *Apostolic Tradition*, but doubtful in Cyprian, of private consumption of reserved eucharistic elements, clearly did not persist in the Church, and may never have been widespread practice. Even if a family or household devotion rather than

41 Cf. A. Stewart-Sykes, *Hippolytus, On the Apostolic Tradition* (New York, NY: St Vladimir's Seminary, 2001), p. 146.

42 Cf. Bradshaw *et al.*, *Apostolic Tradition*, pp. 146–9; P. F. Bradshaw, *Eucharistic Origins* (London: SPCK, 2004), p. 50.

an individual one, this use of the sacrament does not occur in a context of public worship. Ancient precedent for a custom akin to the modern rite of extended communion therefore rests entirely on *Trad. ap.* 28, and effectively on a single transmission thereof, i.e. the Sahidic, on which the Arabic and Ethiopic texts are dependent. Origen is the earliest extant critic of reservation, which he regards as contrary to the dominical institution of the eucharist.[43] Many contemporary Christians might well agree with him, in some if not all the circumstances in which the reserved sacrament is used.

The fundamental issue with extended communion concerns the nature of the eucharist. Where the celebration is understood as a function of an ordained priest, then the essential action could be deemed complete in the prayer of consecration, and the distribution of the elements to a congregation which was not present at the Anaphora would not be problematic. However, when the eucharist is understood as the act of the gathered church, at which the priest presides as a function of his or her pastoral office in the community, but the congregation as a whole is the celebrant, then distribution of the elements to a different congregation, which is not the celebrant, becomes problematic.

A secondary issue concerns the nature of the consecration of the elements, and is bound up with the doctrine of transubstantiation: whether or not the bread and wine retain, beyond the celebration of the eucharist at which they are offered and blessed, the ritual significance conferred on them; and therefore whether or not the elements can meaningfully be consumed on a subsequent occasion. It is this aspect of extended communion which has perhaps dominated the debates unduly, particularly on account of the legacy of ecclesiastical and civil legislation governing not only the worship of the Church of England but the furnishing of church buildings.

Extended communion has been an emotive issue in Anglicanism, not least on account of the repudiation at the Reformation of the doctrine of transubstantiation, and of medieval devotions to the reserved sacrament.[44] This is reflected in Article XXV, *On the Sacraments*:

> *Sacramenta non in hoc instituta sunt a Christo ut spectarentur, aut circumferrentur, sed ut rite illis uteremur.*

---

43 *Homilia in Leviticum*, 5.
44 Cocksworth, *Eucharistic Thought*, pp. 130–31; W. H. G. Thomas, *The Principles of Theology* (London: Vine, 1930), pp. 345–64; Hargrave, *Who Will Preside?*, pp. 8–9.

> The Sacraments were not ordained of Christ to be gazed upon, or to be carried about, but that we should duly use them.

By *uteremur*, "use", when applied to the eucharist, we should presumably understood "eat and drink" the elements of bread and wine, the purpose for which their consecration was originally intended, rather than as an object of devotion to be exhibited or carried in processions such as had been customary on the feast of Corpus Christi. Conversely, this Article also insists that the elements be used *ut rite*, rightly, or reverently, and not carried out of church for profane use. *Circumferentur*, carried about, does not refer necessarily or specifically to conveying the elements from the place in which they were consecrated to another, for devotional, ritual, consumption there. Similarly, the water from the font should be used for the administration of baptism, and not for any other form of ritual washing or asperging, or for nourishing flowers sacrilegiously arranged in the font. Also prohibited, of course, would be the use of sacramental elements as charms or amulets, or in any other form of magic or witchcraft, but this proscription would not have been a novelty of the Reformation.

Article XXVIII, *Of the Lord's Supper*, expresses essentially the same principle, if a little more explicitly. After an explicit repudiation of transubstantiation, as not merely not proven on the basis of Scripture, but also as being contrary to the teaching of Scripture, the Article concludes:

> *Sacramentum Eucharistiae, ex institutione Christi, non servabatur, circumferebatur, elevabatur, nec adorabatur.*
>
> The Sacrament of the Lord's Supper was not by Christ's ordinance reserved, carried about, lifted up, or worshipped.

It is, at least primarily, reservation of the elements, for use as a devotional object outside the eucharist, which is at issue here. The historical context is the repudiation of a variety of medieval practices, in which the Host was an object of extra-liturgical devotion, and lay worshippers witnessed the consecration and, until this and other manual acts were prohibited, the elevation, but rarely partook of the elements.[45] There are two issues of concern here. One is to do with the doctrine of

---

45   E. J. Bicknell, *A Theological Introduction to the Thirty-Nine Articles of the Church of England* (London: Longman, Green and Co., 1955), pp. 365, 402; cf. E. Duffy, *The Stripping of the Altars* (New Haven, CT: Yale University Press, 1992), pp. 23–30, 95–102.

transubstantiation, which the reformers repudiated and with which extra-liturgical devotions to the reserved sacrament were associated. It is perhaps for this reason that reservation for any purpose continues to be opposed by many evangelicals.[46] The second issue is that of communicant worshippers not partaking of the elements when attending the celebration of the eucharist, but rather viewing them as an object of devotion. This was of particular concern to Cranmer, and, by introducing a vernacular order for the eucharist and abolishing ancillary rites, such as the distribution of holy bread to non-communicating worshippers, he hoped to encourage lay people to communicate more frequently. The introduction of vernacular rites did not have the desired effect in this respect, which led Cranmer to compose the offices of Morning and Evening Prayer, so that services of the word would be central to public worship.[47]

The 1549 Book of Common Prayer made provision by rubric for the priest to take consecrated elements to the sick at the conclusion of the eucharist; alternatively to celebrate the eucharist with the sick person and any others attending if there had been no public celebration that day. The 1552 Book of Common Prayer made no explicit provision either for reservation or for celebration of the eucharist in the home of the sick, but ambiguously instructed the curate to "minister" communion to the sick. While pyxes for the storage of the reserved elements were destroyed during the reign of Edward VI and of Elizabeth I, it is unclear what provision governed the communion of the sick until 1662. Unused bread and wine were by rubric allocated to the curate, and this was clarified in 1662 to mean unconsecrated provisions, not consecrated elements. It is therefore argued that this rubric was never intended to prohibit reservation for the purpose of communicating the sick and housebound.[48] The earlier rubric of 1549 had directed that communion be taken to the sick immediately upon the conclusion of the celebration of the eucharist, or at least the same day, in which case a (hanging) pyx would not have been required for its storage. Article XXVIII of course presupposes that relevant rubrics in the current Book of Common Prayer would apply, but there is no explicit prohibition of

46   Cocksworth, *Eucharistic Thought*, pp. 130–31; Griffith Thomas, *Principles*, pp. 345–64; Hargrave, *Who Will Preside?*, pp. 8–9.

47   D. N. J. MacCulloch, *Thomas Cranmer* (New Haven, CT: Yale University Press, 1996), pp. 510–11; cf. Duffy, *Stripping of the Altars*, p. 464.

48   F. Procter and W. H. Frere, *A New History of the Book of Common Prayer* (London: Macmillan, 1951), pp. 501–2.

reservation in the Article.[49] Reservation was undoubtedly practised clandestinely in both England and Scotland during the Commonwealth, and possibly at other times during the late sixteenth and seventeenth centuries, irrespective of the legal position and how it was understood. Reservation continued in use in the proscribed Scottish Episcopal Church after 1689, becoming essential to its sacramental life after the Penal Laws of 1764.[50] The 1662 Book of Common Prayer provided for an abbreviated celebration of the eucharist in the homes of the sick. A rubric stipulated that any consecrated elements remaining after the distribution at a public celebration of the eucharist be consumed in church immediately after the Blessing. While it has been argued that the rubric is intended merely to prohibit the profane use of consecrated elements, and does not exclude reservation of such as would be distributed to the sick the same day,[51] it has also been deemed to constitute a clear legal and liturgical impediment to reservation, at least for as long as the Book of Common Prayer was the only authorized liturgy in the Church of England.

Whether these Articles and the rubrics to the order of the eucharist in the Book of Common Prayer were understood to proscribe reservation in all circumstances and for all purposes, or whether these provisions were simply ignored from time to time by some clergy, remains uncertain. What is clear, though, is that whatever rules may be in force have been promulgated by ecclesiastical authority, subject to the royal supremacy, and therefore lie within the sphere of matters on which the Church can, in terms of Article XX, regulate its life and worship in conformity and continuity with Scripture.

Reservation of the eucharistic elements, and their storage in consecrated buildings, is an issue on which the legal technicalities and arguments have acquired a life of their own, quite apart from the theological and pastoral concerns.[52] This alone has maximized the potential for endless and intractable discussion, as the number of lengthy hearings concerning aumbries, hanging pyxes, and tabernacles in Consistory Courts during the late nineteenth and early to mid twentieth centuries testifies. In many, if not most, cases, the issue has been extra-liturgical devotions to the reserved sacrament at least as much as

---

49 Bicknell, *Articles*, p. 401; *pace*, Griffith Thomas, *Principles*, pp. 388–407.
50 Tovey, *Communion*, p. 26.
51 Procter and Frere, *Book of Common Prayer*, pp. 501–2.
52 G. H. Newsom, *Faculty Jurisdiction in the Church of England* (London: Sweet and Maxwell, 1988), pp. 130–33; cf. E. G. Moore and T. Briden, *Introduction to English Canon Law* (London: Mowbrays, 1985), pp. 79–81, 96–7.

reservation for communion of the sick. Questions of faculty jurisdiction and ecclesiastical furnishings need therefore concern us no further.

The proposed rite for communion of the sick from the reserved sacrament, which the Archbishops of Canterbury and York had declared theologically permissible in 1900, was a factor in the rejection of the revised Prayer Book by parliament in 1928.[53] Opposition was, however, diminished in subsequent decades by the practicalities of ministry in ever larger hospitals. The pastoral ministry of deaconesses, and, many decades later, the ordination of women to the diaconate, together with the increasing involvement of lay people in the pastoral care of the sick and housebound, brought the issue of communion from the reserved sacrament to further prominence and urgency by the second half of the twentieth century. It was ultimately pastoral considerations which led to the unambiguous authorization of reservation and of the handling and administration of the consecrated elements by lay ministers.

Despite the rejection of the proposed revisions to the Book of Common Prayer in 1928, the process of liturgical revision continued during the twentieth century. Local experimentation, with or without episcopal initiative or consent, often preceded legislation and official liturgical provision. During this period the sacrament was reserved in increasing numbers of churches, and usually reached the Consistory Courts only when this proved contentious in the parish. The sick and housebound were undoubtedly communicated from the reserved sacrament in many places while the legalities of the practice were in dispute. A rubric in Series 2, promulgated in 1966, was interpreted as authorizing communion of the sick from the reserved sacrament, and therefore to have rescinded the earlier prohibition of reservation.[54] This interpretation was disputed, but preserved substantially unaltered in Series 3, published in 1973. The Alternative Service Book of 1980 made provision for an abridged celebration of the eucharist to be used in ministry to the sick.[55] An authorized liturgy for communion of the sick from the reserved sacrament was published in 1983, which made explicit allowance for this ministry to be exercised by licensed lay people.[56] The rite is subsidiary to and dependent on the eucharist, and derives its meaning from the corporate act of worship during which the elements

---

53 Tovey, *Extended Communion,* p.119.
54 Cocksworth, *Eucharistic Thought,* p. 130; cf. Moore and Briden, *Canon Law,* pp. 79–81.
55 P. 118, n. 23.
56 *Ministry to the Sick* (London: Church House Publishing, 1983); Newsom, *Faculty Jurisdiction,* pp. 130–33.

are consecrated, and in which the person receiving the reserved sacrament thereby symbolically participates.

Liturgically, "Communion administered from the reserved sacrament to those unable to attend the eucharistic celebration is rightly understood as an extension of that celebration."[57] This rite enables the sick or otherwise housebound worshipper to be incorporated into the eucharistic act of the congregation of which he or she is a member. The consecrated elements, and the ministers who bring them, represent to the communicant the Body of Christ in the sacrament, and in its manifestation in the Church, local and universal, and serve to transcend his or her separation from the worshipping community in the eucharist. Provision for communion from the reserved sacrament is envisaged for those unable through illness or other incapacity to attend the eucharist, and not as a substitute for celebration in parish churches on Sundays when no priest is available.[58] Whether the same notion of representation as gives meaning to communion of the sick can be applied to a gathered community, whose separation consists in the absence of a priest, is another question. This would imply that the gathered community receiving the reserved sacrament is not that in which the eucharist is celebrated, but becomes symbolically identified with it, and is linked through it to the universal Church. Whether this is at all appropriate needs to be considered carefully.

Extended communion was for the first time officially sanctioned in the Church of England in 1979, when the Bishop of Carlisle authorized its use in the parish of Ulverston, with its several scattered congregations.[59] That this is a strongly evangelical parish demonstrates the extent to which the theological issues of previous generations, perhaps even of several centuries, could become relativized in the face of practical pastoral challenges. This does not mean that extended communion has ceased to be contentious, still less that it has become acceptable to all evangelicals, or for that matter to other Anglicans.[60]

The process of composing the rite of extended communion, and obtaining synodical approval for its use, was long and convoluted, and contributed directly to question of lay presidency at the eucharist being raised in the General Synod of the Church of England in 1994.[61]

---

57   *ARCIC. The Final Report* (London: SPCK, 1981), p. 23.

58   *Renewing the Anglican Eucharist*, p. 10.

59   D. A. Smethurst, *Extended Communion* (Bramcote: Grove Books, 1986).

60   Cf. A. J. Hughes, *Public Worship and Communion by Extension* (Cambridge: Grove Books, 2002).

61   Tovey, 'Extended Communion', pp. 129–37.

Continuing controversy surrounding extended communion in public worship is such that the authorized rite may be used only with the explicit consent of the diocesan bishop, which will be granted for no more than a limited period, on an "exceptional and provisional" basis.[62] This indicates less than full acceptance of the rite, and of the theological and liturgical principles underlying it. Furthermore, this liturgy is permitted only in public worship, and is expressly forbidden in informal contexts such as house groups.[63]

Ancient as some incomplete and uncertain precedents may be, extended communion is theologically, liturgically, and pastorally unsatisfactory as a regular form of congregational Sunday worship. It is seldom if ever embraced enthusiastically, and it continues to attract strong and trenchant opposition:

> The theological nonsense of the 'reserved sacrament', where authorized 'lay' people take the consecrated elements from some centre to dispersed churches – as clear a denial of these churches' priesthood and body-of-Christness as one could imagine.[64]

As a celebration of the eucharist, extended communion is incomplete, in that it entails disjunction between the act of consecration and the distribution and consumption of the elements; the gathered community which partakes of the elements is not the gathered community which celebrated the eucharist at which they were consecrated. Furthermore, while the authorized rite provides for readings from the Lectionary and a sermon, unless the authorized minister or another is competent and authorized to preach, the ministry of the word is also deficient. Many Christians may experience extended communion as an adequate and spiritually satisfactory form of worship, making the eucharist present and accessible to people and communities who would otherwise be deprived, and in some sense be separated from full participation in the Body of Christ. While it would be difficult to deny these benefits, the dependence on an absent priest could perpetuate notions of quasi-magical power in the consecration of the elements, and in the priesthood

---

62 *Public Worship with Communion by Extension*, Notes and Guidelines issued by the House of Bishops, 33.

63 *Public Worship with Communion by Extension*, 32.

64 J. D. G. Dunn, 'Whatever Happened to the Lord's Supper?' *Epworth Review* 19 (1992): 46.

which administers such rites.[65] It also distorts the principle that celebrating the eucharist is an act of the gathered church, not of the priest who presides. Where adequate provision for ministry of the word, as essential a component of Christian worship as the sacraments, is not ensured, these problems could be compounded. These perceptions, even if not distortions inherent in the rite, are contrary to the doctrine of the eucharist and to the catholic tradition of priesthood and ministry, which has been inherited and continued in Anglicanism. If extended communion is to be justified, therefore, these perceptions must not merely be overcome, but pre-empted altogether.

A second, but for many also quite fundamental, issue of contention regarding extended communion is that the elements become an embodiment or "vehicle" of Christ,[66] almost to the exclusion of the Church and the gathered congregation being so understood. While this may not necessarily imply transubstantiation in the strict sense, it would nonetheless be incompatible with the eucharistic theology of at least some Anglicans. The Common Worship rite seeks to circumvent this by emphasizing the connection between the congregation receiving the elements and the celebration of the eucharist at which they were consecrated, to the extent that this is expounded more prominently in the rite than is the connection with the death and resurrection of Jesus Christ. This would seem aberrant, in that it gives the impression that the recipients of extended communion are dependent more on the congregation in which the eucharist is celebrated than they are on the saving work of Christ.

It would be worth considering whether the actual and potential aberrations surrounding extended communion might be avoided if greater emphasis were placed on the sense in which the whole Church is understood to be mystically present with the gathered congregation at each celebration of the eucharist. While the Book of Common Prayer invokes "Angels and Archangels, and ... all the company of heaven", other rites, including several of the provisions available in Common Worship, make more explicit the claim to be joining with the whole Church, heavenly and earthly, in and through the eucharistic act. There is clearly a dimension of eschatological anticipation in such phrases as

---

65 Dallen, *Priestless Sundays*, p. 117; Hughes, *Public Worship*, pp. 24–32; cf. Harvey, *Priest or President*, p. 29.

66 W. Temple, *Christus Veritas* (London: Macmillan, 1930), pp. 240–41.

"we, in the company of all the saints",[67] but this is not at all inappropriate. The invocation of the whole Church in the immediate celebration of the eucharist is explicit in

> With your whole Church throughout the world
> we offer you this sacrifice of praise
> and lift our voice to join the eternal song of heaven.[68]

This is implied also in "We, your holy Church, acclaim you",[69] in which the gathered congregation, through the presiding priest, speaks for the whole Church. While explicit reference is made to supernatural or mythical beings, as well as to

> all who served you on earth
> and worship you now in heaven,[70]

any conceptualization of eternity must include those Christians who presently live and worship God on earth. There must therefore be some room for a notion of those to whom the elements are subsequently to be distributed being mystically or spiritually present at a celebration of the eucharist at which the bread and wine are consecrated. But, if this is to be pastorally as well as theologically meaningful, it would need to be expounded in the rite of extended communion.

While it may be possible to resolve some of the issues at the level of theological abstraction, this would not address the pastoral concerns which have been raised about extended communion. Pastoral oversight cannot be exercised by remote control or by mystical means, but only by the physical and visible presence of a person exercising pastoral care in the community. In Anglicanism the cure of souls is shared by the bishop with the priest entrusted with oversight of the particular parish or other pastoral unit. Consecrated elements cannot represent the priest any more than they can proclaim the ministry of the word or exercise pastoral care. Extended communion can therefore not substitute at all adequately for priestly ministry in and to the community, and its expression in presidency at the eucharist in which that community participates.

---

67 Common Worship. Order 1, Prayer B; cf. more explicit future expectation in Prayers E, F, and G.

68 Common Worship. Order 1, Prayer H.

69 Common Worship. Order 1, Extended Preface for Trinity Sunday, and for All Saints' Day.

70 Common Worship. Order 1, Extended Preface for All Saints' Day.

While there may be circumstances in which occasional use of extended communion would be justified, there is no sense in which this could or should become normative in any congregation. As well as the theological and pastoral issues discussed, there is the practical consideration that geographical distance can be a major obstacle to conveying the elements from the place of consecration to the community to receive them; even if not an issue in England this would certainly apply in many other parts of the Anglican Communion.

If there is no priest in the community, and no possibility of providing one from outside or ordaining one from within, then consideration of lay eucharistic presidency cannot be precluded on the basis that extended communion is a viable alternative. Before turning our attention to lay presidency, however, there remain further alternatives to be considered.

A Eucharist-like Meal, *Agape*, or Love Feast

Fellowship meals are as ancient as Christianity, and are well attested both in Judaism and in the wider Graeco-Roman world. The Jewish Passover meal was a particular, annual, example of this, and the Christian eucharist another. The process whereby the ritual meal, with token consumption of consecrated bread and wine, came to be separated from the fellowship meal of the ancient Christian communities, is a matter on which scholars differ, and whether or not the two meal types can in fact be distinguished in the New Testament and such early patristic accounts as the *Didache*, and even the much later *Apostolic Tradition*, is disputed.[71]

The love-feast was introduced to English Christianity by the early Methodists, who adopted a Moravian custom. It was for many years a central but exclusive act of Methodist piety, combining a revivalist prayer meeting with a ritual fellowship meal, consisting of bread and water to maintain a clear distinction from the eucharist, in theory if not always in practice or in popular perception.[72] More recent, and perhaps of more direct relevance to the contemporary revival or innovation, whichever it may be, is a Latin American practice inspired by Roman Catholic liberation theology. This is a ritual fellowship meal, often consisting of bread and wine, celebrated in "base communities" where there is no priest to preside at the eucharist.[73] Unlike the Methodist

---

71 Bradshaw, *Eucharistic Origins*.
72 Tovey, 'Extended Communion', pp. 91–104.
73 Boff, *Ecclesiogenesis*, pp. 61–75.

custom, this practice is intended as a substitute for the eucharist, with a form of ritualized eating and drinking in conscious emulation, if not of the contemporary mass, then of a construction of the ancient Christian eucharist or *agape*.

A similar ritual fellowship meal has become popular in some charismatic and radical house churches, and in other informal groups, within several denominations, including the Church of England and other Anglican provinces. Such a meal has also been used as a substitute for the eucharist in ecumenical contexts in places where intercommunion was not yet authorized. "Alpha" courses are frequently accompanied by communal, and to greater or lesser degrees ritualized, eating and drinking. While not conceived as a substitute for the eucharist, nor even necessarily drawing participants into sacramental worship,[74] these meals can in many respects resemble the *agape* as it has come to be understood.

In the Church of England, a combination of a communal meal or *agape* with the eucharist has become popular.[75] Particular provision was made for it during Holy Week in *Lent, Holy Week, Easter*.[76] This is clearly a eucharist, presided over by a priest, but celebrated in a context which has become unusual, in that it is combined with a fellowship meal of ordinary food, and is usually held not in a church building but in some other domestic or public place. Whatever informality and flexibility may be brought into the celebration, this event remains a eucharist, and canon law and the rubrics require that it be presided over by a priest. This is therefore not an alternative rite for use in the absence of a priest, but has made the format of a ritualized fellowship meal familiar, and perhaps acceptable where it might otherwise not be.

The *agape* has also been suggested for use in church plants, should a celebration of the eucharist under lay presidency not be permitted.[77] Lay presidency at the eucharist and extended communion alike are not permitted in house churches, church plants, or other informal gatherings under the auspices of the Church of England. As well as circumventing the lack of a priest, it could be argued that the *agape* might serve a positive purpose in such contexts as church plants, particularly if these

74 Cf. L. Urwin, 'Fresh Expressions through Sacraments', *Mission-Shaped Questions*, ed. S. J. L. Croft (London, Church House Publishing, 2008).

75 B. T. Lloyd, *Agapes and Informal Eucharists* (Bramcote: Grove Books, 1973); *Celebrating the Agape Today* (Bramcote: Grove Books, 1986).

76 (London: SPCK, 1986), pp. 97–8.

77 G. E. D. Pytches and B. Skinner, *New Wineskins* (Guildford: Eagle Press, 1991), pp. 32–3.

include people with little or no previous acquaintance with Christian worship. A less formal and more open ritual fellowship meal might avoid having to address questions of baptism and admission to communion, and also familiarize recent adherents with aspects of Christian doctrine and liturgy. Questions would, however, remain to be answered, as to whether such an approach is likely to integrate newcomers effectively, leading them to commitment and, where necessary, to baptism, and to full participation in the eucharistic life and work of their local Christian communities. Furthermore, the propriety from all perspectives of a ritual meal which in significant ways resembles and even imitates the eucharist, needs carefully to be considered.

The practice of a ritual fellowship meal which is not a eucharist rests upon the supposition that the Early Church maintained a clear distinction between the eucharist and the common meal, often referred to as the *agape*. While this was a major component in Dom Gregory Dix's reconstruction of the ancient eucharistic rites in his influential *The Shape of the Liturgy*,[78] whether or not this distinction can be sustained has been brought into question in more recent scholarship. With the benefit of access to a wider diversity of literary sources, liturgical historians have argued that the ancient eucharist was very much more varied, both in form and in the elements blessed and consumed, than had hitherto been supposed.[79] The evidence in ancient sources of diversity in liturgical practice cannot simply be categorized into two types of ritual, one of which was the eucharist as has been continued in the Church, while the other was a fellowship meal discontinued at some stage.[80] Nor, even if the rites can be distinguished, can the role of presidency at the two be separated: the same social forces and cultural conventions, as well as theological rationale, would have governed all gatherings of the ancient Church. It is more likely that, for practical reasons as much as any other, the eucharist came to be celebrated apart from a corporate meal, than that there ever was a distinct, non-eucharistic corporate ritual meal.

While the *agape* as a form of worship to be promoted within the Church of England has its champions,[81] the question must remain what

---

78 See esp. pp. 96–102.
79 Bradshaw, *Eucharistic Origins*; B. D. Chilton, *A Feast of Meanings* (Leiden: E. J. Brill, 1994).
80 Cf. Cyprian, *Epistula.* 63, *Ad Caecilium*, 16.1.
81 B. T. Lloyd, *Agapes and Informal Eucharists* (Bramcote: Grove Books, 1973); *Celebrating the Agape Today* (Bramcote: Grove Books, 1986); cf. Tovey, 'Extended Communion'.

function it serves. Whereas in the Roman Catholic base communities without a priest this rite is experienced as "sacramentally incomplete",[82] it is perhaps more highly valued in communities of a Protestant character and among previously unchurched people. Where it is an informal, or, more accurately, less overtly formal, substitute for the eucharist, questions must be asked about the role of the eucharist itself in forming that community as a manifestation of Christ's Church. On the other hand, if divine grace is experienced through the *agape*, and the act of worship and the elements function as vehicles of Christ's presence in the community, then it needs to be asked whether this rite does not in fact constitute a celebration of the eucharist.

Whether the *agape* can be distinguished from the eucharist, either historically or in the spiritual and corporate experience of contemporary worshippers, is doubtful.[83] This is a matter of perception as well as of intention, and, where a celebration of the eucharist is denied, then the impression of a charade or parody may be created. This is not to deny the pastoral value of fellowship meals in Christian communities, preceded, accompanied, or followed by whatever form of worship. However, once the form of the eucharist is imitated, irrespective of who is presiding, distinguishing the rite from the celebration of the eucharist becomes problematic.

Analogous in some ways to the *agape* would be the medieval custom of distributing blessed bread, as distinct from the consecrated elements, to the congregation at the conclusion of the eucharist.[84] This practice was abolished by Cranmer, as part of his drive to persuade the laity of England to make their communion more regularly. A similar custom is observed in some Eastern Orthodox churches, and at least on occasion extended to noncommunicants. While noncommunicants are given a physical symbol of being blessed through feeding, this is a subordinate rite and emphasizes a hierarchy between communicating and non-communicating worshippers. It is doubtful whether any pastoral need would be addressed by as ambiguous a gesture as distributing blessed or unblessed bread, other than the consecrated elements, at a celebration of the eucharist. Whether food on which a blessing is invoked in a corporate ritual meal would be significantly different, especially in communities denied the celebration of the eucharist, needs to be considered with care.

---

82   Boff, *Ecclesiogenesis*, pp. 72–3.

83   Cf. Tovey, 'Extended Communion', pp. 216, 220.

84   Duffy, *Stripping of the Altars*, pp. 125–7.

There may well be considerable pastoral and heuristic value in occasionally celebrating the eucharist in the context of a fellowship meal, and in a setting appropriate to and convenient for corporate dining. Whether a ritualized meal which in some ways resembles the eucharist, but is not identified as a celebration of the eucharist, is at all desirable is another matter. As a substitute for a eucharist when there is no priest available, an *agape* could effectively function as a celebration of the eucharist, and be identified and experienced as such. To authorize such a rite would therefore amount to authorizing lay presidency without acknowledging it as such. Unless there is a virtue to be made of ambiguity, then it would almost certainly be better to authorize lay eucharistic presidency and be honest about it, and to issue guidelines as to how it is to be conducted. Before this is considered further, however, there remains a further alternative to be scrutinized.

Spiritual Communion
The 1549 Book of Common Prayer encouraged those unable to attend the eucharist on account of sickness, or physically unable to consume the elements, to eat and drink spiritually by repentance, and thereby to receive the benefits of communion. This rubric was published alongside that making provision for the priest to administer communion to the sick from the reserved sacrament immediately upon conclusion of the eucharist. This was not included in the 1552 Book of Common Prayer, but, in the Book of Common Prayer of 1662 this form of spiritual communion, under direction from the Curate, is enjoined for those unable to partake of the eucharist. Spiritual communion as a private devotion for those Christians who are unable to attend the eucharist, for reasons of sickness or geographical separation from the worshipping community, has continued to be advocated in pastoral ministry and in theological reflection.[85]

A modern development perhaps of the notion of spiritual communion, is that of the broadcast eucharist. Presumably, when a celebration of the eucharist is chosen for transmission in preference to a service of the word, some thought is given to the ways in which listeners and viewers participate, when not physically part of the gathered congregation in the church or studio. At least one broadcasting company with ecclesiastical sponsorship provides a website from which viewers can download orders of service, according to the rites of the Episcopal Church of the

---

85 Cf. W. Temple, *Thoughts on Some Problems of the Day* (London: Macmillan, 1931), p. 111.

United States, and other material which may assist their devotions.[86] It is claimed that, for most viewers, the weekly broadcast is, of their own choice, their only contact with any religious organisation. In other words, the spiritual lives of these Christians entail no membership of any gathered community or participation in the corporate life of any church. If this is a manifestation of the "believing without belonging" supposedly characteristic of religion in a consumerist culture,[87] it needs to be asked whether such private devotions assisted by the broadcast media constitute communion in any meaningful sense. Whatever sense of relating to God such worshippers may experience, they do not seem to relate at all to the Church as the Body of Christ on earth.

The broadcast eucharist has been developed further in the United States by a United Methodist minister who describes himself as "Anglican in my Sacramentology". The Revd Dr Gregory S. Neal of the North Texas Conference encourages users of his website, entitled "Holy Communion On the Web", to "partake in your own home, via the internet". As well as audio-visual clips, texts of the rites used, sermons, and other accompanying documents are provided, including "Theological Reflections Regarding The Internet and The Means of Grace". Apart from navigating the website, it seems that the potential for using the mouse and keyboard, or even voice-activated software, for interactive participation in the eucharist is not exploited. Communicants are to provide their own bread, "any kinds of bread: a hotdog bun, a piece of sliced bread, a biscuit, a dinner roll, pita bread, a tortilla", and wine or grape juice. A page of instructions on "How To Prepare The Elements for Holy Communion" is provided, but it is not stipulated whether these are to be placed in any particular strategic position relative to the cyber-communicant's computer. It is anticipated, however, that these instructions might become obsolete at some point in the future. "Some day it may well be possible to 'beam' the bread and wine through the internet to communicants but as of today this is still beyond our technological capability."

Several possible questions arise, most of which would normally be more appropriate to satire than to serious theological discourse. All but the most deist of theologians would be reluctant to argue with "grace can function in the virtual realm without too much difficulty", but the

---

86 www.tveucharist.org

87 G. Davie, *Religion in Britain since 1945* (Oxford: Blackwell, 1994); 'From Obligation to Consumption', in *The Future of the Parish System*, ed. S. J. L. Croft (London: Church House Publishing, 2006), pp. 33–5.

implication that a new generation of magic can transform the elements via cyberspace is a travesty of the eucharist in every possible sense. Even in traditions which adhere to the doctrine of transubstantiation this would be regarded as crude and superstitious, the stuff of science fiction not of Christian worship – even if alternative universes have their place in Christian cosmology and eschatology. Even more aberrant is the notion of the eucharist as a private cult, disembodied from the corporate worship of a flesh-and-blood Christian community. In fairness to Dr Neal it should be acknowledged that he does not regard this approach to the eucharist as at all ideal, and in his theological reflection he emphasizes the importance of the corporate aspect of the eucharist which cannot be downloaded from the internet.[88] Nevertheless, the approach to the eucharist offered on this website can only seem bizarre, if not abhorrent, to Christians accustomed to more conventional modes of worship. Irrespective of whether the eucharistic elements can be transubstantiated or otherwise consecrated through the airwaves or via cyberspace, questions need to be asked about the act of communion involved. Even though the technology is available (in at least some places, mainly in the developed world) for the downloaded texts and images to be projected onto a large screen for a group to participate together, there is no sense in which presidency at such a celebration of the eucharist could be exercised in a pastorally meaningful way. A crucial question must surely be whether such use of the media leads those who use it into meaningful Christian worship and fellowship in the life of a local church.

In an age when "cyberchurches" and virtual congregations are spoken of quite casually by some who regard themselves as at the forefront of evangelism and church growth, the promotion of a spiritual life devoid of interpersonal contact and community life and worship, particularly in the eucharist, would seem both theologically unsound and pastorally irresponsible.

> Virtual reality is no substitute for the Real Presence of Christ in the Eucharist, the sacramental reality of the other sacraments, and shared worship in a flesh-and-blood human community. There are no sacraments on the Internet; and even the religious experiences possible

---

88 www.revneal.org/onlinecommunion.html (and links).

there by the grace of God are insufficient apart from real-world interaction with other persons of faith.[89]

The geekish individualism encouraged by such products as internet communion [*sic*] services denies both the fundamental human need for community integration and interaction, and is contrary to the doctrines of the Church and the eucharist. Such a rite should be regarded as less acceptable than extended communion, and less acceptable also than lay presidency at a eucharist celebrated by a gathered church.

The use of broadcasting and the internet to draw people into Christian fellowship, of which the eucharist is the symbol and consummation, cannot be accomplished by simulating – or rather debasing – what is fundamentally an act of corporate worship into a private cult, in which the television or computer screen becomes an electronic tabernacle. Effective and appropriate use of these media for the purposes of mission and evangelism must of necessity consist primarily of proclamation of the word, thereby to draw into the sacramental life of the Church those reached by this ministry.

> Although the virtual reality of cyberspace cannot substitute for real interpersonal community, the incarnational reality of the sacraments and the liturgy, or the immediate and direct proclamation of the gospel, it can complement them, attract people to a fuller experience of the life of faith, and enrich the religious lives of users. ... [P]astoral planning should consider how to lead people from cyberspace to true community and how, through teaching and catechesis, the Internet might subsequently be used to sustain and enrich them in their Christian commitment.[90]

Whatever the potential of broadcasting and the internet for Christian mission and evangelism, these media cannot substitute for the physical, human, reality of the Church and its corporate life. This of course does not answer how this corporate life is to be celebrated and given expression in the eucharist if there is no priest present. There can be no such thing as a virtual priest, and we therefore need to return to the question of whether there could be a lay president at the eucharist.

---

89 Pontifical Council for Social Communications, 'The Church and Internet', http://www.vatican.va/roman_curia/pontifical_councils/pccs/documents/rc_ pc_pccs_doc_20020228_church-internet_en.html

90 Pontifical Council for Social Communications, 'The Church and Internet'.

Conclusions

Several responses to the inability of existing clergy to preside at every celebration of the eucharist needed or desired in the congregations in their care have been identified.[91] These are not necessarily mutually exclusive. The various rites and devotions are not necessarily understood in the same way by ministers and worshippers using them from divergent theological perspectives, or in different cultural contexts. Evaluating them theologically and pastorally is therefore a matter of some complexity. There would be some consensus that the celebration of the eucharist is the ideal form of worship, and any derived rite no more than an inadequate substitute. While spiritual Communion and the ministry of the word are valid, and in themselves essential to Christian spiritual life, neither on its own can compensate for a celebration of the eucharist. Extended communion and the *agape*, insofar as the latter is intended as a substitute for the eucharist, are theologically and pastorally problematic. Neither in itself ensures the effective ministry of the word, and both can be perceived to parody the eucharist. Communion via the internet is little short of a theological abomination. Visiting priests can preside and preach at the eucharist, but cannot exercise effective pastoral oversight, even if they can form a tangible link with the wider Church. While ordination of local Christian leadership can present practical difficulties, this measure is theologically sound, and would seem the most satisfactory alternative to authorized lay presidency at the eucharist. It is to the merits of authorized lay presidency, as it has been proposed in various parts of the Anglican Communion, that we must now turn our attention.

---

91   Cf. also Tovey, 'Extended Communion'.

6

Proposals for Authorized Lay Eucharistic Presidency in the Context of Mission

Lay presidency at the eucharist is neither as new, nor as peculiarly evangelical, nor as recent, a notion in Anglicanism as is sometimes assumed to be the case. We have already noted that, in the early years of the twentieth century, Bishop Azariah of Dornakal in India proposed that authorized lay presidency be considered in certain circumstances, where communities would not otherwise be able to celebrate the eucharist. While this was not taken further at the time, it was in India that Anglicans, or former Anglicans, first became part of a church in which lay eucharistic presidency was practised. When the Church of South India was established in 1947, lay ministers who had been licensed to preside at the eucharist, such as formerly Methodist local preachers, continued to do so until the practice was phased out with the ordination of local church leaders to the diaconate and presbyterate.[1] While some Anglicans persist in considering themselves not to be in full communion with the Church of South India, the fact remains that, for a time, lay ministers could, and presumably did, on occasion officiate at the eucharist in what had formerly been Anglican churches, in a body which has close and enduring ties with the Anglican Communion.

The authorization of diaconal presidency at the eucharist in the Anglican Church in Kenya in 1985[2] was not preceded, accompanied or followed by any theological discussion in the wider Anglican Communion. This development would seem to be premised upon what had for centuries been almost universal Anglican custom, that of regarding the diaconate as a brief probationary and transitional phase in a process all but inevitably culminating in ordination to the presbyterate. Deacons are accordingly permitted, with the explicit consent of their bishop, to preside at the eucharist where there is no priest available to do so. The authority conferred through ordination to the presbyterate is anticipated in the grant of an episcopal licence. This is not a case of lay

---

1   L. Newbigin, 'Lay Presidency at the Eucharist', *Theology* 99 (1996): 366.
2   C. O. Buchanan, *News of Liturgy* 126 (1985): 3–4.

presidency, in that deacons are ordained clergy, and in that deacons who receive this episcopal dispensation are expected to be ordained to the priesthood within a period of probably no more than a year. What is significant is that the bishop confers, by his own mandate, an authority he would normally confer at ordination to the presbyterate, in which he acts for the whole Church, with the active consent of the gathered congregation, and the participation of the presbyters present. The nature and scope of episcopal authority would therefore seem a crucial issue here, as indeed it usually is where lay presidency at the eucharist is proposed.

We will consider first the proposition presented at the Anglican Congress in Toronto in 1963, and then the specific proposals to authorize lay presidency at the eucharist in South America and Australia, before treating the less specific suggestions emanating from the church planting movement in England and elsewhere.

The Toronto Anglican Congress, 1963:
The Challenge of the Frontiers – Training for Action

The Anglican Congresses held in London in 1908, Minneapolis in 1954, and Toronto in 1963, are an all but forgotten episode in global Anglican history. They were born of the recognition that an exclusively episcopal gathering such as the Lambeth Conference could not be truly representative of the Communion, particularly during a period when many dioceses not only in Africa and Asia but also in Canada and the Antipodes were presided over by English bishops, as indeed they continue to be in South America. The Congresses were consultative rather than legislative gatherings, in many ways complementary to and informing the agenda of the subsequent Lambeth Conferences. While a further Anglican Congress, to be held in Cape Town, South Africa, was at one stage scheduled for 2008, to coincide with the Lambeth Conference, no further such gatherings have taken place since the formation of the Anglican Consultative Council in 1970. The recognition that Anglicanism was a global rather than an English Christian movement, with its agenda and priorities to be framed accordingly, is the context in which authorized lay presidency at the eucharist was first proposed in a quasi-official organ of the Communion.

The proposal was presented by Canon Frank Synge, at the time Principal of Christchurch Theological College in New Zealand. He had previously served in South Africa, including a period as Principal of St Paul's Theological College in Grahamstown. Synge's critique of the received Anglican tradition on ministry is that it "stems from an insufficiently high doctrine of the Church and an insufficiently high doctrine of episcopacy and an unwarrantably high doctrine of the presbyterate".[3] He argues that the authority to preside at the eucharist is not inherent in the presbyterate, but is a function delegated by the bishop. In contrast to the three orders of bishop, priest, and deacon identified in the Ordinal, and the popular modern adaptation which adds the order of laity, Synge argues that there are two orders of ministry: those of the episcopate and the laity.[4] Presbyters, and by implication deacons, are lay people to whom the bishop has delegated specific functions, but they are not the only laity to whom the administration of the sacraments and other aspects of ministry can be delegated. Presiding at the eucharist for the entire diocese is the bishop's duty and prerogative, and it is essential that this take place in each community on each Sunday. Where the bishop cannot be present he is responsible for ensuring that a deputy takes his place, and there should be no requirement that this deputy be a priest.[5] Rather than being presidents at the eucharist, presbyters should, as delegates of the bishop, exercise a more concentrated preaching and teaching ministry in the communities in their care.[6]

While Synge's proposals were not implemented in any part of the Anglican Communion, they demonstrate that the case for lay presidency at the eucharist can be argued from an Anglo-Catholic as well as from an evangelical perspective. Synge's concerns were not to do with theological casuistry, but with pastoral provision for eucharistic worship in communities remote from the ministry of their bishop, and remote also from the ministry of a priest. The theological and ecclesiological issues he raises are of considerable importance not only for addressing questions to do with the ministry of word and sacraments but also how the Church conducts its business in every aspect of its life.

Few today would argue with Synge's insistence that the laity are an order of ministry in the Church. There are of course practical as well as theological questions to be asked about how this applies when the boundaries of the Church are fluid and indistinct. Baptism does not indicate unequivocal commitment to the life, worship, and ministry of

---

3   F. C. Synge, 'The Challenge of the Frontiers', in *Anglican Congress 1963* (Toronto: Editorial Committee, 1963), p. 160.

4   'Challenge of the Frontiers', p. 159.

5   'Challenge of the Frontiers', p. 161.

6   'Challenge of the Frontiers', p. 162.

the Church, other than as a theological principle. The same observation, however regrettable, is true also of confirmation. It could therefore in effect be only certain selected, as well as self-selected, members of the laity to whom the bishop could delegate ministerial functions. For the order of laity to be a meaningful concept in the life and ministry of the Church, it will be necessary for the ritual and sacramental, and particularly the initiatory, regime of Anglican provinces to be reconciled with practical reality. The alternative, as with so many proposals for all varieties of lay ministry, would be to create a hierarchy of categories among the laity, from those who have effectively been clericalized without ordination, through those who function as lay members of their communities, to those who are baptized but nominal members, effectively on the fringes of their church.

Synge's typology is more deeply problematic both in his elevation of the episcopate and in his effective denigration of the presbyterate, and, by implication, of the diaconate. The Book of Common Prayer and the Ordinal unambiguously identify the orders of bishop, priest, and deacon, and it is difficult to envisage how any Anglican ecclesiology can justifiably deviate from this. The orders of presbyter and deacon are integral to the life and ministry of the Church, and cannot be reduced to arbitrary extensions of the bishop's ministry. We have already noted that there is considerable ambivalence and ambiguity in the Catholic tradition regarding the episcopate, as to whether it is a distinct order of ministry apart from the presbyterate, or a higher office and ministry within the order of priests. The case for monarchical episcopacy at a very early date in history of the Church, functioning independently of any body of presbyters, has been argued quite cogently in recent scholarship.[7] Even if there were to develop a consensus in support of this position, the reconstruction of the earliest Christian communities would fall some way short of the concentration of power in the hands of a monarchical bishop, such as was later advocated by Ignatius of Antioch, and which Synge seems to regard as the definitive model for the Church. While clergy normally function under the authority of their bishop, and are issued with a bishop's licence, this is not universally the case. As well as royal peculiars in England, there are colleges and other institutions independent of diocesan structures, in which priests function without the oversight of a bishop. While such priests will have been ordained by a bishop, and bishops are invited to administer confirmation and orders where appropriate, they exercise no jurisdiction or pastoral

---

7   R. A. Campbell, *The Elders* (Edinburgh: T & T Clark, 1994).

oversight of such communities. Furthermore, the ministry of word and sacrament does not cease in a diocese when the see is vacant. Nor do clergy who move from one diocese to another require any further ordination by the bishop under whom they will serve; the authority conferred at their ordination remains valid. While deacons and priests are not free to preach, administer the sacraments, or exercise pastoral care as they wish, wherever and whenever they wish, they nonetheless receive an authority at ordination which is indelible. And there are occasions on which clergy function, quite legitimately, in places to which they are not licensed by the bishop. Therefore it cannot be legitimate to reduce priestly ministry to the exercise of functions delegated by the bishop.

As well as being fundamentally discontinuous with catholic and Anglican tradition, Synge's model of the Church and its ministry would seem contrary to the collegial patterns of ministry to which Anglicans in most parts of the world are increasingly committed. Synodical government moderates episcopal authority, but in many places provides far too little protection against the abuses of autocracy. While Synge is undoubtedly correct that the Church is not a democracy, his emphasis on the Church as the whole people of God is not well served by a model of overweening episcopal monarchy.

Synge's twin concerns, that pastoral provision be made for the regular celebration of the eucharist in all Anglican communities, and that more effective teaching be delivered in those communities, undoubtedly command unqualified assent. But his model of the Church is questionable, both in terms of continuity with the received tradition and in that it takes insufficient account of the dangers inherent in concentrating power in the hands of individuals, including bishops. The laity will be better equipped to be the people of God, and an order of ministry in and of the Church, if they are enabled and encouraged by presbyters and deacons whose own ministry is recognized as integral to the life of the Church, and who are not reduced to being brokers of remote and arbitrary episcopal authority.

Both theologically and pastorally, the approach to sacramental ministry advocated by Synge would not seem a sound basis for introducing lay presidency at the eucharist.

The Province of the Southern Cone of America (Iglesia Anglicana del Cono Sur de America)

The proposal for authorized lay eucharistic presidency in South America emerged from a particular pastoral and missionary context. Notwithstanding the presence of English communities in the major seaports and other commercial centres of Latin America, with their long-established Anglican chaplaincies, the province of the Southern Cone is substantially the fruit of relatively recent, and overwhelmingly evangelical, missionary enterprises. Whatever the merits of the missionary methods used, the perhaps unforeseen result was the emergence of remote and scattered communities of recent converts, whom the priests available could not serve adequately, pastorally or liturgically,[8] and presumably also catechetically.

That priestly presidency at the eucharist was and would remain normative, was not in question, and adequate pastoral provision for all congregations was the declared objective of the province.[9] Authorization of lay presidency was considered as an interim measure, until such time as the necessary provision of ordained pastoral ministry was realized. The ordination of recent converts to local ministries was not considered appropriate, when the suitability of individuals was not yet fully ascertained and the resources for their training were not available.[10] Regular celebration of the eucharist was nonetheless considered vital to spiritual growth in these communities. Authorized lay presidency, for a limited period, and with clear criteria for licensing, was regarded as the least unsatisfactory option available in the circumstances.[11] After the proposal was brought forward by the diocese in Chile, a consultation with other Anglican provinces was undertaken, before the matter was brought before the 1986 session of the provincial synod. Here it reached a simple majority, but not the two-thirds majority required, and was therefore narrowly defeated. In the twenty years since, the proposal has not been revived, and there are no plans to do so, but the subject does continue to be discussed from time to time.[12] Irrespective of whether or not a proposal to authorize lay presidency at the eucharist returns to the synod of this particular province, the question has been posed in the

---

8   A. L. Hargrave, *But Who Will Preside?* (Nottingham: Grove Books, 1990), pp. 3–4.

9   Hargrave, *Who Will Preside?*, p. 6.

10   Hargrave, *Who Will Preside?*, pp. 9–10.

11   Hargrave, *Who Will Preside?*, p. 7.

12   Presiding Bishop Gregory Venables, private correspondence.

light of pastoral circumstances which may not be untypical of Anglican communities in other parts of the developing world. It is therefore worth exploring more fully the theological and pastoral issues involved in this particular case.

It is immediately evident that the province of the Southern Cone sought to reach a decision on what was recognized to be an extraordinary proposal, in consultation with the wider Anglican Communion. This was not a militant evangelical crusade to undermine the ordained ministry, but a carefully and perhaps reluctantly considered approach to a real and challenging pastoral situation. The preference for authorized lay presidency was undoubtedly shaped by the evangelical tradition of the province, but also by entirely practical considerations. Extended communion would not have been theologically acceptable, but neither would this have been logistically feasible in the particular geographical circumstances, with remote and inaccessible communities to whom consecrated elements could not be safely or efficiently conveyed.[13] Similarly, peripatetic priests visiting these communities in order to preside at the eucharist were not a viable option, as there were insufficient numbers of clergy available to make this an effective pastoral as well as sacramental ministry.[14] There is no suggestion that a ritual fellowship meal, which would not be a eucharist, might have been held in Anglican congregations, as is practised in Roman Catholic base communities without a priest.[15] No mention is made as to how the ministry of the word might have been provided in congregations without a priest, and presumably also very often without a lay person able to deliver preaching, catechetical instruction, and teaching in the faith. This must presumably have presented at least as great a challenge to the dioceses, even with competent lay people to assist their few priests serving remote and scattered congregations.

The reluctance of the bishops to ordain recent converts, whether from indigenous religions or even from other Christian denominations, can certainly be appreciated, even if such reluctance is informed by the latent or overt anti-catholicism of many conservative Anglican evangelicals. It was felt that ordination of local church leaders would be premature, particularly given the lack of educational and training resources available to equip the laity for ministry, and to prepare those so called

---

13   Hargrave, *Who Will Preside?*, pp. 8–9.
14   Hargrave, *Who Will Preside?*, pp. 7–8.
15   L. Boff, *Ecclesiogenesis* (Maryknoll, MD: Orbis, 1986); cf. I. Fraser, 'Liberating Faith', *ER* 44 (1982): 58–64.

for ordination.[16] A fundamental question seems to be, whether temporarily authorized lay presidency would adequately address the same reservations as were expressed about proceeding to ordain the local leaders concerned. It would seem quite evident that the proposed authorization of lay eucharistic presidency would not have addressed an urgent need for competent ministry of the word, sound catechesis, and continuing education in the faith. Whether implementation of this proposal would have met the short-term spiritual and liturgical needs of the congregations so to be served, without creating or precipitating further, and perhaps foreseeable, pastoral problems, needs also to be considered.

The levels of superstition likely in communities such as those described are unlikely to be ameliorated by making the eucharist more common and devoid of the mystique surrounding infrequent celebration with a priest.[17] If the concern was that former Roman Catholics would retain the understanding of the mass as perpetuated in the popular piety in which they were reared, or that syncretistic ideas might infiltrate from indigenous religions, then it would have been highly unlikely that making a recent convert the ritual functionary who administered the sacrament in his (or her?) local community, remote from the supervision of the bishop and clergy, could have avoided precisely such developments. On the contrary, the remoteness of pastoral supervision would have meant that the associated problems would have been more likely to have emerged undetected, and could have escalated to the point where bishops would have had little option but to impose discipline. Any form of censure would almost certainly have been perceived as unjust, and quite probably have led to schism and the formation of syncretistic cults in places where there had been Anglican congregations.

This might well raise serious questions about the propriety of conferring ritual authority on uneducated local leadership, particularly recent converts whose suitability for ordination has not yet been adequately tested. Such reservations might not be universally shared, and we have noted Roland Allen's critique of the monopolization by missionaries of leadership in newly formed Christian communities, even for a short period.[18] If the relinquishment of oversight in newly formed

16 Hargrave, *Who Will Preside?*, pp. 9–10.
17 Cf. Hargrave, *Who Will Preside?*, pp. 7–8.
18 Cf. R. Allen, *Missionary Methods* (London: World Dominion, 1960), pp. 105–7; V. J. Donovan, *Christianity Rediscovered* (London: SCM Press, 1982), pp. 122–8, 149–59.

Christian communities is indeed an imperative of the gospel, as Allen argued, but it is intended that these congregations would remain integral to the Anglican dioceses in which they were established, then it would surely be better to ordain the local leaders to the diaconate and presbyterate than to license them to an ambivalent, temporary, vulnerable, and easily misunderstood state, in which they would exercise the pastoral and liturgical roles of a priest, but not the teaching office. Furthermore, the pastoral consequences of issuing, and then withdrawing, licences seem not to have been adequately considered, even if the concept of a licence was adequately understood in such communities. In a patriarchal culture, in which the distinction between personal status and public office is not recognized, and retirement and resignation from office, or relinquishment of a particular role, not the established custom, the revocation of a licence to preside at the eucharist would be experienced as degradation and humiliation. In societies in which religion is not isolated from other aspects of communal or private life, degradation in the church would resonate throughout the family and social networks of the person concerned.

While the case for lay presidency in the particular circumstances of Anglican congregations in South America, and perhaps by analogy elsewhere,[19] has been powerfully argued, it does not seem that this would have been a more satisfactory option than the risks of premature ordination of uneducated lay people. Whatever questions there may be as to the educational level and teaching competence required before ordination to the priesthood,[20] the answer must surely be contextual, and not divorced from the needs of the communities to be served. Questions to do with Christian commitment and maturity in newly formed congregations of recent converts may be even more difficult to answer satisfactorily. Whether a concern to preserve the doctrinal orthodoxy

19 Buchanan, *News of Liturgy* (1985); C. J. Cocksworth, *Evangelical Eucharistic Thought in the Church of England* (Cambridge: Cambridge University Press, 1993), pp. 169–70; cf. W. S. Adams, 'The Eucharistic Assembly – Who Presides?', *ATR* 64 (1982): 312–13.

20 S. Escobar, 'Mission in Latin America', *Missiology* 20 (1992): 249; *The Theology of Ordination* (London: Church Information Office, 1975), p. 56; R. Hooker, *The Lawes of Ecclesiastical Polity*, 5.81.1–2,5,8–13,16–17; H. C. B. Green, *Lay Presidency at the Eucharist?* (London: Darton, Longman and Todd, 1994), pp. 15–16; H. Küng, *Why Priests?* (London: Collins, 1971), p. 64; K. Leech, *Spirituality and Pastoral Care* (London: Sheldon, 1986), pp. 127–36; J. F. Puglisi, *The Process of Admission to Ordained Ministry* (Collegeville, IN: Liturgical Press, 1996–2001);

which has evolved in the Church and culture from which the missionaries emanate, in this case the evangelical wing of the Church of England, is at all legitimate, is an issue on which there are likely to be strongly held differences of opinion.

The dilemma with which the province of the Southern Cone of America was confronted during the 1980s was relevant to the Church anywhere else in the world where it is engaged in mission and the formation of new communities of recent converts, if not to Christianity then at least to a particular expression thereof found within the breadth of Anglicanism. The courage fully to indigenize the ministry and to allow an authentic contextualization of the Gospel to emerge, as advocated by Roland Allen and many contemporary missiologists, conflicts quite radically with a determination to preserve and to universalize and absolutize a particular Western interpretation of the Gospel, whether it be catholic or evangelical. The negotiation of this dialectic is the context in which questions of ministry are explored and debated. The case for authorized lay presidency at the eucharist would seem insufficiently cogent, both theologically and pastorally, whatever position one takes on the nature of the church to emerge out of missionary enterprises.

The Diocese of Sydney, Australia

The diocese of Sydney in Australia has long represented what has been perceived as an ultra-Protestant fringe of Anglicanism, where a distinctive conservative evangelicalism has been combined with rigid adherence to the Book of Common Prayer. Their interpretations of the Bible and the Book of Common Prayer may alike be tendentious, and account for the historically somewhat liminal place this diocese has taken in the Anglican Communion, and even in the Anglican Church of Australia, including the province of New South Wales over which the Archbishop of Sydney is Metropolitan. This liminality has been given concrete expression in the long-term support offered by the diocese of Sydney to the schismatic ecclesial group known as the Church of England in South Africa, which maintained close ties with the apartheid regime but has never been part of the Anglican Communion. This isolation of the diocese of Sydney has in recent years been transformed, with the emergence of the conservative, and predominantly evangelical, "Global South" bloc in Anglican Communion affairs. The current

---

J. Roffey, 'The Theology and Practice of Lay Ministry', *St Mark's Review* 138 (1989): 20.

Archbishop of Sydney, Dr Peter Jensen, has been prominent behind such initiatives as the proposed Anglican Covenant, the 2008 Global Anglican Future Conference (GAFCON), held in Jerusalem in defiance of the clearly stated wishes of the Anglican Bishop in Jerusalem, and the self-styled Fellowship of Confessing Anglicans (FOCA) which emerged from it. These moves have all been precipitated by a common abhorrence of homosexuality, and have brought together primates and other bishops deeply divided on other issues such as the ordination of women, polygamy among Christians, and, indeed, lay presidency at the eucharist.[21] But developments in the diocese of Sydney have nonetheless acquired an importance for the Anglican Communion, and must be considered in this light.

The authorization of lay presidency at the eucharist was first considered by the Sydney diocesan synod in 1977, and endorsed in principle in 1985. As this conflicted with the canon law of the Anglican Church of Australia, it could not be implemented in practice, but the matter remained under consideration. The diocesan doctrine commission found in 1993 that there were no theological reasons against lay presidency, and strong arguments in favour thereof.[22] A bill to authorize both preaching and administration of holy communion by deacons and lay persons was brought before the Sydney diocesan synod in 1995, and referred to the Appellate Tribunal of the Anglican Church of Australia. The Tribunal ruled in 1997 that any such change could be implemented by ordinance of a diocesan synod only if first authorized by a canon adopted by the General Synod of the Anglican Church of Australia. The Sydney diocesan standing committee nonetheless proceeded with the matter, and submitted to the diocesan synod a measure to authorize lay and diaconal preaching and administration of holy communion, subject to an archbishop's licence and the consent of the vestry of the parish or other pastoral charge concerned. This was passed in 1999,[23] but the then archbishop, Dr Harry Goodhew, withheld the assent required by the constitution of the Anglican Church of Australia, and it therefore could not take effect. Archbishop Goodhew

---

21 Cf. N. H. Taylor, 'Some Observations on Theological Method, Biblical Interpretation, and Ecclesiastical Politics in Current Disputes in the Anglican Communion', *Theology* 111 (2008): 51–8.

22 At this stage the language of presidency was still employed. In subsequent discussion "administration" of holy communion has been the preferred terminology, and this will be respected in this treatment.

23 Preaching and Administration of Holy Communion by Lay Persons and Deacons Ordinance 1999.

published the reasons for his decision. Notwithstanding the almost two-thirds majority vote in the synod, and acknowledging the force of the arguments presented (from which he personally dissented), and mindful also of the potential implications for the Anglican Church of Australia and the wider Anglican Communion, he deferred to the opinion of the Appellate Tribunal that a general synod canon would be required to authorize such an innovation.[24]

Notwithstanding the ruling of the Appellate Tribunal, and the unaltered canon law of the Anglican Church of Australia on this point, Archbishop Jensen is committed to pursuing the authorization of lay administration of holy communion.[25] In 2004 the diocesan standing committee recommended that synod, rather than reintroducing legislation to authorize lay and diaconal administration, should "discourage any disciplinary action against those involved in such administration by a deacon or layperson".[26] The intention was to create a proverbial space in which the requisite changes in canon law could be anticipated, and to offer deacons and lay people who so acted, and the incumbent of the pastoral charge concerned, some protection from sanctions which they might otherwise incur. The matter was referred back to the standing committee by the diocesan synod, and the same year the general synod of the Anglican Church of Australia rejected a measure to amend the canon law so as to enable the diocese of Sydney to proceed with authorizing lay administration of holy communion without fear of legal sanctions. The 2008 Synod passed the resolution that Synod:

> a) Accepts the report concerning legal barriers to lay and diaconal administration of the Lord's Supper which was submitted to the 3rd session of the 47th synod, and
> b) Affirms again its conviction that lay and diaconal administration of the Lord's Supper is consistent with the teaching of Scripture, and
> c) Affirms that the Lord's Supper in this diocese may be administered by persons other than presbyters

---

24 Decision Concerning the Preaching and Administration of Holy Communion by Lay Persons and Deacons Ordinance 1999.

25 P. F. Jensen, 'Lay Administration of Holy Communion', Address to the Clergy of the Diocese of Newcastle, 2004, p. 3.

26 Lay and Diaconal Administration of Holy Communion. Report of Standing Committee 2004.

and requests the Diocesan Secretary to send a copy of The Lord's Supper in Human Hands to all bishops who attended the GAFCON.

While reaffirming in principle the commitment of the diocese to authorised lay administration of the sacraments, this implements no change in practice, and the matter remains at a legal impasse which reflects the deep theological divisions within the Anglican Church of Australia.

The more immediate intention is to distinguish between preaching and administration of the sacraments by deacons and by lay people, and to consider first the extension of diaconal ministries.[27] This is a potentially significant development, in that women have in recent years been ordained to the diaconate in the diocese of Sydney. Furthermore, diaconal presidency at the eucharist has been authorized elsewhere in the Anglican Communion, in the province of Kenya, since 1985, and is practised in some of the Lutheran churches of northern Europe with which the Anglican provinces in Europe have entered into full communion, as with other denominations with which the Anglican Communion has long enjoyed close ecumenical ties, such as the Moravians. There may, moreover, be some ancient precedent for this. διάκονος emerges in the New Testament in the non-technical and often even menial sense of a servant, as was current Greek usage, but is also applied by Paul of his own apostolic ministry and the leadership exercised in the Church by others.[28] While this is not the only title used, and cannot be equated with the later office of deacon, it does demonstrate that the connotations of service were not incompatible with the exercise of authority and oversight. As mentioned above, the Arabic transmission of the *Apostolic Tradition* could suggest that, in the absence of the bishop, a presbyter or deacon alike may deputize for him in the act of blessing.[29] It is less than certain that this refers to presiding at a celebration of the eucharist, rather than administering elements previously consecrated by the bishop.

While the ministry of the deacon has undoubtedly mutated considerably over the centuries, and the office has at times undoubtedly

---

27   P. G. Bolt *et al.*, *The Lord's Supper in Human Hands* (Sydney: Australian Church Record/Anglican Church League, 2008); esp. G. N. Davies, 'The Athorisation of a Deacon to Administer the Holy Communion', pp. 68-76.

28   Rom. 16.1; 1 Cor. 3.5; 2 Cor. 3.6; 6.4; 11.23; 1 Thess. 3.2; cf. Phil. 1.1.

29   28.4–5. Cf. A. Stewart-Sykes, *Hippolytus, On the Apostolic Tradition* (New York, NY: St Vladimir's Seminary, 2001), p. 46; P. F. Bradshaw *et al.*, *The Apostolic Tradition* (Minneapolis, Fortress, 2002), p. 151.

been a powerful one, all extant evidence suggests that the liturgical role of the deacon has always been subordinate to that of the bishop and presbyters. The leadership and oversight exercised by the deacon in the absence of the bishop or presbyter has always been limited to bringing the benefits of their sacramental action to individuals and groups who would otherwise be excluded, most notably in conveying consecrated eucharistic elements to the sick and housebound. The question of whether extension of diaconal ministry to include presidency at the eucharist would be consistent with the recovery of the distinctive character of the diaconate over the past century and more needs to be considered with great care. While it could affirm the ministry of deacons in significant and powerfully symbolic ways, and end the practice of ordaining people to the presbyterate simply in order that they may administer the sacraments, it could also collapse once again the distinction between priest and deacon which has been re-established in recent years.[30]

The largely urban diocese of Sydney lacks neither the clergy nor the financial resources to provide an adequate ministry of word and sacrament by its ordained clergy. Promotion of lay administration of holy communion is theologically driven, from within a conservative evangelical tradition, which could in some respects at least be described as more Protestant than Anglican, despite its professed adherence to the Book of Common Prayer. It is admitted that "there is no decisive biblical text available" to resolve this issue.[31] The agendum is accordingly founded on a somewhat tendentious reading of Reformation history, the Book of Common Prayer, and the Ordinal. It is assumed that the death of Edward VI disrupted the divinely ordained course of the English reformation, from which it never recovered its true direction or momentum.[32] There is no historical or theological basis for regarding the reign of Edward VI as definitive for Anglicanism for all time, or his death as having disrupted a continuous or consistent process of reform which it is the mission of the diocese of Sydney to revive and bring to

---

30 *Deacons in the Ministry of the Church* (London: Church House Publishing, 1988); J. M. Barnett, *The Diaconate* (London: Continuum, 1995); R. Brown, *Being a Deacon Today* (Norwich: Canterbury Press, 2005); O. F. Cummings, *Deacons and the Church* (New York, NY: Paulist Press, 2004); E. P. Echlin, *The Deacon in the Church Past and Future* (New York, NY: Alba, 1971).

31 Jensen, 'Lay Administration', p. 7.

32 The dependence of Jensen on D. N. J. MacCulloch, *Thomas Cranmer* (New Haven, CT: Yale University Press, 1996), is overt. See 'Lay Administration', pp. 5–7.

completion. The definitive editions of the Book of Common Prayer and the Ordinal were promulgated in 1662, under the restored monarchy following the death of Cromwell, and these became definitive only because they remained in use, whereas previously editions had been superseded with the accession of new monarchs. While much of Cranmer's composition is retained from previous prayer books, his texts were clearly subject to revision.[33] The Articles of Religion were promulgated in their final form in 1571, and are a product of the Elizabethan settlement. These defining texts of Anglicanism all quite explicitly preclude any possibility of authorized lay administration of the eucharist. To presume that this was motivated only by a desire to preserve doctrinal purity, and can therefore now be waived,[34] would seem a curiously liberal hermeneutic for a conservative evangelical diocese, known for its preoccupation with the purity of its distinctive and eccentric doctrinal tradition, in which male headship and other selected "biblical" principles are viewed as of perpetual validity.

The agenda of the diocese of Sydney, under its current Archbishop, is to resume and bring to its completion the process of reformation disrupted by the deaths of Edward VI and Cranmer. Reform is to be continued along a theological trajectory in continuity with Cranmer. The task of tracing the fluctuations in Cranmer's theological thinking during his lifetime is somewhat speculative,[35] but to project how his cognitive processes would have continued during his later years, had Queen Mary not brought these to a fiery conclusion, is to enter the realms of fantasy. It must be doubtful whether such an approach renders appropriate honour to Cranmer, even if a logical conclusion to his theological journey could be reconstructed. However significant a figure Cranmer may be in Anglican history, the English Reformation was never simply the implementation of his theology in the life, worship, ministry, and governance of the Church of England. It was a larger, longer, politically and diplomatically as well as theologically negotiated process, in which liturgical conformity embraced, but never concealed, theological diversity.[36] Furthermore, it is not legitimate to treat Cranmer's recorded theological opinions as though they express the

---

33 Cf. F. Procter and W. H. Frere, *A New History of the Book of Common Prayer* (London: Macmillan, 1951); B. D. Spinks, *sacraments, Ceremonies and the Stuart Divines* (Aldershot: Ashgate, 2002).

34 Jensen, 'Lay Administration', p. 3.

35 Cf. C. A. Haigh, *English Reformations* (Oxford: Clarendon Press, 1993).

36 E. Duffy, *The Stripping of the Altars* (New Haven, CT: Yale University Press, 1992); Haigh, *Reformations*.

definitive doctrine and discipline of the Anglican Communion; the distinction must be recognized between Cranmer's private opinions, however trenchantly expressed, and the succession of measures taken by the Convocations and parliament, and by successive monarchs, in which Cranmer and other Archbishops of Canterbury played their official role, and which cumulatively formed the doctrine and discipline of the Church of England over a period of centuries.

Even if Cranmer were to be regarded as definitive for Anglicanism for all time and in all places, he would provide rather less support for deviation from the Book of Common Prayer – which lay administration of holy communion would undoubtedly be – than is claimed.[37] Celebration of the eucharist is certainly an ecclesial act, and precisely for that reason it may not be administered by anyone not authorized so to do. Cranmer, in a text considered above, argued that royal appointment was sufficient authority to assume an ecclesiastical office, without the necessity of ordination. This exception applied only to the action of a crowned and anointed monarch, within his or her jurisdiction, and is therefore dependent on the doctrine of royal supremacy. Such a theological basis for any measure would be contrary both to the secular constitution of the dominion of Australia, even if the British monarch is head of state, and to the constitution of the disestablished Anglican Church of Australia. In such a dispensation "lawful authority" must be internal to the ecclesial body itself, and the Appellate Tribunal has ruled that lawful authority lies with the General Synod and Canon Law of that church. This may be an authority outside and above the jurisdiction of any single bishop or archbishop, but whether this would equate the role of General Synod with that of a crowned monarch, as envisaged by Cranmer, is another question. If lawful authority were to permit certain lay people to assume the functions of the priesthood, they would, in terms of Cranmer's theology, thereby become priests, irrespective of whether or not any bishop were to ordain them to that order of ministry. Cranmer provides no theological basis for administration of the eucharist by lay people, but for lay people to be appointed to ecclesiastical office, and therefore to become priests or bishops, with or without undergoing ordination.

Rigid adherence to the Book of Common Prayer is not consistently observed in making the case for lay administration of holy communion. It is entirely clear from the rubrics to the order of holy communion that this rite is to be administered by a priest – which undoubtedly means a

---

37   Cf. Jensen, 'Lay Administration', pp. 5–6.

person ordained to the priesthood by a bishop.[38] The priesthood of all Christians is nowhere articulated, or even reflected, anywhere in the Book of Common Prayer or the Ordinal, or in the Articles of Religion. Furthermore, the Lectionary drafted by Cranmer to accompany the 1549 Book of Common Prayer, and substantially unaltered until 1871, appoints 1 Pet 2 to be read at Evening Prayer on 18 April, 17 August, and 14 December, and Revelation not to be read at all at the daily Offices. The passages expressing the notion of the priesthood of the whole Church are nowhere appointed for reading at the eucharist. "Priest" in the Book of Common Prayer therefore denotes quite clearly a presbyter or bishop. Many, of catholic as well as of evangelical persuasion, would prefer the term presbyter to priest, as indeed did Hooker.[39] But "Priest" is undoubtedly usage of the Book of Common Prayer and the Ordinal; "Minister" has a somewhat ambiguous usage, denoting presbyters and deacons, and at times specifically the officiating priest at holy communion.

Interpretation of the Book of Common Prayer, and more specifically the Ordinal, has been crucial to opposition to the ordination of women in the diocese of Sydney, as is illustrated by a report on the issue in 1991. This argued that women could not be ordained to the diaconate, not only on biblical grounds including Genesis 2 and 3 as well as New Testament texts to do with "male headship", but also because the Ordinal includes the prayer that those just ordained as deacons "may so well behave themselves in this inferior Office, that they may be found worthy to be called unto the higher Ministries of the Church".[40] Women have more recently been ordained to the diaconate in Sydney, but the 2006 session of diocesan synod reaffirmed its consistent rejection of ordination of women to the priesthood by a more than overwhelming majority. The most recent proposals to authorize lay people and deacons to administer holy communion would have allowed women to exercise this role, which would apparently not be construed as violating the principle of male headship. Despite this provision, it is hardly surprising that authorization of lay administration of holy communion is perceived as a device to avoid ordaining women to the priesthood.[41]

---

38 As is acknowledged by J. Woodhouse, "Lay Administration of the Lord's Supper", *The Lord's Supper in Human Hands*, pp. 9-14.

39 *Laws*, 5.78.2-3.

40 The Ordination of Women to the Priesthood, 1991.

41 A. Marriage, *The People of God* (London: Darton, Longman and Todd, 1995), p. 142; S. K. Pickard and L. Johnston, 'Lay Presidency at Holy Communion', *St Mark's Review* 161 (1995): 41; cf. Roffey, 'Lay Ministry'.

The declared objective of authorizing deacons and lay people to administer holy communion is to facilitate the missionary agenda of the diocese, to which the regular worship of established congregations is considered "almost irrelevant" by the current Archbishop.[42] If the regular ministry of word and sacraments in the gathered Christian communities of the diocese of Sydney is "almost irrelevant", and for that reason can be delegated to lay people because the clergy have more important things to do, this raises significant theological questions. At the level of ecclesiology, the nature of the Church as the Body of Christ is called into question, if the eucharist is so marginal to Christian life, identity, and spirituality.[43] It suggests also an uncritical acquiescence in the hyper-individualistic outlook of secular modernity and postmodernity, which ignores community and is oblivious to the corporate nature of Christian identity and authentic spirituality, to which the eucharist is central and essential. As a theology of the laity, it denigrates the people of God to whom the "almost irrelevant" ministry of word and sacrament is entrusted, while clergy are engaged in the ministry which really matters. At the level of missiology, it reflects a bourgeois Protestant post-Enlightenment obsession with the individual, and a preoccupation with winning individual souls for Christ without adequate regard for the community into which they are to be incorporated if their conversions are to be sustained.[44] It disregards also the role of ritual in creating and sustaining community, a social reality from which no ecclesial group, however Protestant, is exempt.[45] For mission and evangelism to be at all effective, the corporate nature of human identity, even in the modern world, and the social nature of religious conversion, must be appreciated. This may not in itself answer the questions to do with the administration of the sacraments, but it does suggest that the issues need to be refocused if the ritual and corporate life of the Church are to play their necessary part in effective evangelism.

It is not envisaged that delegation to lay people of functions such as preaching and administering holy communion in Sunday worship would

---

42 Jensen, 'Lay Administration', p. 3.

43 Cf. N. N. Afanasiev, *The Church of the Holy Spirit* (Notre Dame, IN: University of Notre Dame Press, 2007).

44 Cf. R. A. Straus, 'Religious Conversion as a Personal and Collective Accomplishment', *Sociological Analysis* 40 (1979): 158–65; D. A. Snow and R. Machalek, 'The Convert as a Social Type', in *Sociological Theory 1983*, ed. R. Collins (San Francisco, CA: Jossey Bass, 1983), pp. 261–76.

45 Cf. R. K. Fenn, *The Return of the Primitive: A New Sociological Theory of Religion* (Aldershot: Ashgate, 2001).

involve any participation in the pastoral oversight exercised by the Archbishop and clergy of the diocese of Sydney. Power would remain vested in an exclusive male cadre, formed principally and definitively at Moore Theological College in the very particular and narrow theological tradition which Sydney represents. It is precisely in order to maintain dogmatic rigour and monolithic theological purity that the ordination of local church leaders will not be considered. This is justified on the basis of the Ordinal, which describes the ministry of a priest in terms which most approximate those of the incumbent of a parish.[46] This observation is undoubtedly accurate, but, as the Archbishop himself observes, there are other forms of priestly ministry exercised "in connection with the Christian community which is being served",[47] and there has never been a time when the ordination of priests was administered only to those who had been appointed to incumbencies of parishes. The presbyterate is inherently collegial, and has always embraced some variety of gifts and ministries.

It is asserted that to delegate the ministry of the word, including preaching, to lay people, while reserving the ministry of the sacraments to the clergy, gives the impression of exalting the sacrament above the proclamation of the word.[48] Evangelicals would maintain, to the contrary, that the word is supreme, and the sacraments are dependent on the word for their life-giving meaning. Therefore to allow the higher ministry to lay people, while reserving the inferior to clergy, is inconsistent.[49] It is not necessary to argue on the basis of a hierarchy of word over sacrament, or of the ministers of one over those of the other, to recognize that there is a degree of inconsistency here. The ministries both of word and of sacrament are integral and essential to Anglican worship and spirituality; neither is in fact derivative from the other, historically or theologically, but both are dependent on the other for the fullness of their meaning and its realization in the life of the Church.

The appropriate person to exercise a particular ministry is a matter not merely of hierarchy and status, but of relationships and of gifts and abilities, which are to be recognized and reflected in the authority conferred by the Church. The argument of the superiority of the ministry of the word to that of the sacraments has its own internal, if somewhat perverse, logic, but it overlooks crucial aspects of both ministries. The

---

46 Jensen, 'Lay Administration', p. 6.
47 Jensen, 'Lay Administration', pp. 6–7.
48 Jensen, 'Lay Administration', pp. 8–10.
49 Jensen, 'Lay Administration', pp. 8–9.

ministry of the sacraments is more closely bound with the corporate identity and life of the community celebrating the eucharist than is that of the word, simply because of the power of its symbolism as well as of the gifts required. Throughout Christian history, there has been an important role in the ministry of the word for clergy, and often for lay people, who do not share in the cure of souls of the communities to which they preach. Licensed preachers, such as those licensed by the Archbishops of Canterbury, have exercised a significant role in the spiritual and liturgical life of the Church of England, outside any relationship of pastoral oversight. Some of these have been lay members of the universities rather than clerics. Furthermore, in the ancient Church such significant lay figures as Justin, Tertullian, and Origen played an immensely important role in teaching and, indeed, defining, the Christian faith, even if this may not have been exercised in the context of liturgical preaching. This may not equate with the modern case of lay ministers licensed to preach in the churches of which they are members, but, if they exercise a pastoral role alongside, or in the absence of, the priest inducted to the cure of souls, there may be little justification for withholding ordination. The presbyterate has always been collegial, and never monarchical, and the Ordinal does not presuppose that it ought to be otherwise.

The entrenchment and concentration of power in the hands of an ordained, exclusively male, and theologically monolithic, cadre in the diocese of Sydney represents a fundamental contrast to the expansion of lay ministry in Anglican parishes elsewhere in the Communion over the past century and more. Preaching and administration of holy communion by lay people would seem not to be about empowerment of lay people for ministry; rather, the semi-clericalization of selected lay people, who in many other parts of the Anglican Communion would almost certainly be ordained, would perpetuate their subjugation to a repressive and exclusive, theologically monolithic, ecclesiastical regime.[50] It would seem a reflection of the degree to which radical Protestantism, represented by the diocese of Sydney, has uncritically absorbed secularized and deritualized modern Western bourgeois culture, that its liturgical worship should be denigrated as "almost irrelevant", and that administration of holy communion by lay women should not be seen as violating the principle of male headship which the diocesan hierarchy holds sacred.

---

50   Cf. Pickard and Johnston, 'Lay Presidency'; H. I. J. Southern, 'Anglicanism Sydney Style', *Theology* 107 (2004): 117–24.

Advocacy of lay administration of holy communion in the diocese of Sydney seems, therefore, to be founded on premises irreconcilable with the Anglican tradition. As well as disregarding the Church Universal and the pre-Reformation heritage of the Church of England, this programme rests on a tendentious reading of the Reformation and subsequent Anglican history and theology, and in particular of the Book of Common Prayer and the Ordinal. The proposal to authorize lay and diaconal preaching and administration of Holy Communion is motivated not by pastoral necessity, but by a theological agenda contentious and divisive even within the spectrum of Anglican evangelicalism, and fundamentally discontinuous with the breadth and the spirit of the Anglican reformation.

The Church-Planting Movement and "Fresh Expressions of Church"

A recent development in the Church of England, at least partly inspired by the apparent success of evangelical missions in South America and led by some veterans thereof,[51] is the church-planting movement.[52] This has been defined as "the transfer of part of a congregation in an area of need with the evangelistic expectation that new people will find faith and the renewal of their spiritual lives".[53] Chapels of ease have for centuries provided venues for worship, according to the rites of the Church of England and under the auspices of the parish church, in places convenient and accessible to parishioners. Church plants, on the other hand, are separate from and sometimes hostile to established parishes,[54] and not necessarily governed by Anglican standards in worship, doctrine, and discipline.[55]

This approach was described as consumerist and fractious in the foreword to the book which has in some respects become the manifesto of the church-planting movement.[56] Some proponents envisage that

51 G. E. D. Pytches and B. Skinner, *New Wineskins* (Guildford: Eagle Press, 1991).

52 *Breaking New Ground: Church Planting in the Church of England* (London: Church House Publishing, 1984); R. Hopkins, *Church Planting* (Nottingham: Grove Books, 1988); *Planting New Churches*, ed. R. Hopkins and T. Anderson (Guildford: Eagle Press, 1991); G. Lings, *New Ground in Church Planting* (Cambridge: Grove Books, 1994).

53 G. L. Carey, 'Church Planting, Ecclesiology and Mission', in *Planting New Churches*, ed. R. Hopkins and T. Anderson (Guildford: Eagle Press, 1991), p. 22.

54 Carey, 'Church Planting', pp. 27–8.

55 Carey, 'Church Planting', pp. 29–30.

56 J. Tiller, 'Preface', to G. E. D. Pytches and B. Skinner, *New Wineskins* (Guildford: Eagle Press, 1991).

church plants could be led by persons without Anglican convictions or commitment, and unwilling to accept Anglican ordination, or to subscribe in any way to the doctrine and discipline of the Church of England.[57] There should be no restraints upon such people preaching, conducting worship or performing rituals,[58] presumably propagating their own opinions rather than Christian doctrine as received and taught in the Church of England. This evident permissiveness is remarkably disconsonant with the repressive attitude the same people take towards those who differ with their views on such matters as homosexuality and the ordination of women. The evident assumption that the leaders of church plants exercising this freedom would necessarily be orthodox and conservative evangelicals is at the very least naïve. Once this freedom is granted, there can in reality be little if any restriction on the forms of worship practised, no control of the teaching delivered, or of the lifestyle advocated. The liberty claimed by certain evangelicals to establish communities of their kind wherever they will, could allow all manner of organisations to operate under the auspices of the Church of England, with the potential for cults, abuse, and scandal. If Anglican worship, doctrine, and discipline are regarded as dispensable, the question needs to be asked why it is proposed to establish such groups within the Church of England rather than independently.

It has been described as an "anomaly" that lay leaders are not authorized to preside at the eucharist in cell churches, and claimed that this will inevitably become the established practice in the near future.[59] On what basis established Anglican practice should be regarded as anomalous is not explained. The confidence, and even the aspiration, that these groupings will become normative in the Church of England is not shared by others committed to such initiatives.[60] When efforts are being made to proclaim the gospel and create communities into which "unchurched" people and families can be drawn, and there become more familiar with and absorb the values which the Church of England

---

57 Pytches and Skinner, *New Wineskins*, p. 24. Cf. A. M. Lord, *Spirit-Shaped Mission* (Milton Keynes: Paternoster Press, 2005).

58 Pytches and Skinner, *New Wineskins*, p. 16.

59 D. C. James, 'Cell Future', in *The Future of Ministry: Look Ahead 25 Years*, ed. G. Wakefield (Cambridge: Grove Books, 2004), pp. 20–21.

60 Cf. S. J. L. Croft, 'Serving, Sustaining, Connecting', in *The Future of the Parish System*, ed. S. J. L. Croft (London: Church House Publishing, 2006), pp. 75–90; R. Gamble, 'Doing Traditional Church Really Well', in *The Future of the Parish System*, ed. S. J. L. Croft (London: Church House Publishing, 2006), pp. 93–109.

upholds, and be drawn into its worship and corporate life, and these are proving effective, then there seems little justification in accommodating sectarian groups within the Church of England or any other Anglican body.

The church-planting programme has become quasi-institutionalized within the Church of England through the adoption by General Synod of *Mission-shaped Church* in 2004, and the subsequent establishment of an official structure to promote "fresh expressions of church". The general principle is that groups and activities would be organised, within the Church of England but not necessarily integrated within its parochial structures, and not bound by its doctrine and discipline, particularly in their worship. It is in this context, and without further theological or ecclesiological reflection, that lay eucharistic presidency is, at least implicitly, advocated: "New expressions of church may raise practical difficulties about authorized ministry, but, if they are to endure, they must celebrate the Eucharist."[61] The propriety of establishing "fresh expressions" without the pastoral oversight of a priest competent to teach sound Christian doctrine and administer the sacraments in a responsible fashion, and attend to the pastoral needs of people with little or no previous Christian involvement, is not even considered. The importance of these issues has been cogently argued, not from a hostile or reactionary Anglo-Catholic perspective, but from an unqualified commitment to effective evangelism and church planting, by the evangelical priest at that time leading the Fresh Expressions initiative:

> the health and well being of the Church is best served through the ordination of particular people to ... ministries of service and leadership within the community. The call to sustain and enable missionary communities, which is at the heart of the call to be a priest, cannot easily be separated from presiding at the Eucharist.[62]

The approach to church growth expounded in *Mission-Shaped Church* has been criticized as, *inter alia*, consumerist and postmodern.[63] Permissiveness and antinomianism in matters of church order, doctrine, and administration of the sacraments, are suggestive of a modern Western individualism, by no means confined to evangelicals, which is

---

61 *Mission-Shaped Church: Church Planting and Fresh Expressions of Church in a Changing Context* (London: Church House Publishing, 2004), p. 101.

62 Croft, 'Serving', p. 86.

63 J. M. Hull, *Mission-Shaped Church* (London: SCM Press, 2006); cf. Tiller, 'Preface' to Pytches and Skinner, *New Wineskins*.

potentially highly destructive of the Church, and of the people involved. Liturgical conformity and continuity give tacit expression in worship to the corporate nature of Christian identity. It would be extremely difficult for "fresh expressions" and innovative approaches to instil a sense of common identity beyond the immediate group. Where the eucharist is perceived as a private devotion, rather than as an act of the Church Universal, manifested in the gathered congregation, then it is fundamentally impoverished in every respect. The eucharistic theology, devoid of any ecclesiology, which recognizes no constraints on individual autonomy and self-expression, cannot inform or shape worship which can meaningfully be an act of the whole Church.[64] Where the Church of England is understood to exist only as a bureaucracy and fundraising mechanism to support the activities of those engaged in mission, and this mission is narrowly conceived as the conversion of individuals, rather than as building the Church, then the most that can be created is an amorphous and fissiparous entity, prone to schism and unable to nurture in the faith those brought into its fellowship.[65] Where Anglicanism is viewed as an enemy, mission under the auspices of the Church of England is likely to fail.

The "Fresh Expressions" initiative has, on its website[66] and in its publications,[67] reflected far greater consciousness of and commitment to the Anglican heritage, and is concerned as far as possible to ensure that "fresh expressions ... remain part of the Church of England as a whole and not spin off into their own denomination as has happened so often in the past".[68] While questions may be raised as to how integral a part of the Church of England, and how authentically Anglican, some of these groups are likely to be, the ecclesiological issues are among the "hard questions" currently being addressed.[69] In this context the anomalies likely to arise in the creation of "fresh expressions of church", and the nurture of those drawn into these groups, are considered, and while the dearth of eucharistic worship is lamented, the question of lay presidency

---

64   Cf. A. T. Hanson, *Church, Sacraments and Ministry* (London: Mowbrays, 1975), pp. 105–6.

65   Cf. P. D. L. Avis, *A Ministry Shaped by Mission* (London: T & T Clark, 2005).

66   www.freshexpressions.org.uk

67   S. J. L. Croft (ed.), *The Future of the Parish System* (London: Church House Publishing, 2006).

68   Croft, 'Serving', p. 77.

69   S. J. L. Croft (ed), *Mission-shaped Questions* (London: Church House Publishing, 2008).

is not raised.[70] The creation of "pioneer ministries", to which candidates may be ordained, as well as being recruited from parochial and other ministries within the wider Church, should enable the sacramental needs of the new communities to be met, if they are ordained or commissioned in sufficient numbers. This step should also ensure that the teaching delivered is in conformity with the doctrine of the Church of England, and pastoral care exercised to the standards expected of its clergy.[71]

Considerable steps have been taken in recent decades to make the worship of the Church of England more flexible and amenable to particular needs, and particularly to facilitate the introduction of hitherto unchurched people and families to Christian worship. Social and cultural grounds may well exist for making provision for further innovation and diversity for the purposes of mission, but where the intention is to establish groups inimical to Anglicanism, their presence within the Church of England and access to its resources cannot be justified. There is legally protected freedom of belief and association in the United Kingdom, and those who do not identify with the Anglican heritage are free to establish their own communities outside the Church of England. A "fresh expression" which does not identify with the Church catholic and universal, and with the Church of England and the wider Anglican Communion in particular, can, should, and probably inevitably will, either become yet another sect, or bifurcate and perish in the attempt.

The question of lay eucharistic presidency within a church-planting or "fresh expressions" context is fundamentally one of the nature of the communities being created. Where there is no community there can be no eucharist. Where a community is formed within the Church of England, however distinctive it may be in its patterns of worship and other aspects of its life, it is essential that it be conscious of its membership of a larger and wider Church, and committed to growing in union with the Church of which it is a part. This necessarily and inevitably entails accepting some of the discipline of the Church of England. There should be no question of the leadership in any such group being vested in a person who is not committed to being fully a part of the Church of England, and there can be no justification for any congregation to be without the ministry of a priest. The particular needs of new communities may be best served by clergy specially trained for

---

70   L. Urwin, 'What is the Role of Sacramental Ministry in Fresh Expressions of Church?', in S. J. L. Croft (ed.), *Mission shaped Questions*, (London: Church House Publishing, 2008), pp. 29–41.

71   Dioceses, Pastoral and Mission Measure 2007; cf. Croft, 'Serving', pp. 84–6.

this work, and pastoral oversight will certainly require particular skills and sensitivity, but no less commitment to or integration in the life of the wider Church. Particular liturgical skills and sensitivity, as well as some flexibility, will be needed in leading worship, including the celebration of the eucharist. The liturgical presidency exercised in such communities must surely be pastoral and priestly.

Conclusions

The specific proposals to authorize lay eucharistic presidency, within an Anglican ecclesiastical body, have been found to be theologically and pastorally inadequate, and premised upon questionable mission strategies. The argument from an Anglo-Catholic perspective depended upon too autocratic a model of episcopacy, but addressed substantially the same pastoral needs in essentially the same way as the variety of evangelical proposals considered. These have not emanated from traditional Anglican evangelicalism, which has preserved the essentials of catholic Christianity since the Reformation. Rather, they have emanated from a conservative Protestant evangelicalism, to which Catholic and Anglican tradition are considered at best incidental and disposable. However urgent and sincere the commitment to mission, without a robust Church with a clear sense of its identity before God and a pervading consciousness of its universal nature, and ministries of word and sacrament which give expression to these, there can be no viable community into which those reached by mission can be incorporated, sustained, and nurtured in their Christian lives.

While the particular arguments for introducing lay eucharistic presidency in different parts of the Anglican Communion have been found theologically inadequate and pastorally inappropriate, there remain to be considered in the next chapter a number of further theological issues relevant to the question, but not directly raised in any of the preceding cases.

7

Theological Arguments for Lay Presidency at the Eucharist

Some theological arguments for lay eucharistic presidency have been considered in previous chapters, where they have been applied in particular pastoral and missionary contexts. Those discussions will be repeated in this chapter only in so far as is necessary to give coherence to the arguments to be considered here. These arguments are not necessarily any less valid or forceful, but are also less directly related to the catholic and Anglican heritage of the Church of England, or to mission in the Anglican Communion.

Perhaps the strongest argument for lay presidency at the eucharist is that the validity of the sacrament depends not on the person who presides, but on the grace of God. The corollary, that any baptized Christian may therefore preside at the eucharist,[1] has all but unanimously been rejected by the Fathers and by almost all subsequent ecclesiastical authorities, in virtually all Christian traditions. The corollary depends on following through the logic of the argument in isolation from any consideration of the nature of the eucharist, any discussion as to whom the rite belongs under God, and any deliberation on the place of order in the life of the Church, and particularly in the celebration of the eucharist.[2] The discussion in this chapter will be concerned essentially with these issues.

Baptism and the Priesthood of all Christians
The eucharist is an act of the Church, and the Church in its terrestrial manifestation is constituted by all baptized Christians. That baptism is not merely a rite of initiation into membership of the Church, but also an induction into the priestly people of God, is increasingly recognized

---

1   A. Marriage, *The People of God* (London: Darton, Longman and Todd, 1995), p. 151; A. Smithson, 'Lay Presidency', *Theology* 101 (1998): 12–13; cf. I. Fraser, 'Liberating Faith', *ER* 44 (1982): 63.

2   Cf. A. E. Harvey, *Priest or President?* (London: SPCK, 1975), p. 31; B. T. Lloyd, *Lay Presidency at the Eucharist?* (Nottingham: Grove Books, 1977), pp. 7–8; L. Newbigin, 'Lay Presidency at the Eucharist', *Theology* 99 (1996): 369.

in Christian theology, and given verbal and often visual expression in contemporary liturgies. Not only do baptismal rites emphasize the priestly identity of all Christians, but so also do ordination rites. In Common Worship, the rite of baptism makes no more than a passing reference to a "royal priesthood" at the introductory bidding to the intercessions, and there are references to the duties of worship and service in the baptism and confirmation rites, and possibly priestly allusions in the provision for anointing. In the Common Worship Ordinal, there is greater emphasis on the royal priesthood of the Church, in the bishop's introduction to the rites for the ordination of deacons and priests, and in the opening paragraph of the prayer of ordination for all three orders. The ministry of bishops, presbyters, and deacons takes its place within the priesthood which is common to all Christians by virtue of their baptism, and this is a principle to which the Church of England at least is clearly committed in its liturgy.

We have noted that this priesthood is rooted in the New Testament, and is therefore an inalienable aspect of Christian identity. Passages in 1 Peter and Revelation,[3] considered above, refer to a corporate priestly identity, whose function certainly includes the worship of God, but does not entail a ritual or liturgical role for any individual member of that priesthood. The "priesthood of all believers", rooted in baptism, has accordingly never been understood to confer liturgical office on any or all Christians, even if it is the basis on which individuals may be called to particular forms of service, and constitutes the community from and in which they are called to ministry.[4] While conferring no office beyond the corporate priesthood of the baptized, this priesthood and membership of the people of God, the Body of Christ, has its own distinctive value, without which the particular, lay or ordained, ministries to which individual ·Christians are called would not be possible.[5] It is perhaps a reflection on the individualism of modern and postmodern Western culture, as well as of the negative connotations which the term "lay" has acquired in contemporary parlance, that the

---

3   1 Pet. 2.5, 9; Rev. 5.10.

4   Tertullian, *Exhortione Castitatis*; Luther, *Institutiones Ministeriae* 3; R. T. Beckwith, *Priesthood and sacraments* (Abingdon: Marsham Manor, 1964), p. 16; *Eucharistic Presidency: A Theological Statement by the House of Bishops of the General Synod* (London: Church House Publishing, 1997), p. 53; H. C. B. Green, *Lay Presidency at the Eucharist?* (London: Darton, Longman and Todd, 1994), p. 17.

5   Cf. S. K. Wood, 'Presbyteral Identity Within Parish Identity', in *Ordering the Baptismal Priesthood*, ed. S. K. Wood (Collegeville, IN: Liturgical Press, 2003), pp. 175–94; H. Küng, *Why Priests?* (London: Collins, 1971), esp. pp. 80–81.

corporate identity of the Christian priesthood has been neglected, and is often not readily appreciated in many parts of the Church today.

The fragmented and often fissiparous state of the Church poses further challenges, practical as much as theological, for any theology of ministry founded on baptism, at least within any ecclesiology concerned with the catholicity of the Church. That there is, and can only be, one baptism in Christ, despite the divided nature of the Church, is acknowledged in principle, both within the ecumenical community of the World Council of Churches, and in the official teaching of nearly all Christian denominations,[6] not least in the teaching of the Second Vatican Council on behalf of the Roman Catholic Church.[7] This has not overcome the deep and long-standing divisions within the Christian Church, and the plain fact is that the Church does not present a common or united image of itself to the world.

The claim that "any baptized Christian" can represent the catholicity of the Church is problematic, quite apart from the contingent claim that baptism confers and constitutes authority to preside at the eucharist.[8] This is not a question of the validity of baptism or of orders, but of whether, in the divided state of the Church, such a claim can be at all realistic. This concerns relationships within the Church, and between different denominations in a divided Church, and whether and how representation of Christ can be perceived and recognized in such a situation: "To preside is about representing Christ in a particular way, and it says something about the Eucharist being the heart of the whole Church, universal as well as local."[9] Acknowledgement of a common baptism does not mean that all Christians, or all Christian denominations, understand baptism in the same way, and this can in itself present something of a problem. In traditions in which believers' baptism is normative, and in principle entails unequivocal and informed adult commitment to the life and witness of the Church, baptism can

---

6   *Baptism, Eucharist and Ministry* (Geneva: WCC, 1982), Baptism IV C.15.

7   *Unitatis Redintegratio* 3.22–3.

8   T. Bradshaw, *The Olive Branch* (Carlisle: Paternoster Press, 1992), p. 195; A. L. Hargrave, *But Who Will Preside?* (Nottingham: Grove Books, 1990), p. 8.

9   K. W. Stevenson, *Do This: The Shape, Style and Meaning of the Eucharist* (Norwich: Canterbury Press, 2002), p. 86; cf. *The Theology of Ordination: A Report by the Faith and order Advisory Group of the Board for Mission and Unity* (London: Church Information Office, 1975), p. 55; G. W. Lathrop, *Holy Things* (Minneapolis, MN: Fortress Press, 1998), pp. 180–203; W. Temple, *Christus Veritas* (London: Macmillan, 1930), p. 163; J. Tiller, *A Strategy for the Church's Ministry* (London: Church Information Office, 1983), p. 121.

quite readily be associated with ministry, and this perhaps contributes to the acceptance of lay presidency at the eucharist in the Baptist and many Pentecostal traditions. On the other hand, where baptism has become an infancy rite, and is frequently administered without any commitment on the part of the parents to living out their own baptism in the worship and fellowship of the Church, or to nurturing their child in the faith and in the community of the local church, then the association of baptism with priesthood and ministry becomes, to all intents and purposes, very much more tenuous. Even where infant baptism is restricted to the children of committed and active members of the church, it remains problematic at what point a baptized Christian can consciously and meaningfully assume a representative role on behalf of Christ and the Church.

Baptism is the rite of initiation into the Church, and confers a common identity and a corporate priesthood on all Christian people, but does not make every individual Christian a priest in the sense of being a minister of the word and sacraments.[10] That which is common to all Christians does not enable any individual member of the Church to function as the representative of the entire Body, unless such a representative role is acknowledged, both by those represented and by those to whom representation is made. The task of representation of Christ and the Church needs to be considered further, but baptism and the corporate priesthood of all Christians cannot be the sole criterion of representation. Even were the reunification of the Church to be realized, baptism could not enable any individual to assume a representative role on behalf of the Church. If presidency involves representation of Christ and the Church, then baptism alone therefore cannot be the sole basis for authorization to preside at the eucharist.[11]

Representation of Christ

The Church, as the Body of Christ, corporately represents Christ as his visible and active presence in the world. Corporate entities act in and through designated representatives. Such representative persons embody the ethos and ideals of the corporate body they represent, in relating on behalf of that body both with its members and with the surrounding society. Given the dual nature of the Church, representation of the

---

10   Cf. J. Taylor, *Clerus Domini*, 5.9.
11   Cf. D. J. Davies, 'Some Historical and Theological Arguments Against', in *Lay Presidency at the Eucharist?* ed. B. T. Lloyd (Bramcote: Grove Books, 1977), p. 24; Newbigin, 'Lay Presidency'.

terrestrial community to God and to the world is inextricably bound with representation of God to the Church and to the world.

In catholic tradition and in Anglican ecclesiology, the episcopate embodies the fullest representation of Christ, both in the leadership and pastoral oversight of the Church, and in embodying it in relations with the surrounding society. It is accordingly upon bishops that the primary responsibility for liturgical acts on behalf of the Church is bestowed.[12] This includes both the ministry of the word and exposition of Christian doctrine, and the administration of the sacraments, and in particular baptism, the eucharist, and orders. It is a long-established practice that much of this responsibility is delegated to the college of presbyters, particularly in the subsidiary communities within the diocese in which an individual presbyter shares with the bishop the cure of souls. While the priest has become the usual, but not the normative, administrator of baptism, the administration of confirmation is reserved to the bishop. While confirmation may be a lesser and subsidiary rite to baptism, and is accordingly argued not to require the ministry of the bishop, administration by the bishop nonetheless is significant in that it powerfully demonstrates that those confirmed are committing themselves to, and being commissioned for, witness and ministry as lay members of the Church universal.

The bishop is similarly the normative president at the eucharist, and other priests would not normally preside when the bishop is present. In sharing the cure of souls in a parish, the incumbent exercises a delegated authority received from the bishop, which certainly includes the ministry of word, sacraments, and pastoral care. This commissioning for ministry in a particular place, in a distinctive relationship with the bishop, cannot be equated with the authority to preside at the eucharist which presbyters receive at ordination, even though the exercise of presbyteral ministry normally takes place under the authority of the bishop. Nevertheless, what has become something of a truism in Anglican theology, that the authority to represent Christ and the Church universal through presiding at the eucharist is a function of delegation by the bishop, is something of an overstatement.[13] Monarchical episcopacy is

---

12 P. D. L. Avis, *A Ministry Shaped by Mission* (London: T & T Clark, 2005), p. 92. Cf. F. C. Synge, 'The Challenge of the Frontiers', in *Anglican Congress 1963* (Toronto: Editorial Committee, 1963), pp. 155–64.

13 R. Hooker, *Of the Lawes of Ecclesiastical Polity*, 5.78, 80; Avis, *Ministry*, p. 82; Bradshaw, *Olive Branch*, p. 195; C. J. Cocksworth, *Evangelical Eucharistic Thought in the Church of England* (Cambridge: Cambridge University Press, 1993), pp. 170, 223–4; B. Cooke, *Ministry to Word and Sacraments* (Philadelphia, PA:

not of the essence of Christianity; corporate life as the Body of Christ is. The bishop acts within a college of presbyters, all of whom have been commissioned for ministry of the word and sacraments. In Anglicanism this commissioning takes place through ordination by the bishop, acting as a representative, together with the gathered congregation, of the universal Church. To claim that the bishop could or should delegate to deacons or lay people the function of presiding at the eucharist, on the same basis as he or she delegates that function to presbyters,[14] is to misconstrue the nature both of episcopacy and of the presbyterate. Licensing of clergy by the bishop is not an alternative to, or substitute for, ordination, but is a commission to exercise the authority conferred at ordination in a particular place, and in a particular relationship with the bishop and other clergy of the diocese and pastoral charge.

This is not to claim that episcopal ordination is essential to salvation, or to grace being received through the sacraments. It is a matter of how the corporate life of the Church is sustained, in the gathered congregation in which the eucharist is celebrated, but also in the local church embodied in the diocese, and in the universal Church, whose presence is invoked in every celebration. Anglicanism has sustained these relationships through ensuring that the eucharist is presided over by a priest who not merely represents Christ by virtue of his or her baptism, but embodies the apostolic ministry sustained in the Catholic Church through the sacrament of orders, and is explicitly authorized to act on behalf of the universal Church in the ministry of word and sacraments, and in conscious communion with the wider Church. This is not to deny that grace would be received through a sacramental act administered by a layperson, or in an ecclesial body in which the ministry is not conceived or constituted on the same basis. But it is to suggest that any loosening of the bonds which the ordained ministry

---

Fortress Press, 1976), pp. 643–5; G. Dix, *The Shape of the Liturgy* (London: Dacre, 1945), p. 270; P. McPartlan, *Sacrament of Salvation* (Edinburgh: T & T Clark, 1995); R. C. Moberly, *Ministerial Priesthood* (London: SPCK, 1969), pp. 258–61; cf. R. P. Greenwood, *Transforming Priesthood* (London: SPCK, 1994), pp. 155–79; Lloyd, *Lay Presidency?*, pp. 8–9; Newbigin, 'Lay Presidency', pp. 369–70; K. Rahner, *Bishops* (London: Burns and Oates, 1964); M. Thurian, *Priesthood and Ministry* (London: Mowbrays, 1983), pp. 122–3; Tiller, *Strategy*, p. 121.

14 Cf. W. H. Griffith Thomas, *The Principles of Theology* (London: Vine, 1930), pp. 36–7; H. Küng, *The Church* (London: Burns and Oates, 1968), pp. 439–43; T. Pitt, *At the Head of the Table, or Under the Carpet?* (York: Dean and Chapter of York, 1994), p. 12; Synge, 'Challenge'.

embodies may not be conducive to the unity or the mission of the Church.[15] Furthermore, where a sacramental act is performed by one not commissioned so to do on behalf of the Church, this could violate the unity of the Church, divide the community, and compromise its witness.

That ordination has a particular significance for representation of Christ is a long-established, if not always well-defined, principle of Anglican theology of ministry, reflected in the Ordinal.[16] Divine commission and representation of the Church are inextricably linked, but the priest is not a mediator or broker upon whose ritual functions and observances the laity depend for their access to God, still less for their salvation. "[T]he ministerial priest is but the divinely appointed and empowered organ of the whole priestly body",[17] and cannot represent Christ unless at the same time representing the Church, the Body of Christ. At ordination the priest receives a commission and authority conferred by God, through the agency of the bishop and the gathered congregation, representing Christ and the universal Church. This authority does not derive from the local community, or even from the universal Church, but from God, to be exercised in and on behalf of the local community and the universal Church.[18] In the eucharist the priest forms a link between the gathered community and the universal Church, not merely in its terrestrial manifestation but in its mystical essence as the Body of Christ, transcending space and time. "Ordained Presidency is vital, for it symbolizes the unity of each eucharist with

---

15 Temple, *Christus Veritas*, p. 163; pace, Marriage, *People*, p. 151.

16 Hooker, *Laws*, 5.77; F. D. Maurice, *The Kingdom of Christ* (London: Rivington, 1842), pp. 298–300; H. Aldenhoven, 'Presidency at the Eucharist in the Context of the Theology of Icons', *ATR* 84 (2002): 705; M. D. Chapman, 'Preparing for Judgement', *Modern Believing* 37 (1996): 10–16; Cooke, *Ministry*, pp. 643–5; A. A. K. Graham, 'Should the Ordained Ministry Now Disappear'? in *The Sacred Ministry*, ed. G. R. Dunstan (London: SPCK, 1970), pp. 51–2; G. Guiver, 'The Priest as Focus', in *Priests in a People's Church*, ed. G. Guiver (London: SPCK, 2001), pp. 127–38; R. P. C. Hanson, *Christian Priesthood Examined* (Guildford: Lutterworth, 1979), pp. 99–102; D. W. Hardy, *Finding the Church* (London: SCM Press, 2001), p. 93; J.-M. R. Tillard, *Church of Churches* (Collegeville, Liturgical, 1992), pp. 190–97; H. M. Wybrew, *Called to Be Priests* (Oxford: SLG Press, 1989), p. 5.

17 C. Gore, *The Body of Christ* (London: John Murray, 1901), p. 271; cf. Moberly, *Priesthood*, p. 68.

18 Taylor, *Clerus Domini*, 6.7; 7.2; A. A. K. Graham, 'Postscript', in *Priesthood Here and Now*, ed. M. Bowering (Newcastle: Diocese of Newcastle, 1994), pp. 179–81; D. N. Power, *Ministers of Christ and His Church* (London: Geoffrey Chapman, 1969), p. 166; cf. Moberly, *Priesthood*, pp. 99–125.

others that are taking place, have taken place, and will take place – in the communion of saints."[19]

Ordination does not confer magical power of any kind. Christ's death can be recalled in a gathered community of Christians whether or not there is a bishop or presbyter present. The sacramental use of bread and wine, and their ritual, spiritual but essentially symbolic, transformation, are not an exercise of supernatural power, but of Christ's presence in and with those gathered in his name. The dominical injunction to "Do this in remembrance of me"[20] is obeyed, and Christ's promise to be present where two or three are gathered in his name[21] is fulfilled. As a vehicle and sacrament of salvation, therefore, the eucharist can be celebrated without an ordained priest, and the tradition at least as ancient as Tertullian, considered above, cannot be controverted. However, this does not mean that a lay person could appropriately be the normative president at the eucharist, as Tertullian was equally clear.[22] The role of the priest in the eucharist represents and embodies aspects of the mystery of salvation which would not otherwise be apparent, and without which the celebration would be denuded of something of its significance; not necessarily in terms of communion with God, but certainly in terms of communion with the universal Church. As a symbol of the unity of the Church, and its continuity through the ages of Christian history, the priest ordained in the apostolic succession represents something of the essential nature of the Church, vital to Anglican identity, which is lacking where the unity and universality of the Church are not embodied.

The Argument from Clinical Baptism

Baptism, as the rite of initiation into the Church, and the sacrament of dying and rising with Christ,[23] came from ancient times to be regarded as essential to human salvation. It is not necessary to discuss whether or not babies and children were baptized in the apostolic Church, or at what stage infant baptism became normative, still less to assume that ancient Christian practice was uniform.[24] Nor do we need to consider

---

19   Stevenson, *Do This*, p. 6.

20   Lk. 22.19; 1 Cor. 11.24, 25.

21   Mt. 18.20.

22   *Ex. cast.* 7.3–4.

23   Rom. 6.3-4; Col. 2.12.

24   G. R. Beasley-Murray, *Baptism in the New Testament* (Exeter: Paternoster Press, 1962); J. Jeremias, *Infant Baptism in the First Four Centuries* (London: SCM Press, 1960); *The Origins of Infant Baptism* (London: SCM Press, 1963); K. Aland, *Did*

the emergence of death-bed baptism, a practice whereby adult converts postponed their baptism until they believed their death was imminent, as a means to guarantee their salvation through baptism, while minimising the risk of sin after baptism, and the judgement they might thereby incur. The theology behind this may be in every respect questionable, but the idea nonetheless became established that baptism ought to be administered, as a matter of urgency, to persons associated with the Church who were in imminent danger of death.

With high infant mortality rates in ancient society, and indeed until very recently in modern society, newborn babies were with good reason regarded as being in danger of imminent death. It was therefore considered imperative that baptism not be deferred until Easter, or whatever other date in the liturgical calendar may have been considered appropriate, but be administered as soon as possible after birth, so that if the baby died his or her salvation would nonetheless be assured. It is of course entirely possible that many an unfortunate infant died as a direct or indirect consequence of being submerged in cold water on a winter's day, or for that matter in tepid and infested water in other climatic conditions, but it was presumably of considerable comfort to their families that they had died baptized, and accordingly assured of salvation. Before ridiculing the religiosity which informed this practice, we should take cognisance of the perverted and insidious belief that babies who died unbaptized would inevitably be damned, propagated by no less a figure of Western Christian history than Augustine of Hippo: *Infantes non baptizati ... damnantur*, "Infants who are not baptized ... are damned."[25] It is consequently hardly surprising that baptism came to be hastened, as insurance against damnation rather than as governing life in the Church and in the world.

The sense of urgency which accompanied and followed childbirth during the medieval period was such that often baptism was not deferred until the next Sunday or saint's day, or, at times, even until the parish priest could be called upon to administer the rite. If a priest were not immediately available to baptize the child, then very often the rite would be administered by the midwife, in the home rather than at the font in the parish church. There was ancient provision for baptism to be conducted by a lay Christian, if there were no priest available and the

---

the *Early Church Baptise Infants?* (London: SCM Press, 1963); D. F. Wright, *What has Infant Baptism done to Baptism?* (Aldershot: Ashgate, 2005).

25 *De peccatorum meritis*, 16.21; *Enchiridion* 93; cf. *Epistula* 116.16.

candidate was in danger of dying unbaptized.[26] There were those authorities, however, who objected to the rite's being administered by women,[27] while others allowed for non-Christian "Jews or pagans" to administer the baptism, provided they used the formula of the Catholic Church.[28] Emergency or clinical baptism of course diminished the rite, not so much because it was conducted by a layperson, but because the essential aspect of incorporation into the Church was not given liturgical expression, unless the child survived and was subsequently brought to the church. What originated as an emergency provision, however well conceived or otherwise, seems to have become not the exception when a life was in danger but a widespread general practice. How common the practice was is impossible to determine, but the *Sarum Manual* included what were almost certainly not the only set of instructions for administration of emergency baptism.[29] Concern for salvation in the afterlife superseded initiation into the terrestrial Church, and a perfunctory rite in a domestic setting often replaced the public liturgy of baptism.

Despite significant changes in sacramental theology introduced at the Reformation, baptism by lay people, when the life of an unbaptized person was deemed to be in peril, continued to be authorized in the Church of England, with the 1549 edition of the Book of Common Prayer including rubrics directing how the rite should be administered. These rubrics were not included in the 1552 or 1559 editions, but midwives continued to be licensed to baptize during the reign of Elizabeth I.[30] Baptism by lay men and women is defended by Hooker, but not as a guarantee of salvation for those who would otherwise die unbaptized.[31] Baptism by lay people was forbidden by James I in 1604, and this prohibition remained in force through the ecclesiastical vicissitudes of the ensuing decades.[32] In the Book of Common Prayer the rubrics for the Publick baptism of Infants direct that the rite be administered by a priest, but in the rite of Private Baptism of Children

26 Augustine, *Ep.* 9.44; Tertullian, *Bapt.* 17.2.

27 Tertullian, *Virg.*; Epiphanius, *Pan.* 1,2.

28 Thomas Aquinas, *Summa* 3a.67.5.

29 J. D. C. Fisher, *Christian Initiation* (London: SPCK, 1965), pp. 175–77.

30 F. Procter and W. H. Frere, *A New History of the Book of Common Prayer* (London: Macmillan, 1951), pp. 585–7; B. D. Spinks, *Sacraments, Ceremonies and the Stuart Divines* (Aldershot: Ashgate, 2002), pp. 34–35.

31 *Laws*, 5.48–49; 60–62.

32 Cf. Procter and Frere, *Book of Common Prayer*, pp. 585–88; Spinks, *Sacraments*, pp. 34–5.

reference is made to a "lawful Minister" if the curate is not available. Such lawful minister is undoubtedly a deacon or priest, but baptism administered by a lay person, however unlawful or irregular, continued to be recognized as valid, both legally and liturgically.[33] This ambivalence is reflected also by Jeremy Taylor, who argued that the legal position was indeterminate, but "since the keys of the kingdom of heaven be most notoriously and signally used in baptism ... it may be of ill consequence to let them be usurped by hands to whom they were not consigned".[34] By this he means that anyone not ordained to the apostolic ministry should not normally be permitted to administer baptism, but he stops short of proscribing the practice entirely.

One of the revisions included in the proposed Prayer Book of 1928 was provision for a lay person to baptize in an emergency, should no "lawful Minister" be available. This must be taken to reflect the mind and will of the Church of England, even if not of parliament, during the lengthy process of revision and the abortive legislative procedures which followed, and indeed during subsequent decades. The Alternative Service Book and Common Worship have made unambiguous provision for lay people to baptize in an emergency where there is no priest or deacon available, but also emphasize that the salvation of the person in danger of death would not be contingent upon baptism. Emergency baptism is a pastoral provision for the care of the family during a time of extreme stress, and not a theological or liturgical prerequisite to salvation, but only to participation in the terrestrial life of the Church.

It has been argued that clinical baptism constitutes a precedent for lay presidency at the eucharist, and it is considered inconsistent that administration of one sacrament by lay people be permitted and the other prohibited.[35] The principle of establishing a theological precedent on the basis of a derived rite, whose continuation is motivated by pastoral compassion rather than theological or liturgical necessity, must be questionable. As has been observed previously, the removal of liturgical functions from the laity, as of private and extra-liturgical devotions, was the product of the Reformed tradition, with its ethos of the supremacy of the ministry of the word. Any correlation between

---

33   Procter and Frere, *Book of Common Prayer*, pp. 592–3.

34   *Clerus Domini*, 4.14.

35   Bradshaw, *Olive Branch*, pp. 195; Küng, *Church*, pp. 443; A. Rowthorn, *The Liberation of the Laity* (Wilton, CT: Morehouse–Barlow, 1986), p. 126; Thurian, *Priesthood*, p. 124.

baptism and the eucharist, and the authority to administer these rites on behalf of the Church, needs to be more carefully considered.

While the dominical injunction to baptize is in the gospels directed to the apostles,[36] there is no suggestion anywhere in the New Testament that its administration was ever restricted to them. On the contrary, there is no explicit account in Acts of any of the Twelve administering baptism. Whatever ambivalence may be reflected in the account of the apostles' sending Peter and John to Samaria to follow up the mission of Philip (Acts 8.4-8, 14-17), the reception of the Holy Spirit by the converts upon whom the apostles imposed their hands does not invalidate the baptism administered by Philip. There is no suggestion that Philip's subsequent baptism of the Ethiopian official (Acts 8.27-39) was in any way deficient. Philip had, in any event, been set apart for ministry along with Stephen and others (Acts 6.1–6), albeit not the same ministry as the apostles exercised.

In Acts 10.23-48 Peter preaches to the centurion Cornelius and the gathered members of his household, at the conclusion of which the Holy Spirit descends upon them. Peter accordingly directs that those who have received the Spirit be baptized, but does not baptize them himself. This suggests that the actual baptism was carried out by subordinates, who immersed the converts on Peter's instructions. As well perhaps as enabling women to be baptized by women, this arrangement would have preserved Peter's dignity as he oversaw the rite. This may reflect a more widespread process, whereby apostles and other principal missionaries remained somewhat aloof from the mechanical processes of baptism, but would nevertheless have retained oversight of and responsibility for the administration of the rites (cf. Acts 2.38-41).

A similar custom may lie behind Paul's claim that he did not personally baptize many of the Corinthian Christians (1 Cor. 1.13-17). However widely this passage may have come to be understood as demonstrating the superiority of proclamation of the word to administration of the sacraments, this is not Paul's purpose in the text. While he administered relatively few baptisms in Corinth, these are conspicuously those of prominent householders and their families: Crispus, Gaius, and Stephanas. This does not imply that Paul was not responsible for the baptism of other converts, administered by subordinates, such as Aquila and Priscilla, Silas and Timothy, during his mission to Corinth. Perhaps he condescended to baptize personally

---

36   Mt. 28.16-19; Mk 16.14-16. Cf. G. Wingren, *Gospel and Church* (Edinburgh: Oliver and Boyd, 1964), p. 13.

people of potential usefulness to the furtherance of his mission, but by the time he wrote 1 Corinthians he may regret having done this. Paul is not concerned with the priority of proclaiming the gospel, so much as with distancing himself from the divisions which had surfaced in the church.

However the portrayal of Peter and Paul be interpreted, the custom clearly evolved at an early date of bishops supervising the baptism of initiates into the Church, while deacons and presbyters immersed the initiates and came also to administer some of the subsidiary rites, such as anointing and clothing. This pattern is attested as early as Justin Martyr, in a passage we have considered above,[37] and is described in considerable detail in the *Apostolic Tradition* 19–21 and related literature. Delegation by the bishop is quite evident in the extant baptism rites of the ancient Church, but equally clear is the oversight by the bishop of the entire initiation process.[38]

The basis for comparison between baptism and the eucharist, other than that both are sacraments of the Church, inaugurated by Jesus Christ in the gospels, and which, in most but not all ancient and modern liturgies involve the invocation of supernatural power over the elements and their human recipients, is unclear. The principle that "No unbaptized person should be left to die while desiring baptism but beyond the reach of an ordained minister",[39] does not extend to the eucharist, as this is not an initiatory rite. However comforting a last eucharist or Viaticum might be, this would not change the status of the recipient in relation to the Church, and has never been understood to determine salvation or damnation. The eucharist is about sustaining the continuing life and witness of the Church and of individual Christians in the world, and as such is not analogous to baptism. Regular eucharistic celebration in Christian communities is routine, and not in itself an emergency. Even if the absence of a priest may be occasioned by an emergency, a single occasion on which a congregation is unable to celebrate the eucharist does not constitute an emergency, even if it is a deprivation. While the routine separation of a gathered Christian community from the ministry of a priest would be an issue to be

---

37   *1 Apologia* 61.

38   A. Kavanagh, *Confirmation* (New York, NY: Pueblo, 1988); B. D. Spinks, *Early and Medieval Rituals and Theologies of Baptism*; *Reformation and Modern Rituals and Theologies of Baptism* (Aldershot: Ashgate, 2006).

39   *Eucharistic Presidency*, p. 57; cf. Davies, 'Historical and Theological Arguments', p. 25.

addressed, it is not comparable with the pastoral need to admit a dying person to the Church through baptism.

The rubrics in *Common Worship Initiation Services* authorising lay people, including Readers, to baptize in an emergency, require that the rite be completed, liturgically if not sacramentally, by registering the baptism and, should the baptisand live, presenting him/her to the priest and congregation for incorporation into the Church. In this prescription Common Worship stands fully in continuity with the Book of Common Prayer. A lay person who administers baptism is required to account for this to the parish priest, not only as a matter of courtesy or liturgical correctness, but to ensure that appropriate pastoral care is offered to the affected family, and in recognition that baptism is an act of the Church. The bishop, and in his absence the priest, is the normative officiant of baptism, irrespective of who administers the rite in any particular circumstances.

Ecclesiastical Authority and Spiritual Power

In traditional societies ritual function is often if not always translated into social power, the role of mediating between the community and its deities, harnessing benevolent supernatural power on its behalf, and opposing the machinations of malevolent powers, all contributing to the prestige and influence of the priest or shaman.[40] Fear of supernatural power translates into fear of the person perceived to wield or control it, and his or her power in the community – or expulsion from it. It would be naïve to imagine that such beliefs and cosmology have had no part in shaping Christian doctrine, piety, and liturgy.[41] We do not need to judge the piety and devotions of our forebears in the faith, but merely to recognize that we live in a very different world to theirs, and the modern Western intelligentsia at least has a very different approach to religious belief and practice. Nevertheless, the Church needs to reflect theologically upon how the power of God relates to its liturgical and spiritual life, and to the ministry of its clergy.

---

40 E. Durkheim, *The Elementary Forms of Religious Life* (London: Allen and Unwin, 1964); G. van der Leeuw, *Religion in Essence and Manifestation* (London: Allen and Unwin, 1964); I. M. Lewis, *Ecstatic Religion* (London: Routledge, 1989); I. M. Lewis, *Religion in Context: Cults and Charisma* (Cambridge: Cambridge University Press, 1986).

41 H.-J. Klauck, *Magic and Paganism in Early Christianity* (Minneapolis, MN: Fortress Press, 2003); R. E. de Maris, *The New Testament in Its Ritual World* (London: Routledge, 2008).

It is perhaps a reflection of the superficially deritualized nature of modern Western cultures, or rather the perceived lack of meaning and power in ritual, that social control is thought possible without maintaining liturgical hegemony. Where Protestantism and secularism have diminished the intercessory and representative role of the ministry, and the dependence of the laity on the ritual actions of the clergy, it may be possible for rites denuded of their power to be delegated or even surrendered to lay people without incurring any corresponding loss of authority in the community.

We have noted in the preceding discussion that, in the diocese of Sydney, the Archbishop expects to retain absolute authority in doctrine and discipline, and to rule the diocese through the clergy, while at the same time handing over the liturgical functions of the priests to selected lay people. Authority is vested in and founded upon the proclamation and exposition of the word, and is perceived to require no counterpart in the corporate life and worship of the communities ruled. In the less Westernized context of South America, we observed that proponents of lay presidency at the eucharist were more conscious of the social function of ritual and the authority wielded by its functionaries, and were accordingly more cautious in their proposals. The approach proposed was to demystify the eucharist, at least partly through delegating to the lay leadership of communities the authority to preside at its celebration, thereby creating a very different liturgical experience to that to which their converts had been accustomed in the Roman Catholic Church. An absence of dedicated buildings, consecrated vessels, and other liturgical objects could similarly have contributed to altering the religious experience of the worshippers. The likelihood would have been, either that lay eucharistic presidents remote from episcopal and presbyteral oversight would rapidly have acquired the aura, as would the rites they administered and the elements they handled, or that alternative outlets for magic and superstition would have been found if they failed to do so.

In the case of "fresh expressions" of church, the variety makes generalization impossible, but there may nonetheless be common elements. Both the superficially deritualized culture of contemporary Western society and the disaffection with the established patterns of Christian worship (to which it has become fashionable to pander in the Church of England) which gives rise to such phenomena, seem very often to generate an alternative ritual system, in which different cultic objects and practices are used alongside or in place of traditional symbols. Consumerism tends to locate meaning in the individual participant and the connection he or she makes with his or her chosen sense of deity, rather than in corporate life. Accepting the ministry of a priest, or even a lay president, for a celebration of the eucharist may therefore represent something of a compromise. Ironically, this may lead to a resurgence of beliefs and cultic practices more primitive, and more superstitious, than those which have been rejected or marginalized.

It is argued by some proponents of lay presidency that ordination acknowledges rather than confers spiritual gifts and does not confer magical powers.[42] Whether any Christian before the Enlightenment would have believed this with any conviction, however, is open to question. The Church has always maintained a distinction between mantic or magical power, such as perceived to be at work in shamans, and authority conferred on clergy to undertake ritual, teaching, and pastoral functions on behalf of the community. This may have had as much to do with maintaining difference from pagan cults as it did with the ancient Christian understanding of supernatural power, but the Church nonetheless inherited from Judaism unequivocal belief in the sovereignty of God. Manipulation of God through ritual was therefore, theoretically at least, not an option open to any Christian, however widespread such practices may have been in Graeco-Roman paganism. This does not mean that the celebration of the eucharist, or of baptism, or of orders, was without any counterpart in divine presence or action in the community, but the power of liturgical functionaries was moderated by this doctrine. A ritual such as ordination functions as a rite of passage, from one status and role in the community to another. However much the decision to ordain is founded upon discernment of particular gifts in the candidate, the reality of God's action in the rite is not to be ignored either.

However alien to educated modern minds this may be, the continuing prevalence of such religiosity in many parts of the world today cannot be ignored. Whether it is entirely absent from modern and postmodern Western societies, must also be questioned in the light of the growth of religious movements, Christian and otherwise, which propound quite explicit notions of personalized spiritual power, possession, and the use of ritual to engage with benevolent and malevolent spiritual forces. Bourgeois rationalism, whether in the form of secularism or of evangelical fundamentalism, may therefore be a declining minority worldview even in modern Western societies. The credibility of

---

42 Griffith Thomas, *Principles*, pp. 323–4; Marriage, *People*, p. 182; cf. K. Rahner, *Theological Investigations*, 19 (London: Burns and Oates, 1983), p. 67.

Christian witness depends on teaching which relates popular religiosity to the liturgical life of the Church, and does so in a theologically coherent manner. This requires that the social and theological significance of Christian rituals be taken seriously.

Few in the modern, developed, world would dispute that ordination does not confer supernatural powers, and we have noted that ancient catholic tradition is very careful to distinguish the ritual life of the Church from magic. The Ordinal is nonetheless explicit in conferring authority in and on behalf of the Church, as well as invoking the Holy Spirit for the office and work of a priest.[43] However symbolic the invocation of the Spirit may be,[44] the liturgical rite is significant for defining and giving meaning to the life of the gathered community, as well as those who serve as bishop, presbyter, and deacon within and on behalf of the Church. The liturgical and sacramental ministry of the bishop, acting collegially with the presbyters and the gathered congregation in the name of God and of the universal Church, is categorically different to the, essentially secular, legal process of issuing a licence. Even where a commissioning rite for licensing lay ministers is administered by or on behalf of the bishop, this is fundamentally different to ordination, as has been recognized at least since the time of the *Apostolic Tradition*. To advocate a legal transaction as a substitute for the sacramental liturgy of the Church[45] is to profane the ministry both of the bishop and of the lay person so authorized to preside over the gathered congregation in the celebration of the eucharist.[46] Furthermore, those ordained to the priesthood, as to the diaconate and the episcopate, thereby enter a new relationship, with the community they serve, but also with their fellow deacons, priests, or bishops, and especially with the presbyteral and episcopal colleges which they join, with the universal Church, and, in the case of deacons and priests, with their bishop. Ordination is a rite of passage, directly relevant to the ministry to be exercised, and it is entirely appropriate that empowerment by the Holy Spirit for this ministry be invoked in the rite.[47] Correspondingly, it would

---

43   Cf. Hooker, *Laws*, 5.77.8.

44   Cf. Griffith Thomas, *Principles*, pp. 316–17, 323–4.

45   Marriage, *People*, p. 152; J. Pryor, 'Lay Presidency and the Ordained Ministry Today', *St Mark's Review* 138 (1989): 17.

46   P. Gibson, 'The Presidency of the Liturgy', in *A Kingdom of Priests*, ed. T. J. Talley (Nottingham: Grove Books, 1988), p. 35.

47   R. R. Gaillardetz, 'The Ecclesiological Foundations of Ministry Within an ordered Communion', in *ordering the baptismal Priesthood*, ed. S. K. Wood

seem inappropriate that any person should be authorized or invited to assume particular functions in the community, without first entering those relationships, before the Church, through the bishop, college of presbyters, and gathered congregation, invokes the Holy Spirit upon him or her for the ministry to which he or she is called.

Ministry and Patriarchy

How the Church relates to the society of which its members are a part may be intractably problematic.[48] That the Christian Church emerged in a highly stratified and patriarchal society, and that this impacted very directly on its growth, and also on the patterns of worship and ministry which took shape during the early centuries, is scarcely to be denied. This is most evident in the exclusively male ordained ministry which characterized the Catholic Church until the middle of the twentieth century, and which continues to be defended in many Anglican provinces, as well as in the official teaching of the Roman Catholic Church, and to be presupposed without discussion in the Eastern and Oriental Orthodox Churches. Irrespective of whether the emphasis placed on the role of women in the ministry of Jesus,[49] and in leadership roles in the Early Church,[50] is always historically sound, historical reconstruction alone cannot resolve the issue for the life of the Church today.[51] The Church today needs to take responsibility for reflecting theologically on its heritage, and on how it relates to the cultures of the societies in which it has evolved and in which it lives and bears witness to Christ today.

Issues to do with patriarchy cannot be reduced to questions concerning the role of women in the ministry of the Church, even if some feminists saw potential in lay presidency at the eucharist as a

---

(Collegeville, IN: Liturgical, 2003), p. 40; J. D. Zizioulas, *Being as Communion* (New York, NY: St Vladimir, 1985), pp. 214–15.

48   Cf. H. R. Niebuhr, *Christ and Culture* (New York, NY: Harper and Row, 1951).

49   S. R. Kraemer and M. R. D'Angelo (eds), *Women and Christian Origins* (Oxford: Oxford University Press, 1999); E. Moltmann-Wendel, *The Women around Jesus* (New York, NY: Crossroad, 1986); E. Schüssler Fiorenza, *In Memory of Her* (London: SCM Press, 1983).

50   Rom. 16: K. E. Corley, *Private Women, Public Meals* (Peabody, MA: Hendrickson, 1993); W. Cotter, 'Women's Authority Roles in Paul's Churches', *NovT* 36 (1994): 350–72; S. Heine, *Women and Early Christianity* (London: SCM Press, 1987); Kraemer and A'Angelo, *Women*; Schüssler Fiorenza, *In Memory*; K. J. Torjesen, *When Women were Priests* (San Francisco, CA: Harper, 1993).

51   N. H. Taylor, 'Paul for Today', *Listening* 32:1 (1997): 22–38.

vehicle for declericalizing a patriarchal Church.[52] The whole question of whether order, in the sense of structured and authoritative ministries, is essential to the nature of the Church, needs to be considered. Where the abolition of the ordained ministry has been proposed within Anglicanism,[53] this has not been to do with equality between men and women, but with the eradication of structures deemed to be unattested in the New Testament, and the pursuit of a phantom idyll of egalitarian collectivism in the Early Church, in which no correlation existed between pastoral and liturgical roles in the community. That such reconstructions are historically unsound in every respect has been demonstrated in earlier chapters, and, furthermore, those who advocate such positions are not necessarily uncommitted to the principle of male headship.[54] We have noted also what is at the very least a common perception, that there is in the diocese of Sydney a perverse correlation between advocacy of lay administration of holy communion, and rejection of the ordination of women to the presbyterate, or to use the terminology of the Book of Common Prayer, the priesthood.

While modern reaction against authoritarianism and patriarchy are identified as contributing to the declining status of the clergy, and challenges to their prerogatives in Christian life and worship,[55] it has not been only on feminist, socialist, or other egalitarian premises that the case for lay presidency at the eucharist has been argued. Ironically, perhaps, the case has also been argued on what are essentially patriarchal grounds:

> [T]hat heads of families and rulers of nations should have special status in the worship of God is a feature of human society almost everywhere except in the Christian Church; and the barriers to the free integration of the natural order into God's kingdom can hardly be lowered, much less done away, until the representatives of the former are admitted into the heart of Man's relationship with God. And this means not simply a seat on church councils but the right to perform certain offices, such as presiding at the Eucharist, and teaching, which are at present confined to 'professional' ministers.[56]

---

52   M. Furlong, in *The Tablet*, 26 March 1994: 384.

53   J. Goldingay, *Authority and Ministry* (Nottingham: Grove Books, 1976), p. 24.

54   This position would be well represented among conservative evangelicals within the Church of England, including members of Reform and the Church Society.

55   Graham, 'Ordained Ministry', pp. 45–7.

56   J. A. Baker, *The Foolishness of God* (London: Darton, Longman and Todd, 1970), pp. 352–3.

Notwithstanding the way patriarchal household structures shaped patterns of ecclesiastical governance and liturgical office in the ancient Church,[57] the uncritical sanctification of patriarchal structures, in the family as elsewhere in society, would be contrary to the emancipatory emphasis of much recent theology.[58] While crowned and anointed monarchs have, since Constantine, exercised a not always benign oversight of the Church within their realms, Catholic tradition has nonetheless consistently distinguished between the temporal oversight of the Christian sovereign and the liturgical ministry of bishops and priests. This separation between the Crown and the ministry of word and sacraments is articulated by Hooker.[59] The same separation between king and cult is attested in the Old Testament, particularly in the deuteronomistic tradition. Samuel warns Saul of the consequences of his usurpation of the functions of priesthood (1 Sam. 13.9-15), and, despite the royal patronage of the first Temple, there remains a strong prophetic tradition of resistance to the state cult and its ideology.[60] The experience of the Maccabees at a much later period may also be instructive. Having led Judaea to liberation from Seleucid rule, the Hasmonaean family acquired both the kingship and the high priesthood, which proved not merely deeply divisive in the nation, but profoundly corrupting, and contributed to the circumstances precipitating the Roman conquest.[61]

In resisting the coalescence of priesthood with monarchy, the Church has preserved some measure of independence and critical distance from the political rulers of the states in which it has functioned. This has proved vital to the integrity of its witness, particularly in times of oppression and tyranny. There would seem to be little justification for dissolving the distinction between Church and state by surrendering liturgical presidency over corporate worship, including the Christian sacraments, to political leaders. The spectre of brutal and repressive dictators elevating the sacramental elements in their bloodstained hands,

---

57   R. W. Gehring, *House Church and Mission* (Peabody, MA: Hendrickson, 2004); W. A. Meeks, *The First Urban Christians* (New Haven, CT: Yale University Press, 1983); R. H. Williams, *Stewards, Prophets, Keepers of the Word* (Peabody, MA: Hendrickson, 2006).

58   E.g. L. Boff, *Ecclesiogenesis* (Maryknoll, NY: Orbis, 1986); Schüssler Fiorenza, *In Memory of Her*.

59   *Laws*, 8.

60   Cf. N. K. Gottwald, *The Hebrew Bible* (London: SCM Press, 1986).

61   See 1–2 Maccabees; Josephus, *Antiquitates Iudaeorum* 13–16; L. L. Grabbe, *Judaism from Cyrus to Hadrian* (London: SCM Press, 1991); P. Sacchi, *The History of the Second Temple Period* (Sheffield: Sheffield Academic Press, 2000).

and appropriating the liturgy of the Church for their own aggrandizement and the entrenchment of their power, would seem too offensive to contemplate. It may be a neurotic, or even a self-deluding, sensitivity, but the well-established Christian tradition that those who wage war, however justly, should not also administer the Body and Blood of Christ in the eucharist, is surely not without merit. There is simply no possibility that such an arrangement, or what would become a state cult in the most benign of democracies, would further the work of the Church. The Church is nowhere coterminous with the state, and its rites and sacraments should not be surrendered to political rulers.

A subsidiary question might be the place the eucharist would take in a multicultural and pluralist society. In the United Kingdom, the monarch is crowned and anointed by the Archbishop of Canterbury. Whatever pagan overtones the coronation rituals may retain, it is an unambiguously Christian rite, constitutionally binding the sovereign to the Church of England, whose Supreme Governor he or she is, and on behalf of which the title *Defensor Fidei*, Defender of the Faith, has been somewhat dubiously appropriated. But the monarch is nonetheless essentially a secular, titular, ruler, and exercises no priestly role in the Church of England, and still less in the Church of Scotland. The Christian and Anglican heritage of England, and the less overt Christian and Presbyterian establishment in Scotland, exist in some tension with the multicultural religious and secular British society. Were the sovereign to preside over a national eucharist of any kind, this would alienate a significant proportion of the population not only from the monarchy but from the entire political order of the United Kingdom, which is constitutionally tied to the Crown, and symbolically subservient to the monarch as a representative person of the nation.

At first sight there may be a stronger case for the celebration of the eucharist in the family. But the family is a very much more contested and ambiguous entity than is often presumed. The assumption that the head of the family is the dominant male has been challenged not only by the growing equality and reciprocity between husband and wife, but also by the fragmentation of family life and emergence of single-parent families, and indeed same-sex partnerships. However much the holy family of Nazareth may be deemed to incarnate an ideal of family life, consecrated by Jesus through birth into an earthly family, for many women and children in particular the family is the locus of repression, exploitation, and abuse. To sacralize tyranny, and the often unaccountable power which heads of traditional families wield, would pose, albeit on a smaller scale, precisely the dangers of endowing heads of state and other political rulers with sacerdotal legitimacy. Those who in some societies commit or instigate "honour killings" and similar abominations are hardly fit to represent Christ to their families or to the world. Notwithstanding the significance of the household, and the role of the Christian householder, in the Early Church, as discussed in earlier chapters, the Church has remained distinct, and not surrendered its identity or its ritual life to the heads of families among its members. The local community of the church is not dissolved into the family gatherings of its members, but sustained through the gathering of single people and families alike for its corporate worship. However benign its structures and relationships, and however appropriate and beneficial corporate prayer may be to Christian family life, the family is nonetheless not the appropriate eucharistic community.

It is difficult to envisage how the gospel can be served by patriarchy in the home, or sacerdotal patriarchy in the state, at a time when at least some in the Church are seeking to recover the serving aspect of ministry.[62] However much patriarchal or autocratic rule in the family or in the state may be articulated in terms of service, to God and to those dominated, this is subterfuge or self-delusion on the part of its apologists. Service involves the renunciation of power, the acceptance of accountability, and the subordination of self-interest to the needs of those served. The tension between service and authority is to be recognized, as an all but unavoidable dilemma of ministry in the Church. Neither the abolition of ordered ministry in the name of egalitarian anarchy, nor the dissolution of ecclesiastical order into the patriarchal structures of the family or the state, can further the work of the gospel.

Tradition, Continuity, and Reception

As with any change proposed to the life of the Church, the question of compatibility with Christian doctrine and the received tradition arises. That the eucharist should be presided over by an ordained priest is far from being an article of faith. That Christians should celebrate the eucharist is rooted in the gospels, and has been received by the Church as fulfilment of an explicit commandment of Christ.

Our survey of catholic tradition, however selective, has shown that order has always been fundamental to the life of Christian communities, and been reflected in their worship. Order cannot be equated with the

---

62 Greenwood, *Transforming Priesthood*; E. Schillebeeckx, *Ministry: Leadership in the Community of Jesus Christ* (New York, NY: Crossroad, 1981).

ordained ministry of bishops, presbyters, and deacons; rather, the emergence and crystallization of this structure of Christian ministry represents a theologically rationalized stabilization of the order which had governed the life of the Church from the beginning.

We have observed also that the early Church resisted superstitious interpretations of its rituals, and in particular of the eucharist. Presidency was never a matter of endowment with supernatural power or the capacity to harness it, but a function of order. The person who exercised the highest degree of pastoral oversight in the community presided over its worship, and in particular the administration of the sacraments. While teaching authority has also been a function of pastoral oversight, there has always been a place in the life of the Church for theologians and teachers whose ministry does not include the pastoral oversight of communities, and these have often been laity rather than clergy.

While the Reformation in England was far from being a single or coherent process, continuity with the ancient Church was consciously maintained, and this was understood to include the threefold orders of ministry of the word and sacraments, conferred through episcopal ordination. While the historical premises of Anglican order came to be questioned in the light of critical scholarship, until recently the continuation of this dispensation has not been questioned.

The nineteenth century saw the beginnings of quite significant change in Anglicanism. While clergy were sent to serve English congregations abroad at a much earlier date, and the first bishops for dioceses in territories independent of the British Crown were consecrated at the end of the eighteenth century, it was the nineteenth century which saw the Church of England transformed into the nucleus of an international Communion of dioceses and ecclesiastical provinces in which Anglican order and worship were continued, and propagated in mission to people whose culture and heritage were not British.[63] During the same period there was increasing polarization between the catholic and evangelical wings of the Church of England, and liturgical conformity was strained to the extent that revision to the Book of Common Prayer came to be seen as imperative. Critical scholarship, increasingly international and independent of ecclesiastical control, began to make its impact on the interpretation of Scripture and the reconstruction of Christian tradition, undermining many of the certainties about catholic order and the

---

63 W. M. Jacob, *The Making of the Anglican Church Worldwide* (London: SPCK, 1997).

sacraments which had prevailed in the Church of England through the Reformation period.

The twentieth century saw further tensions and diversification in the Anglican Communion, as the newer provinces increasingly asserted their independence of the Church of England, elected their own bishops, and sought to contextualize the gospel, and their life and worship, in their own social and cultural setting. Two issues in particular continue to divide the Anglican Communion very deeply, not only between provinces, but within them, and within dioceses and parishes. The ordination of women to the presbyterate and to the episcopate is viewed by some as a violation of catholic tradition, and a departure from the essentially male character of the apostolic ministry. Human sexuality, most prominently the public acceptance of homosexual relationships in the Church, and particularly among the clergy, but also polygamy among Christians, continues to be an issue on which some are willing to divide the Church.

We do not need to discuss here the merits of any position taken on any of these issues, or to reflect on the ways in which the debates and conflicts have been managed in different parts of the Anglican Communion, to recognize the reality of these controversies and divisions, and the fundamentally different theological positions and methods which inform them. For this reason we began this study with some consideration of Anglican theological method, in order to approach the question of lay presidency at the eucharist in a manner which was academically sound, but which also acknowledged the authority of Scripture and the role of human reason and catholic tradition in evolving Anglican theology.

Our examination of Scripture, Catholic tradition, and the Anglican theological heritage has shown that many of the arguments, or perhaps rather presuppositions, against authorizing lay people to preside at the eucharist are not sound, or at least are not articulated with sufficient care and conceptual precision. That presidency and pastoral oversight have always been functions of order, and that liturgical leadership is an aspect of pastoral *episcope*, is quite clear. But that orders have always been conferred through episcopal ordination is another matter entirely.

In the absence of any explicit directive in Scripture, the authority to decide any change in order lies with the Church, save only that any such change should be consistent with Scripture. As we have noted, Scripture reflects the lives of Christian communities founded on order, but does not stipulate any particular order as definitive for the whole Church for all time. The catholic order which emerged at an early date, and which has mutated through the centuries in response to changing circumstances, has become the basis for catholic and particularly Anglican ecclesiology, though regrettably in ways which have often contributed to neglect of the laity and their role in the life of the Church. The more recent emphasis on baptism and the priesthood of all Christians has been a necessary corrective to this, but not the basis for fundamental reversal of order.

The Church could, in principle, authorize the administration of the sacraments, and in particular the eucharist, by lay people. But determining at what level of governance any such decision is to be made is fundamentally problematic. It has been a tactic of conservative Anglo-Catholic intransigence over the ordination of women to appeal to the entirely phantom concept of an ecumenical Church Council as the only body with the authority to make such a decision. Alternatively, appeal is made directly to the pope, whose official teaching is that Anglican orders are "absolutely null and utterly void".

Clearly, any decision has in fact to be made within the Anglican Communion. Neither the Lambeth Conference nor any other organ of the Communion has any legislative function, and this means it is impossible for global Anglicanism to reach a collective decision except by informal consent. While we have noted a near consensus that lay presidency at the eucharist should not be authorized, and that more presbyters should be ordained to ensure adequate provision for the administration of the sacraments, this does not amount to a collective decision of the Anglican Communion. It is within the synodical processes of the individual provinces of the Communion, or groups of provinces in the case of England, Ireland, Canada, Australia, Nigeria, and the United States, that the issue will need to be considered if any change in order is to be implemented. We have noted that this has already taken place in Kenya, and has been considered and rejected in Latin America and Australia.

A model which has been found useful in some parts of the Anglican Communion, where divergent but intransigently held opinions are maintained on issues of order, is "Reception". This has been the basis hitherto of accommodation within the Church of England of incompatible positions on the ordination of women to the priesthood. The limits of accommodation are likely to be tested with the consecration of women to the episcopate, and the greater difficulties that would create for the oversight of communities in which their authority and ministry are not acknowledged. Reception is the process – in principle open-ended – whereby theological truth is sought through permitting a contentious change to be introduced, so that discernment can be made in the light of experience as to whether the innovation reflects the will of God, so far as this can be ascertained, and is conducive to the mission of the Church.

The theological and pastoral arguments offered in support of authorizing lay presidency at the eucharist, which have been considered in this and the preceding chapter, have seemed deficient both in pastoral insight and in ecclesiological foundation. It would seem, therefore, that, despite the weakness of some of the arguments against authorising lay eucharistic presidency in Anglican communities, the arguments in favour are at least as inadequate, and do not have the support of Scripture, human reason or catholic tradition. If implemented, it seems likely that lay presidency would undermine the unity, solidarity, and mission of the Church. Nevertheless, the need, and gospel requirement, for Christian communities to celebrate the eucharist cannot be ignored. Whether, therefore, lay presidency should be provisionally authorized, subject to a process of reception, must therefore be considered.

8

The Current Position in the Anglican Communion, and Outstanding Issues

The current legal position in the Church of England is as stated in Canon B12.1: "No person shall consecrate and administer the holy sacrament of the Lord's Supper unless he shall have been ordained priest by episcopal ordination in accordance with the provisions of Canon C1." It was not until *Eucharistic Presidency* was published by the House of Bishops in 1997 that the question was systematically addressed. This was produced in response to a resolution of General Synod in 1994, in the context of the debate about extended communion. It is noteworthy that this debate was occasioned by the decline in clergy numbers in the Church of England, and the consequent need for alternative provision for the eucharist in communities without priests. The resolution requesting that the House of Bishops address the issue, significantly, recognized lay presidency as "incompatible with the Anglican tradition", but also identified a need for clarification of the roles of clergy and laity in the eucharist. The Bishops affirmed the traditional Anglican position, and recommended the ordination of appropriately identified and trained local church leaders to self-supporting ministries, rather than authorizing presumably substantially the same local lay leadership to preside at the eucharist. While extended communion is not discussed in the same detail, it was in the context of the synodical debate on authorizing this practice that the Bishops were asked to address the question of lay presidency, and *Eucharistic Presidency* was drafted with this issue fully in mind.[1]

While *Eucharistic Presidency* was intended to close debate on the subject, at least within the Church of England, the reality is that it has not done so. As well as the moves, discussed in a previous chapter, to authorize lay administration of holy communion in the diocese of Sydney in Australia, the issue has emerged in the context of the church-planting movement and the "Fresh Expressions of Church" initiative in

---

1   *Eucharistic Presidency: A Theological Statement by the House of Bishops of the General Synod* (London: Church House Publishing, 1997), p. 61.

the Church of England. It remains, furthermore, an issue of eucharistic theology and ecclesiology, and the questions to do with provision for the celebration of the eucharist in all Anglican congregations have not yet been adequately addressed by the ordination of various self-supporting clergy. But neither the proposals formed in response to pastoral or missionary need, nor those theologically driven, have resolved the question. Rather than attempting to do so in this final chapter, however, we will identify and explore some of the outstanding issues which need to be resolved before the question of authorized lay eucharistic presidency can definitively be addressed.

The State of the Anglican Communion

The question of authorized lay presidency at the eucharist was presented to the Anglican Communion by the Province of the Southern Cone of America in 1986. The Anglican Consultative Council meetings in 1984[2] and 1987,[3] and the Lambeth Conference in 1988,[4] recognized the pastoral problem which the church in South America, and also Anglican communities in other parts of the world, were facing. The Anglican Consultative Council and the Lambeth Conference all favoured provision for regular celebration of the eucharist through the ordination to the priesthood of suitable local people, even though these might not meet the normal criteria of ordination. This approach was favoured also by the International Anglican Liturgical Consultation of 1995, which notably also rejected the use of extended communion as a means of eucharistic provision for congregations without priests.[5]

The conclusions of *Eucharistic Presidency* might therefore seem to represent something of an Anglican consensus, at least outside certain evangelical circles in which the diocese of Sydney has become the standard-bearer. Whatever position one may take on the relationship between this tendency and the mainstream of Anglicanism, the theological issues driving the ecclesio-political agenda, or being exploited in those causes, require careful examination. It is recognized that this is a question not of doctrine, but of discipline, and therefore subject to change and innovation in the evolving tradition of the Church.

---

2   *Bonds of Affection* (London: Anglican Consultative Council, 1984), p. 65.

3   *Many Gifts, One Spirit* (London: Anglican Consultative Council, 1987), p. 57.

4   *Lambeth Conference 1988* (London: Anglican Consultative Council, 1988), Mission and Ministry Report, §205.

5   *Renewing the Anglican Eucharist*, ed. D. R. Holeton (Cambridge: Grove Books, 1996), p. 11; *Anglican Orders and Ordination*, ed. D. R. Holeton (Cambridge: Grove Books, 1997).

The question needs to be whether a departure from the long-established custom, not merely of the Anglican Communion but of the universal Church, well rooted in Scripture and tradition, can be justified in changed circumstances, while maintaining allegiance to Scripture and continuity within the Anglican tradition.

While there is a clear majority position in the Anglican Communion, this falls somewhat short of consensus. There are those determined to pursue lay presidency, whether canonically authorized or not, either in the cause of a theological agenda to bring the Reformation to its conclusion, or in conscious or unconscious disregard for the wider Church, and for canonical authority in the local church. This raises specific issues of Anglican polity and governance, and of the parameters of acceptable diversity within the Anglican Communion. These same issues are raised by the debates about the ordination of women, particularly to the presbyterate and the episcopate, and about human sexuality, both within the Church of England and in the wider Anglican Communion. The same principles of course apply to such issues as liturgical reform and the remarriage of divorcees, but these tend not to be quite so emotive, except within fairly narrow circles.

The then Archbishop of Sydney in 1999 withheld his assent to a resolution of his diocesan synod authorizing lay and diaconal presidency and preaching, citing "the impact on the Australian Church and the wider Communion" and his responsibility as a bishop to a larger community than his own diocese.[6] At a time when the Anglican Communion is struggling to maintain unity while addressing issues of sexuality, and has still not resolved the conflicts and divisions aroused by the ordination of women, a moratorium on moving from debate to implementation on this issue might well be appropriate. Clarifying the theological issues, and the methods by which they are addressed, many of which impinge on the other contentious debates, may nonetheless be a service to the Anglican Communion, especially as the issues of method and of substance seem inextricably linked. At the time of writing it remains to be seen whether an Anglican Covenant or other such protocol is able to define, for the adherence of all parties, the level and the forum in which particular issues of contention are to be authoritatively resolved.

The present task therefore is to identify and tentatively to explore some of the theological issues, acknowledged or otherwise, which

---

6   Decision Concerning the Preaching and Administration of Holy Communion by Lay Persons and Deacons Ordinance 1999.

continue to impinge on the debate on authorizing lay presidency at the eucharist.

The Theology and Ministry of the Laity

It has been noted that the laity, as an order of ministry in the Church, rather than as the recipients of the ministry of the clergy, has been emphasized in recent theology, and also in modern Anglican liturgies, in particular Initiation but also the Ordinal. The laity are understood as all baptized Christians, who are in principle committed to the faith and the way of life reflected in the vows made at baptism. This is problematic in a number of respects. As is generally recognized, this definition includes the ordained clergy among the laity, and emphasizes that their ministry is offered from within and on behalf of the laity. While the theological truth of this is not to be disputed, or even diminished, it does not form an adequate basis for defining or understanding the distinctive function of the laity within the Church and in God's saving work in the world. This is an issue to which we shall return shortly.

A rather different problem with the definition of the laity as all the baptized, is that, outside traditions which stipulate "believers' baptism", this includes babies and young children who have not reached the point of responsible adult commitment. While those nurtured within the Church and educated in the faith may be deemed to be in a process of formation as Christian laity, this does not apply to the many who are baptized in infancy, or for that matter at any stage in life, but whose membership of the Church is nominal, whose families have no intention of nurturing them in the faith, and who are unlikely to reach any point of commitment to the gospel and the life of the Church unless they subsequently experience renewal or even conversion during their adolescent or adult lives. To describe such recipients of baptism as laity has recently been questioned:

> the minimum requirement *in addition to baptism* for identification as a lay person includes a conscious, willing and mature participation (appropriate to life stage) in regular corporate worship, service to others (both inside and outside the church), and commitment to learning with a view to deepening faith and Christian practice.[7]

As baptism in Anglicanism is predominantly a birth rite, in itself it effects no transition into active involvement in the life of the Church.

---

7   W. Dackson, 'Toward a Theology of the Laity', unpublished paper (2007), p. 8.

This is not to deny that baptism is the sole and definitive rite of Christian initiation, or, perhaps more accurately, initiation into the Church. But in Christian communities into which membership is, if not formally conferred through birth, then at least in effect a direct consequence of birth into a Christian family, or even into a nominally Christian society, baptism cannot function meaningfully as a rite of Christian profession and commitment.

Confirmation may be the more appropriate liturgical rite of entry into the laity. Responsible adult profession of Christian faith is made before the bishop and the gathered congregation, and commitment pledged to the life and witness of the Church. There has been an unfortunate tendency, over a period of centuries, for confirmation to degenerate into a derivative rite of admission to communion, upon which the status of adult communicant has become contingent in matters of church governance. With the increasing admission of children to communion on the basis of their baptism rather than confirmation, the latter rite is rapidly losing even this distinctive character, without having acquired any clear alternative and coherent significance.[8] The sacrament of confirmation has mutated over the centuries, and has no clear and unambiguous purpose rooted in Scripture or undivided ancient tradition. It would therefore be amenable to a new purpose and significance in the life of the Church, as a Christian rite of passage into adulthood. The profession of faith and allegiance which characterizes confirmation in the Western Church could appropriately, and without any fundamental departure from established tradition, become the occasion on which baptized Christians become members of the laity, and assume the responsibilities which this entails. This would be fully consonant with the recommendation of the 1968 Lambeth Conference that "Each province or regional Church be asked to explore the theology of baptism and confirmation in relation to the need to commission the laity for their task in the world, and to experiment in this regard."[9]

If this were to be meaningfully implemented, however, it would require a renewed commitment and rigour, on the part both of the Church and of candidates, to catechetical instruction preceding confirmation.[10] Furthermore, the role of the bishop in the rite should be

---

8   Cf. *The Lambeth Conference 1968* (London: SPCK), p. 37; J. D. C. Fisher, *Confirmation* (London: SPCK, 1968); A. Kavanagh, *Confirmation* (New York, NY: Pueblo, 1988).

9   Resolution 25.

10   Cf. *Lambeth Conference 1968*, Resolution 27.

emphasized as representing the universal Church, not because it is liturgically or sacramentally necessary, which it clearly is not, but because it demonstrates the commitment of the Church to supporting the life, ministry, and witness of its lay members.

The last century has seen an exponential increase in the range of activities in the life of the Church in which lay people have exercised leadership, and also in the numbers of both men and women who have assumed such responsibilities. Despite this, and perhaps precisely because this has consisted largely in incremental delegation to lay people of functions which there are no longer sufficient numbers of clergy to perform, the identity and vocation of the lay Christian, both in terms of Anglican ecclesiology and ecumenically, remain vague and ambiguous, if not undefined. The process which has brought increasing numbers of lay Christians into ministerial roles in the life of the Church has not been guided so much by theological insight into the significance of baptism, as by declining clergy numbers. There is a clear need for a more thorough and coherent theology of the laity, in the context of which the role of lay Christians in the life of the Church, and in the world, can be explored in relation to the ministry of word and sacrament, and in relation to the ministry of the ordained.[11]

It has become something of a theological truism that "All Christians share in the priesthood of their Lord".[12] While it has been objected that Christ's priesthood, as expounded in the New Testament, is unique, and shared with no human being,[13] the notion of the entire Church as a priesthood is well established in Christian theology, and rooted in the New Testament.[14] Whether this should properly be described as Christ's priesthood, if this were understood to mean the same priesthood as Christ exercises, is perhaps of secondary importance. It is of course true, as has been noted above, that the priesthood of all Christians alluded to

---

11 Cf. *Ordination and the Church's Ministry: A Theological Evaluation* (London: Church House Publishing, 1990) 31; *All Are Called: Towards a Theology of the Laity* (London: Church Information Office, 1985).

12 *Lambeth Conference 1968*, p. 100; *Baptism, Eucharist and Ministry* (Geneva: WCC, 1982), Ministry 1–6; cf. N. N. Afanasiev, *The Church of the Holy Spirit* (Notre Dame, IN: University of Notre Dame Press, 2007); T. F. O'Meara, *Theology of Ministry* (New York, NY: Paulist Press, 1983), p. 210; J. D. Zizioulas, *Being as Communion* (New York, NY: St Vladimir Press, 1985), pp. 215–16.

13 H. R. McAdoo, *The Eucharistic Theology of Jeremy Taylor Today* (Norwich: Canterbury Press, 1988), p. 100, citing Heb. 7.24; cf. H. Küng, *The Church* (London: Burns and Oates, 1968), p. 363; J. M. R. Tillard, *What Priesthood Has the Ministry?* (Nottingham: Grove Books, 1973), pp. 14–27.

in 1 Pet. 2.5, 9 and Rev. 1.6; 5.10; 20.6 is a corporate identity, the activities associated with which are worship and witness, which cannot be equated with the self-sacrificial priesthood of Christ articulated in Hebrews. This priesthood nonetheless relates to Christ, and can therefore appropriately be described as his. The point is that Christians, through baptism, share corporately in a priestly character and service defined in relation to Christ. In the Common Worship Ordinal of the Church of England the bishop states that "In baptism, God calls his people to follow Christ, and forms them into a royal priesthood", within which the ordained ministry are called to serve. Priesthood in this sense does not imply liturgical office, but it does imply corporate Christian identity and the obligations of worship and service in the world.

The corporate identity of the Church as a priesthood[15] derives from different traditions in the New Testament to Paul, who describes the Church as the Body of Christ, to which the gifts of the Holy Spirit are given, conferred on individual Christians to be exercised within and on behalf of the Body as a whole.[16] Ministry, empowered by the Spirit, therefore cannot be directly equated with priesthood, though clearly there are commonalities between these images of the Church. Subsequent theology has sought to integrate these traditions, and it is perhaps the confusion of priesthood with ministry which has contributed most deleteriously to the clericalization of the Church. Conversely, it has also meant that the role of the laity has been secularized and profaned, and this requires remedial attention.

While priesthood, when applied to the laity, may be a quality of collective identity rather than a function within or on behalf of the Church, ministry by its definition implies commitment and action.[17] "Ministry is God-given work for the cause of God that is acknowledged by the Church."[18] The issue at present is not the corporate priesthood of the Church in which lay Christians share, but what the ministry of the laity is, within and on behalf of the Church, and empowered by the Holy Spirit. Here it is not feasible or justifiable to restrict "ministry" to the proclamation of the word, administration of the sacraments, and

---

14   1 Pet. 2.5, 9; Rev. 5.10.

15   1 Pet. 2.5, 9; Rev. 1.6; 5.10; 20.6.

16   Rom. 12.4-5; 1 Cor. 10.17; 11.29; 12.12-28; Eph. 1.23; 2.16; 4.4-16; Col. 1.18.

17   P. D. L. Avis, *A Ministry Shaped by Mission* (London: T & T Clark, 2005), p. 54; cf. O'Meara, *Theology*, p. 210.

18   Avis, *Ministry*, p. 58; cf. T. P. Rausch, 'Ministry and Ministries', in *Ordering the Baptismal Priesthood*, ed. S. K. Wood (Collegeville, MN: Liturgical Press, 2003), pp. 52–67.

pastoral oversight.[19] This would be to restrict ministry to what have until recently been exclusively clerical functions, and to perpetuate the secularization and profanation of other activities engaged in by lay people, guided and empowered by the Holy Spirit, in conscious or subconscious fulfilment of their Christian vocation. We need therefore to ask: what is the specific role entrusted distinctively and pre-eminently to lay Christians, not so much in the liturgy as in the ministry of the Church in the saving work of God in the world?

It has traditionally been recognized that, for the majority of lay Christians, their vocation and mission consist primarily in their lives in the world, in family life and in their places of work, but also in the community, in charities and organisations concerned with what it has become popular to call "civil society", and in politics.[20] This has meant that, with the exception of such public office holders as church wardens, and people with particular skills such as organists, the church has been the place at which Christians have gathered for corporate worship, but not the context in which their Christian commitment is lived out and their vocation fulfilled during the week. In other words, lay Christians are present and active alongside their neighbours in all aspects of community life, not excluding their workplaces, and it is there that their witness is proclaimed and their ministry exercised, in often intangible and subconscious ways, but faithfully and meaningfully.

Declining clergy numbers have made the Church increasingly dependent on lay people, certainly in ways which never strictly required the presence or action of a priest or deacon, but also in liturgical and pastoral activities which have traditionally been the function of the clergy. In absorbing the time and energy of increasing numbers of lay people, the Church has in many ways turned in on itself, and thereby arguably accelerated its own decline. While it is observed that secular as well as religious voluntary organisations have declined more rapidly than the churches,[21] the question needs to be asked whether the Church, in monopolizing the spare time of its more committed and public spirited lay members, is thereby contributing to the decline of voluntary associations and charities, through which its lay people previously

---

19 Cf. Avis, *Ministry*.

20 Cf. *Lambeth Conference 1968*, pp. 96–7; *All are Called*, p. 67; *Theology of Ordination*, p. 8.

21 G. Davie, 'From Obligation to Consumption', in S. J. L. Croft (ed.), *The Future of the Parish System*, (London: Church House Publishing, 2006), pp. 33–5; M. W. Percy, 'Many Rooms in My Father's House', in Croft (ed.), *The Future of the Parish System*, p. 6.

exercised their mission in the world and made the contacts on which evangelism depends. This theologically ill-considered development has denuded the Church of its most effective agency in its mission outward to the world.[22]

The increasing delegation to lay ministers of roles hitherto exercised all but exclusively by clergy has been undertaken with inadequate theological reflection on the nature of priesthood and the ministry of the laity. The time and energy of committed Christian laity is increasingly absorbed into the institutional life of the Church, and in liturgical leadership, to compensate for the lack of clergy. A direct consequence of this has been that lay Christians are no longer as active or as prominent in the wider community, and the value of such time and energy as they do expend in voluntary involvement with the wider community is increasingly deemed secular, if not profane, and irrelevant to their lives and ministry as Christian laity. The presence and the influence of the Church in society are accordingly diminished, and its mission impeded. The reaction of the Church to decline, both in clergy numbers and in lay adherence, has generated a collective introversion which, unless reversed, will aggravate and perpetuate the decline.

It has increasingly been recognized in recent years that there are lay Christians whose gifts and vocation ought to be acknowledged and affirmed, and indeed empowered, through ordination to the diaconate and presbyterate. Nevertheless, this should not be seen as the natural or appropriate, still less a spiritually or theologically necessary, culmination in the ecclesiastical lives of all baptized Christians. The pressures on lay people in many places to concentrate on church activities such time and energy as are not consumed by their employers is an inappropriate and ineffective panacea to decline, both in clergy numbers and in lay adherence to the local church. A more robust theology of the laity is needed, which will resist the clericalization[23] of those whose gifts and ministry lie in being and representing the Church in the world, and doing so in ways which are less overt than the ministry of the clergy in the wider community. Genuine and sustained renewal in the life of the Church is more likely to be achieved if the laity are freed to exercise their ministry as laity, being an active Christian presence and influence in all aspects of society and community life.

---

22 Cf. W. Ind, *Towards a Theology of the People of God* (Truro: Truro Diocesan Board of Finance, 2001), p. 27.

23 Cf. S. K. Pickard and L. Johnston, 'Lay Presidency at holy communion', *St Mark's Review* 161 (1995): 15.

A further consequence of clericalizing selected lay Christians has been both confusion of identity and roles between clergy and laity, which many may see as an innocuous or even a beneficial development. It has also been argued, on sociological grounds, that this would be fundamentally destructive both of the Church and of the society it serves and to which it is called to bear witness.[24] We have seen this in the collective introversion, and even sectarianism, of many congregations, where collapsing the distinction between clergy and laity has led to neglect of the ministry of the latter. As well as being damaging to the laity, this tendency is destructive of clerical identity and vocation. There is a real danger of priests in particular becoming reduced to ritual functionaries, whose perceived role in the community is the performance of archaic and quasi-magical acts, divorced from the religious experience and spiritual needs of Christians, and indeed of their secularized neighbours, in the modern world. "There comes a point where the practical distinction between minister and layman is the ability to say one prayer at the communion service ... it is not surprising that there are voices which say the distinction is meaningless."[25]

The increasing delegation of liturgical leadership to lay people is a particularly conspicuous form of clericalization of selected laity.[26] Lay presidency at the eucharist would exacerbate this tendency, and aggravate its consequences both for clerical identity and for the ministry of the laity. It would at the very least be arguable that abolition of the ordained ministry altogether would be the logical and even necessary consummation of this process,[27] even if such a measure is not consciously envisaged. While in the diocese of Sydney the question of authorizing lay administration of holy communion has been driven by a clear theological agenda, elsewhere the proposal has been made with little if any theological reflection, or even consciousness that there are theological, pastoral, and missiological issues to be considered with care. Impetuosity is perhaps characteristic of the church-planting movement, or at least is certainly widely attested in such circles, and the wilful disregard for theological as well as practical issues in sustaining

---

24 D. Martin, *The Breaking of the Image* (Oxford: Blackwell, 1980), pp. 13, 37, 55.

25 C. O. Buchanan, 'Some Anglican Historical Perspectives', in B. T. Lloyd (ed.), *Lay Presidency at the Eucharist?* (Bramcote: Grove Books, 1977), p. 14; cf. A. E. Harvey, *Priest or President?* (London: SPCK, 1975), p. 29; B. T. Lloyd (ed.), *Lay Presidency at the Eucharist?* (Nottingham: Grove Books, 1977), pp. 9–10.

26 Pickard and Johnson, 'Lay Presidency', p. 15.

27 Cf. J. Goldingay, *Authority and Ministry* (Nottingham: Grove Books, 1976), p. 24.

conversions and building communities has contributed to the failure of mission in many places.

The completeness of the Church, the effective exercise of its ministry, and the fulfilment of its mission in the world, require that lay Christians be released and empowered to live out their vocation as laity in the world.[28] The integrity and value of the vocation of lay Christians is to be affirmed and emphasized, in interdependence with the ministry of the ordained. This will not be accomplished by defining the clergy as a sub-species of the laity, however valid this may be as a theological corollary of baptism. In so far as clergy are also laity, they cannot be in an interdependent or symbiotic relationship with the laity as a whole. There must therefore be a distinction, at least in emphasis, between the vocation of the lay Christian and those of deacon, presbyter, and bishop. The integrity of lay Christian identity and ministry should not be maintained by diverting the time and energy of lay people from their engagement with the world to ecclesiocentric activities. The ministry of word and sacraments, including presidency at the eucharist, is a clerical rather than a lay vocation, and those called to exercise it ought to be ordained to the diaconate and presbyterate. The complementarity of lay and clerical vocations requires that some distinction between them be maintained.

Diaconate, Priesthood and Episcopacy

We have noted that the elevation of episcopal ordination as the defining criterion of valid ministry is a misconstrual of the notion of apostolic succession, established in catholic thought during the sixteenth century, when the Council of Trent reacted to the emergence of Protestant churches and sought to reform those churches still in communion with the Church of Rome. Continuity with the Apostolic Church is defined through faithfulness to the gospel, and is maintained in doctrine rather than in the ordering of ministry. God's grace given and received in the eucharist can therefore never be dependent upon the validity attributed to the ministry of the person who presides.

The role of the deacon in the eucharist has traditionally been subordinate to that of the bishop, or in his absence the presiding presbyter. The deacon assists in the celebration of the eucharist, but is not authorized to consecrate the elements in the absence of a priest. The usage of διάκονος in early Christianity was clearly rather wider than

---

28 Cf. D. N. Power, *Ministers of Christ and His Church: The Theology of the Priesthood* (London: Geoffrey Chapman, 1969), p. 174.

this. Paul uses the term of Christ (Rom. 15.8), and also of people of some prominence and influence in their communities (cf. Rȯm. 16.1), and, not least, of himself and his associates in the work of apostleship (1 Cor. 3.5, 6; 2 Cor. 3.6; 6.4; 11.15; 1 Thess. 3.2). The connotations of the term are therefore not necessarily servile.[29] While the diaconate became at an early date an office defined by assistance to the bishop, primarily administrative but also pastoral and liturgical, we can be by no means certain that officers of the church who used the title διἀκονος never presided at the eucharist.

From the fifth century the diaconate became increasingly, but never exclusively, a transitional stage towards ordination to the presbyterate, and gradually lost its distinctive significance. This transitional character remained normative until quite recently. In 1967 Pope Paul VI, acting on the recommendation of the Second Vatican Council,[30] restored the diaconate as a permanent and distinctive order of ministry, to which married men could be ordained.[31] This development has influenced thinking within the Anglican Communion, particularly in provinces willing to ordain women to the diaconate but not to the presbyterate or episcopate. In the Church of England and some other provinces of the Communion, the admission of women to the diaconate entailed ordaining deaconesses who had hitherto been regarded as laity rather than as clergy. Whether the diaconate was envisaged as transitional or permanent, those ordained to this ministry did not become ministers of the sacrament except in the subordinate roles which deacons had traditionally exercised.

We have noted that the Anglican Church in Kenya made canonical provision in 1985 for deacons to be authorized by their bishops to preside at the eucharist where no priest was available. In this, deacons were permitted to anticipate their ordination to the presbyterate by exercising an authority not yet conferred through ordination. The intention of the diocese of Sydney, however, is that deacons, including women for whom ordination to the priesthood is not to be countenanced, would become authorized to administer holy communion.[32] Two distinct issues arise here. The propriety of deacons

---

29   J. N. Collins, *Diakonia* (New York, NY: Oxford University Press, 1990); E. P. Echlin, *The Deacon in the Church Past and Future* (New York, NY: Alba, 1971).

30   *Lumen Gentium*, 29.

31   *Sacrum Diaconam Ordinem*.

32   P. G. Bolt *et al.*, *The Lord's Supper in Human Hands* (Sydney: Australian Church Record, 2008).

anticipating their ordination to the presbyterate is a question which may not directly affect the character of the diaconate where it is still understood as a transitional process in the formation of priests. However, where administration of the sacraments becomes a proper function of the diaconate, the question of altering the character of the diaconate does arise. If the diaconate were to be assimilated into the presbyterate, in terms of liturgical function if not of pastoral authority in the congregation, then the distinctive character of that order, emphasized in modern Ordinals, could be diminished. As with the laity, the integrity and the unique value and witness of diaconal ministry, in its social, pastoral, and administrative expressions, would seem to be best served by maintaining its distinctiveness from the priesthood.

Of the orders of ministry, it is the presbyterate which has come to be most closely associated with presidency at the eucharist. We have observed that this was not the original function of presbyters, but one which gradually devolved to them as congregations multiplied under the care of single bishops. Presiding at the eucharist was an aspect of pastoral oversight in the community, rather than being a distinctive ritual function. From the second century, notions of priesthood came to be attached to Christian bishops and presbyters, until the language of priesthood eclipsed that of eldership in defining the ministry of presbyters. There are questions to do with episcopacy to which we shall need to return shortly, but for the present priesthood and presbyterate must be considered.

The concept and theology of priesthood have been challenged and eroded by recent developments in church life, many of which have been pragmatic and reactive, rather than theologically motivated. The development and expansion of lay ministries, in response to declining clergy numbers and without adequate theological reflection, has created the perception that the distinctive nature of priesthood consists in the power to consecrate the eucharistic elements: the one function that is reserved to presbyters and bishops.[33] The increasing delegation to lay people of liturgical as well as pastoral roles in the congregation, without due attention to the implications, theological and practical, for both clergy and laity, has brought the purpose and significance of ordination into question. "[W]e seem perilously near to discovering that the concept of ordination has already been evacuated of much of its meaning."[34] This perception has been created across the ecclesiastical

---

33 *Lambeth Conference 1968*, p. 101.
34 Lloyd, *Lay Presidency?*, pp. 9–10.

spectrum, as much in traditions where sacerdotal notions of priesthood would be anathema as in traditions in which, in popular religiosity as well as in abstract theology, this sacramental power was understood to be of the essence of priesthood.[35]

It is perhaps not so much the sacrament of ordination which has given rise to this problem as the sacerdotal concept of priesthood which has become attached to the presbyterate. Lack of clarity and of careful theological reflection on the theology of ministry, not least that of the laity, has in recent decades aggravated an ancient, but nonetheless anachronistic, misconception of the apostolic ministry. Sacerdotal notions of priesthood, with which the doctrine of transubstantiation and sacrificial interpretations of the eucharist are closely associated, entered Christian ministry well after the orders of bishop, presbyter, and deacon had become established and stabilized in the ancient Church.[36] Sacerdotal conceptions of priesthood therefore need to be subordinated to the more ancient conception of "apostolic ministry",[37] rooted in relationships with and in ecclesial communities, and to a clear and holistic theology of the Church, or repudiated altogether.

The centrality of the celebration of the eucharist to the ministry of presbyters, which would be recognized across the spectrum of theologies of ministry,[38] must be the same centrality as the eucharist commands in the lives of all Christians, defining the Church rather than its individual members.[39] The eucharist expresses Christian identity and vocation as the Body of Christ, present and active in the world. The vocation of the

---

35 Cf. Buchanan, 'Anglican Historical Perspectives', p. 14; Harvey, *Priest*, p. 29; L. Newbigin, 'Lay Presidency at the Eucharist', *Theology* 99 (1996): 366–70.

36 Cf. P. McPartlan, *sacrament of Salvation: An Introduction to Eucharistic Ecclesiology* (Edinburgh: T & T Clark, 1995), pp. 1–44; Power, *Ministers*, pp. 163–67; H. Küng, *Why Priests?* (London: Collins, 1971); E. Schillebeeckx, *Ministry* (New York, NY: Crossroad, 1981); *The Church with a Human Face* (London: SCM, 1985); R. E. Brown, *Priest and Bishop* (London: Geoffrey Chapman, 1971); A. T. Hanson, *The Pioneer Ministry* (London: SPCK, 1961); R. P. C. Hanson, *Christian Priesthood Examined* (Guildford: Lutterworth, 1979).

37 Power, *Ministers*, p. 163; cf. R. C. Moberly, *Ministerial Priesthood* (London: SPCK, 1969); T. Pitt, *At the Head of the Table, or Under the Carpet?* (York: Dean and Chapter of York, 1994), p. 14.

38 C. J. Cocksworth and R. Brown, *Being a Priest Today* (Norwich: Canterbury Press, 2002); R. P. Greenwood, *Transforming Priesthood* (London: SPCK, 1994), pp. 141–80; Moberly, *Ministerial Priesthood*, pp. 259–65.

39 Cf. K. W. Stevenson, *Do This: The Shape, Style and Meaning of the Eucharist* (Norwich: Canterbury Press, 2002), p. 86; M. Thurian, *Priesthood and Ministry* (London: Mowbrays, 1983), p. 121.

Christian, ordained and lay alike, is therefore reflected in, but not defined by, participation in the eucharist or a distinctive role in its celebration.

A redefinition of the presbyterate is needed, in terms both of essence and of function, in the context of which the liturgical ministry of the priest can be located and explored.[40] Perhaps the most significant recent contribution has been that of Christopher Cocksworth and Rosalind Brown, which has the considerable merit of embracing some breadth of the Anglican spectrum.[41] Leading worship and in particular presiding at the eucharist are located in a wider context of relationships and spirituality, so that the liturgical role of the presbyter is an act of service and an expression of spiritual and pastoral relationships with God and the community. There remains the danger of defining the clergy as "everything the laity are and more", which inevitably generates at the very least the perception of a spiritual hierarchy and clerical elitism. A model which speaks of the ordained as being "everything the laity are in essence, but distinct in function" may be able to avoid this.

The distinction made by Jeremy Taylor in the seventeenth century, between *vis* and *facultas* "to intervene between God and the people",[42] may avoid ascribing connotations of magical power to the priesthood, but it does not in itself explain why this *facultas* is restricted to the ordained priesthood if the clergy are not endowed with a distinctive *vis*. The dependence of ministerial priesthood on the priesthood of Christ,[43] and on the power of the Holy Spirit, however true in itself, does not account for this empowerment being restricted to bishops and presbyters. A distinction between powers and functions conferred by Jesus on his disciples during his earthly ministry, and continued within the apostolic ministry, on the one hand, and the conferral of the Holy Spirit on the Church at Pentecost, on the other,[44] would be impossible to sustain with any confidence on the basis of critical scholarship. There may nonetheless be theological value in this distinction, and it may point to a truth about the Church and its ministry which no amount of

---

40 Cf. M. Downey, 'Ministerial Identity', in *Ordering the Baptismal Priesthood*, ed. S. K. Wood (Collegeville, MN: Liturgical Press, 2003), pp. 3–25.

41 Cocksworth and Brown, *Being a Priest*.

42 *Clerus Domini*, 7.3. Cf. W. Temple, *Thoughts on Some Problems of the Day* (London: Macmillan, 1931), p. 110.

43 F. D. Maurice, *The Kingdom of Christ. 2* (London: Rivington, 1858), 125–6, 149. Cf. S. W. Sykes, 'The Theology of Priesthood', *Sewanee Theological Review* 43 (2000): 121–9.

44 Cf. Taylor, *Clerus Domini*, 8.1.

historical reconstruction could sustain. A distinction between the apostolic ministry, represented particularly by bishops, but also by presbyters, with deacons in a supporting capacity, and the life and ministry of the Church, each rooted and founded in Christ and empowered in distinctive ways by the Holy Spirit, may prove helpful in defining a theology of priesthood for the modern Church,[45] if it can be done in such a way as not to denigrate the identity and ministry of the laity.

Where it is maintained that priesthood is not defined by its functions, but by some abstract essence,[46] this ontology all but invariably becomes the basis not only for a spiritual hierarchy, but also for reserving certain functions to bishops and presbyters in particular, but also to deacons. If this priestly attribute is not an endowment with supernatural power, then what precisely it is needs to be defined: how it distinguishes clergy from the laity, and how the Church is served by this peculiar ethereal quality being visited upon some but not all its members. Whether such notions of priesthood are attested prior to the introduction of sacerdotal notions to ecclesiastical office is, furthermore, doubtful. Bishops, presbyters, deacons, and laity alike are defined by their relationships with God and one another, and, secondarily, by the ministries within and on behalf of the Church which they offer. Personal qualities and attributes, and even spiritual attainments, can be no more than signs of vocation and of endowment by the Holy Spirit for the fulfilment of that vocation and the exercise of ministry. If priests "personify the embodiment in the Church of God's work to bring truth and healing to the world", and ordination serves or effects this "personification",[47] then it needs to be explained why the eucharist in particular, of all acts or functions of ministry, requires the action of such a "personification".

If the orders of bishop, presbyter, and deacon are defined by relationship and function, then there needs to be some consonance and consistency between the two. In so far as presiding at the eucharist has been understood as a function of pastoral relations and representation of Christ and of the universal Church, then this role is to be exercised by persons whose lives and ministry embrace and reflect these relationships. Where there is disjunction between relationships and liturgical

45   Cf. Power, *Ministers*, p. 166.

46   Hanson, *Christian Priesthood*, p. 108; H. M. Wybrew, *Called to Be Priests* (Oxford: SLG Press, 1989), p. 3; cf. K. Leech, *Spirituality and Pastoral Care* (London: Sheldon Press, 1986), pp. 127–36.

47   D. W. Hardy, *Finding the Church* (London: SCM Press, 2001), p. 93.

function, this would seem to be most satisfactorily resolved through ordaining to the presbyterate those who exercise the pastoral ministry and oversight of a priest in their communities, not to elevate them above the laity but to distinguish them in identity and function from those whom they are to serve.

It has been argued that, in continuity with the Reformed tradition, preaching, as well as administering the sacraments, should be restricted to the ordained clergy.[48] If this were to be implemented, Readers and other lay ministers licensed to preach ought to be ordained, and thereby to become ministers of the sacraments as well as of the word. While the complementarity of word and sacrament is to be acknowledged, it needs also to be recognized that the ministry of the word has not always been as closely bound to pastoral relationships as that of the sacraments. While pastoral relations are undoubtedly a powerful and dynamic influence upon preaching and other forms of Christian teaching, catechesis and preaching do not inherently reflect or express such relationships. Furthermore, the word can be proclaimed, by clergy or lay preachers alike, outside of the structures of pastoral relationships. It would therefore seem more appropriate that Readers and other lay ministers licensed to preach be ordained, if, but only if, they are exercising a pastoral ministry which would appropriately be expressed in the administration of the sacraments, or if they otherwise display clear signs of vocation to the diaconate and presbyterate.

If the authority of the apostolic ministry derives from God or Christ, apart from the Church,[49] then it could be argued that only a priest can "give sacramental expression to Christ's priestly action".[50] This would be consistent with the notion of *facultas* which Jeremy Taylor associates with the priesthood. In the eucharist, the priest would, in terms of this conception of apostolic ministry, represent Christ to the Church rather than the Church to Christ. However, this raises a further question as to how a ministry that derives from Christ relates to the notion of the Church as the Body of Christ. While some caution must be exercised in conflating theological metaphors, the principle that Christ is present in the gathered congregation, and that all Christians have received the Holy Spirit at baptism, cannot be ignored. There must therefore be some

---

48 D. J. Davies, 'Some Historical and Theological Arguments Against', in *Lay Presidency at the Eucharist?* ed. B. T. Lloyd (Bramcote: Grove Books, 1977), p. 25.

49 So *Ministry and Ordination: A Statement on the Doctrine of the Ministry Agreed by the Anglican–Roman Catholic International Commission* (London: SPCK, 1973), p. 7.

50 B. Cooke, *Ministry to word and sacraments* (Philadelphia, PA: Fortress Press, 1976), p. 645.

doubt as to whether vocation and authority deriving from God, through Christ and the Holy Spirit, can ultimately be distinguished from vocation and authority derived from the Church, the Body of Christ endowed with the Holy Spirit.[51]

Where the representative nature of priesthood is emphasized,[52] it needs to be explained in what ways a priest can represent God to the Church which are impossible for a lay person, and why only a priest can represent the Church in the eucharistic prayer. The problem is particularly acute when different Christians, and different Anglicans, understand the priest to be representing Christ in different ways, whether it be the ministry of the word or that of the sacrament,[53] or even in radical or conventional forms of pastoral care. The priest is certainly not the only possible representative of the universal Church in space and time.[54] Still less can a priest be considered the only possible or legitimate representative of God in and to the world. The Early Church, like ancient Israel previously, recognized that the gift and vocation of prophecy were not necessarily conferred on priests or other cultic functionaries, however unwelcome such a gift may have been to its recipient and to the community alike. We have noted the evidence that, in at least some ancient churches, prophets were recognized as having the authority to assume the liturgical, and no doubt other, functions of bishops and presbyters, however much this authority may have been contested. While ancient prophecy may not be a complete or adequate analogy for any form of charisma which may be encountered in the Church today, we still need to recognize God's independence of and sovereignty over the structures of the Church, and therefore the possibility that gifts and vocation may be conferred on persons whom the Church has not ordained, or even on persons in whom those gifts and vocation are not acknowledged by canonical authority. While we may be confident that God normatively operates through the Church, and its established structures and its ordained and lay ministers, it would nonetheless be presumptuous to claim that the particular gifts conferred at ordination are never bestowed outside the rite.[55] It would be more

---

51 Cf. J. Dallen, *The Dilemma of Priestless Sundays* (Chicago, IL: Liturgy Training Publications, 1994), p. 119.

52 C. Gore, *The Body of Christ* (London: John Murray, 1901), p. 271; J. B. Lightfoot, *Saint Paul's Epistle to the Philippians* (London: Macmillan, 1896), pp. 181–269; Hanson, *Christian Priesthood*, pp. 99–102.

53 Cf. Avis, *Ministry*, pp. 72–6.

54 Cf. R. Moloney, *The Eucharist* (London: Geoffrey Chapman, 1995), p. 204.

55 Hooker, *Laws*, 5.77.2; Avis, *Ministry*, pp. 81–2.

accurate to say that ordination is the liturgical process in and through which the Church acknowledges vocation and intercedes for the gifts to fulfil the ministry to which deacons, presbyters, and bishops are called.

The collegial and relational nature of the presbyterate is perhaps an obstacle to a clear and unambiguous definition of the priesthood, at least in functional terms. Collegiality implies some degree of diversity and complementarity, and this includes the gifts and ministries exercised by presbyters. The notion of priesthood reflected, if not implied, in the Ordinal most closely approximates that of incumbent of a parish, which is in itself entirely reasonable in that it would have been to the beneficed parochial ministry that the overwhelming majority of clergy have been ordained through most of Anglican history. Nevertheless, while incumbency may embody quite distinctively the relationships and ministry of a priest, it has never been normative or definitive of Anglican ministry. The ordained ministry has been defined in terms of lifelong vocation to service of the word, sacraments, and pastoral oversight in the universal Church.[56] Not all priests will, or ever have, exercised all of these ministries simultaneously to the same local community, and the diversity of their functions mean that for at least some there will be an emphasis on one aspect or another, and for others "community" will be defined in a much less rigid way. As well as sector ministries, in which scope for ministry of the word and sacraments may be very limited, there are forms of ministry appropriately exercised by presbyters which relate not to gathered communities of lay Christians but, intangibly, to the Church as a whole through the contemplative life of religious orders, or in spiritual, theological, or administrative support of bishops and other clergy.[57] The wholeness of the priestly ministry is to be found not in the role of any individual presbyter, or even any single bishop, but in the complementarity of their diverse gifts and roles in the one ministry.

The ordained ministry, in particular that of presbyters and deacons, is distinguished from the temporary assumption of functions or duties, or a limited range of ministerial activities, by the lifelong commitment to a distinctive vocation, acknowledged by the Church in and through the sacrament of orders. The propriety in theology and in pastoral practice

---

56 *The Theology of Ordination: A Report by the Faith and Order Advisory Group of the Board for Mission and Unity*, GS 281 (London: Church Information Office, 1975), p. 9; Avis, *Ministry*, p. 116.

57 Hooker, *Laws*, 5.80.3–13; cf. R. R. Gaillardetz, 'The Ecclesiological Foundations of Ministry within an Ordered Communion', in *Ordering the Baptismal Priesthood*, ed. S. K. Wood (Collegeville, MN: Liturgical, 2003), pp. 26–51; Zizioulas, *Being*.

of temporary licences to perform the duties of a priest has been questioned in this study. The near consensus within the Anglican Communion, and to a lesser degree ecumenically, seems to be that those who exercise pastoral oversight should also preside at the celebration of the eucharist in the communities they serve, and should be ordained to the presbyterate.[58] Perhaps it is time to consider also ordaining those who preach,[59] at the very least those whose role in the community extends beyond the pulpit to some level of pastoral care and responsibility. Here a crucial issue must be the way in which the ministry of the lay minister who preaches and exercises pastoral care relates to that of the presbyter who shares with the bishop the cure of souls in that community. Where pastoral care becomes shared oversight, then it would surely be appropriate for the lay minister concerned to be ordained into the presbyteral college.

We have noted that the relationship between the presbyterate and the episcopate is more complex and more ambiguous than is generally supposed in catholic ecclesiology, particularly in the Eastern and Oriental Orthodox churches. Historically, the emergence of the monarchical episcopate has tended to be viewed as a development from a corporate presbyterate.[60] This reconstruction is supported largely on the basis of the essential similarity between the qualities expected in candidates for episcopal and presbyteral office in the Pastoral letters. More recently, a contrary theory has been propounded, that householders hosting Christian congregations exercised what was effectively a monarchical episcopate from the first, and that a presbyterate emerged subsequently, under diverse influences including the ascendancy of a single bishop over different congregations in a particular city.[61] We do not need to resolve the historical question here,

58 *Eucharistic Presidency*, p. 55; S. J. L. Croft, 'Serving, Sustaining, Connecting', in *The Future of the Parish System*, ed. S. J. L. Croft (London: Church House Publishing, 2006), p. 86; Dallen, *Priestless Sundays*, pp. 121–2; H. C. B. Green, *Lay Presidency at the Eucharist?* (London: Darton, Longman and Todd, 1994); Pitt, *At the Head of the Table*.

59 Cf. Davies, 'Historical and Theological Arguments', pp. 23–5.

60 H. F. von Campenhausen, *Ecclesiastical Authority and Spiritual Power in the Church of the First Three Centuries* (London: A. & C. Black, 1969); E. Käsemann, 'Ministry and Communion in the New Testament', *Essays on New Testament Themes* (London: SCM Press, 1964), pp. 63–94; J. D. G. Dunn, *Unity and Diversity in the New Testament* (London: SCM Press, 1977).

61 R. A. Campbell, *The Elders* (Edinburgh: T & T Clark, 1994). Cf. R. W. Gehring, *House Church and Mission* (Peabody, MA: Hendrickson, 2004).

nor to assume that there was a single pattern of development which culminated and stabilized in the threefold orders of catholic ministry. It is not possible, however plausible the latter theory, to demonstrate either that the monarchical episcopate was universally established during the first generation of the Church, or that it originated through appointment by the apostles, however these be defined. Nor can it be established that all subsequent presbyteral and diaconal, as well as episcopal, ministry derived either directly from the apostles or from bishops they had appointed.

We have noted also the further ambivalence in the medieval Western Church, where the episcopate and presbyterate were understood to be a single order of priesthood. In other words, a bishop was no more than a priest who had been appointed to high administrative office, and acquired thereby the wealth, status, and power of a feudal lord. It was not until the Council of Trent that the episcopate was definitively established as a distinct order of ministry, and ordination and certain other functions reserved to bishops. During the Reformation period, or at the very least the early decades thereof, ambiguity about the relationship between priesthood and episcopate was experienced in both catholic and Reformed ecclesiology, even if ultimately resolved in different ways. Anglicanism adopted a catholic position, one which had not been established in doctrine while the Church of England was in communion with the see of Rome.

One of the earliest proposals for authorized lay presidency at the eucharist was premised, as we have noted above, not upon evangelical or Protestant convictions, but on a catholic principle that all ministry derives from the bishop. Where the bishop is unable to preside in person at a celebration of the eucharist within his diocese, it is his prerogative and his duty to appoint another to do so, and the person so delegated need not be a presbyter.[62] This notion of episcopacy, however uncritically accepted in many Anglo-Catholic circles, and more widely, is unsupported by the historical evidence, and explicitly denies the integrity of the ministry of presbyters.

However valuable an institution episcopacy has become for Anglicans, as also for many Lutheran traditions, and increasingly for other Protestants, and however willingly many presbyters acquiesce in the notion of their ministry as consisting entirely in substituting for their remote or absent bishops,

---

62 F. C. Synge, 'The Challenge of the Frontiers', in *Anglican Congress 1963* (Toronto: Editorial Committee, 1963), pp. 155–64.

[a] theological or dogmatic distinction is impossible to draw not only because *episkopoi* and presbyters were originally differentiated either differently from today or not at all, but because there are no specific episcopal functions which have not, in the course of Church history, been legitimately assumed by priests.[63]

These functions include both confirmation and ordination. Apostolic succession, and the legitimacy or validity of priestly ministry, do not depend on episcopal ordination.

The ambiguity of the relationship between the episcopate and the presbyterate needs to be acknowledged and accepted, and resolved in an essentially collegial relationship between bishops and the priests of their dioceses. This is not a denial of the primacy of bishops within their jurisdiction, but it does emphasize the collegiality of priestly ministry in which bishops share. It has become fashionable to describe the ministry of some priests, especially those who lead team ministries which include other presbyters, as in some sense episcopal. The ambivalence between priest and bishop can therefore be reflected in the ministry of both. And, in a deeper sense, ambivalence in both identity and function is essential to the identity of all called to Christian ministry, and especially bishops and presbyters who distinctively represent God to their fellow human beings, and their fellow human beings to God.

Theological Education, Ministerial Formation, and the Diversity of Ordained Ministries

The notions of theological education and ministerial formation are a relatively recent innovation in Anglicanism. Theology was not taught to undergraduates in the English universities until the nineteenth century. The oldest Anglican theological college, Codrington College in Barbados, was established in 1745, on property bequeathed to the Society for the Propagation of the Gospel along with the invidious legacy of slave ownership. Theological colleges were not established in England until the middle of the nineteenth century,[64] and reflect and embody in their architecture and their ethos a pseudo-monastic version

---

63 Küng, *Church*, p. 430. Cf. K. Rahner, *Theological Investigations. 19* (London: Burns & Oates, 1983).

64 M. D. Chapman, 'Living the Truth: Cuddesdon in the History of Theological Education', in M. D. Chapman (ed.), *Ambassadors of Christ*, (Aldershot: Ashgate, 2004), pp. 1–22; D. A. Dowland, *Nineteenth-Century Anglican Theological Training* (Oxford: Clarendon Press, 1997).

of the Victorian neo-Gothic romanticism of their period. It was not until the twentieth century that this particular approach to ministerial formation came to be regarded, particularly among the staff and alumni of such institutions, as essential to the preparation for ministry of candidates for ordination. Contrary to what is widely believed, and even aggressively asserted in some circles, attendance at a residential theological college has never been a legal prerequisite to ordination in the Church of England, even if it has become official policy for certain categories of ordinands.[65] Canon law requires that the candidate

> ... be sufficiently instructed in Holy Scripture and in the doctrine, discipline, and worship of the Church of England.[66]

The "doctrine, discipline, and worship of the Church of England" are defined as "set forth in the Thirty-nine Articles of Religion, The Book of Common Prayer, and the Ordinal".[67] How this learning is to be acquired, other than to the satisfaction of the bishop, is not stipulated.

These observations notwithstanding, most ordinands in the Church of England and in other provinces of the Communion during the past century have undergone some form of residential training, in which community life and worship has been emphasized alongside academic and pastoral training and spiritual formation. This approach to ministerial training has been called into question in recent years, for several reasons. The public school dormitory environment is at the very least unsuitable for an increasing proportion of mature ordinands, and the pseudo-monastic regime is grotesquely inappropriate for ordinands with families, in particular parents with young children. The extent to which such institutions have been able to adapt to changing circumstances remains a matter of contention. Whether the pseudo-monastic model was ever appropriate for ministerial formation, is, furthermore, open to question. Well-connected ordinands who had already been sheltered from ordinary life by social background, isolated from parochial church life since commencing preparatory school and reared in the religion of the public school chapel and Oxford or Cambridge college could hardly be prepared for any aspect of pastoral ministry by a pseudo-monastic residential theological college. It is unlikely to be a coincidence that the period when the theological

---

65   *Ministry in the Church of England* (London: Church House Publishing, 2005).

66   Canon C4 1 (amended 1991).

67   Canon C7 (amended 1972).

colleges flourished was also that in which the Church of England experienced its most drastic decline.

Residential training is almost invariably an impossible undertaking for ordinands who remain in secular employment and envisage ministry in a self-supporting capacity. While this is an impediment to ordination that some vested interests would wish to see entrenched, the mind of the Church has been otherwise. In the Church of England there have over the last 30 years been published a series of substantial reports into the nature of ministry and the educational and training requirements for equipping men and, more recently, women to serve effectively in the diaconate and presbyterate.[68] It is now nearly 80 years since the Lambeth Conference first considered self-supporting ordained ministries,[69] and 50 since the bishops declared that "there is no theological principle which forbids a suitable man [*sic*] from being ordained priest while continuing in his lay occupation", and recommended that provinces explore ways of widening their ministry, "not as a substitute for the full-time ministry of the Church, but as an addition to it".[70] In 1968 the bishops gathered at Lambeth reaffirmed this resolution, and urged that "a wider and more confident use" be made of "supplementary ministry".[71] The theological principle ought therefore to be well-established in the Anglican Communion that, notwithstanding the financial and pastoral needs which have been experienced in many parts of the Church in recent decades, the broadening of the presbyterate is a desirable development.

If it is accepted that patterns of self-supporting ordained ministry are theologically and pastorally beneficial to the life of the Church, it would stand to reason that modes of ministerial formation designed, however appositely or otherwise, for young unmarried men training for the full-time ministry would be inappropriate for candidates of different backgrounds preparing for other forms of ministry. It is not necessary here to rehearse the benefits to the Church of being served by priests and deacons whose theological education and ministerial formation has been rooted in the worshipping community of their local church, and has not

---

68   J. Tiller, *A Strategy for the Church's Ministry* (London: Church Information Office, 1983); *Education for the Church's Ministry: The Report of the Working Party on Assessment* (London: Church Information Office, 1987); *Formation for Ministry Within a Learning Church: The Structure and Funding of Ordination Training* (London: Church House Publishing, 2004).

69   Lambeth Conference 1930, Resolution 65.

70   Lambeth Conference 1958, Resolution 89.

71   Lambeth Conference 1968, Resolution 33.

entailed the disruption of their family lives. The only disadvantage of part-time, non-residential training programmes is that ordinands in full-time employment do not have the time or the leisure to undertake the volume of reading and concentrated study which can reasonably be expected of full-time students; nor do they enjoy the same opportunities for fellowship and interaction with each other, but at least their spirituality is formed in an environment relevant to the exercise of their future ministry.

We have noted that there has been considerable disagreement, both historically and in recent theologies of ministry, as to the level of academic competence needed to function effectively in the ordained ministry, as indeed also in lay ministries. There has been considerable consultation on these issues through the Theological Education for the Anglican Communion (TEAC) working party established by the Primates' Conference in 2003. This body has produced quite complex and detailed recommendations for a comprehensive range of learning processes to be required of those training for and beginning ministry as laity, deacons, priests, and bishops.[72]

Disagreement concerning the educational needs of clergy has extended to whether or not a presbyter requires sufficient theological proficiency to preach.[73] While none would dispute that preaching should normally be integral to the ministry of a priest, as indeed is stipulated in the Ordinal, there remains doubt as to whether this is essential. This is a matter not only of the person's intellectual grasp of Christian doctrine, and capacity to articulate it within and outside the liturgy, but also of the educational level of the community and its needs in Christian teaching. We have observed that some proposals for authorized lay presidency at the eucharist have not considered adequately the need for communities to receive regular and adequate ministry of the word. This is a need which must be addressed when ordination of local church leaders, or their authorization as lay leaders to preside at the celebration of the eucharist, is considered. At the same time, the need to be measured is fundamentally contextual, and the academic, pastoral, and spiritual aspects of the formation process undertaken must also be contextually appropriate.

While issues to do with theological education may apply most obviously to the ministry of the word, they are relevant also to the exercise of pastoral care and oversight, and therefore cannot be ignored

---

72   www.aco.org/ministry/theological/teac/grids.index.cfm
73   Hooker, *Laws*, 5.81; Küng, *Why Priests?*, pp. 60–64.

where liturgical presidency is concerned. This applies equally whether the minister concerned is a lay person, deacon, presbyter, or even bishop.

Word, Sacrament, and Pastoral Care

Who should or may preside at the celebration of the eucharist on any particular occasion in any particular community is a question fundamentally of who is the appropriate minister of the sacraments in that particular context. We have noted that liturgical presidency and pastoral oversight have been inextricably linked since the earliest days of the Church. The teaching office and the ministry of the word were closely associated, but not as closely identified, with pastoral oversight and the ministry of the sacraments. The link has been disrupted in the Western Church largely on account of medieval conceptions of priesthood and the episcopate. The episcopate became increasingly an administrative, and often military, office, all too often denuded of its pastoral and spiritual functions, and bishops, when present at the eucharist, came to preside from their thrones, and sometimes to preach, while another priest conducted the service. The sacerdotal attributes which accrued to the presbyterate, and the increasing tendency for priests to function independently of their bishop and the presbyteral college, changed the character of the ministry, particularly of priests not competent to preach or not inducted to the cure of souls. While the reformed Church of England at least attempted to ensure that clergy were effective ministers of the word as well as of the sacraments, and took some steps towards ensuring that the cure of souls was exercised in parishes, it was not until very much more recently that the liturgical and pastoral ministry of bishops was restored to its proper prominence.

The relationship between ministry of word and of sacrament, and of pastoral care, "those primary, public and mandated tasks of the Church",[74] needs to be explored, in the context both of priesthood and of lay ministry. Ministry of word and sacrament, and pastoral oversight of communities, are all of the essence of priestly ministry, but all have come increasingly to be shared with lay people in different ways.[75] It needs to be considered not only which ministries ought properly to be exercised by a deacon, presbyter, or bishop, and which ministers ought accordingly to be ordained, but also whether lay Christians are being

---

74 Avis, *Ministry*, p. 49.
75 Cf. Avis, *Ministry*; Greenwood, *Transforming Priesthood*; Power, *Ministers*, pp. 167, 173.

diverted from their proper witness and ministry in the world to service the structures of the Church.

In Anglicanism the fundamental unity and parity between word and sacrament has traditionally been emphasized;[76] even if evangelicals have wished to assert the primacy of the word, the unavoidable historical reality is that the sacraments were celebrated in the Church before the books of the New Testament were written, and were well established in Christian liturgy before the canon of the New Testament was fixed. The parity, and perhaps more importantly the interdependence, between word and sacrament has been perceived to have been distorted, not only by authorizing lay people to preach but not to preside at the eucharist, but also by the trend of recent decades towards more frequent celebrations of the eucharist, with fewer services focused primarily or exclusively on the ministry of the word. Advocates and opponents alike of authorized lay presidency at the eucharist have wrestled with the question as to why liturgical preaching, at the eucharist as well as at the Office or other services of the word, can be delegated to a lay person, but not presiding at the eucharist.[77]

The practice of what was in effect delegated presidency, whereby bishops sat on their thrones "presiding" while a presbyter "celebrated" the eucharist, which originated in the medieval Church and persisted in Anglicanism after the Reformation, and has not yet been fully eradicated, may have contributed to this. The practice of bishops' "presiding" and preaching while another priest "celebrated" the eucharist may or may not have contributed to the perception that the ministry of the word is superior to that of the sacraments, but it is far from being a healthy precedent for any kind of delegation, even if such a practice could be attested in the ancient Church.[78] It is now generally recognized that presidency cannot be delegated, and cannot be separated from the words and acts which constitute the prayer of consecration. Even where it is still argued that parish clergy exercise a liturgical presidency delegated to them by their bishops, it is no longer considered appropriate that presidency be delegated when the bishop is present.

---

76 Pickard and Johnson, 'Lay Presidency', p. 14.

77 Cf. *Eucharistic Presidency*, p. 56; Cocksworth and Brown, *Being a Priest*, pp. 74–80; P. F. Jensen, 'Lay Administration of Holy Communion', Address to the Clergy of the diocese of Newcastle (2004), pp. 8–10; Pickard and Johnson, 'Lay Presidency'.

78 Cf. P. F. Bradshaw, *Liturgical Presidency in the Early Church* (Bramcote: Grove Books, 1983).

While presidency cannot be exercised apart from conducting the eucharistic rite as a whole, including the prayer of consecration, this does not exclude delegation to others of subordinate roles in the act of worship. Even if it is normative that the president should also preach, nobody would suggest that this should invariably be the case. Presidency can therefore include oversight of the ministry of the word, without necessarily exercising that ministry personally at a particular celebration of the eucharist. Presidency therefore entails being responsible for what is read and preached in public worship, without necessarily delivering the ministry of the word.[79] In ancient Christian tradition teaching authority was shared more widely, and such figures as Justin Martyr, Tertullian, Clement of Alexandria, and Origen exercised considerable influence if not official teaching authority as laymen. We have noted that there is some uncertainty as to whether such lay teachers were permitted to preach at the eucharist or at any other act of liturgical worship, but their significance for the transmission of Christian doctrine can nonetheless not be ignored. The administration of the sacraments has historically been very much more closely bound up with pastoral oversight of the congregation than has ministry of the word, and lay theologians and teachers have contributed significantly, and independently of ecclesiastical office, to the development of Christian doctrine without exercising liturgical presidency. Ancient tradition would therefore tell strongly against the logic that if lay people can preach they can also be authorized to administer the sacraments. Nevertheless, when the ministry of the word is exercised by those who exercise pastoral oversight of the community, there can be little justification for withholding ordination of such ministers to the ministry of word and sacraments.

Theology of the Eucharist

A comprehensive treatment of eucharistic theology, whether specifically Anglican or more inclusively Catholic or ecumenical, is not necessary for the purposes of this study. The only aspect of the theology of the eucharist relevant to the present purpose is whether or not, and in what way, the eucharist itself determines who may preside at its celebration. In other words, the question is whether the celebration of the eucharist requires that a particular person, and specifically an episcopally ordained priest, preside.

---

79 Cocksworth and Brown, *Being a Priest*, pp. 74–80.

There are undoubtedly some Anglo-Catholics who believe that the priesthood is endowed with supernatural or quasi-magical powers, and that these powers are conferred at ordination, provided of course that the rite be administered by a (male) bishop consecrated in the apostolic succession. Where it is believed that these powers are essential to the celebration of the eucharist, and for that matter other sacraments, these rites are not valid or effective without the ministry of an officiating priest. Even if this has been the conviction of the majority of Christians in both East and West since early in the medieval period, if not earlier, such beliefs are not consonant with the doctrine of the Church of England, or of any other Anglican province. Such notions of priesthood and the sacraments would be regarded by most Anglican theologians as incompatible with the Book of Common Prayer, the Ordinal, and the Articles of Religion. Whether or not such beliefs can legitimately be extrapolated from Scripture, they are quite clearly not expounded there so explicitly as to constitute the body of belief that can be deemed to be "necessary unto eternal salvation", as defined in Article VI.

There are of course those Anglicans and other Christians who sincerely believe that a doctrine of transubstantiation is implicit, if not explicit, in the "last supper" narratives in the canonical gospels. For these, transubstantiation would indeed be an article of faith. This is clearly not how the relevant passages have been understood and interpreted in the authoritative statements of Anglican doctrine, as transubstantiation is explicitly repudiated in Article XXVIII. *Of the Lord's Supper*:

> *Panis et vini transubstantiation in eucharistia ex sacris literis probari non potest. Sed apertis Scripturae verbis adversatur, sacramenti naturam evertit, et multarum superstitionum dedit occasionem.*

> Transubstantiation (or the change of the substance of Bread and Wine) in the Supper of the Lord cannot be proved by Holy Writ; but is repugnant to the plain words of Scripture, overthroweth the nature of a sacrament, and hath given occasion to many superstitions.

So far as this Article is concerned, therefore, not only can the doctrine of transubstantiation not be established on the basis of Scripture, as would be required for the doctrine to be accepted in terms of Article VI, but it is declared inconsistent with Scripture, and therefore beyond the remit of the Church in defining its teaching and ordering its worship, as stipulated in Article XX. Nor would the doctrine of transubstantiation be supported by critical New Testament scholarship, so as to challenge the tradition of the Church. Anthropologically informed exegesis would be particularly aware of the diverse and not mutually exclusive ways in which divine presence is experienced in physical matter in different cultures.[80] Even were it possible for transubstantiation to be extrapolated from the relevant passages in the New Testament, this would not form a sufficient basis for the doctrine to be accepted in the Anglican Communion on the same basis as it is the official teaching of the Roman Catholic Church. Nor would the doctrine in and of itself require that an episcopally ordained priest preside at every celebration of the eucharist.

The eucharist is ultimately dependent on the grace of God, and not on the power of the person, bishop, priest, deacon, or lay, whether male or female, who officiates at the rite. Arguments about the validity of ministry in terms of who was ordained by whom, and according to which rite, have been shown to be anachronistic, if not spurious. Apostolic succession is not constituted by the transmission of supernatural power through episcopal ordination. Even if the dominical injunction to celebrate the eucharist was addressed specifically and exclusively to the apostles, its celebration is an act of the Church as a whole, which the apostles gathered at the "last supper" represent and embody. It is the gathered congregation as a whole which celebrates the eucharist, and which embodies the presence of the whole Church, living and departed, not the officiating bishop of presbyter.

Bishops and presbyters are able to represent Christ and the Church in distinctive ways, at the celebration of the eucharist and in other acts of liturgical presidency, and indeed also in mission and pastoral ministry. However much value is attached to this, and however much power is experienced in the symbolism, these notions of priesthood cannot in themselves determine who may preside at the eucharist. At the same time, the doctrines of the eucharist, the Church, and Christian ministry represented are not lightly to be discarded.

Defining the Eucharistic Community

Much of the debate concerning authorized lay presidency at the eucharist, and indeed extended communion and, to a lesser extent, the ordination of self-supporting clergy, has concerned the right, and indeed the necessity, of Christian communities to celebrate the eucharist. More attention has been given to how this is to be accomplished than to defining which gatherings form an appropriate context for the

---

80   Cf. F. J. King, *More than a Passover* (Frankfurt: Peter Lang, 2007).

celebration of the eucharist.[81] This is particularly relevant to such informal meetings within and alongside parochial congregations as fellowship and Bible study groups, sometimes called house churches, and also to some "fresh expressions of church" which may or may not constitute coherent communities. Notwithstanding the dominical saying, "Wherever two or three are gathered in my name, I am in their midst" (Mt. 18.20), which does not allude directly or necessarily even indirectly to the eucharist, there has been a history of sensitivity in the Church of England, reflected in the rubrics in the Book of Common Prayer, to celebrations of the eucharist with very small numbers of communicants or other worshippers present. This is not a matter simply of numbers, or whether the whole Church can be truly and effectively represented in a small gathering, but, more importantly, of how such a gathering relates to the Church catholic.

Where there has been any discussion of the appropriate setting for the celebration of the eucharist, notions of church have tended to be all but exclusively parochial.[82] In Anglicanism, the diocese is the definitive, local, eucharistic community; parishes and other worshipping communities are derivative, and this must apply in principle also to chaplaincies and peculiars outside diocesan structures.[83] The persistence of ideas of church associated with Ignatius of Antioch may be regarded as archaic, in that bishops have become remote from the sacramental and pastoral lives of most Christians. Nevertheless, the celebration of the eucharist at which the bishop presides, with the college of presbyters and the laity of the diocese gathered, is an ideal of catholicity, locally embodied, which should not be altogether lost.

While catholicity may be essential to communion,[84] and whatever the theological and ecclesiological value attached to the diocese, the parish has become for all practical purposes the local church in Anglicanism, and indeed the equivalent pertains in most Christian denominations. The functions of the presbyter who shares with the bishop the cure of souls in the parish, is in many ways essentially episcopal. The rector or vicar exercises pastoral care and oversight, teaches the faith, gathers the congregation for worship, and, increasingly, coordinates the ministry of those, lay as well as ordained, who share in this work. Unless the

---

81 Cf. Lloyd, *Lay Presidency?*, pp. 7–8.

82 Cf. *Mission-Shaped Church: Church Planting and Fresh Expressions of Church in a Changing Context* (London: Church House Publishing, 2004).

83 G. R. Evans, *Authority in the Church* (Norwich: Canterbury Press, 1990), p. 31; cf. O'Meara, *Theology*, p. 184.

84 Cf. Zizioulas, *Being*, pp. 141–59, 249–53.

Church of England, and other Anglican provinces, are to divide their dioceses into very much smaller units, the eucharist in the absence of the bishop will remain normative. The issue is therefore not whether the parish will function as the primary eucharistic community for most Christians, but, if it is not served by a full-time priest, inducted to the cure of souls, whether and how the eucharist is to be celebrated.

Largely as a consequence of the charismatic movement, smaller and less formal groups, meeting generally on weekday evenings in private homes, have become popular in many Anglican parishes, of all ecclesiastical persuasions. As well as structured or unstructured prayer and fellowship, Bible studies and other forms of discussion have been the principal activities of these groups. It has not been uncommon for some to request the parish priest to celebrate the eucharist with them from time to time. Extended communion, however, is forbidden to such groups in the Church of England.[85] Some have adopted a reconstructed *agape* meal as a form of worship. Others have called for the lay leaders of these groups, or their hosts, to be authorized to preside at a celebration of the eucharist. Here the issue is not only whether lay people should be so authorized, in such groups or more widely, but whether such groups are the appropriate context for a celebration of the eucharist.[86] If such celebrations are appropriate, and quite apart from the issue of lay presidency, the question arises as to whether it would be more appropriate that the priest be invited, to represent and embody, and to maintain and reinforce, the place of the group within the parish, the diocese, and the wider Church, and to give expression to its commitment to being a part of the life of the local church in the diocese and the parish.[87]

This issue becomes particularly acute with the church-planting movement within the Church of England, and also in other Anglican provinces. Hitherto, the principal places of worship have been parish churches, and it is here that Christians have gathered to celebrate the eucharist. Whereas other defined communities, such as schools, colleges, and hospitals, may have chapels for their worship, and to meet their particular spiritual needs, and have their own priests appointed and licensed to serve them, in the Church of England they are nonetheless subject to the jurisdiction of the incumbent of the parish in which they are located, unless granted a royal charter or exempted by the diocesan

---

85 Rubrics and Bishops' Guidelines to *Public Worship with Communion by Extension.*
86 Cf. *Theology of Ordination*, p. 58.
87 Cf. *Theology of Ordination*, p. 59.

bishop under the Extra-Parochial Ministry Measure 1967.[88] Chapels of ease are legally and in practice an extension of the parish church; even if in time many have become separate parishes, they remain integral to the parochial system of the Church of England, and to the diocese of which they are a part. The eucharist may be celebrated in private chapels only with explicit authorization from the bishop, and then not as a substitute for residents' participating in the regular worship of the parish.[89]

The creation of "fresh expressions of church", within the Church of England though not necessarily within its parochial system, represents a significant departure from long-established Anglican practice. It is not so much that patterns of worship may be abhorrent to more traditional Anglicans, but that worshipping groups are being created which have no defined social identity. Whereas a school or college chapel represents that particular community at worship, and ministers to its particular spiritual needs, and parish churches aspire to do the same for the entire local community, "fresh expressions" are gatherings of individuals who have no collective identity or purpose outside their particular meetings. Careful consideration is needed as to whether such groups should celebrate the eucharist apart from the regular worship of the parish in which they are located, at least on a regular basis. It is reckless, and increases the already considerable likelihood of "fresh expressions" becoming schismatic sects, to suggest that the absence of a priest should be no obstacle to regular celebration of the eucharist.[90] If the Church of God is to be built up rather than divided through "fresh expressions", then it would almost certainly be judicious as well as theologically appropriate to ensure that they are served by presbyters and deacons who are fully integrated into the life of their dioceses, to proclaim the word and administer the sacraments while exercising pastoral oversight, and thereby effectively to integrate these groups and those who join them fully into the wider Church.

Summary

This chapter has not so much reached conclusions as raised questions, about some of which Anglicans are deeply divided. These need to be addressed before a definitive answer to the question of lay presidency at the eucharist can be reached. The questions may usefully be summarized as follows:

---

88   Canon B41 2.–3.

89   Canon B41 1.

90   *Mission Shaped Church*, p. 101.

1. Is the current state of the Anglican Communion conducive to resolving this issue? If it is not possible for the Communion to reach a common mind, reached and expressed through its Instruments, what would the potential consequences be of individual dioceses and provinces reaching their own decisions and acting on them? Is the issue that urgent, or so fundamental to the truth of the gospel, that unilateral action could justifiably be contemplated?

2. Is it appropriate, and conducive to the mission of the Church, that the laity be increasingly drawn into the ministerial roles which ought to enable and support them in their witness in the world?

3. What is the proper ministry of deacons, presbyters, and bishops, and how is this most appropriately expressed in the eucharist?

4. What levels of theological education, and what patterns of ministerial formation, are necessary or appropriate to equip men and women for the ministry of word and sacrament, and the exercise of pastoral care and oversight, in the contexts in which they are called to serve?

5. How do the ministries of word, sacrament, and pastoral oversight relate? When are they most adequately and appropriately exercised by a bishop, presbyter, or deacon? What is the appropriate role of the laity in these ministries?

6. Does the theology of the eucharist, as received and transmitted in Anglicanism, require that the celebration be presided over, on all or particular occasions, by any particular minister of the Church?

7. In which gathered communities is the Church embodied and represented in its catholicity? In which contexts is a celebration of the eucharist appropriate? How is the catholicity of the Church best embodied in these celebrations?

9

Concluding Reflections

This study has treated an issue, perhaps less prominent and sensational, but no less potentially divisive of the Anglican Communion than questions surrounding sexuality and the ordination of women. It is no coincidence that lay presidency at the eucharist has been most strenuously advocated in parts of the Communion in which women are not ordained to the priesthood, and whose leaders have been strident and perhaps opportunistic in exploiting disputes concerning homosexuality to extend their influence into other provinces. This is not a climate or a context conducive to addressing issues with profound implications for the Anglican Communion, its ministry, and its sacramental life, as well as its developing relationships with other Christians. This is illustrated by the level of theological ineptitude and noncommunication evident in the current debates within Anglican bodies, official and otherwise, about sexuality.[1] Whether the proposed Anglican Covenant will provide an adequate framework both for addressing contentious theological issues and for managing relations between provinces in which different positions predominate, is far from certain.

In this situation, it is perhaps prudent not to attempt conclusions when the premises upon which they are founded would not be recognized by all parties to the debate about lay presidency. But perhaps there are issues which it has been possible to clarify, and some contentious but ultimately irrelevant issues which it has been possible, if not to exclude altogether, then at least to place in perspective. Whether this has contributed to the creation of a common ground on which Anglicans of all persuasions would be able to engage and move forward together remains to be seen. But this is the spirit in which these concluding reflections, and the book as a whole, are offered.

We have noted that order has been integral to the life of the Church from its inception, and was reflected in the liturgical worship as well as other aspects of the corporate life of the ancient Christian congregations.

---

1   N. H. Taylor, 'Some Observations on Theological Method, Biblical Interpretation, and Ecclesiastical Politics in Current Disputes in the Anglican Communion', *Theology* 111 (2008): 51–8.

The Church has never been free of patriarchal structures,[2] and those which evolved in the Early Church acquired a theological significance as they crystallized into the catholic order which Anglicanism has inherited and maintained. This enables the exercise of authority and ministry in the life of the Church to be measured in the light of the gospel. It does not mean that from the foundations of the Church there have always been bishops, presbyters, and deacons ordained in the apostolic succession, or that the eucharist has invariably been presided over by an episcopally ordained priest. But the origins of the structures and offices which evolved are attested, as is the eucharistic theology in terms of which sacramental ministry has been defined. The continuation of the ministries of bishops and presbyters, in whom custody of the liturgical and sacramental life of the Church, as well as its teaching office, is vested, was fundamental to the unique character of the English Reformation, and the Anglicanism which emerged and evolved out of it. The ministry of deacons and the laity has not been acknowledged or maintained with the same consistency through history, and this is a loss which the Church in recent decades has rightly sought to address.

While this has been denied by some of its protagonists, lay presidency at the eucharist would entail a radical deviation from Anglican order, however widespread it may be in some of the Protestant denominations which emerged at the Reformation and subsequently. The ordination of women did not in any way alter the nature of the ministry and the liturgical life of the Church, which have been so central to the development and self-understanding of Anglicanism. However central sexuality may be to questions of Christian morality, it does not concern the character of Christian ministry. The authorization of lay presidency at the eucharist, however, would constitute a fundamental redefinition of Christian priesthood, as well as altering the character and orientation of lay ministry. This does not mean that such a change cannot be contemplated within Anglicanism, or even necessarily that such a change would not be desirable. But the magnitude of the issue needs also to be recognized.

For some proponents of change, the authorization of lay presidency at the eucharist would be little more than a matter of expediency. For

---

2   Cf. A. D. Clarke, *Serve the Community of the Church* (Grand Rapids, MI: Eerdmans, 2000); D. N. Power, *The Eucharistic Mystery* (Dublin: Gill & Macmillan, 1992), p. 59; R. A. Campbell, *The Elders* (Edinburgh: T & T Clark, 1994); R. W. Gehring, *House Church and Mission* (Peabody, MA: Hendrickson, 2004); R. H. Williams, *Stewards, Prophets, Keepers of the Word* (Peabody, MA: Hendrickson, 2006).

others it represents the logical – even necessary – continuation of the English Reformation, even if this means deviating from the Anglican order to which the overwhelming majority remain committed, and for whom lay eucharistic presidency would be "destructive of the values which the ordained ministry exists to conserve".[3]

Our review of both theological arguments and of specific proposals for authorized lay eucharistic presidency, as also of the range of alternative provisions for worship in the absence of a priest exercising the cure of souls in a particular community, has tended towards negative conclusions, as much on pastoral as on theological grounds. There can be no substitute for the celebration of the eucharist, but neither can there be any substitute for the competent and regular ministry of the Word. Nor can there be any substitute for the presence of a priest exercising pastoral oversight in the congregation. In principle, therefore, we have come to support the prevailing consensus in the Anglican Communion, that the training and ordination of local church leaders to the diaconate and the presbyterate is the most appropriate approach to the provision for ministry of word, sacrament, and pastoral care, in each congregation.

Having reached this position, it is nonetheless necessary to recognize that the question of lay presidency at the eucharist is a second-order issue.[4] The dominical injunction to celebrate the eucharist, however this be reconstructed historically, and however interpreted ontologically, is primary. This principle was recognized most notably by conservative catholic and evangelical theologians in the Church of England collaborating after the collapse of the Anglican–Methodist unity proposals during the 1960s.[5] Where a Christian community does not have a priest, provision for the regular celebration of the eucharist, as for ministry of the word and pastoral oversight, is the responsibility of the bishop to whom the cure of souls reverts. The deployment of a full-time priest and the development of ordained non-stipendiary ministries would not be mutually exclusive options, and while the latter in particular would take time to implement, the lack of a priest in the community is nonetheless temporary. Contingency arrangements during the interim period would vary according to circumstances, but there would be little justification, and considerable risk, in dispensing with order in such a situation.

---

3   W. Temple, *Christus Veritas* (London: Macmillan, 1930), p. 163; cf. P. Gibson, 'The Presidency of the Liturgy', in *A Kingdom of Priests*, ed. T. J. Talley (Nottingham: Grove Books, 1988), p. 55.

4   Cf. J. B. Lightfoot, *Saint Paul's Epistle to the Philippians* (London: Macmillan, 1896), p. 266; Temple, *Christus Veritas*, p. 163.

5   C. O. Buchanan, *et al.*, *Growing Into Union* (London: SPCK, 1970), pp. 86–7.

There remains the question, by no means hypothetical, of unforeseeable and uncontrollable circumstances, in which a group of lay Christians is severed from the life and ministry of the Church. The church in Japan persisted from the sixteenth to the nineteenth century without the ministry of ordained bishops, presbyters, and deacons, and other Christian groups have either been formed or become isolated from the wider Church in extraordinary circumstances, occasioned by war or other forms of social upheaval, and been constrained to be church for an indefinite period. In such circumstances it would be extremely difficult to deny that lay presidency at the eucharist would be appropriate and even necessary.[6]

While the celebration of the eucharist by the Church as a whole does not depend on the participation of any individual Christian or community, this needs to be balanced by the need of these individuals and communities for the spiritual sustenance which the eucharist provides. Notwithstanding the possibilities of spiritual communion, or even the ambiguous possibility of the *agape*, actual participation in the eucharist in what would inevitably be straitened circumstances, could not justifiably be denied. Such an act would not be a case for wanton schism, or of an "emergency" analogous to clinical baptism.[7] Rather, it would be a case of remaining faithful, and believing that the "grace represented by the presbyter's ministry of presiding"[8] has been given to that community, albeit without episcopal ordination. The remembrance of Christ's death in the celebration of the eucharist is a higher obligation than observance of Church order, and, where extraordinary circumstances arise, and communities are constrained to be church in isolation from the fellowship and ministry of the Church catholic, then "'the spirit' and not the letter must decide" when, how, and by whom the ministry of word and sacrament should be exercised.[9]

---

6   H. C. B. Green, *Lay Presidency at the Eucharist?* (London: Darton, Longman and Todd, 1994), pp. 3–4, 8; Lightfoot, *Philippians*, p. 266; cf. H. Küng, *The Church* (London: Burns & Oates, 1968), p. 443; E. Schillebeeckx, *Ministry: Leadership in the Community of Jesus Christ* (New York, NY: Crossroad, 1981), pp. 72–3, 138–9.

7   Cf. A. Rowthorn, *The Liberation of the Laity* (Wilton, CT: Morehouse-Barlow, 1986), p. 126; W. Temple, *Thoughts on Some Problems of the Day* (London: Macmillan, 1931), p. 111.

8   R. D. Williams, 'Theological Resources for Re-Examining Church', in *The Future of the Parish System*, ed. S. J. L. Croft (London: Church House Publishing, 2006), p. 56.

9   Lightfoot, *Philippians*, p. 266; cf. Tertullian, *De Exhortatione Castitatis* 7.

Bibliography

Achtemeier, P. J. (1996) *1 Peter* (Minneapolis, MN: Fortress Press).

Adam, A. K. M. (2006) *Faithful Interpretation: Reading the Bible in a Postmodern World* (Minneapolis, MN: Fortress Press).

Adam, D. (1994) 'The Priest and Prayer', in *Priesthood Here and Now*, ed. M. Bowering (Newcastle: Diocese of Newcastle), pp. 59–63.

Adams, W. S. (1982) 'The Eucharistic Assembly – Who Presides?' *Anglican Theological Review*, 64: 311–21.

Afanasiev, N. N. (2007) *The Church of the Holy Spirit.* (Notre Dame, IL: University of Notre Dame Press).

Aland, K. (1963) *Did the Early Church Baptise Infants?* (London: SCM Press).

Aldenhoven, H. (2002) 'Presidency at the Eucharist in the Context of the Theology of Icons', in *Anglican Theological Review*, 84: 703–12.

All are Called: Towards a Theology of the Laity (1985) (London: Church Information Office).

Allchin, A. M. (1988) *Participation in God: A Forgotten Strand in Anglican Tradition* (London: Darton, Longman and Todd).

Allen, R. (1930) *The Case for Voluntary Clergy* (London: Eyre and Spottiswoode).

Allen, R. (1960) *Missionary Methods: St Paul's or Ours?* (London: World Dominion).

Allison, C. F. (1975) 'What is a Priest? Another Anglican View', in *To Be A Priest: Perspectives on Vocation and Ordination*, eds R. E. Terwilliger and U. T. Holmes (New York, NY: Seabury Press), pp. 11–20.

Allmen, J.–J. v. (1981) 'The Communal Character of Public Worship in the Reformed Tradition', in *Roles in the Liturgical Assembly*, ed. M. J. O'Connell (New York, NY: Pueblo Press), pp. 1–111.

Alviar, J. J. (1993) *Klesis: the Theology of the Christian Vocation According to Origen* (Dublin: Four Courts Press).

Anderson, H. and Foley, E. (2001) *Mighty Stories, Dangerous Rituals: Weaving Together the Human and the Divine* (San Francisco, CA: Jossey Bass).

Anglican Orders and Ordination: Essays and Reports from the Interim Conference at Jarvenpää, Finland, of the International Anglican Liturgical Consultation, 4–9 August 1997 (1997), ed. D. R. Holeton (Cambridge: Grove Books).

Anglican–Lutheran Dialogue: The Report of the European Commission (1982) (London: SPCK).

An Anglican–Methodist Covenant: Common Statement of the Formal Conversations Between the Methodist Church of Great Britain and the Church of England (2001) (London: Methodist Publishing House/Church House Publishing).

Anglican–Methodist Unity: Report of the Anglican–Methodist Unity Commission. Part 2: The Scheme (1968) (London: SPCK and Epworth Press).

Anglican–Roman Catholic International Commission: The Final Report (1981) (London: SPCK).

Ashwin, V. (1994) 'Serve Them with Joy', in *Priesthood Here and Now*, ed. M. Bowering (Newcastle: Diocese of Newcastle), pp. 121–8.

Atkins, P. (2004) *Memory and Liturgy: The Place of Memory in the Composition and Practice of Liturgy* (Aldershot: Ashgate).

Atkinson, N. T. (1997) *Richard Hooker and the Authority of Scripture, Tradition and Reason: Reformed Theologian of the Church of England?* (Carlisle: Paternoster Press).

Atta-Bafoe, V. R., Tovey, P. N. (1990) 'What Does Inculturation Mean?', in *Liturgical Inculturation in the Anglican Communion*, ed. D. R. Holeton (Nottingham: Grove Books), pp. 14–16.

Atteridge, H. W. (1989) *The Epistle to the Hebrews* (Philadelphia, PA: Fortress Press).

Aune, D. E. (1997) *Revelation 1–5* (Waco, TX: Word Books).

Avis, P. D. L. (1992) *Authority, Leadership and Conflict in the Church* (London: Mowbrays).

Avis, P. D. L. (2000) *The Anglican Understanding of the Church: An Introduction* (London: SPCK).

Avis, P. D. L. (2002) *Anglicanism and the Christian Church: Theological Resources in Historical Perspective* (London: T & T Clark).

Avis, P. D. L. (2004) 'The Episcopal Ministry Act of Synod: A "Bearable Anomaly?"', in *Seeking the Truth of Change in the Church*, ed. P. D. L. Avis (London: T & T Clark), pp. 152–70.

Avis, P. D. L. (2004) 'Reception: Towards an Anglican Understanding', in *Seeking the Truth of Change in the Church*, ed. P. D. L. Avis (London: T & T Clark), pp. 19–39.

Avis, P. D. L. (2005) *A Ministry Shaped by Mission* (London: T & T Clark).

Baker, J. A. (1970) *The Foolishness of God* (London: Darton, Longman and Todd).

Barker, M. (2007) *Temple Themes in Christian Worship* (London: T & T Clark).

Baker, T. G. A. (1977) *Questioning Worship* (London: SCM Press).

Balasuriya, T. (1979) *The Eucharist and Human Liberation* (London: SCM Press).

Ballard, P. (2000) 'The Emergence of Pastoral and Practical Theology in Britain', in *The Blackwell Reader in Pastoral and Practical Theology*, eds J. Woodward and S. Pattison (Oxford: Blackwell), pp. 59–70.

Banks, N. (1994) 'Parish Priest', in *Priesthood Here and Now*, ed. M. Bowering (Newcastle: Diocese of Newcastle), pp. 64–73.

Banks, R. (1980) *Paul's Idea of Community* (Exeter: Paternoster Press).

Baptism, Eucharist and Ministry (1982). World Council of Churches, Faith and Order Paper No. 111 (Geneva: WCC).

Baptism, Eucharist and Ministry 1982–1990: Report on the Process and Responses (1990). World Council of Churches, Faith and Order Paper No. 149 (Geneva: WCC).

Barbara June SLG. (2001) 'Simple Gifts: Priesthood in a Praying Community', in *Priests in a People's Church*, ed. G. Guiver (London: SPCK), pp. 63–71.

Barclay, J. M. G. (1996) *Jews in the Mediterranean Diaspora* (Edinburgh: T & T Clark).

Barker, M. (2003) *The Great High Priest: The Temple Roots of Christian Liturgy* (London: T & T Clark).

Barnett, J. M. (1995) *The Diaconate: A Full and Equal Order* (London: Continuum).

Barrett, C. K. (1973) *A Commentary on the Second Epistle to the Corinthians* (London: A. and C. Black).

Barrett, C. K. (1978) 'Shaliah and Apostle', in *Donum Gentilium*, ed. E. Bammel *et al* (Oxford: Clarendon Press), pp. 88–102.

Barrett, C. K. (1983) *Church, Sacraments and Ministry in the New Testament* (Exeter: Paternoster Press).

Barrett, C. K. (1994, 1998) *Acts of the Apostles* (Edinburgh: T & T Clark).

Bartchy, S. S. (2002) 'Divine Power, Community Formation, and Leadership in the Acts of the Apostles', in *Community Formation in the Early Church and in the Church Today*, ed. R. N. Longenecker (Peabody, MA: Hendrickson), pp. 88–104.

Bartlett, A. B. (2007) *A Passionate Balance: The Anglican Tradition* (London: Darton, Longman and Todd).

Bartlett, D. L. (1993) *Ministry in the New Testament* (Minneapolis, MN: Fortress Press).

Bauckham, R. J. (1988) Tradition in Relation to Scripture and Reason', in *Scripture, Tradition and Reason*, eds. R. J. Bauckham and B. Drewery (Edinburgh: T & T Clark), pp. 117–45.

Bauer, W. F. (1971) *Orthodoxy and Heresy in Earliest Christianity* (Philadelphia, PA: Fortress Press).

Bayes, P. (2004) *Mission-Shaped Church: Missionary Values, Church Planting and Fresh Expressions of Church* (Cambridge: Grove Books).

Beare, F. W. (1987) *Matthew* (Peabody, MA: Hendrickson).

Beasley-Murray, G. R. (1962) *Baptism in the New Testament* (Exeter: Paternoster Press).

Beckford, J. A. (1978) 'Accounting for Conversion', in *British Journal of Sociology*, 29: 249–62.

Beckwith, R. T. (1964) *Priesthood and Sacraments: A Study of the Anglican–Methodist Report* (Abingdon: Marsham Manor).

Beckwith, R. T. (2003) *Elders in Every City: The Origin and Role of the Ordained Ministry* (Carlisle: Paternoster Press).

Bell, C. M. (1992) *Ritual Theory, Ritual Practice* (New York, NY: Oxford University Press).

Benenden, P. von (1987) 'Haben Laien die Eucharistie ohne Ordinierte gefeiert? Zu Tertullians » De exhortatione castitatis« 7,3', in *Archiv für Liturgiewissenschaft*, 29: 31–46.

Berger, P. L. (1967) *The Sacred Canopy* (New York, NY: Doubleday).

Berger, P. L. (1969) *A Rumor of Angels: Modern Society and the Rediscovery of the Supernatural* (New York, NY: Doubleday).

Best, E. (1972) *A Commentary on the First and Second Epistles to the Thessalonians* (London: A. and C. Black).

Best, E. (1998) *Ephesians* (Edinburgh: T & T Clark).

Bicknell, E. J. (1955) *A Theological Introduction to the Thirty-Nine Articles of the Church of England* (London: Longman, Green and Co.).

Bieler, A. and Schottroff, L. (2007) *The Eucharist: Bodies, Bread, and Resurrection* (Minneapolis, MN: Fortress Press).

Biggar, N. (2006) 'The Ethical "Use" of Scripture', in *The Authority of Scripture: A Report of the Church of Ireland Bishops' Advisory Commission on Doctrine*, ed. R. Clarke (Dublin: Church of Ireland), pp. 141–63.

Birchall, M. (1985) 'The Case for Corporate Leadership in the Local Church', in *All are Called: Towards a Theology of the Laity*, ed. P. C. Rodger (London: Church Information Office), pp. 52–6.

Blasi, A. J. (1991) *Making Charisma* (New York, NY: Peter Lang).

Boff, L. (1986) *Ecclesiogenesis: The Base Communities Reinvent the Church* (Maryknoll, MN: Orbis).

Bolt, P., Thompson, M. and Tong, R. (2008) *The Lord's Supper in Human Hands: Who Should Administer?* (Sydney: Australian Church Record / Anglican Church League).

Booty, J. E. (1979) 'Richard Hooker', in *The Spirit of Anglicanism*, ed. W. J. Wolf (Edinburgh: T & T Clark), pp. 1–45.

Booty, J. E. (1987) 'The Judicious Mr Hooker and Authority in the Elizabethan Church', in *Authority in the Anglican Communion*, ed. S. W. Sykes (Toronto: Anglican Book Centre), pp. 94–115.

Borsch, F. H. (1975) 'The Priest as Professional', in *To Be A Priest: Perspectives on Vocation and Ordination*, eds R. E. Terwilliger and U. T. Holmes (New York, NY: Seabury Press), pp. 111–16.

Bouley, A. (1981) *From Freedom to Formula: The Evolution of the Eucharistic Prayer from Oral Improvisation to Written Texts* (Washington DC: Catholic University of America Press).

Bourke, M. M. (1975) 'The Priesthood of Christ', in *To Be A Priest: Perspectives on Vocation and Ordination*, eds R. E. Terwilliger and U. T. Holmes (New York, NY: Seabury Press), pp. 55–62.

Bouyer, L. (1975) 'The Priest and the Eucharist', in *To Be A Priest: Perspectives on Vocation and Ordination*, eds R. E. Terwilliger and U. T. Holmes (New York, NY: Seabury Press), pp. 103–10.

Bowe, B. E. (1988) *A Church in Crisis: Ecclesiology and Paranaesis in Clement of Rome* (Minneapolis, MN: Fortress Press).

Bowen, J. R. (1968) 'The Church of the Province of East Africa', in *Modern Anglican Liturgies: 1958–1968*, ed. C. O. Buchanan (London: Oxford University Press), pp. 70–7.

Bowering, M. (1994) 'Under Authority with Authority', in *Priesthood Here and Now*, ed. M. Bowering (Newcastle: Diocese of Newcastle), pp. 89–97.

Boyarin, D. (1999) *Dying for God: Martyrdom and the Making of Christianity and Judaism* (Stanford, CA: Stanford University Press).

Bradbury, N. (2000) Ecclesiology and Pastoral Theology', in *The Blackwell Reader in Pastoral and Practical Theology*, eds J. Woodward and S. Pattison (Oxford: Blackwell), pp. 173–81.

Bradshaw, P. F. (1971) *The Anglican Ordinal: Its History and Development from the Reformation to the Present Day* (London: SPCK).

Bradshaw, P. F. (1983) *Liturgical Presidency in the Early Church* (Bramcote: Grove Books).

Bradshaw, P. F. (1988) 'Ordinals', in *The Study of Anglicanism*, eds S. W. Sykes and J. E. Booty (London: SPCK), pp. 143–53.

Bradshaw, P. F. (1989) 'The Participation of Other Bishops in the Ordination of a Bishop in the *Apostolic Tradition* of Hippolytus', in *Studia Patristica*, 18: 335–8.

Bradshaw, P. F. (1990) *Ordination Rites of the Ancient Churches of East and West* (New York, NY: Pueblo Press).

Bradshaw, P. F. (1991) 'Daily Prayer', in *The Identity of Anglican Worship*, eds K. W. Stevenson and B. D. Spinks (London: Mowbrays), pp. 69–79.

Bradshaw, P. F. (1998) '"*Ubi eucharistia, ibi ecclesia*": Ecclesiological Reflections on Ministry, Order, and the Eucharist', in *Our Thanks and Praise: The Eucharist in Anglicanism Today*, ed. D. R. Holeton (Toronto: Anglican Book Centre), pp. 51–65.

Bradshaw, P. F. (2002) *The Search for the Origins of Christian Worship: Sources and Methods for the Study of Early Liturgy* (London: SPCK).

Bradshaw, P. F. (2004) *Eucharistic Origins* (London: SPCK)

Bradshaw, P. F., Johnson, M. E. and Phillips, L. E. (2002) *The Apostolic Tradition* (Minneapolis, MN: Fortress Press).

Bradshaw, T. (1992) *The Olive Branch: An Evangelical Anglican Doctrine of the Church* (Carlisle: Paternoster Press).

Branick, V. (1989) *The House Church in the Writings of Paul* (Wilmington, DE: Glazier).

Breaking New Ground: Church Planting in the Church of England (1984) (London: Church House Publishing).

Brent, A. (1995) *Hippolytus and the Roman Church in the Third Century: Communities in Tension Before the Emergence of the Monarch-Bishop* (Leiden: E. J. Brill).

Brightman, F. E. (1899) 'The Sacramentary of Serapion of Thmuis', *Journal of Theological Studies*, 1: 247–77.

Brilioth, Y. (1956) *Eucharistic Faith and Practice, Evangelical and Catholic* (London: SPCK).

Brooks, R., and Vasey, M. (1990) 'What is the Relation between Formation and Inculturation?', in *Liturgical Inculturation in the Anglican Communion*, ed. D. R. Holeton (Nottingham: Grove Books), pp. 23–6.

Brown, D. W. (2001) '*Phronesis*, Development, and Doctrinal Definition', in *International Journal for the Study of the Christian Church*, 1: 70–85.

Brown, R. (2005) *Being a Deacon Today: Exploring a Distinctive Ministry in the Church and in the World* (Norwich: Canterbury Press).

Brown, R. E. (1971) *Priest and Bishop: Biblical Reflections* (London: Geoffrey Chapman).

Brown, R. E. (1979) *The Letters of John* (New York, NY: Doubleday).

Brown, R. E. (1994) *The Death of the Messiah* (New York, NY: Doubleday).

Brown, R. E. and Meier, J. P. (1983) *Antioch and Rome* (London: Geoffrey Chapman).

Browning, D. (2000) 'Pastoral Theology in a Pluralistic Age', in *The Blackwell Reader in Practical and Pastoral Theology*, eds J. Woodward and S. Pattison (Oxford: Blackwell), pp. 89–103.

Bruce, S. (1995) *Religion in Modern Britain* (Oxford: Oxford University Press).

Bruce, S. (1996) *Religion in the Modern World: From Cathedrals to Cults* (Oxford: Oxford University Press).

Bruce, S. (2002) *God is Dead: Secularization in the West* (Oxford: Blackwell).

Bryant, R. (1994) 'Study the Scriptures', in *Priesthood Here and Now*, ed. M. Bowering (Newcastle: Diocese of Newcastle), pp. 129–37.

Brydon, M. A. (2006) *The Evolving Reputation of Richard Hooker: An Examination of the Responses, 1600–1714* (Oxford: Oxford University Press).

Buchanan, C. O. (1975) *Further Anglican Liturgies: 1968–1975* (Bramcote: Grove Books).

Buchanan, C. O. (1977) 'Some Anglican Historical Perspectives', in *Lay Presidency at the Eucharist?* ed. B. T. Lloyd (Bramcote: Grove Books), pp. 11–19.

Buchanan, C. O. (ed.), (1987) *Modern Anglican Ordination Rites*, Alcuin/GROW Liturgical Studies, 3 (Bramcote: Grove Books).

Buchanan, C. O. (1994) 'Issues of Liturgical Inculturation', in *Anglican Liturgical Inculturation in Africa*, ed. D. Gitari (Bramcote: Grove Books), pp. 9–19.

Buchanan, C. O. (2007) 'Questions Liturgists would like to ask Justin Martyr', in *Justin Martyr and His Worlds*, ed. S. Parvis and P. Foster (Minneapolis, MN: Fortress Press), pp. 152–9.

Buchanan, C. O. (ed.) (1985) *Latest Anglican Liturgies: 1976–1984* (London: SPCK).

Buchanan, C. O., Mascall, E. L., Packer, J. I. and Leonard, G. D. (1970) *Growing Into Union: Proposals for Forming a United Church in England* (London: SPCK).

Burston, R. (1994) 'Country Incumbent', in *Priesthood Here and Now*, ed. M. Bowering (Newcastle: Diocese of Newcastle), pp. 79–88.

Burtchaell, J. T. (1992) *From Synagogue to Church: Public Services and Offices in the Earliest Christian Communities* (Cambridge: Cambridge University Press).

Caird, G. B. (1984) *The Revelation of St John the Divine* (London: A. and C. Black).

Calvin, J. (1960) *Institutes of the Christian Religion* (Philadelphia, PA: Westminster Press).

Campbell, R. A. (1994) *The Elders: Seniority within Earliest Christianity* (Edinburgh: T & T Clark).

Campenhausen, H. F. v. (1969) *Ecclesiastical Authority and Spiritual Power in the Church of the First Three Centuries* (London: A. and C. Black).

Card, T. (1988) *Priesthood and Ministry in Crisis* (London: SCM Press).

Carey, G. L. (1991) 'Church Planting, Ecclesiology and Mission', in *Planting New Churches*, ed. R. Hopkins and T. Anderson (Guildford: Eagle Press), pp. 21–32.

Carey, G. L. (2004) *Know the Truth* (London: HarperCollins).

Carr, A. W. (1989) *The Pastor as Theologian: The Integration of Pastoral Ministry, Theology and Discipleship* (London: SPCK).

Casey, P. M. (1998) *Aramaic Sources of Mark's Gospel* (Cambridge: Cambridge University Press).

Chadwick, H. (1997) Reception', in *Christian Life and Witness*, ed. C. M. N. Sugden and V. Samuel (London: SPCK) , pp. 200–13.

Chapman, M. D. (1996) 'Preparing for Judgement: A Theology for Ministry', in *Modern Believing*, 37: 10–16

Chapman, M. D. (1997) *By What Authority? Authority, Ministry and the Catholic Church* (London: Darton, Longman and Todd).

Chapman, M. D. (2004) 'Living the Truth: Cuddesdon in the History of Theological Education', in *Ambassadors of Christ*, ed. M. D. Chapman (Aldershot: Ashgate), pp. 1–22.

Chapman, M. D. (2006) *Anglicanism: A Very Short Introduction* (Oxford: Oxford University Press).

Chapman, M. D. (2007) *Bishops, Saints and Politics: Anglican Studies* (London: T & T Clark).

Charley, J. W., ed. (1973) *Agreement on the Doctrine of the Ministry*. Grove Booklet on Ministry and Worship, 22 (Bramcote: Grove Books).

Chester, S. J. (2003) *Conversion at Corinth* (London: T & T Clark).

Chesworth, J. (2002) 'Anglican Liturgical Reform in Kenya: Some Reflections', in *Encounter*, 2: 9–18.

Chidester, D. S. (1984) 'The Challenge to Christian Ritual Studies', in *Anglican Theological Review*, 66: 23–34.

Chilton, B. D. (1994) *A Feast of Meanings: Eucharistic Theologies from Jesus through the Johannine Circle* (Leiden: E. J. Brill).

Chow, J. K.–M. (1992) *Patronage and Power: Studies in Social Networks in Corinth* (Sheffield: Sheffield Academic Press).

Chupungco, A. J. (1982) *Cultural Adaptation of the Liturgy* (New York, NY: Paulist Press).

Churches Respond to BEM (1986–88). Faith and Order Papers, 129, 132, 135, 137, 143, 144, ed. M. Thurian (Geneva: World Council of Churches).

Clarke, A. D. (2000) *Serve the Community of the Church: Christians as Leaders and Ministers* (Grand Rapids, MI: Eerdmans).

Clarke, K. H. (1990) *Called to Minister? A Consideration of Vocation to the Ordained Ministry* (Belfast: Church of Ireland Evangelical Fellowship).

Coakley, S. (2000) 'Lay and Ordained Ministry: Some Theological Reflections', in *Sewanee Theological Review*, 43: 207–13.

Cocksworth, C. J. (1991) 'Eucharistic Theology', in *The Identity of Anglican Worship*, eds K. W. Stevenson and B. D. Spinks (London: Mowbrays), pp. 49–68.

Cocksworth, C. J. (1993) *Evangelical Eucharistic Thought in the Church of England* (Cambridge: Cambridge University Press).

Cocksworth, C. J. (1997) *Holy, Holy, Holy: Worshipping the Trinitarian God* (London: Darton, Longman and Todd).

Cocksworth, C. J., Brown, R. (2002) *Being a Priest Today: Exploring Priestly Identity* (Norwich: Canterbury Press).

Cohen, S. J. D. (1989) 'Crossing the Boundary and Becoming a Jew', in *Harvard Theological Review*, 82: 13–33.

Collins, J. N. (1990) *Diakonia: Re-Interpreting the Ancient Sources* (New York, NY: Oxford University Press).

Collins, R. F. (1999) *First Corinthians* (Collegeville, MN: Liturgical Press).

Common Worship: Initiation Services (1998) (London: Church House Publishing)

Common Worship: Initiation Services: Rites on the Way (2004). Church of England Liturgical Commission, GS 1546 (London: General Synod of the Church of England).

Common Worship: Pastoral Services (2000) (London: Church House Publishing).

Congar, Y. (1957) *Lay People in the Church* (London: Bloomsbury).

Congar, Y. M. J. (1959) *Lay People in the Church: A Study for a Theology of Laity* (London: Geoffrey Chapman).

Congregation for the Doctrine of the Faith, Letter to Bishops, 'The Minister of the Eucharist' (1983) in *Origins*, 13 (15 September): 229–33.

Congregation for the Doctrine of the Faith, Letter to Edward Schillebeeckx, 'Who Can Preside at the Eucharist' (1985) in *Origins*, 14 (24 January): 523, 525.

Conversations between the Church of England and the Methodist Church (1963) (London: Church Information Office and Epworth Press).

Conzelmann, H. G. (1987) *Acts of the Apostles* (Philadelphia, PA: Fortress Press).

Cooke, B. (1976) *Ministry to Word and Sacraments*. (Philadelphia, PA: Fortress Press).

Corley, K. E. (1993) *Private Women, Public Meals: Social Conflict in the Synoptic Tradition* (Peabody, MA: Hendrickson).

Cotter, W. (1994) 'Women's Authority Roles in Paul's Churches: Countercultural or Conventional?', in *Novum Testamentum*, 36: 350–72.

Cottrell, S. (1996) *Sacrament, Wholeness and Evangelism: A Catholic Approach* (Cambridge: Grove Books).

Coulton, N. (1994) 'Calling', in *Priesthood Here and Now*, ed. M. Bowering (Newcastle: Diocese of Newcastle), pp. 4–12.

Countryman, L. W. (1999) *Living on the Border of the Holy: Renewing the Priesthood of All* (Harrisburg, PA: Morehouse).

Countryman, L. W. (2003) *Interpreting the Truth: Changing the Paradigm of Biblical Studies* (Harrisburg, PA: Trinity Press International).

Cranfield, C. E. B. (1963) *Mark* (Cambridge: Cambridge University Press).

Cranfield, C. E. B. (1975, 1979) *Romans* (Edinburgh: T & T Clark).

Cranmer, T. (1846) *Miscellaneous Writings and Letters of Thomas Cranmer*, ed. J. Edmund (Cambridge: Cambridge University Press).

Cray, G. (2006) 'Focusing Church Life on a Theology of Mission', in *The Future of the Parish System: Shaping the Church of England for the Twenty-First Century*, ed. S. J. L. Croft (London: Church House Publishing), pp. 61–74.

Crisis for Confirmation (1967), ed. M. C. Perry (London: SCM Press).

Crockett, W. R. (1989) *Eucharist: Symbol of Transformation* (Collegeville, MN: Pueblo Press).

Croft, S. J. L. (1999) *Ministry in Three Dimensions: Ordination and Leadership in the Local Church* (London: Darton, Longman and Todd).

Croft, S. J. L. (2006) 'Many Rooms in my Father's House: The Changing Identity of the English Parish Church', in *The Future of the Parish System: Shaping the Church of England for the Twenty–First Century*, ed. S. J. L. Croft (London: Church House Publishing), pp. 178–82.

Croft, S. J. L. (2006) 'Serving, Sustaining, Connecting: Patterns of Ministry in the Mixed Economy Church', in *The Future of the Parish System: Shaping the Church of England for the Twenty–First Century*, ed. S. J. L. Croft (London: Church House Publishing), pp. 75–90.

Croft, S. J. L. (ed.) *Mission–shaped Questions: Defining Issues for Today's Church* (London: Church House Publishing).

Cullmann, O. (1953) *Peter: Disciple – Apostle – Martyr* (London: SCM Press).

Cummings, O. F. (2004) *Deacons and the Church* (New York, NY: Paulist Press).

Cundy, I. P. M. (2006) 'Reconfiguring a Diocese towards Mission', in *The Future of the Parish System: Shaping the Church of England for the Twenty–First Century*, ed. S. J. L. Croft (London: Church House Publishing), pp. 152–69.

Dackson, W. (2004) *The Ecclesiology of Archbishop William Temple* (Lewiston, NY: Edwin Mellen Press).

Dackson, W. (2007) 'Toward a Theology of the Laity'. Unpublished paper.

Dallen, J. (1994) *The Dilemma of Priestless Sundays* (Chicago, IL: Liturgy Training Publications).

Daly, C. B. (1993) *Tertullian the Puritan and His Influence* (Dublin: Four Courts Press).

Davie, G. (1994) *Religion in Britain Since 1945: Believing Without Belonging* (Oxford: Blackwell).

Davie, G. (2006) 'From Obligation to Consumption: Understanding the Patterns of Religion in Northern Europe', in *The Future of the Parish System: Shaping the Church of England for the Twenty–First Century*, ed. S. J. L. Croft (London: Church House Publishing), pp. 33–45.

Davie, P. (1983) 'Faith and the Future', in *Pastoral Care and the Parish*, ed. D. Nicholls (Oxford: Blackwell).

Davies, D. J. (1977) 'Some Historical and Theological Arguments against', in *Lay Presidency at the Eucharist?* ed. B. T. Lloyd (Bramcote: Grove Books), pp. 20–5.

Davies, W. D. and Allison, D. C. (1991–1997) *Matthew* (Edinburgh: T & T Clark).

Deacons in the Ministry of the Church (1988), GS 802, ed. T. J. Bavin (London: Church House Publishing).

Dexter, F. (1994) 'Pastor', in *Priesthood Here and Now*, ed. M. Bowering (Newcastle: Diocese of Newcastle), pp. 105–12.

Dickens, A. G. (1964) *The English Reformation* (London: Batsford).

Dillistone, F. W. (1955) *Christianity and Symbolism* (London: SCM Press).

Dillistone, F. W. (1986) *The Power of Symbols* (London: SCM Press).

Dix, G. (1945) *The Shape of the Liturgy* (London: Dacre).

Dix, G. (1946) *The Theology of Confirmation in Relation to Baptism* (London: Dacre).

Dix, G. and Chadwick, H. (1991) *The Treatise on the Apostolic Tradition of St Hippolytus of Rome, Bishop and Martyr* (London: Alban).

Donahue, J. R. and H., D. J. (2002) *The Gospel of Mark* (Collegeville, MN: Liturgical Press).

Donovan, V. J. (1982) *Christianity Rediscovered: An Epistle from the Masai* (London: SCM Press).

Douglas, M. (1966) *Purity and Danger* (London: Penguin).

Dowland, D. A. (1997) *Nineteenth–Century Anglican Theological Training: The Redbrick Challenge* (Oxford: Clarendon Press).

Downey, M. (2003) 'Ministerial Identity: A Question of Common Foundations', in *Ordering the Baptismal Priesthood: Theologies of Lay and Ordained Ministry*, ed. S. K. Wood (Collegeville, MN: Liturgical Press), pp. 3–25.

Doyle, D. M. (2000) *Communion Ecclesiology: Visions and Versions* (Maryknoll, NY: Orbis).

Driver, T. F. (1998) *Liberating Rites: Understanding the Transformative Power of Ritual* (Oxford: Westview Press).

Duffy, E. (1992) *The Stripping of the Altars: Traditional Religion in England, c. 1400 – c. 1580* (New Haven, CT: Yale University Press).

Dugmore, C. W. (1942) *Eucharistic Doctrine in England from Hooker to Waterland* (London: SPCK).

Dugmore, C. W. (1958) *The Mass and the English Reformers* (London: Macmillan).

Dulles, A. (1987) *Models of the Church* (New York, NY: Doubleday).

Dulles, A. R. (1997) *The Priestly Office: A Theological Reflection* (New York, NY: Paulist Press).

Dunn, J. D. G. (1977) *Unity and Diversity in the New Testament* (London: SCM Press)

Dunn, J. D. G. (1988) *Romans* (Waco, TX: Word Books).

Dunn, J. D. G. (1991) *The Partings of the Ways: Between Christianity and Judaism, and Their Significance for the Character of Christianity* (London: SCM Press).

Dunn, J. D. G. (1992) 'Whatever happened to the Lord's Supper?', in *Epworth Review*, 19(1): 35–48.

Dunn, J. D. G. (1998) *The Theology of Paul the Apostle* (Edinburgh: T & T Clark).

Durkheim, E. (1964) *The Elementary Forms of Religious Life* (London: Allen and Unwin).

Dyson, A. O. (1985) 'Clericalism, Church and Laity', in *All Are Called: Towards a Theology of the Laity*, ed. P. C. Rodger (London: Church Information Office), pp. 13–17.

Echlin, E. P. (1971) *The Deacon in the Church Past and Future* (New York, NY: Alba).

Echlin, E. P. (1974) *The Story of Anglican Ministry* (Slough: St Paul).

Education for the Church's Ministry: The Report of the Working Party on Assessment (1987). ACCM, 22 (London: Church Information Office).

Ehrhardt, A. A. T. (1958) *The Apostolic Ministry* (Edinburgh: Oliver and Boyd).

Eichhorn, K. A. A. L. ([1898] 2007) *The Lord's Supper in the New Testament* (Atlanta, GA: Scholars Press).

Eliade, M. (1958) *Rites and Symbols of Initiation: The Mysteries of Birth and Rebirth* (New York, NY: Harper).

Ellingworth, P. (1993) *The Epistle to the Hebrews* (Grand Rapids, MI: Eerdmans).

Elliott, J. H. (2000) *1 Peter* (New York, NY: Doubleday).

Elliott, M. (2006) 'Scripture and Revelation', in *The Authority of Scripture: A Report of the Church of Ireland Bishops' Advisory Commission on Doctrine*, ed. R. Clarke (Dublin: Church of Ireland), pp. 67–101.

Elliott, N. (1994) *Liberating Paul* (New York, NY: Crossroad).

Elliott, P. (1994) 'Ordination Revisited', in *Priesthood Here and Now*, ed. M. Bowering (Newcastle: Diocese of Newcastle), pp. 165–71.

Episcopal Ministry (1990), Archbishops' Group on the Episcopate (London: Church House Publishing).

Escobar, S. (1992) 'Mission in Latin America: An Evangelical Perspective', *Missiology: An International Review*, 20: 241-53.

Etchells, D. R. (1985) 'Towards a Theology of Laos', in *All are Called: Towards a Theology of the Laity*, ed. P. C. Rodger (London: Church Information Office), pp. 29–34.

Etchells, D. R. (1995) *Set My People Free: A Lay Challenge to the Churches* (London: CollinsFount).

Etzioni, A. (1975) *A Comparative Analysis of Complex Organizations* (New York, NY: Free Press).

The Eucharist of the Early Christians (1978), ed. W. Rordorf (New York, NY: Pueblo).

Eucharistic Presidency: A Theological Statement by the House of Bishops of the General Synod (1997), GS 1248 (London: Church House Publishing).

Evans, C. F. (1990) *Luke* (London: SCM Press).

Evans, E. (1964) *Tertullian's Homily on Baptism* (London: SPCK).

Evans, G. R. (1990) *Authority in the Church: A Challenge for Anglicans* (Norwich: Canterbury Press).

Evans, G. R. (1997) *The Reception of the Faith* (London: SPCK).

Faulkner, R. K. (1981) *Richard Hooker and the Politics of a Christian England* (Berkeley, CA: University of California Press).

Fee, G. D. (1987) *The First Epistle to the Corinthians* (Grand Rapids, MI: Eerdmans).

Feeley–Harnik, G. (1981) *The Lord's Table: Eucharist and Passover in Early Christianity* (Philadelphia, PA: University of Pennsylvania Press).

Fenn, R. K. (1995) *The Persistence of Purgatory* (Cambridge: Cambridge University Press).

Fenn, R. K. (1997) *The End of Time: Religion, Ritual, and the Forging of the Soul* (London: SPCK).

Fenn, R. K. (2001) *The Return of the Primitive: A New Sociological Theory of Religion* (Aldershot: Ashgate).

Ferguson, E. (1963) 'Jewish and Christian Ordination', in *Harvard Theological Review*, 56: 13–19

Ferguson, E. (1975) 'Laying on of Hands: Its Significance for Ordination', in *Journal of Theological Studies*, 26: 1–12.

Feulner, H.–J. (1997) *Das 'Anglikanische Ordinale': Eine liturgiegeschichtliche und liturgietheologische Studie* (Neuried: Ars Una).

Fiddes, P. S. (2000) *Participating in God: A Pastoral Doctrine of the Trinity* (London: Darton, Longman and Todd).

Finger, R. H. (2007) *Of Widows and Meals: Communal Meals in the Book of Acts* (Grand Rapids, MI: Eerdmans).

Fisher, J. D. C. (1965) *Christian Initiation: Baptism in the Medieval West* (London: SPCK).

Fisher, J. D. C. (1968) *Confirmation: Then and Now* (London: SPCK).

Fitzmyer, J. A. (1981–85) *Luke* (New York, NY: Doubleday).

Fitzmyer, J. A. (1993) *Romans* (New York, NY: Doubleday).

Fitzmyer, J. A. (1998) *Acts* (New York, NY: Doubleday).

Flanagan, K. (1991) *Sociology and Liturgy: Re-Presentations of the Holy* (London: Macmillan).

Ford, D. F. (1999) *Self and Salvation: Being Transformed*, eds C. Gunton and D. W. Hardy. Cambridge Studies in Christian Doctrine. (Cambridge: Cambridge University Press).

Formation for Ministry within a Learning Church: The Structure and Funding of Ordination Training (2004) (London: Church House Publishing).

Fowl, S. E. (1998) *Engaging Scripture: A Model for Theological Interpretation* (Oxford: Blackwell).

Fowl, S. E. (2000) 'The Role of Authorial Intention in the Theological Interpretation of Scripture', in *Between Two Horizons: Spanning New Testament Studies and Systematic Theology*, eds J. B. Green and M. Turner (Grand Rapids, MI: Eerdmans), pp. 71–87.

Fox, R. L. (1986) *Pagans and Christians* (London: Penguin).

Fox, Z. (2003) 'Laity, Ministry, and Secular Character', in *Ordering the Baptismal Priesthood: Theologies of Lay and Ordained Ministry*, ed. S. K. Wood (Collegeville, MN: Liturgical Press), pp. 121–51.

France, R. T. (2002) *The Gospel of Mark* (Grand Rapids, MI: Eerdmans).

Francis, J. M. M. (1996) *Reflections on Non–Stipendiary Ministry as Ministry in Secular Employment* (Sunderland: University of Sunderland).

Fraser, I. (1982) 'Liberating Faith: Basic Christian Communities and the Eucharist', in *Ecumenical Review*, 44: 58–64.

Frend, W. H. C. (1965) *Martyrdom and Persecution in the Early Church* (Oxford: Blackwell).

Frend, W. H. C. (1984) *The Rise of Christianity* (London: Darton, Longman and Todd).

Freyne, S. V. (1968) *The Twelve: Disciples and Apostles* (London: Sheed and Ward).

Fuchs, L. F. (2008) *Koinonia and the Quest for an Ecumenical Ecclesiology: From Foundations through Dialogue to Symbolic Competence for Communionality* (Grand Rapids, MI: Eerdmans).

Fuller, R. H. (1988) 'Scripture', in *The Study of Anglicanism*, ed. S. W. Sykes and J. E. Booty (London: SPCK), pp. 79–90.

Fuller, R. H. (1988) 'Scripture, Tradition and Priesthood', in *Scripture, Tradition and Reason*, eds R. J. Bauckham and B. Drewery (Edinburgh: T & T Clark), pp. 101–14.

Furnish, V. P. (1984) *II Corinthians* (New York, NY: Doubleday).

Gaillardetz, R. R. (2003) 'The Ecclesiological Foundations of Ministry within an Ordered Communion', in *Ordering the Baptismal Priesthood:*

Theologies of Lay and Ordained Ministry, ed. S. K. Wood (Collegeville, MN: Liturgical Press), pp. 26–51.

Gamble, R. (2006) 'Doing Traditional Church really Well', in *The Future of the Parish System: Shaping the Church of England for the Twenty–First Century*, ed. S. J. L. Croft (London: Church House Publishing), pp. 93–109.

Garnsey, P. D. A. (1970) *Social Status and Legal Privilege in the Roman Empire* (Oxford: Clarendon Press).

Garrow, A. J. P. (2004) *The Gospel of Matthew's Dependence on the Didache* (London: T & T Clark).

Gassmann, G. (1993) *Documentary History of Faith and Order, 1963–1993* (Geneva: World Council of Churches).

Gehring, R. W. (2004) *House Church and Mission: The Importance of Household Structures in Early Christianity* (Peabody, MA: Hendrickson).

Gennep, A. v. (1960) *The Rites of Passage* (London: Routledge and Kegan Paul).

Gessell, J. M. (1975) 'The Priest as Authority on the World', in *To be a Priest: Perspectives on Vocation and Ordination*, eds R. E. Terwilliger and U. T. Holmes (New York, NY: Seabury Press), pp. 117–24.

Gibaut, J. S. (2000) *The Cursus Honorum: A Study of the Origins and Evolution of Sequential Ordination* (New York, NY: Peter Lang).

Gibbs, M. (1985) 'Ministries outside the Parish', in *All Are Called: Towards a Theology of the Laity*, ed. P. C. Rodger (London: Church Information Office), pp. 22–6.

Gibbs, M. (1985) 'The Spiritual Growth of the Laity', in *All Are Called: Towards a Theology of the Laity*, ed. P. C. Rodger (London: Church Information Office), pp. 57–62.

Gibson, P. (1988) 'The Presidency of the Liturgy', in *A Kingdom of Priests: Liturgical Formation of the People of God*, ed. T. J. Talley (Bramcote: Grove Books), pp. 31–8.

Gibson, P. (1990) 'What is the future role of liturgy in Anglican unity?', in *Liturgical Inculturation in the Anglican Communion*, ed. D. R. Holeton (Bramcote: Grove Books), pp. 17–22.

Gibson, P. (2002) *Anglican Ordination Rites*. Grove Worship Series, 168 (Cambridge: Grove Books).

Gill, R. M. (1981) *Prophecy and Praxis: The Social Function of the Churches* (London: Marshall, Morgan and Scott).

Gill, R. M. (1988) *Beyond Decline: A Challenge to the Churches* (London: SCM Press).

Gill, R. M. (1993) *The Myth of the Empty Church* (London: SPCK).

Gill, R. M. (2003) *The 'Empty' Church Revisited* (Aldershot: Ashgate).

Gitari, D., Ed. (1994) *Anglican Liturgical Inculturation in Africa: The Kanamai Statement 'African Culture and Anglican Liturgy'.* Alcuin/GROW Liturgical Studies, vol. 28 (Bramcote: Grove Books).

Gofton, A. (1994) 'Growing Stronger and More Mature', in *Priesthood Here and Now*, ed. M. Bowering (Newcastle: Diocese of Newcastle), pp. 4–12.

Goldingay, J. (1976) *Authority and Ministry* (Bramcote: Grove Books).

Goodacre, D. (1994) 'Counsellor', in *Priesthood Here and Now*, ed. M. Bowering (Newcastle: Diocese of Newcastle), pp. 113–20.

Goodman, M. D. (1994) *Mission and Conversion* (Oxford: Clarendon Press).

Gordon–Taylor, B. (2001) 'Detachment in Priesthood and Community', in *Priests in a People's Church*, ed. G. Guiver (London: SPCK), pp. 115–24.

Gordon–Taylor, B. (2001) 'The Priest and the Mystery: A Case of Identity', in *Priests in a People's Church*, ed. G. Guiver (London: SPCK), pp. 3–23.

Gore, C. (1889) *The Ministry of the Christian Church* (London: Rivington).

Gore, C. (1901) *The Body of Christ: An Enquiry Into the Institution and Doctrine of Holy Communion* (London: John Murray).

Gore, C. (1919) *The Church and the Ministry* (London: Longman).

Gorman, M. J. (2001) *Cruciformity: Paul's Narrative Spirituality of the Cross* (Grand Rapids, MI: Eerdmans).

Gorringe, T. J. (1990) *Discerning Spirit: A Theology of Revelation* (London: SCM Press)

Gospel Parallels: A Comparison of the Synoptic Gospels (1992), ed. B. H. Throckmorton (Nashville, TN: Nelson).

Gottwald, N. K. (1986) *The Hebrew Bible* (London: SCM Press).

Grabbe, L. L. (1991) *Judaism from Cyrus to Hadrian* (London: SCM Press).

Graf, F. (2002) 'Theories of Magic in Antiquity', in *Magic and Ritual in the Ancient World*, eds P. Mirechi and M. Meyer (Leiden: E. J. Brill), pp. 93–104.

Graf, H. J. (1981) 'Priestless Sunday Services with Communion and Resulting Problems. A Report on an Ongoing Controversy', in *East Asian Pastoral Review*, 18: 175–89.

Graham, A. A. K. (1970) 'Should the Ordained Ministry now Disappear?', in *The Sacred Ministry*, ed. G. R. Dunstan (London: SPCK), pp. 45–53.

Graham, A. A. K. (1994) 'Postscript', in *Priesthood Here and Now*, ed. M. Bowering (Newcastle: Diocese of Newcastle), pp. 172–83.

Graham, E. L. (1996) *Transforming Practice: Pastoral Theology in an Age of Uncertainty* (London: Mowbrays).

Graham, E. L. (2000) 'Practical Theology as Transforming Practice', in *The Blackwell Reader in Pastoral and Practical Theology*, eds J. Woodward and S. Pattison (Oxford: Blackwell), pp. 104–17.

Grant, R. M. (1964) *The Apostolic Fathers* (New York, NY: Nelson).

Gray, D. C. (1991) 'Liturgy and society', in *The Identity of Anglican Worship*, eds K. W. Stevenson and B. D. Spinks (London: Mowbrays), pp. 135–43.

Gray, D. C. (2005–6) *The 1927-28 Prayer Book Crisis* (Cambridge: Grove Books).

Green, E. M. B. (1964) *Called to Serve* (London: Hodder and Stoughton).

Green, H. C. B. (1994) *Lay Presidency at the Eucharist?* (London: Darton, Longman and Todd).

Green, J. B. and Turner, M. (eds) (2000) *Between Two Horizons: Spanning New Testament Studies and Systematic Theology* (Grand Rapids, MI: Eerdmans).

Green, W. B. (1975) 'On Vocation', in *To Be A Priest: Perspectives on Vocation and Ordination*, eds R. E. Terwilliger and U. T. Holmes (New York, NY: Seabury Press), pp. 133–40.

Greenwood, R. P. (1994) *Transforming Priesthood: A New Theology of Mission and Ministry* (London: SPCK).

Greenwood, R. P. (2002) *Transforming Church: Liberating Structures for Ministry* (London: SPCK).

Griffiss, J. E. (1997) *The Anglican Vision* (Boston, MA: Cowley Press).

Grimes, R. L. (1990) *Ritual Criticism: Case Studies in the Practice, Essays on Its Theory* (Columbia, SC: University of South Carolina Press).

Gruenwald, I. (2003) *Rituals and Ritual Theory in Ancient Israel* (Leiden: E. J. Brill).

Guiver, G. (2001) 'Priest and Victim', in *Priests in a People's Church*, ed. G. Guiver (London: SPCK), pp. 73–82.

Guiver, G. (2001) 'The Priest as Focus', in *Priests in a People's Church*, ed. G. Guiver (London: SPCK), pp. 127–38.

Haenchen, E. (1971) *Acts* (Oxford: Blackwell).

Hagstrom, A. A. (2003) 'The Secular Character of the Vocation and Ministry of the Laity: Toward a Theology of Ecclesial Lay Identity', in *Ordering the Baptismal Priesthood: Theologies of Lay and Ordained*

Ministry, ed. S. K. Wood (Collegeville, MN: Liturgical Press), pp. 152–74.

Hahnenberg, E. P. (2003) *Ministries: A Relational Approach* (New York, NY: Crossroad)

Haigh, C. A. (1993) *English Reformations: Religion, Politics and Society Under the Tudors* (Oxford: Clarendon Press).

Hannaford, R. (1991) 'Towards a Theology of the Diaconate', in *The Deacon's Ministry*, ed. C. Hall (Leominster: Gracewing), pp. 25–44.

Hannaford, R. (2004) 'Communion and the Kingdom of God', in *Seeking the Truth of Change in the Church*, ed. P. D. L. Avis (London: T & T Clark), pp. 75–100.

Hanson, A. T. (1961) *The Pioneer Ministry* (London: SPCK).

Hanson, A. T. (1975) *Church, Sacraments and Ministry* (London: Mowbrays).

Hanson, R. P. C. (1979) *Christian Priesthood Examined* (Guildford: Lutterworth Press).

Harding, L. S. (2000) 'What have We been telling Ourselves about the Priesthood?', in *Sewanee Theological Review*, 43: 144–66.

Hardy, D. W. (2001) *Finding the Church: The Dynamic Truth of Anglicanism* (London: SCM Press).

Hargrave, A. L. (1990) *But Who Will Preside?* Grove Worship 113 (Nottingham: Grove Books).

Harrington, D. J. (1991) *Matthew* (Collegeville, MN: Glazier Press).

Hart, T. (2000) 'Tradition, Authority, and a Christian Approach to the Bible as Scripture', in *Between Two Horizons: Spanning New Testament Studies and Systematic Theology*, eds J. B. Green and M. Turner (Grand Rapids, MI: Eerdmans), pp. 183–204.

Hartman, L. (1997) *'Into the Name of the Lord Jesus': Baptism in the Early Church* (Edinburgh: T & T Clark).

Harvey, A. E. (1975) *Priest or President?* (London: SPCK)

Hastings, A. (1996) *The Church in Africa, 1450–1950* (Oxford: Clarendon Press).

Hatchett, M. J. (1988) 'Prayer Books', in *The Study of Anglicanism*, ed. S. W. Sykes and J. E. Booty (London: SPCK), pp. 121–33

Haugaard, W. P. (1968) *Elizabeth and the English Reformation* (Cambridge: Cambridge University Press).

Hawthorne, G. F. (1983) *Philippians* (Waco, TX: Word Books).

Hayes, A. L. (2002) 'Christian Ministry in Three Cities of the Western Empire (160 – 258 C.E.)', in *Community Formation in the Early Church and in the Church Today*, ed. R. N. Longenecker (Peabody, MA: Hendrickson), pp. 129–56.

Heaney, S. E. (2008) *Contextual Theology for Latin America: Liberation Themes in Evangelical Perspective* (Milton Keynes: Paternoster).

Hefling, C. (2003) 'What Do We Bless and Why?', in *Anglican Theological Review*, 85: 87–96.

Hegg, D. W. (1999) *Appointed to Preach: Why Ordination Matters* (Fearn: Christian Focus).

Heine, S. (1987) *Women and Early Christianity: Are the Feminist Scholars Right?* (London: SCM Press).

Hengel, M. (1977) *Christ and Power* (Philadelphia, PA: Fortress Press).

Hengel, M. (1979) *Acts and the History of Early Christianity* (London: SCM Press).

Herbert, G. (1981) *The Country Parson, The Temple* (New York, NY: Paulist Press).

Herman, G. (1987) *Ritualised Friendship and the Greek City* (Cambridge: Cambridge University Press).

Herron, T. J. (1989) 'The More Probable Date of the First Epistle of Clement to the Corinthians', in *Studia Patristica*, 21: 106–21.

Higgins, A. J. B. (1952) *The Lord's Supper in the New Testament* (London: SCM Press).

Higham, F. (1962) *Catholic and Reformed: A Study of the Anglican Church 1559–1662* (London: SPCK).

Hill, C. J. (2004) 'Reception and the Act of Synod', in *Seeking the Truth of Change in the Church*, ed. P. D. L. Avis (London: T & T Clark), pp. 101–22.

Hill, R. (1994) 'Tending the Flock of God', in *Priesthood Here and Now*, ed. M. Bowering (Newcastle: Diocese of Newcastle), pp. 13–20.

Hillerdal, G. (1962) *Reason and Revelation in Richard Hooker* (Lund: Gleerup).

Hiltner, S. (2000) 'The Meaning and Importance of Pastoral Theology' in *The Blackwell Reader in Pastoral and Practical Theology*, ed. J. Woodward and S. Pattison (Oxford: Blackwell), pp. 27–48.

Hinchliff, P. B. (1963) *The Anglican Church in South Africa* (London: Darton, Longman and Todd).

Hind, J. (2004) 'Reception and Communion', in *Seeking the Truth of Change in the Church*, ed. P. D. L. Avis (London: T & T Clark), pp. 40–57.

Hoffman, L. A. (1979) 'Jewish Ordination on the Eve of Christianity', in *Studia Liturgica*, 13: 11–41.

Holeton, D. R. (1988) 'The Formative Character of the Liturgy', in *A Kingdom of Priests: Liturgical Formation of the People of God*, ed. T. J. Talley (Bramcote: Grove Books), pp. 8–14.

Holeton, D. R., ed. (1990) *Liturgical Inculturation in the Anglican Communion, Including the York Statement 'Down to Earth Worship'*. Alcuin / GROW Liturgical Studies, vol. 15 (Bramcote: Grove Books).

Holeton, D. R. *et al.* (1993) *Growing in Newness of Life: Christian Initiation in Anglicanism Today* (Toronto: Anglican Book Centre).

Holmberg, B. (1980) *Paul and Power* (Minneapolis, MN: Fortress Press).

Holmes, U. T. (1975) 'The Priest as Enchanter', in *To Be A Priest: Perspectives on Vocation and Ordination*, eds R. E. Terwilliger and U. T. Holmes (New York, NY: Seabury Press), pp. 173–81.

Hooker, M. D. (1991) *The Gospel According to Mark* (London: A. and C. Black).

Hooker, R. (1907) *Ecclesiastical Polity* (London: J. M. Dent).

Hope, D. E. (1985) 'Liturgy – the Work of the People?', in *All Are Called: Towards a Theology of the Laity*, ed. P. C. Rodger (London: Church Information Office), pp. 47–51.

Hopkins, R. (1988) *Church Planting: Models for Mission in the Church of England* (Bramcote: Grove Books).

Hopkins, R. (1989) *Church Planting: Some Experiences and Challenges* (Bramcote: Grove Books).

Horrell, D. G. (1996) *The Social Ethos of the Corinthian Correspondence: From Paul to 1 Clement* (Edinburgh: T & T Clark).

Houlden, J. L. (1974) 'Liturgy and her Companions: A theological appraisal', in *The Eucharist Today*, ed. R. C. D. Jasper (London: SPCK), pp. 168–76

Hovda, R. W. (1976) *Strong, Loving, and Wise: Presiding in Liturgy* (Collegeville, MN: Liturgical Press).

Hughes, A. J. (2002) *Public Worship and Communion by Extension* (Cambridge: Grove Books).

Hull, J. M. (2006) *Mission–Shaped Church: A Theological Response* (London: SCM Press).

Humphrey, C. and Laidlaw, J. (1996) *The Archetypal Actions of Ritual: A Theory of Ritual Illustrated by the Jain Rite of Worship* (Oxford: Clarendon Press).

Ind, W. (2001) *Towards a Theology of The People of God: Our Story* (Truro: Truro Diocesan Board of Finance).

Ind, W. (2007) *With God We Can... : The People of God Journeying On* (Truro: Truro Diocesan Board of Finance).

Inge, J. (1994) 'Best Powers of Mind and Spirit', in *Priesthood Here and Now*, ed. M. Bowering (Newcastle: Diocese of Newcastle), pp. 148–57.

Ingle–Gillis, W. C. (2007) *The Trinity and Ecumenical Church Thought* (Aldershot: Ashgate).

Inziku, J. (2005) *Overcoming Divisive Behaviour: An Attempt to Interpret 1Cor 11,17–34 from Another Perspective* (Frankfurt a. M.: Peter Lang).

Isichei, E. A. (1995) *A History of Christianity in Africa: From Antiquity to the Present* (London: SPCK).

James, D. C. (2004) 'Cell Future', in *The Future of Ministry: Look Ahead 25 Years*, ed. G. Wakefield (Cambridge: Grove Books), pp. 16–22.

James, P. (1993) *Liturgical Presidency* (Bramcote: Grove Books).

Janowitz, N. (2002) *Icons of Power: Ritual Practices in Late Antiquity* (University Park, PA: Pennsylvania State University Press).

Jeanes, G. P. (1995) 'A Reformation Treatise on the Sacraments', in *Journal of Theological Studies*, 46: 149–90.

Jeanes, G. P. (2008) *Signs of God's Promise: Thomas Cranmer's Sacramental Theology and the Book of Common Prayer* (London: T & T Clark, 2008).

Jeanrond, W. G. (1989) 'Community and Authority: The Nature and Implications of the Authority of the Christian Community', in *On Being the Church: Essays on the Christian Community*, eds C. E. Gunton and D. W. Hardy (Edinburgh: T & T Clark), pp. 81–109.

Jeffers, J. S. (1991) *Conflict at Rome* (Minneapolis, MN: Fortress Press).

Jefford, C. N. (2006) *The Apostolic Fathers and the New Testament* (Peabody, MA: Hendrickson).

Jensen, P. F. (2004) 'Lay Administration of Holy Communion'. Address to the Clergy of the Diocese of Newcastle.

Jeremias, J. (1960) *Infant Baptism in the First Four Centuries* (London: SCM Press).

Jeremias, J. (1963) *The Origins of Infant Baptism* (London: SCM Press).

Jeremias, J. (1966) *The Eucharistic Words of Jesus* (London: SCM Press).

Jewel, J. (1969) *An Apologie or Aunswer in Defence of the Church of England, 1562* (London: Scolar).

Jewel, J. (1974) *An Apology of the Church of England*, trans. J. E. Booty (Charlottesville, VA: University Press of Virginia).

Jewett, R. (1993) 'Tenement Churches and Communal Meals in the Early Church: The Implications of a Form–Critical Analysis of 2 Thessalonians 3:10', in *Biblical Research*, 38: 23–43.

Jewett, R. (2007) *Romans* (Minneapolis, MN: Fortress Press).

Johnson, L. T. (1992) *Acts* (Collegeville, MN: Liturgical Press).

Johnson, L. T. (1996) *Letters to Paul's Delegates: 1 Timothy, 2 Timothy, Titus* (Valley Forge, PA: Trinity Press International).

Johnson, L. T. (2002) *1 and 2 Timothy* (New York, NY: Doubleday).

Jones, C. P. M. *et al* (1992) *The Study of Liturgy* (London: SPCK).

Jones, N. L. (2002) *The English Reformation: Religion and Cultural Adaptation* (Oxford: Blackwell).

Kavanagh, A. (1988) *Confirmation: Origins and Reform* (New York, NY: Pueblo Press).

Kaye, B. N. (2002) *Anglicanism in Australia: A History* (Melbourne: Melbourne University Press).

Käsemann, E. (1964) *Essays on New Testament Themes* (London: SCM Press).

Kelly, J. N. D. (1969) *A Commentary on the Epistles of Peter and Jude* (London: A. and C. Black).

Kelly, J. N. D. (1980) *Early Christian Creeds* (Harlow: Longman).

Kenney, P. (1994) 'Confessor', in *Priesthood Here and Now*, ed. M. Bowering (Newcastle: Diocese of Newcastle), pp. 41–50.

King, F. J. (2007) *More than a Passover: Inculturation in the Supper Narratives of the New Testament* (Frankfurt: Peter Lang).

Kings, G., Morgan, G., Gitari, D., (2001) *Offerings from Kenya to Anglicanism: Liturgical Texts and Contexts Including "A Kenyan Service of Holy Communion"*. Joint Liturgical Studies, vol. 50 (Cambridge: Grove Books).

Kirigia, J. K. (2002) 'Liturgical Development in the Anglican Church of Kenya', in *Encounter*, 2: 1–8.

Kitagawa, J. (1975) 'Priesthood in the History of Religions', in *To Be A Priest: Perspectives on Vocation and Ordination*, eds R. E. Terwilliger and U. T. Holmes (New York, NY: Seabury Press), pp. 45–54.

Kitchen, M. (1991) 'The Bible in Worship', in *The Identity of Anglican Worship*, eds K. W. Stevenson and B. D. Spinks (London: Mowbrays), pp. 36–48.

Klauck, H.–J. (1981) *Hausgemeinde und Hauskirche Im frühen Christentum* (Stuttgart: Verlag Katholisches Bibelwerk).

Klauck, H.–J. (1982) *Herrenmahl und hellenistischer Kult: Eine religionsgeschichtliche Untersuchung zum ersten Korintherbrief* (Münster: Aschendorf).

Klauck, H.–J. (2003) *Magic and Paganism in Early Christianity*. (Minneapolis, MN: Fortress Press).

Klawans, J. (2006) *Purity, Sacrifice, and the Temple: Symbolism and Supercessionism in the Study of Ancient Judaism* (Oxford: Oxford University Press).

Klobbenborg Verbin, J. S. (2000) *Excavating Q* (Edinburgh: T & T Clark).

Koester, H. H. (1980/82) *History and Literature of Early Christianity* (Philadelphia, PA: Fortress Press).

Kraemer, S. R. and D'Angelo, M. R. (1999) *Women and Christian Origins* (Oxford: Oxford University Press).

Kruse, C. G. (1983) *New Testament Models for Ministry: Jesus and Paul* (Nashville, TN: Nelson).

Küng, H. (1968) *The Church* (London: Burns and Oates).

Küng, H. (1971) *Why Priests?* (London: Collins).

La Verdiere, E. (1996) *The Eucharist in the New Testament and in the Early Church* (Collegeville, MN: Liturgical Press).

Lacey, T. A. (1910) *A Roman Diary, and Other Documents Relating to the Papal Inquiry Into English Ordinations, MDCCCXCVI* (London: Longman).

The Lambeth Conference 1948 (London: SPCK).

The Lambeth Conference 1968: Resolutions and Reports (London: SPCK).

Lampe, G. W. H. (1967) *The Seal of the Spirit* (London: SPCK).

Lampe, P. (1991) 'The Corinthian Dinner Party: Exegesis of a Cultural Context', in *Affirmation*, 4: 1–16.

Lancel, S. (2002) *St Augustine* (London: SCM Press).

Lartey, E. Y. (1997) *In Living Colour: An Intercultural Approach to Pastoral Care and Counselling* (London: Cassell).

Lartey, E. Y. (2000) 'Practical Theology as a Theological Form', in *The Blackwell Reader in Pastoral and Practical Theology*, eds J. Woodward and S. Pattison (Oxford: Blackwell), pp. 128–34.

Lasswell, H. D., and Kaplan, A. (1952) *Power and Society* (London: Routledge and Kegan Paul).

Lathrop, G. W. (1998) *Holy Things: A Liturgical Theology* (Minneapolis, MN: Fortress Press).

Laud, W. (1901) *A Relation of the Conference Between William Laud Late Archbishop of Canterbury and Mr. Fisher the Jesuit*, ed. C. H. Simpkinson (London: Macmillan).

Laurance, J. D. (1984) *'Priest' as Type of Christ: The Leader of the Eucharist in Salvation History According to Cyprian of Carthage* (New York, NY: Peter Lang).

Laws, S. (1980) *The Epistle of James* (London: A. and C. Black).

Leech, K. (1985) *True God: An Exploration in Spiritual Theology* (London: Sheldon Press).

Leech, K. (1986) *Spirituality and Pastoral Care* (London: Sheldon Press).

Leeder, L. (1991) 'The Diaconate in the Church of England: a Legal Perspective', in *The Deacon's Ministry*, ed. C. Hall (Leominster: Gracewing), pp. 123–46.

Leeuw, G. v. d. (1964) *Religion in Essence and Manifestation* (London: Allen and Unwin).

Legrand, H.–M. (1979) 'The Presidency of the Eucharist according to Ancient Tradition', in *Worship*, 53: 413–38.

Lenski, G. (1967) *Power and Privilege* (New York, NY: Free Press).

Lent, Holy Week and Easter (1986) (London: SPCK).

Leonhard, C. (2006) *The Jewish Pesach and the Origins of the Christian Easter* (Berlin: de Gruyter).

Lewis, I. M. (1986) *Religion in Context: Cults and Charisma* (Cambridge: Cambridge University Press).

Lewis, I. M. (1989) *Ecstatic Religion: A Study of Shamanism and Spirit Possession* (London: Routledge).

Léon-Dufour, X. (1982) *Sharing the Eucharistic Bread: The Witness of the New Testament* (Mahwah, NJ: Paulist Press).

Lightfoot, J. B. (1896) *Saint Paul's Epistle to the Philippians* (London: Macmillan).

Lindars, B. F. C. (1972) *The Gospel of John* (London: Marshall, Morgan and Scott).

Lings, G. (1994) *New Ground in Church Planting* (Cambridge: Grove Books).

Lings, G. (2006) 'Fresh Expressions Growing to Maturity', in *The Future of the Parish System: Shaping the Church of England for the Twenty-First Century*, ed. S. J. L. Croft (London: Church House Publishing), pp. 138–51.

Linyard, F. and Tovey, P. N. (1994) *Moravian Worship*. Grove Worship (Bramcote: Grove Books).

Lloyd, B. T. (1973) *Agapes and Informal Eucharists* (Bramcote: Grove Books).

Lloyd, B. T. (ed.) (1977) *Lay Presidency at the Eucharist?* Grove Liturgy Studies, vol. 8 (Bramcote: Grove Books).

Lloyd, B. T. (1986) *Celebrating the Agape Today* (Bramcote: Grove Books).

Lohse, E. (1951) *Die Ordination im Spätjudentum und im Neuen Testament* (Berlin: Evangelische Verlagsanstalt).

Longenecker, R. N. (2002) *Community Formation in the Early Church and in the Church Today* (Peabody, MA: Hendrickson).

Lord, A. M. (2005) *Spirit–Shaped Mission: A Holistic Charismatic Missiology* (Milton Keynes: Paternoster Press).

Lubac, H. de (1949) *Corpus Mysticum: L'Eucharistie et L'Eglise Au Moyen Age* (Paris: Étude historique).

Lukes, S. M. (1974) *Power: A Radical View* (London: Macmillan).

Luz, U. (2002) *Das Evangelium Nach Matthaus* (Berlin: Benziger Bros.).

Luz, U. (2002) *Matthew 8–20* (Minneapolis, MN: Fortress Press).

Lyon, B. (2000) 'What is the Relevance of Congregational Studies for Pastoral Theology?', in *The Blackwell Reader in Pastoral and Practical Theology*, eds J. Woodward and S. Pattison (Oxford: Blackwell), pp. 257–71.

MacCulloch, D. N. J. (1996) *Thomas Cranmer: A Life* (New Haven, CT: Yale University Press).

MacDonald, M. Y. (1988) *The Pauline Churches: A Socio–Historical Study of Institutionalization in the Pauline and Deutero–Pauline Writings* (Cambridge: Cambridge University Press).

MacMullen, R. (1974) *Roman Social Relations* (New Haven, CT: Yale University Press).

MacMullen, R. (1981) *Paganism in the Roman Empire* (New Haven, CT: Yale University Press).

Macmurray, J. (1961) *Persons in Relation* (London: Faber and Faber).

Macquarrie, J. (1975) 'Priestly Character', in *To Be A Priest: Perspectives on Vocation and Ordination*, eds R. E. Terwilliger and U. T. Holmes (New York, NY: Seabury Press), pp. 147–54.

Maier, H. O. (2002) *The Social Setting of the Ministry as Reflected in the Writings of Hermas, Clement and Ignatius* (Waterloo: Wilfred Laurier University Press).

Maitland, S. (1985) 'A Case History of Structural Oppression', in *All Are Called: Towards a Theology of the Laity*, ed. P. C. Rodger (London: Church Information Office), pp. 18–21.

Malina, B. J. (1986) *Christian Origins and Cultural Anthropology* (Atlanta, GA: John Knox Press).

Malinowski, B. K. (1965) 'The Role of Magic and Religion', in *Reader in Comparative Religion*, eds W. A. Lessa and E. Z. Vogt (New York, NY: Harper and Row), pp. 63–71.

Maltby, J. (1998) *Prayer Book and People in Elizabethan and Early Stuart England* (Cambridge: Cambridge University Press).

Marcus, J. (2000) *Mark* (New York, NY: Doubleday).

Maris, R. E. de. (2008) *The New Testament in Its Ritual World* (London: Routledge).

Markschies, C. (1999) *Between Two Worlds: Structures of Early Christianity* (London: SCM Press).

Marriage, A. (1995) *The People of God: A Royal Priesthood* (London: Darton, Longman and Todd).

Marshall, I. H. (1978) *The Gospel of Luke* (Grand Rapids, MI: Eerdmans).

Marshall, J. S. (1963) *Hooker and the Anglican Tradition: An Historical and Theological Study of Hooker's Ecclesiastical Polity* (London: A. and C. Black).

Marshall, M. (1975) 'The Re–Ordering of the Ministry', in *To be a Priest: Perspectives on Vocation and Ordination*, eds R. E. Terwilliger and U. T. Holmes (New York, NY: Seabury Press), pp. 163–72.

Martin, D. (1978) *A General Theory of Secularization* (Oxford: Blackwell).

Martin, D. (1980) *The Breaking of the Image: A Sociology of Christian Theory and Practice* (Oxford: Blackwell).

Martineau, R. A. S. (1981) *The Office and Work of a Priest* (London: Mowbrays).

Mason, K. S. (1992) *Priesthood and Society* (Norwich: Canterbury Press).

Mathew, G. (1991) 'Whose culture and why?', in *The Identity of Anglican Worship*, eds K. W. Stevenson and B. D. Spinks (London: Mowbrays), pp. 144–55.

Maude, A. (1994) 'Minister to the Sick', in *Priesthood Here and Now*, ed. M. Bowering (Newcastle: Diocese of Newcastle), pp. 74–8.

Maurice, F. D. (1842) *The Kingdom of Christ; or, Hints to a Quaker, Respecting the Principles, Constitution, and Ordinances of the Catholic Church* (London: Rivington).

Mayland, J. (1985) 'An Ecumenical Viewpoint', in *All Are Called: Towards a Theology of the Laity*, ed. P. C. Rodger (London: Church Information Office), pp. 39–43.

Maynagh, M. (2006) 'Good Practice is not what it used to be: Accumulating wisdom for Fresh Expressions of Church', in *The Future of the Parish System: Shaping the Church of England for the Twenty-First Century*, ed. S. J. L. Croft (London: Church House Publishing), pp. 110–24.

Mbiti, J. S. (1971) *New Testament Eschatology in an African Background: A Study of the Encounter Between New Testament Theology and African Traditional Concepts* (London: SPCK).

Mbonigaba, E. G. (1994) 'The Indigenization of Liturgy', in *Anglican Liturgical Inculturation in Africa*, ed. D. Gitari (Bramcote: Grove Books), pp. 20–32.

McAdoo, H. R. (1965) *The Spirit of Anglicanism: A Survey of Anglican Theological Method in the Seventeenth Century* (London: A. and C. Black).

McAdoo, H. R. (1987) 'Authority in the Church; Spiritual Freedom and the Corporate Nature of Faith', in *Authority in the Anglican Communion*, ed. S. W. Sykes (Toronto: Anglican Book Centre), pp. 69–93.

McAdoo, H. R. (1988) *The Eucharistic Theology of Jeremy Taylor Today* (Norwich: Canterbury Press).

McAdoo, H. R. and Stevenson, K. W. (1995) *The Mystery of the Eucharist in the Anglican Tradition* (Norwich: Canterbury Press).

McCauley, R. N. and Lawson, E. T. (2002) *Bringing Ritual to Mind: Psychological Foundations of Cultural Forms* (Cambridge: Cambridge University Press).

McCormick, K. (2000) 'Lay Presidency at the Eucharist? Recent Discussions', in *Sewanee Theological Review*, 43.

McDevitt, A. (1960) 'The Episcopate as an order and Sacrament on the Eve of the High Scholastic Period', in *Franciscan Studies*, 20: 96–148.

McFadyen, A. I. (1990) *The Call to Personhood: A Christian Theory of the Individual in Social Relationships* (Cambridge: Cambridge University Press).

McGowan, A. B. (1999) *Ascetic Eucharists* (Oxford: Oxford University Press).

McPartlan, P. (1995) *Sacrament of Salvation: An Introduction to Eucharistic Ecclesiology* (Edinburgh: T & T Clark).

McPherson, J. M. (1999) 'Lay Presidency by Presbyteral Delegation', in *Anglican Theological Review*, 81: 413–28.

McVann, M. E. (ed.) (1995) *Semeia*, Vol. 67: *Transformations, Passages, and Processes: Ritual Approaches to Biblical Texts* (Atlanta, GA: SBL Press).

Meeks, W. A. (1983) *The First Urban Christians* (New Haven, CT: Yale University Press).

Meeks, W. A. and Wilken, R. L. (1978) *Jews and Christians in Antioch in the First Four Centuries of the Common Era* (Missoula, MT: Scholars Press).

Meissner, W. W. (2000) *The Cultic Origins of Christianity: The Dynamic of Religious Development.* (Collegeville, MN: Liturgical Press).

Melinsky, M. A. H. (1992) *The Shape of the Ministry* (Norwich: Canterbury Press).

Meyers, R. A. (1996) 'Christian Rites of Adolescence', in *Life Cycles in Jewish and Christian Worship*, eds P. F. Bradshaw and L. A. Hoffmann (Notre Dame, IN: University of Notre Dame Press), pp. 55–80.

Michaels, J. R. (1988) *1 Peter* (Waco, TX: Word Books).

Middleton, A. (1995) *Towards a Renewed Priesthood* (Leominster: Gracewing).

Middleton, P. (2006) *Radical Martyrdom and Cosmic Conflict in Early Christianity* (London: T & T Clark).

Ministry and Ordination: A Statement on the Doctrine of the Ministry Agreed by the Anglican–Roman Catholic International Commission (1973) (London: Catholic Truth Society).

Ministry to the Sick (1983) (Oxford: Oxford University Press).

Mission–Shaped Church: Church Planting and Fresh Expressions of Church in a Changing Context (2004) (London: Church House Publishing).

Mitchell, N. (1982) *Cult and Controversy: The Worship of the Eucharist Outside Mass* (New York, NY: Pueblo Press).

Moberly, R. C. (1969) *Ministerial Priesthood: Chapters (Preliminary to a Study of the Ordinal) on The Rationale of Ministry and the Meaning of Christian Priesthood* (London: SPCK).

Mol, H. J. (1976) *Identity and the Sacred* (Oxford: Blackwell).

Moloney, F. J. (1997) *A Body Broken for a Broken People: Eucharist in the New Testament* (Peabody, MA: Hendrickson).

Moloney, R. (1995) *The Eucharist* (London: Geoffrey Chapman).

Moltmann, J. (1977) *The Church in the Power of the Spirit: A Contribution to Messianic Ecclesiology* (London: SCM Press).

Moltmann–Wendel, E. (1986) *The Women Around Jesus* (New York, NY: Crossroad).

Mombo, E. (2007) 'The Windsor Report: A Paradigm Shift for Anglicanism', in *Aniglican Theological Review*, 89: 69–78.

Montefiore, H. W. (1964) *The Epistle to the Hebrews* (London: A. and C. Black).

Moody, C. (1992) *Eccentric Ministry: Pastoral Care and Leadership in the Parish* (London: Darton, Longman and Todd).

Moore, E. G. and Briden, T. (1985) *Introduction to English Canon Law* (London: Mowbrays).

Morisy, A. (2006) 'Mapping the Mixed Economy', in *The Future of the Parish System: Shaping the Church of England for the Twenty–First Century*, ed. S. J. L. Croft (London: Church House Publishing), pp. 125–37.

Mosbech, H. (1948) 'Apostolos in the New Testament', in *ST*, 2: 166–200.

Moule, C. F. D. (1961) *Worship in the New Testament* (London: Lutterworth Press).

Muddiman, J. (2001) *The Epistle to the Ephesians* (London: Continuum).

Muga, Z. (2002) 'The New Kenya Anglican Liturgy', in *Encounter*, 2: 19–45.

Muller, R. A. and Thompson, J. L. (1996) *Biblical Interpretation in the Era of the Reformation*. (Grand Rapids, MI: Eerdmans).

Munz, P. (1952) *The Place of Hooker in the History of Thought* (London: Routledge and Kegan Paul).

Myers, G. (2000) *Using Common Worship: Initiation Services* (London: Church House Publishing).

Ndungane, W. H. N. (2007) 'Grasping the Past: Grabbing Hold of the Future: The Challenge of Afro–Anglicanism', in *Anglican Theological Review*, 89: 21–8.

Neelands, W. D. (1997) 'Hooker on Scripture, Reason, and "Tradition"', in *Richard Hooker and the Construction of Christian Community*, ed. A. S. McGrade (Tempe, AZ: Arizona State University), pp. 75–84.

Neill, S. C. (1963) 'Britain, 1600–1780', in *The Layman in Christian History*, eds S. C. Neill and H.–R. Weber, pp. 191–215 (London: SCM Press)

Neill, S. C. (1965) *Anglicanism* (Harmondsworth: Penguin).

Newbigin, L. (1977) *The Good Shepherd: Meditations and Christian Ministry in Today's World* (London: Mowbrays).

Newbigin, L. (1996) 'Lay Presidency at the Eucharist', in *Theology*, 99: 366–70.

Newsom, G. H. (1988) *Faculty Jursidiction in the Church of England* (London: Sweet and Maxwell).

Neyrey, J. H. (ed.) (1991) *The Social World of Luke–Acts* (Peabody, MA: Hendrickson).

Nichols, B. R. (1996) *Liturgical Hermeneutics: Interpeting Liturgical Rites in Performance* (Frankfurt a. M.: Peter Lang).

Niebuhr, H. R. (1929) *The Social Sources of Denominationalism* (New York, NY: Meridian Press)

Niebuhr, H. R. (1951) *Christ and Culture* (New York, NY: Harper and Row).

Niederwimmer, K. (1998) *The Didache* (Minneapolis, MN: Fortress Press).

Noll, R. R. (1993) *Christian Ministerial Priesthood: A Search for Its Beginnings in the Primary Documents of the Apostolic Fathers* (San Francisco, CA: Catholic Scholars Press).

Nolland, J. C. (1989–93) *Luke* (Waco, TX: Word Books).

Norris, R. A. (1988) 'Episcopacy', in *The Study of Anglicanism*, eds S. W. Sykes and J. E. Booty, (London: SPCK), pp. 296–309.

Northcott, M. (2000) 'Pastoral Theology and Sociology', in *The Blackwell Reader in Pastoral and Practical Theology*, eds J. Woodward and S. Pattison (Oxford: Blackwell), pp. 151–63.

Oakes, P. (2001) *Philippians: From People to Letter* (Cambridge: Cambridge University Press).

Olsson, B. and Zetterholm, M (eds). (2003) *The Ancient Synagogue from Its Origins Until 200 CE* (Stockholm: Almqvist and Wiksell).

Ordination and the Church's Ministry: A Theological Evaluation (1990) (London: Advisory Council on the Church's Ministry).

Osborn, E. F. (1973) *Justin Martyr* (Tübingen: J. C. B. Mohr).

Osborn, E. F. (1997) *Tertullian, First Theologian of the West* (Cambridge: Cambridge University Press).

Osborne, K. B. (2003) 'Envisioning a Theology of Ordained and Lay Ministry: Lay/Ordained Ministry – Current Issues of Ambiguity', in *Ordering the Baptismal Priesthood: Theologies of Lay and Ordained Ministry*, ed. S. K. Wood (Collegeville, MN: Liturgical Press), pp. 195–227.

Osiek, C. (1999) *Shepherd of Hermas* (Minneapolis, MN: Fortress).

Osiek, C. and Balch, D. L. (1997) *Families in the New Testament World* (Louisville, KY: Westminster John Knox Press).

Osiek, C. and MacDonald, M. Y. (2006) *A Woman's Place: House Churches in Earliest Christianity* (Minneapolis, MN: Fortress Press).

O'Donovan, O. M. T. (1986) *On the Thirty Nine Articles: A Conversation with Tudor Christianity* (Exeter: Paternoster Press).

O'Meara, T. F. (1983) *Theology of Ministry* (New York, NY: Paulist Press).

Parsons, M. (1964) *The Ordinal: An Exposition of the Ordination Service*, ed. F. Colquhoun. The Prayer Book Commentaries. (London: Hodder and Stoughton).

Parsons, T. (1954) *Essays in Sociological Theory* (New York, NY: Free Press).

Patterson, S. (2006) 'Scripture and Community', in *The Authority of Scripture: A Report of the Church of Ireland Bishops' Advisory Commission on Doctrine*, ed. R. Clarke, (Dublin: Church of Ireland), pp. 103–39.

Pattison, E. M. (1977) *Pastor and Parish – A Systems Approach.* (Philadelphia, PA: Fortress Press).

Pattison, S. B. (1993) *A Critique of Pastoral Care* (London: SCM Press)

Peabody, R. L. (1968) 'Authority', in *International Encyclopedia of the Social Sciences* (New York, NY: Macmillan), vol. 1, pp. 473–7.

Percy, M. W. (1996) *Words, Wonders and Power: Understanding Contemporary Christian Fundamentalism and Revivalism* (London: SPCK)

Percy, M. W. (1998) *Power and the Church* (London: Cassell).

Percy, M. W. (1999) *Introducing Richard Hooker and the Laws of Ecclesiastical Polity* (London: Darton, Longman and Todd).

Percy, M. W. (2001) *The Salt of the Earth: Religious Resilience in a Secular Age* (London: Sheffield Academic Press).

Percy, M. W. (2006) *Clergy: The Origin of Species* (London: Continuum).

Percy, M. W. (2006) 'Many Rooms in my Father's House: The Changing Identity of the English Parish Church', in *The Future of the Parish System: Shaping the Church of England for the Twenty–First Century*, ed. S. J. L. Croft (London: Church House Publishing), pp. 3–15.

Perham, M. F. (1992) *Lively Sacrifice: The Eucharist in the Church of England* (London: SPCK).

Perham, M. F. (2000) *New Handbook of Pastoral Liturgy* (London: SPCK)

Pickard, S. K. and Johnston, L. (1995) 'Lay Presidency at Holy Communion: An Anglican Dilemma', in *St Mark's Review*, 161: 12–17.

Pickstone, C. (2001) 'The Priest in the Media Age', in *Priests in a People's Church*, ed. G. Guiver (London: SPCK), pp. 33–48.

Pierce, A. (2006) 'Where Are We Now? The Contesting of Biblical Authority in Historical Perspective', in *The Authority of Scripture: A Report of the Church of Ireland Bishops' Advisory Commission on Doctrine*, ed. R. Clarke (Dublin: Church of Ireland), pp. 9–52.

Pinnock, J. (1991) 'The History of the Diaconate', in *The Deacon's Ministry*, ed. C. Hall (Leominster: Gracewing), pp. 9–24.

Pitt, T. (1994) *At the Head of the Table, or Under the Carpet? The Issue of Lay Presidency* (York: Dean and Chapter of York).

Planting New Churches (1991), eds R. Hopkins and T. Anderson. (Guildford: Eagle Press).

Platten, S. (1997) *Augustine's Legacy: Authority and Leadership in the Anglican Communion* (London: Darton, Longman and Todd).

Pollard, A. (1966) *Richard Hooker* (London: Longman, Green and Co.).

Power, D. N. (1969) *Ministers of Christ and His Church: The Theology of the Priesthood* (London: Geoffrey Chapman).

Power, D. N. (1992) *The Eucharistic Mystery: Revitalizing the Tradition* (Dublin: Gill and Macmillan).

Power, D. N. (2003) 'Priesthood Revisited: Mission and Ministry in the Royal Priesthood', in *Ordering the Baptismal Priesthood: Theologies of Lay and Ordained Ministry*, ed. S. K. Wood (Collegeville, MN: Liturgical Press), pp. 87–120.

The Priesthood of the Ordained Ministry (1986), GS 694 (London: Board for Mission and Unity).

Procter, F. and Frere, W. H. (1951) *A New History of the Book of Common Prayer* (London: Macmillan).

Pryor, J. (1989) 'Lay Presidency and the Ordained Ministry Today', in *St Mark's Review*, 138: 12–17.

Public Worship with Communion by Extension (2001) (London: Church House Publishing).

Puglisi, J. F. (1996–2001) *The Process of Admission to Ordained Ministry*. (Collegeville, MN: Liturgical Press).

Pytches, G. E. D. and Skinner, B. (1991) *New Wineskins: A Plea for Radical Rethinking in the Church of England to Enable Normal Church Growth to Take Effect Beyond Existing Parish Boundaries* (Guildford: Eagle Press).

Quesnell, Q. (1983) 'The Women at Luke's Supper', in *Political Issues in Luke–Acts*, eds R. J. Cassidy and P. J. Sharper (Maryknoll, NY: Orbis) pp. 59–79.

Quevedo-Bosch, J. (1994) 'The Eucharistic Species and Inculturation', in *Liturgical Inculturation in the Anglican Communion*, ed. D. R. Holeton (Bramcote: Grove Books), pp. 48–9.

Radner, E. and Turner, P. (2006) *The Fate of Communion: The Agony of Anglicanism and the Future of a Global Church* (Grand Rapids, MI: Eerdmans).

Rahner, K. (1964) *Bishops: Their Status and Function* (London: Burns and Oates).

Rahner, K. (1974) *The Shape of the Church to Come* (New York, NY: Crossroad).

Rahner, K. (1983) *Theological Investigations*, Vol. 19 (London: Burns and Oates).

Räisänen, H. (1986) *Paul and the Law* (Philadelphia, PA: Fortress Press).

Rajak, T. and Noy, D. (1993) '*Archisunagogoi*: Office, Title and Social Status in the Greco-Jewish Synagogue', in *Journal of Roman Studies*, 83: 75–93

Rambo, L. R. (1993) *Understanding Religious Conversion* (New Haven, CT: Yale University Press).

Ramsey, A. M. (1936) *The Gospel and the Catholic Church* (London: Longman).

Ramsey, A. M. (1961) *The Resurrection of Christ: A Study of the Event and Its Meaning for the Christian Faith* (London: SPCK).

Ramsey, A. M. (1991) *The Anglican Spirit* (London: SPCK).

Ramshaw, E. (1987) *Ritual and Pastoral Care*, ed. D. S. Browning. Theology and Pastoral Care (Philadelphia, PA: Fortress Press).

Rankin, D. I. (1995) *Tertullian and the Church* (Cambridge: Cambridge University Press).

Rappaport, R. A. (1999) *Ritual and Religion in the Making of Humanity* (Cambridge: Cambridge University Press).

Ratcliff, E. C. (1966) 'Apostolic Tradition: Questions Concerning the Appointment of the Bishop', in *Studia Patristica*, 8: 266–70.

Rausch, T. P. (2003) 'Ministry and Ministries', in *Ordering the Baptismal Priesthood: Theologies of Lay and Ordained Ministry*, ed. S. K. Wood (Collegeville, MN: Liturgical Press), pp. 52–67.

Reardon, M. A. (1991) *Christian Initiation: A Policy for the Church of England*. General Synod Misc, GS Misc. 365. (London: Church House Publishing).

Redfern, A. (1999) *Ministry and Priesthood* (London: Darton, Longman and Todd).

Renewing the Anglican Eucharist: Findings of the Fifth International Anglican Liturgical Consultation, Dublin, Eire, 1995 (1996), ed. D. R. Holeton (Cambridge: Grove Books).

Rengstorf, K. H. (1934) Apostellw, αποστολος', in *Theological Dictionary of the New Testament*, vol. 1, pp. 399–412.

Richardson, P. (2004) Reception and Division in the Church', in *Seeking the Truth of Change in the Church*, ed. P. D. L. Avis, pp. 123–38 (London: T & T Clark).

Robinson, J. A. T. (1950) *In the End, God. A Study of the Christian Doctrine of the Last Things* (London: James Clarke).

Robinson, J. A. T. (1952) *The Body: A Study in Pauline Theology* (London: SCM Press).

Robinson, J. A. T. (1960) *Liturgy Coming to Life* (London: Mowbrays).

Robinson, J. A. T. (1960) *On Being the Church in the World* (London: SCM Press).

Robinson, J. A. T. (1963) 'The Ministry and the Laity', in *Layman's Church*, ed. T. Beaumont (London: Lutterworth Press), pp. 9–22.

Robinson, J. A. T. (1972) *The Difference in Being a Christian Today* (London: Collins).

Robinson, J. A. T. (1976) *Redating the New Testament* (London: SCM Press).

Rodger, P. C. (1985) 'Bishops, Clergy and Laity', in *All Are Called: Towards a Theology of the Laity*, ed. P. C. Rodger (London: Church Information Office), pp. 35–8.

Roffey, J. (1989) 'The Theology and Practice of Lay Ministry', in *St Mark's Review*, 138: 18–21.

Rowell, D. G. (2004) 'Learning to Live with Difference', in *Seeking the Truth of Change in the Church*, ed. P. D. L. Avis (London: T & T Clark), pp. 139–51.

Rowthorn, A. (1986) *The Liberation of the Laity*. Wilton, CT: Morehouse-Barlow).

Runcie, R. A. K. (1988) *Authority in Crisis? An Anglican Response* (London: SCM Press).

Rupp, E. G. (1963) 'The Age of the Reformation, 1500–1648', in *The Layman in Christian History*, eds S. C. Neill and H.-R. Weber (London: SCM Press), pp. 135–50.

Rusch, W. G. (2004) The Landscape of Reception', in *Seeking the Truth of Change in the Church*, ed. P. D. L. Avis (London: T & T Clark), pp. 1–18.

Russell, A. J. (1980) *The Clerical Profession* (London: SPCK).

Russell, A. J. (1986) *The Country Parish* (London: SPCK).

Ryan, H. T. (1975) 'The Meaning of Ordained Priesthood in Ecumenical Dialogues', in *To Be a Priest: Perspectives on Vocation and Ordination*, eds R. E. Terwilliger and U. T. Holmes (New York, NY: Seabury Press), pp. 91–9.

Sacchi, P. (2000) *The History of the Second Temple Period* (Sheffield: Sheffield Academic Press).

Sagovsky, N. (2000) *Ecumenism, Christian Origins and the Practice of Communion* (Cambridge: Cambridge University Press)

Sainte Croix, G. E. M. de (1981) *The Class Struggle in the Ancient Greek World* (London: Duckworth).

Saller, R. P. (1982) *Personal Patronage under the Early Empire* (Cambridge: Cambridge University Press).

Sanders, E. P. (1983) *Paul, the Law, and the Jewish People* (London: SCM Press).

Sanders, E. P. (1985) *Jesus and Judaism* (London: SCM Press).

Sanders, E. P. (1992) *Judaism: Practice and Belief 63BCE–66CE* (London: SCM Press).

Sanders, E. P. (1994) *The Historical Figure of Jesus* (London: Penguin).

Sawyerr, H. A. E. (1968) *Creative Evangelism: Towards a New Christian Encounter with Africa* (London: Lutterworth Press).

Scarisbrick, J. J. (1984) *The Reformation and the English People* (Oxford: Oxford University Press).

Scharlemann, M. H. (1968) *Stephen: A Singular Saint* (Rome: Pontifical Biblical Institute).

Scheer, A. (1979) 'The Influence of Culture on the Liturgy as shown in the History of the Christian Initiation Rite', in *Structures of Initiation in Crisis*, 122: 14–25.

Schillebeeckx, E. (1981) *Ministry: Leadership in the Community of Jesus Christ* (New York, NY: Crossroad).

Schillebeeckx, E. (1985) *The Church with a Human Face: A New and Expanded Theology of Ministry* (London: SCM Press).

Schmemann, A. (1988) *The Eucharist: Sacrament of the Kingdom* (New York, NY: St Vladimir's Seminary Press).

Schmithals, W. (1971) *The Office of Apostle in the Early Church* (London: SPCK).

Schnackenburg, R. (1965) *The Church in the New Testament* (New York, NY: Herder).

Schoedel, W. R. (1985) *Ignatius of Antioch.* (Hermeneia). (Philadelphia, PA: Fortress Press).

Scholer, J. M. (1991) *Proleptic Priesthood: Priesthood in the Epistle to the Hebrews* (Sheffield: Sheffield Academic Press).

Schüssler Fiorenza, E. (1983) *In Memory of Her: A Feminist Theological Reconstruction of Christian Origins* (London: SCM Press).

Schütz, J. H. (1975) *Paul and the Anatomy of Apostolic Authority* (Cambridge: Cambridge University Press).

Schweizer, E. (1967) *The Lord's Supper According to the New Testament.* (Philadelphia, PA: Fortress Press).

Schweizer, E. (1975) *Church Order in the New Testament* (London: SCM Press).

Seaman, B. (1994) 'Preacher', in *Priesthood Here and Now*, ed. M. Bowering (Newcastle: Diocese of Newcastle), pp. 21–9.

Secor, P. B. (1999) *Richard Hooker: Prophet of Anglicanism* (Tunbridge Wells: Burns and Oates).

Segal, A. F. (1990) *Paul the Convert* (New Haven, CT: Yale University Press).

Selby, M. (2001) 'A Word from One of the Laos', in *Priests in a People's Church*, ed. G. Guiver (London: SPCK), pp. 51–9.

Selby, P. S. M. (1982) *Look for the Living: The Corporate Nature of Resurrection Faith* (London: SCM Press).

Selwyn, E. G. (1961) *The First Epistle of St. Peter*. London: Macmillan

Senior, D. P. (2003) *1 Peter* (Collegeville, MN: Liturgical Press).

Sennett, R. (1980) *Authority* (New York, NY: Vintage).

Shepherd, M. H. (1975) 'Presbyters in the Early Church', in *To Be A Priest: Perspectives on Vocation and Ordination*, eds R. E. Terwilliger and U. T. Holmes (New York, NY: Seabury Press), pp. 71–82.

Shorter, A. (1985) 'Eucharistic Famine in Africa', in *African Ecclesiastical Review*, 27: 131–7.

Shorter, A. (1988) *Toward a Theology of Inculturation* (Maryknoll, NY: Orbis).

Simon, M. (1958) *St Stephen and the Hellenists in the Primitive Church* (London: Longman).

Skinner, J. E. (1987) 'Ideology, Authority, and Faith', in *Authority in the Anglican Communion*, ed. S. W. Sykes (Toronto: Anglican Book Centre), pp. 27–46.

Slee, M. (2003) *The Church of Antioch in the First Century CE* (Sheffield: Sheffield Academic Press).

Smalley, S. S. (2005) *The Revelation to John* (London: SPCK).

Smethurst, D. A. (1986) *Extended Communion: An Experiment in Cumbria* (Bramcote: Grove Books).

Smith, D. E. (2003) *From Symposium to Eucharist* (Minneapolis, MN: Fortress Press).

Smith, J. Z. (1987) *To Take Place: Toward Theory in Ritual* (Chicago, IL: University of Chicago Press).

Smith, J. Z. (1990) *Drudgery Divine* (Cambridge: Cambridge University Press).

Smithson, A. (1998) 'Lay Presidency', in *Theology*, 101: 3–13, 71–2

Snow, D. A. and Machalek, R. (1983) 'The Convert as a Social Type', in *Sociological Theory 1983*, ed. R. Collins (San Francisco: Jossey Bass), pp. 259–89.

Sohm, R. (1892) *Kirchenrecht. I* (Leipzig: Duncker and Humbolt).

Southern, H. I. J. (2004) 'Anglicanism Sydney Style', in *Theology*, 107: 117–24.

Spinks, B. D. (1991) 'The Eucharistic Prayer', in *The Identity of Anglican Worship*, eds K. W. Stevenson and B. D. Spinks (London: Mowbrays), pp. 89–102.

Spinks, B. D. (1991) 'Two Seventeenth Century Examples of *Lex Credendi, Lex Orandi*: The Baptismal and Eucharistic Theologies of Jeremy Taylor and Richard Baxter', in *Studia Liturgica*, 21: 165–89.

Spinks, B. D. (1999) 'Ecclesiology and Soteriology Shaping Eschatology: The Funeral Rites in Perspective', in *To Glorify God*, ed. B. D. Spinks and I. Torrance (Edinburgh: T & T Clark).

Spinks, B. D. (1999) *Two Faces of Elizabethan Anglican Theology: Sacraments and Salvation in the Thought of William Perkins and Richard Hooker* (Lanham, NY: Scarecrow).

Spinks, B. D. (2002) *Sacraments, Ceremonies and the Stuart Divines: Sacramental Theology and Liturgy in England and Scotland, 1603–1662* (Aldershot: Ashgate).

Spinks, B. D. (2006) *Early and Medieval Rituals and Theologies of Baptism: From the New Testament to the Council of Trent* (Aldershot: Ashgate).

Spinks, B. D. (2006) *Reformation and Modern Rituals and Theologies of Baptism: From Luther to Contemporary Practices* (Aldershot: Ashgate).

Spinks, B. D. and Tellini, G. (1991) 'The Anglican Church and Holy Order', in *The Identity of Anglican Worship*, eds K. W. Stevenson and B. D. Spinks (London: Mowbrays), pp. 116–23.

Stancliffe, D. S. (1991) 'Is There an "Anglican" Liturgical Style?', in *The Identity of Anglican Worship*, eds K. W. Stevenson and B. D. Spinks (London: Mowbrays), pp. 124–34.

Stark, R. (1996) *The Rise of Christianity: A Sociologist Reconsiders History* (Princeton, NJ: Princeton University Press).

Stark, W. (1969) *The Sociology of Religion. IV. Types of Religious Man* (London: Routledge and Kegan Paul).

Steinmetz, D. C. (. (1990) *The Bible in the Sixteenth Century* (Durham: Duke University Press).

Stevenson, K. W. (1986) *Eucharist and Offering* (New York, NY: Pueblo).

Stevenson, K. W. (1989) *The First Rites: Worship in the Early Church* (London: Marshall Pickering).

Stevenson, K. W. (1991) 'Anglican Identity: A Chapter of Accidents', in *The Identity of Anglican Worship*, eds K. W. Stevenson and B. D. Spinks (London: Mowbrays), pp. 184–96.

Stevenson, K. W. (1991) 'The Pastoral Offices', in *The Identity of Anglican Worship*, eds K. W. Stevenson and B. D. Spinks (London: Mowbrays), pp. 103–15.

Stevenson, K. W. (2002) *Do This: The Shape, Style and Meaning of the Eucharist* (Norwich: Canterbury Press).

Stewart–Sykes, A. (2001) *Hippolytus, On the Apostolic Tradition* (New York, NY: St Vladimir's Seminary Press).

Stock, N. (1994) 'Minister of the Sacraments', in *Priesthood Here and Now*, ed. M. Bowering (Newcastle: Diocese of Newcastle), pp. 51–8.

Straus, R. A. (1979) 'Religious Conversion as a Personal and Collective Accomplishment', in *Sociological Analysis*, 40: 158–65.

Strecker, G. (1996) *The Johannine Letters* Hermeneia (Minneapolis, MN: Fortress Press).

Sugirtharajah, R. S. (2001) *The Bible and the Third World: Precolonial, Colonial and Postcolonial Encounters* (Cambridge: Cambridge University Press).

Sundkler, B. (1960) *The Christian Ministry in Africa* (London: SCM Press).

Sykes, S. W. (1978) *The Integrity of Anglicanism* (London: Mowbrays).

Sykes, S. W. (1988) 'Episcopacy, Communion and Collegiality', in *Communion and Episcopacy*, ed. J. L. Draper (Oxford: Ripon College Cuddesdon), pp. 35–46.

Sykes, S. W. (1995) *Unashamed Anglicanism* (London: Darton, Longman and Todd).

Sykes, S. W. (1997) *The Story of Atonement* (London: Darton, Longman and Todd).

Sykes, S. W. (2000) 'The Theology of Priesthood', in *Sewanee Theological Review*, 43: 121–9.

Synge, F. C. (1963) 'The Challenge of the Frontiers', in *Anglican Congress 1963: Report of Proceedings* (Toronto: Editorial Committee), pp. 155–64.

Synopsis Quattuor Evangeliorum (1964), ed. K. Aland (Stuttgart: Württembergische Bibelanstalt Stuttgart).

Talley, T. J. (1991) 'The Year of Grace', in *The Identity of Anglican Worship*, eds K. W. Stevenson and B. D. Spinks (London: Mowbrays), pp. 27–35.

Tanner, M. (2004) 'The Episcopal Ministry Act of Synod in Context', in *Seeking the Truth of Change in the Church*, ed. P. D. L. Avis (London: T & T Clark), pp. 58–74.

Taylor, J. (1828) '"Clerus Domini;" or, a Discourse of the Divine Institution, Necessity, Sacredness, and Separation, of the Office Ministerial; together with the Nature and Manner of its Power and Operation: Written by the special Command of King Charles I', in *The Whole Works of the Right Rev. Jeremy Taylor, D.D., Lord Bishop of Down, Connor, and Dromore*, ed. R. Heber (London: Rivington).

Taylor, M. H. (1983) *Learning to Care: Christian Reflection on Pastoral Practice*, ed. D. Blows. New Library of Pastoral Care (London: SPCK).

Taylor, N. H. (1992) *Paul, Antioch and Jerusalem: A Study in Relationships and Authority in Earliest Christianity* (Sheffield: Sheffield Academic Press).

Taylor, N. H. (1995) 'The Social Nature of Conversion in the Early Christian World', in *Modelling Early Christianity*, ed. P. F. Esler (London: Routledge), pp. 128–36.

Taylor, N. H. (1996) 'Palestinian Christianity and the Caligula Crisis. I. Socio-Historical Reconstruction', in *Journal for the Study of the New Testament*, 61: 101–24

Taylor, N. H. (1996) 'Palestinian Christianity and the Caligula Crisis. II. The Markan Eschatological Discourse', in *Journal for the Study of the New Testament*, 62: 13–41.

Taylor, N. H. (1997) 'Paul for Today: Race, Class, and Gender in Light of Cognitive Dissonance Theory', in *Listening: Journal of Religion and Culture*, 32.1: 22–38.

Taylor, N. H. (1999) 'Jerusalem and the Temple in Early Christian Life and Teaching', in *Neotestamentica*, 33: 445–61.

Taylor, N. H. (1999) 'Prolegomena to Reconstructing the Eschatological Teaching of Jesus', in *Neotestamentica*, 33: 145–60

Taylor, N. H. (2002) 'The Contextualisation of Christianity in the Early Church', in *Reflections on Christian Faith: An African Context*, ed. E. R. Johnson (Mutare: Africa University Press), pp. 41–54.

Taylor, N. H. (2003) 'Stephen, the Temple, and Early Christian Eschatology', in *Revue Biblique*, 110: 62–85.

Taylor, N. H. (2008) 'Some Observations on Theological Method, Biblical Interpretation, and Ecclesiastical Politics in Current Disputes in the Anglican Communion', in *Theology*, 111: 51–8.

Temple, W. (1912) 'The Church', in *Foundations: A Statement of Christian Belief in Terms of Modern Thought*, ed. B. H. Streeter (London: Macmillan), pp. 337–60.

Temple, W. (1930) *Christus Veritas* (London: Macmillan).

Temple, W. (1931) *Thoughts on Some Problems of the Day* (London: Macmillan).

Temple, W. (1944) *The Church Looks Forward* (London: Macmillan).

Terwilliger, R. E. (1975) 'What is a Priest? One Anglican View', in *To be a Priest: Perspectives on Vocation and Ordination*, eds R. E. Terwilliger and U. T. Holmes (New York, NY: Seabury Press), pp. 3–10.

Theissen, G. (1982) *The Social Setting of Pauline Christianity* (Edinburgh: T & T Clark).

The Theology of Ordination: A Report by the Faith and Order Advisory Group of the Board for Mission and Unity (1975), GS 281. (London: Church House Publishing).

Thiselton, A. C. (2000) *The First Epistle to the Corinthians* (Grand Rapids, MI: Eerdmans).

Thomas, O. C. (1979) 'William Temple', in *The Spirit of Anglicanism*, ed. W. J. Wolf (Edinburgh: T & T Clark), pp. 101–34.

Thomas, W. H. G. (1930) *The Principles of Theology: An Introduction to the Thirty-Nine Article* (London: Vine).

Thrall, M. E. (1994) *II Corinthians* (Edinburgh: T & T Clark).

Thurian, M. (1983) *Priesthood and Ministry: Ecumenical Research* (London: Mowbrays).

Thurian, M., Wainwright. G. (1983) *Baptism and Eucharist: Ecumenical Convergence in Celebration* (Geneva: World Council of Churches).

Tillard, J.-M. R. (1973) *What Priesthood Has the Ministry.* Grove Booklet on Ministry and Worship, 13 (Bramcote: Grove Books).

Tillard, J.-M. R. (1992) *Church of Churches: The Ecclesiology of Communion.* (Collegeville, MN: Liturgical Press).

Tiller, J. (1983) *A Strategy for the Church's Ministry* (London: Church Information Office).

Tiller, J. (1991) 'Preface', in *New Wineskins: A Plea for Radical Rethinking in the Church of England to Enable Normal Church Growth to Take Effect Beyond Existing Parish Boundaries*, eds G. E. D. Pytches and B. Skinner (Guildford: Eagle Press).

Together in Mission and Ministry: The Porvoo Common Statement with Essays on Church and Ministry in Northern Europe (1993), GS 1083 (London: Church House Publishing).

Toon, P. (1974) *The Ordinal and its Revision.* Grove Booklet on Ministry and Worship, 29 (Bramcote: Grove Books).

Torjesen, K. J. (1993) *When Women Were Priests: Women's Leadership in the Early Church and the Scandal of their Subordination in the Rise of Christianity* (San Francisco, CA: Harper San Francisco).

Tovey, P. N. (1993) *Communion Outside the Eucharist*, Alcuin/Grove 26 (Bramcote: Grove Books).

Tovey, P. N. (2001) *Public Worship with Communion by Extension: A Commentary*, W 167 (Cambridge: Grove Books).

Tovey, P. N. (2004) *Inculturation of Christian Worship: Exploring the Eucharist.* Liturgy, Worship and Society (Aldershot: Ashgate).

Tovey, P. N. (2006) 'The Theory and Practice of Extended Communion, with particular reference to parishes within the Anglican Diocese of Oxford'. Ph. D. diss. Oxford Brookes University"; forthcoming as *The Theory and Practice of Extended Communion* (Aldershot: Ashgate, 2009).

Trigg, J. W. (1983) *Origen: The Bible and Philosophy in the Third-Century Church* (London: SCM Press).

Troeltsch, E. (1931) *The Social Teaching of the Christian Churches* (London: Allen and Unwin).

Turner, V. W. (1969) *The Ritual Process: Structure and Anti–Structure* (New York, NY: Aldine/de Gruyter).

Urwin, L. (2008) 'What is the Role of Sacramental Ministry in Fresh Expressions of Church?', in *Mission–Shaped Questions: Defining Issues for Today's Church*, ed. S. J. L. Croft (London: Church House Publishing), pp. 29–41.

Verner, D. C. (1983) *The Household of God: The Social World of the Pastoral Epistles* (Chico, CA: Scholars Press).

Versnel, H. F. (2002) The Poetics of the Magical Charms', in *Magic and Ritual in the Ancient World*, ed. P. Mirechi and M. Meyer (Leiden: E. J. Brill), pp. 105–58.

Voak, N. (2003) *Richard Hooker and Reformed Theology: A Study of Reason, Will, and Grace* (Oxford: Oxford University Press).

Voak, N. (2008) 'Richard Hooker and the Principle of *Sola Scriptura*', in *Journal of Theological Studies*, 59: 96–139.

Vogel, A. A. (1975) 'Priesthood and the Church as Community', in *To Be A Priest: Perspectives on Vocation and Ordination*, eds R. E. Terwilliger and U. T. Holmes (New York, NY: Seabury Press), pp. 141–6.

Volf, M. (1998) *After Our Likeness: The Church as the Image of the Trinity* (Grand Rapids, MI: Eerdmans).

Wainwright, G. (2003) *Eucharist and Eschatology* (London: Epworth Press).

Wall, R. W. (2000) 'Reading the Bible from within our Traditions: The "Rule of Faith" in Theological Hermeneutics', in *Between Two Horizons: Spanning New Testament Studies and Systematic Theology*, ed. J. B. Green and M. Turner (Grand Rapids, MI: Eerdmans), pp. 88–117.

Wallace-Hadrill, A. (ed). (1989) *Patronage in Ancient Society* (London: Routledge).

Wanamaker, C. A. (1990) *The Epistles to the Thessalonians* (Grand Rapids, MI: Eerdmans).

Wanjiku, P. (2002) 'Liturgical Revision in the Anglican Church of Kenya', in *Encounter*, 2: 46–51.

Ward, H. and Wild, J. (eds) (1995) *Human Rites: Worship Resources for an Age of Change* (London: Mowbrays).

Waterland, D. (1880) *A Review of the Doctrine of the Eucharist* (Oxford: Clarendon Press).

Watts, F. N. and Williams, J. M. G. (1988) *The Psychology of Religious Knowing* (London: Geoffrey Chapman).

Weber, M. (1947) *The Theory of Social and Economic Organization* (New York, NY: Oxford University Press).

Weber, M. (1964) *The Sociology of Religion* (Boston, MA: Beacon).

Webster, J. (2002) 'The "Self–Organizing" Power of the Gospel: Episcopacy and Community Formation', in *Community Formation in the Early Church and in the Church Today*, ed. R. N. Longenecker (Peabody, MA: Hendrickson), pp. 179–93.

Webster, J. B. (1988) 'Ministry and Priesthood', in *The Study of Anglicanism*, ed. S. W. Sykes and J. E. Booty, (London: SPCK), pp. 285–96.

Wedderburn, A. J. M. (1997) *Baptism and Resurrection* (Tübingen: J. C. B. Mohr).

Weil, L. (1975) 'Priesthood in the New Testament', in *To Be A Priest: Perspectives on Vocation and Ordination*, eds R. E. Terwilliger and U. T. Holmes (New York, NY: Seabury Press), pp. 63–70.

Weingrod, A. (1977) 'Patronage and Power', in *Patrons and Clients*, ed. E. Gellner (London: Duckworth), pp. 41–52.

Westphal, G. (1981) 'Role and Limit of Pastoral Delegation to Laymen for the Celebration of the Eucharist in the Protestant Reformed Churches', in *Roles in the Liturgical Assembly*, ed. M. J. O'Connell (New York, NY: Pueblo Press), pp. 275–90.

Whitaker, E. C. (1975) *Sacramental Initiation Complete in Baptism*, 1 (Bramcote: Grove Books).

Whitaker, E. C. (1981) *The Baptismal Liturgy* (London: SPCK).

Whitaker, E. C. and Johnson, M. E. (2003) *Documents of the Baptismal Liturgy* (London: SPCK).

White, S. R. (1996) *Authority and Anglicanism* (London: SCM Press).

White, S. R. (2006) 'Scripture and Experience: A Creative Tension', in *The Authority of Scripture: A Report of the Church of Ireland Bishops' Advisory Commission on Doctrine*, ed. R. Clarke (Dublin: Church of Ireland), pp. 53–66.

Wilhite, D. E. (2007) *Tertullian the African: An Anthropological Reading of Tertullian's Context and Identities* (Berlin: de Gruyter).

Williams, G. H. (1963) 'The Ancient Church, AD 30–313', in *The Layman in Christian History*, ed. S. C. Neill and H.-R. Weber (London: SCM Press), pp. 28–56.

Williams, R. D. (1982) *Eucharistic Sacrifice – The Roots of a Metaphor*, Grove Liturgical Study 31 (Bramcote: Grove Books).

Williams, R. D. (1991) 'Imagining the Kingdom: Some questions for Anglican Worship Today', in *The Identity of Anglican Worship*, eds K. W. Stevenson and B. D. Spinks (London: Mowbrays), pp. 1–13.

Williams, R. D. (2006) 'Theological Education and the Anglican Way', in *Anitepam Journal*, 52: 3–16.

Williams, R. D. (2006) 'Theological Resources for Re-examining Church', in *The Future of the Parish System: Shaping the Church of England for the Twenty-First Century*, ed. S. J. L. Croft (London: Church House Publishing), pp. 49–60.

Williams, R. D. (2007) 'The Bible Today: Reading and Hearing'. Larkin Stuart Lecture, Toronto.

Williams, R. H. (2006) *Stewards, Prophets, Keepers of the Word: Leadership in the Early Church* (Peabody, MA: Hendrickson).

Wilson, B. R. (1969) *Religion in Secular Society* (Harmondsworth: Penguin).

Wilson, B. R. (1982) *Religion in Sociological Perspective* (Oxford: Oxford University Press).

Wilson, G. H. (1936) *The History of the Universities' Mission to Central Africa* (London: Universities' Mission to Central Africa).

Wilson, M. M. H. (1971) *Religion and the Transformation of Society: A Study of Social Change in Africa* (Cambridge: Cambridge University Press).

Wilson, S. G. (1979) *Luke and the Pastoral Epistles* (London: SPCK)

Wingren, G. (1964) *Gospel and Church* (Edinburgh: Oliver and Boyd).

Winkler, G. (1997) *Studies in Early Christian Liturgy and Its Context* (Aldershot: Ashgate).

Winter, B. W. (2001) *After Paul Left Corinth.* (Grand Rapids, MI: Eerdmans).

Wolf, W. J. (1979) 'Frederick Denison Maurice', in *The Spirit of Anglicanism*, ed. W. J. Wolf (Edinburgh: T & T Clark), pp. 49–99.

Wood, S. K. (2000) *Sacramental Orders* (Collegeville, MN: Liturgical Press).

Wood, S. K. (2003) 'Presbyteral Identity within Parish Identity', in *Ordering the Baptismal Priesthood: Theologies of Lay and Ordained Ministry*, ed. S. K. Wood (Collegeville, MN: Liturgical Press), pp. 175–94.

Woodhouse, J. (1995) 'Lay Administration of the Lord's Supper', in *St Mark's Review*, 162: 15–19.

World Council of Churches. (1982) *Baptism, Eucharist and Ministry*. Faith and Order Group, 111 (Geneva: World Council of Churches).

Wright, D. F. (2005) *What Has Infant Baptism Done to Baptism? An Enquiry at the End of Christendom* (Aldershot: Ashgate).

Wright, F. S. (1980) *The Pastoral Nature of Ministry* (London: SCM Press).

Wright, F. S. (1996) *Pastoral Care Revisited* (London: SCM Press).

Wrong, D. H. (1979) *Power* (Oxford: Blackwell).

Wybrew, H. M. (1989) *Called to Be Priests* (Oxford: SLG Press).

York, S. (2000) *Remembering Well: Rituals for Celebrating Life and Mourning Death* (San Francisco, CA: Jossey Bass).

Young, F. M. (1994) 'On Επισκοπος and Πρεσβυτερος', in *Journal of Theological Studies*, 45: 142–8.

Young, F. M. (1997) *Biblical Exegesis and the Formation of Christian Culture* (Cambridge: Cambridge University Press).

Young, F. M. (2002) 'Ministerial Forms and Functions in the Church Communities of the Greek Fathers', in *Community Formation in the Early Church and in the Church Today*, ed. R. N. Longenecker (Peabody, MA: Hendrickson), pp. 157–76.

Zetterholm, M. (2003) *The Formation of Christianity in Antioch* (London: Routledge).

Ziegler, R. F. (2003) 'Should Lutherans Reserve the Consecrated Elements for the Communion of the Sick?', in *Concordia Theological Quarterly*, 67: 131–47.

Zizioulas, J. D. (1985) *Being as Communion: Studies in Personhood and the Church* (New York, NY: St Vladimir Seminary Press).

Zygmunt, J. F. (1972) 'Movements and Motives', in *Human Relations*, 25: 449–67.

Index

1. Biblical References

Exodus
19.6 94
19.24 46
24.8 91
28-29 46

Leviticus
8 85
8.10 51
9 89
13-14 89
14-16 89

Numbers
5 89
16-17 94
27.15-23 51

Deuteronomy
33.8-10 89

Joshua
18-19 89
18.1 89

1 Samuel
1-3 89
10.17-24 89
13.9-15 222

1 Kings
8 89

Ezra
7.1-6 89

Nehemiah
8 89

Psalms
109.8 50

Isaiah
6.1-8 89
53 90-91
60.17 72

Jeremiah
1.1 89

Ezekiel
1.3 89

Amos
7.14 89

Matthew
4.18-22 46
9.9-13 46
10.1-4 35, 46
10.1-2 47
16.18-19 78
18.1-4 35
18.20 210, 259
20.28 90
23.11 35
26.28 91
28.16-19 214

Mark
1.16-20 46
2.13-17 46
3.3-19 35, 46
3.14 46-7
9.34 35
10.45 90
13.1-4 89

14.17 33
14.17-18 34
14.24 90-1
16.14-16 214

Luke
1 89
1.5-27 88
1.5 89
1.57-66 88
5.1-11 46
5.27-32 46
6.13-16 35, 46
6.13 47-8
22.14-38 30
9.1 47
9.46 35
10.1 47-8
22.14 33
22.19 33, 210
22.20 91
22.24-26 35

John
1.29 91
1.35-51 46
2.19 89
3.16 91
6 32
13.2-17.26 30
19.31 32

Acts
1.2 47
1.15-26 35, 49
1.20 50
1.21-22 45
1.25 49-50

313

2. Early Christian and Patristic Authors

3. Anglican Writings

4. Subjects and Names